ALFRED VON SCHLIEFFEN'S
MILITARY WRITINGS

CASS SERIES: MILITARY HISTORY AND POLICY
Series Editors: John Gooch and Brian Holden Reid
ISSN: 1465-8488

This series will publish studies on historical and contemporary aspects of land power, spanning the period from the eighteenth century to the present day, and will include national, international and comparative studies. From time to time, the series will publish edited collections of essays and 'classics'.

1. *Allenby and British Strategy in the Middle East, 1917–1919*
   Matthew Hughes

2. *Alfred von Schlieffen's Military Writings*
   Robert Foley (ed. and trans.)

3. *The British Defence of Egypt 1935–1940: Conflict and Crisis in the Eastern Mediterranean*
   Stephen Morewood

4. *The Japanese and British Commonwealth Armies at War, 1941–1945*
   Tim Moreman

5. *Training, Tactics and Leadership in the Confederate Army of Tennessee: Seeds of Failure*
   Andrew Haughton

6. *Military Training in the British Army, 1940–1944: From Dunkirk to D-Day*
   Tim Harrison-Place

7. *The Boer War: Direction, Experience and Image*
   John Gooch (ed.)

8. *Caporetto 1917: Victory or Defeat?*
   Mario Morselli

9. *Postwar Counterinsurgency and the SAS, 1945–1952: A Special Type of Warfare*
   Tim Jones

ALFRED VON SCHLIEFFEN'S
MILITARY WRITINGS

Translated and Edited by
ROBERT T. FOLEY
*King's College, London and
Joint Services Command and Staff College, Shrivenham*

FRANK CASS
LONDON • PORTLAND, OR

First published in 2003 in Great Britain by
FRANK CASS PUBLISHERS
2 Park Square, Milton Park, Abingdon,
Oxon, OX14 4RN

and in the United States of America by
FRANK CASS PUBLISHERS
270 Madison Ave,
New York NY 10016

Transferred to Digital Printing 2006

Website: www.frankcass.com

Copyright © 2003 R. Foley

British Library Cataloguing in Publication Data

Schlieffen, Alfred, Graf von, 1833–1913
   Alfred von Schlieffen's military writings. – (Cass series.
Military history and policy; no. 2)
   1. Military art and science – Germany
   I. Title II. Foley, Robert T. III. Military writings
355′.02′0943

ISBN10: 0-7146-4999-6 (hbk)
ISBN10: 0-415-40862-8 (pbk)

ISBN13: 978-0-7146-4999-3 (hbk)
ISBN13: 978-0-415-40862-2 (pbk)

ISSN 1465-8488

Library of Congress Cataloging-in-Publication Data

Schlieffen, Alfred, Graf von, 1833–1913
   Alfred von Schlieffen's military writings / translated and edited by Robert T. Foley.
     p. cm. – (Cass series – military history and policy, ISSN 1465-8488; no. 2)
   Includes bibliographical references and index.
   ISBN 0-7146-4999-6 (cloth)
     1. Military art and science. 2. Military doctrine – Germany. I. Foley, Robert T.
II. Title. III. Series.

U41 .S35 2003
355.02 – dc21

2002067623

All rights reserved. No part of this publication may be reproduced, stored in or introduced into a retrieval system or transmitted in any form or by any means, electronic, mechanical, photocopying, recording or otherwise, without the prior written permission of the publisher of this book.

Typeset in 10.5/12pt Classical Garamond by Frank Cass Publishers

Cover illustrations: (above) Generalfeldmarschall Alfred Graf von Schlieffen.

Contents

List of Illustrations   vii
Series Editor's Preface   ix
Preface   xi
Introduction   xv
Note on Equivalent Military Ranks   xxix

Part I: Wargames

Introduction   3
1. General Staff Ride (East), 1894   13
2. General Staff Ride (East), 1897   27
3. General Staff Ride (East), 1899   39
4. General Staff Ride (East), 1901   51
5. General Staff Ride (East), 1903   61
6. Tactical-Strategic Problems, 1892   72
7. Tactical-Strategic Problems, 1896   82
8. Tactical-Strategic Problems, 1903   92
9. Tactical-Strategic Problems, 1905   108
10. *Kriegsspiel*, 1905   119

CONTENTS

Part II: Memoranda

Introduction	143
11. Reports on the Russian Army, 1905	159
12. Memorandum of 1905: The Schlieffen Plan	163
13. Addendum to the Memorandum, 1906	175
14. Comments by Moltke on the Memorandum, *c.*1911	178

Part III: Theoretical Writings

Introduction	183
15. War Today, 1909	194
16. Million-Man Armies, 1911	206
17. Cannae Studies	208
18. The *Feldherr*, 1910	219
19. Helmuth von Moltke	227

Appendices

I.	Schlieffen's Life and Career	235
II.	The General Staff, 1891–1905	238
III.	German Army Corps at Wartime Strength	240
IV.	French Army Corps at Wartime Strength	241
V.	Russian Army Corps at Wartime Strength	242

Notes	243
Select Bibliography	267
Index	273

Illustrations

Between pages 126 and 127

1. *Generalfeldmarschall* Alfred Graf von Schlieffen.
2. Kaiser Wilhelm II with his staff at the 1899 manoeuvres.
3. Kaiser Wilhelm II strikes a dramatic pose at the 1906 manoeuvres.
4. *Generalfeldmarschall* Gottlieb Graf von Haeseler.
5. Kaiser Wilhem II shakes hands with Graf von Haeseler at the 1905 manoeuvres.
6. *General der Kavallerie* Friedrich von Bernhardi, shown during the First World War.
7. An artillery team fires a field gun at the 1902 manoeuvres.
8. Airships.
9. German infantry and field entrenchments.
10. Bavarian cavalrymen advance during the 1906 manoeuvres.
11. Field telephone.
12. Machine-guns firing at the 1905 manoeuvres.
13. Hugo Freiherr von Freytag-Loringhoven.

Images 1–12 are reproduced courtesy of the Imperial War Museum.

Series Editor's Preface

The relationship between military thought and practice has often perplexed historians, indeed soldiers themselves. Those who think about the nature of war are rarely in a position to conduct military operations, and those who do frequently appear incapable of reflecting on their conduct. In one army the connection between thinkers and doers has been closer than in most – the Prussian/German.

The army shaped by von Moltke the Elder (himself a prolific author) produced a range of soldier-intellectuals who held the highest commands. Perhaps the most famous was Field Marshal Graf von Schlieffen (1833–1913). Schlieffen was not a profound thinker but a technocrat. He had attended the *Kriegsakademie* (1859–61) and served as a general staff officer during the Austro-Prussian War (1866) and the Franco-Prussian War (1870–71). Apart from a tour as the commander of the 1st Guard Uhlans (1876–84), his military career was spent on the staff. It was, therefore, the range of a staff officer's problems that gripped his (rather constricted) imagination. In 1891 Schlieffen succeeded as Chief of the General Staff, a post in which he served with dedication and enormous industry for 17 years.

Schlieffen's personal life was bleak. He had no family life to speak of, as his wife had died young. Military professionals can sometimes be obsessive, and Schlieffen was what would now be termed a 'workaholic'. He did nothing in life but work, and regularly set his staff operational problems to be solved on Christmas Day.

The range of Schlieffen's interests and concerns are well conveyed in Robert Foley's fine translation of some of his military writings. It is amazing that they have not appeared in English before. They capture the professional, technical approach of a soldier whose intellectual concerns focused on future planning rather than general reflection. They also enshrine the operational and strategic dilemma that Schlieffen inherited. According to Schlieffen, Moltke had bequeathed a guiding dictum: 'Not *one* method, not *one* means, not *one* expedient, but many' (p. 229). Schlieffen grasped, however, that as armies and the fronts they occupied grew enormously in size, they would have to be controlled, and the expedient he chose was intricate planning. To ensure variety of expedient, Schlieffen selected for his subordinates a governing method.

There is a great deal here for today's professional officers to chew over and debate, especially in those papers dedicated to the operational level of war. Schlieffen attached great importance to staff rides, which have undergone a revival. The attention of historians will be probably caught by Chapter 15, 'War Today, 1909'. Schlieffen clearly understood the impact of firepower on the modern battlefield, that 'wide desert' (p. 198). 'No unit in close order', he averred, 'no man standing free and upright can expose themselves to the rain of shot' (p. 195). Schlieffen placed his faith in the power of artillery to ensure a successful infantry advance that could gain the decisive victory he sought. In the long run, he was right, although the tactical equation was more complicated than he imagined. This is just a hint of the diversity of issues central to the conduct of war contained in this important book. Dr Foley's readable translation, informed by an intimate knowledge of the workings of the German army, deserves to be read by the many involved in the study of the oscillating relationship between military thought and practice.

Brian Holden Reid
Series Co-Editor

Preface

The figure of Alfred von Schlieffen featured prominently in the early years of my doctoral studies. Although I was writing about the concept of attrition in German military thought, Schlieffen's writings stimulated me to think about how warfare was viewed in Wilhelmine Germany. As I began to teach German military history, I realized that his writings were not widely available to today's student: Gerhard Ritter's translation of Schlieffen's eponymous plan had long gone out of print and was not widely available.[1] Crucially, most of Schlieffen's other works had never been translated into English. Although a translated volume of some of his theoretical writings had been published by the US Army's Command and General Staff College in the 1930s, this too was long out of print and difficult to find.[2] Moreover, it contained only a limited number of texts. After reading a lengthy and sometimes ill-informed debate about Schlieffen in the pages of the the *Spectator*,[3] and after the positive response to my translation of Schlieffen's last *Kriegsspiel* (wargame) in the now-defunct *War Studies Journal*,[4] I suspected that a more-comprehensive collection of Schlieffen's writings might be welcomed by students of military history and strategic studies.

With the encouragement and support of Professor Brian Holden Reid, I approached Frank Cass Publishers with the idea of bringing out an edited translation of Schlieffen's key texts. When they agreed, the most immediate challenge was which of Schlieffen's many publications to include. His staff rides, staff problems and *Kriegsspiele*, what I have termed here his 'wargames', were crucial to understanding what it was that Schlieffen was teaching his subordinates in the General Staff. However, these covered several hundred pages in two volumes. This has required me to be selective in what I have included. I have translated here that which I felt to be the most important elements of the staff rides – Schlieffen's final critiques. Unfortunately, this means that the detail of who ordered which unit to do what on a particular day in a certain ride has been lost, but at least Schlieffen's ideas have been brought out. Of Schlieffen's staff problems, I have chosen to translate four as a representative sample. His first and last problems give an idea of how these problems changed over time. Additionally, the four I chose deal with combat on the eastern and western fronts, an invasion of Germany from the north, and an example of how he used history. As Schlieffen's critique to only one *Kriegsspiel* has survived, this made its inclusion imperative.

With Gerhard Ritter's translation of Schlieffen's last great memorandum, the so-called Schlieffen Plan, so difficult to find, I decided to include a new translation of Schlieffen's final version here. While this is not intended to replace Ritter's work, with its translation of all the different versions of the plan, I none the less felt that any volume of Schlieffen's writings would be incomplete without its inclusion. Moreover, I have provided new translations of Schlieffen's addendum to his plan and Helmuth von Moltke the Younger's comments on the memorandum. In addition to these memoranda, I have included two reports to the Chancellor, Bernhard von Bülow, as they cast important light on Schlieffen's impressions of the Russian army on the eve of drafting his plan. Perhaps conspicuous by its absence in this section is Schlieffen's memorandum of 1912. I decided to leave this document out because I wanted to concentrate on those of Schlieffen's works that had significant influence. The 1912 memorandum is largely a restatement of the concepts of the 1905 memorandum and does not appear to have had a great deal of impact on Imperial Germany's decisionmakers.

Given their sheer volume, Schlieffen's writings from his retirement period again offered a challenge. The bulk of his writing, however, consisted of historical studies. As these were not written with the utmost attention to historical methods, I did not think that they would be of interest or of use to most students of the period today. Therefore, I decided to include only portions of one of his historical pieces – the introduction and conclusion from his 'Cannae Studies'. I have included this to give a flavour of his historical writing and also because Schlieffen intended it to serve as more than just a piece of history. With this piece, Schlieffen hoped to prove certain theories about tactical and operational methods. Thus, it was not only historical but theoretical in nature. With his historical studies largely ruled out, the majority of his public writings, this left me with a few pieces that were intended to influence his contemporaries, and I have included translations of these.

Throughout, I have attempted to stay as close as possible in my translation to Schlieffen's original. At times, this has led to somewhat stilted, but I believe still comprehensible, prose. Overall, though, I believe it has worked. In a few other instances, I have regrettably had to change Schlieffen's century-old German words to allow modern-day English speakers to understand Schlieffen's ideas. I have tried to stay as close to Schlieffen's meaning as possible when doing this. However,

PREFACE

differences of interpretation will inevitably arise. All errors and omissions in this work are, of course, my own.

Of course, a work such as this cannot be completed without the assistance of many others. I have already mentioned my debt to Professor Brian Holden Reid for his efforts in getting this project under way. I must also thank Frank Cass Publishers, and in particular their senior book editor, Andrew Humphrys, for their support and patience throughout the time it has taken me to bring the idea to fruition. I am also grateful to the Imperial War Museum for permission to reproduce photographs from their collection. Additionally, many friends and colleagues have aided me in my work, be it with my translation, with reading and commenting on drafts, or, importantly, with encouragement. Those I wish to thank include: Jim Beach, Stephanie Frey, Marcus Funke, James F. Gentsch, John Greenwood, Bruce I. Gudmundsson, Richard Lock-Pullan, Annika Mombauer, Jon Robb-Webb, Martin Robson and Athena Scotis. However, I am especially grateful to Dr Helen McCartney. Not only did she encourage and cajole me to complete this project, along the way taking time from her own work to read and provide insightful comments on my drafts, but she has also had to share me with the ghost of a long-dead German general throughout the process.

Introduction

On the ninety-fifth anniversary of Alfred Graf von Schlieffen's birth, Hans von Seeckt, a successful chief of staff in wartime and the interwar reorganizer of the German army, wrote a piece commemorating 'Schlieffen Day'. Seeckt warned that, with the passing of time, every great personality changes from the man himself into a pure idea and that this is often less than the man himself. He wrote: 'There exists a danger in this formulation of an ideal: It often does the person an injustice. In the place of a rich life comes a fixed idea. This idea is somewhat one-sided and easily leads to false conclusions about a person.' Seeckt cautioned against Schlieffen becoming such a 'fixed idea'. To him, Schlieffen was 'still alive in the heads and hearts of the German General Staff, the German soldiers and the German people'.[1] Schlieffen's pupil wrote that the German army must continue to learn from its old master, believing that three ideas taught by Schlieffen continued to have relevance for the *Reichswehr*:

> The annihilation of the enemy is the goal of warfare, but many routes lead to this end.
> Every operation must be governed by a simple, clear concept. Everything and everyone must be subordinated to this concept of operation.
> The decisive strength must be placed against the decisive point. The result is only to be achieved through sacrifice.

Seeckt felt that if these three concepts were mastered, then 'the idea of Schlieffen would be the idea of victory'.[2]

Seeckt's short piece on Schlieffen not only represents well the prevailing interpretation of the former Chief of the General Staff between the two world wars, but also is illustrative of the tensions inherent in this interpretation. On one hand, the former subordinate and pupil of Schlieffen was conscious that, by 1928, Schlieffen the man was being lost in Schlieffen the idea. Yet, on the other hand, the former head of the *Heeresleitung* and the teacher of the *Reichswehr* had been trained by

Schlieffen himself not to seek out historical truths, but rather to use history for specific purposes.

Defeat in the First World War and the subsequent collapse of Imperial Germany had led German soldiers into a period of intense reflection. However, this reflection was guided by their pre-war training as General Staff officers. Although military history had played an important role in officer education in Germany before the First World War, events were more often than not removed from their context and used for the purposes of learning particular lessons, a process known as the 'applicatory method'.[3] The study of history was less important for understanding what actually had happened than for providing a means of learning particular lessons. The role history played within the General Staff is shown by the approach taken to the study of Napoleon by one promising General Staff historian:

> Which part of this study [of war] is most valuable and improving to the soldier? The fact of knowing accurately the method in which some warlike operation was performed, or of knowing the date of some historical event, cannot be of much advantage to us, for no opportunity is likely to arise to reproduce facts, so to speak, in duplicate; what is of value to the student is to see how things have come to pass and thence to deduce the reason for the results.[4]

Thus it was that the interwar authors, trained as they were in the traditional methods of General Staff history, sought not only the causes for German defeat but, more importantly, lessons from which young officers could learn to fight the next war more effectively. By the time that Seeckt wrote his piece for 'Schlieffen Day', the former General Staff Chief, his ideas and his plan had become a large part of this process. However, the historical context of these factors was increasingly pushed to the background as a Schlieffen myth was developed in interwar Germany.

Indeed, this myth was consciously created to facilitate this process of reflection. First, the members of this so-called 'Schlieffen School' created the idea that Schlieffen had written a perfect plan; a plan that, had it been followed to the letter, would have led to certain German victory in 1914. Taking this assumption as a starting point allowed these authors to lay blame for failure on an individual who had ignored and changed Schlieffen's 'genial' plan (Helmuth von Moltke the Younger, conveniently dead),[5] and it provided a template against which to measure the decisions of wartime leaders.[6] In addition, these authors created the myth that Schlieffen had found the perfect operational methods. This allowed them to use Schlieffen's ideas on the conduct of war as

INTRODUCTION

examples for current practice.[7] Schlieffen's staff problems, General Staff rides, and his solutions to these were shared around the army and ultimately published as a means of reinforcing his ideas.[8] The mythical status afforded Schlieffen in the interwar period is perhaps best symbolized by the foundation of a society in 1921 aimed at circumventing the proscription on the General Staff forced on the German army by the Treaty of Versailles. This organization was named the *Generalstabsverein Graf Schlieffen*, the General Staff Society Graf Schlieffen.[9]

The image of Schlieffen produced by this cracked interpretive lens has given us a distorted image of his ideas and his impact upon the German army. Works on Schlieffen in the interwar period were not designed by their authors to give a truthful picture of Schlieffen, his work, or his place in the Wilhelmine army. Wilhelm Groener, a key member of the Schlieffen School, wrote of his works on Schlieffen and the First World War: 'I do not write for history ... I write for the future, because I fear that our hollow-heads [*Hohlköpfe*] will make improvements for the worse in the strategy of the next war, as it happened in the world war.'[10] Yet, despite the clear purpose behind these works, the 'fixed idea' they gave of Schlieffen is still in use today.

Schlieffen's interwar reputation as a master strategist did not survive the Second World War. This war changed the nature of military history writing, particularly in Germany. With the final destruction of the German military came an end to General Staff history writing. Instead of officers writing for other officers, now civilians wrote in search of the true origins of German militarism and of Germany's defeat in the two wars. Freed from the restraints of traditional *Kriegsgeschichte* (war history), German authors turned instead to look at *Militärgeschichte* (military history), and thus to examine German military history from a wider perspective.[11] Where once highly trained staff officers would examine the merits of this or that tactical or operational decision or plan, now civilian historians explored wider issues, such as the role of the military in German society or the development of a particular military institution.[12]

Schlieffen and his plan did not escape this shift in methodology. Schlieffen's plan was now viewed against the backdrop of German and international politics, and found wanting. It was dismissed, not without justification, as a 'purely military' creation, a 'gambler's throw'.[13] Moreover, Schlieffen's strategic planning was seen as inflexible and out of touch: 'The development of German strategic thought [in the nineteenth century] is marked by a slow hardening of a subtle dialectical approach to military problems into a set of unchallenged axioms.'[14] It was not only Schlieffen's plan that fared less well under the harsh light of this new methodology, the efficacy of Schlieffen's views on the conduct of war were also called into question. Where interwar authors had seen operational efficiency, post-Second World War observers saw dogma leading to defeat.[15]

Indeed, this shift in the focus of military history caused previous writing on Schlieffen to look distinctly parochial. However, despite this, these new military historians relied for the most part on the sometimes simplistic and often distorted image of Schlieffen created by their interwar predecessors. They took for granted the interwar view that Schlieffen's plan of 1905 was the logical and final culmination of years of planning.[16] They accepted, even if they recognized the existence of the Schlieffen School, the interpretation that Schlieffen's fixed views on operational manoeuvre permeated throughout the Imperial army, creating a dogmatic approach to war.[17]

It is only recently that this older image of Schlieffen has begun to be questioned by historians. Schlieffen's ideas have been examined in their own rights and in their proper historical context. They have been analysed in comparison to those of other theorists of their day and, more importantly, within the spectrum of development of the General Staff.[18] Moreover, the course of development of Schlieffen's famous plan, as well as its significance and impact have begun to be carefully studied,[19] and the impact of developments within the broader realm of military theory on Schlieffen's ideas has been looked at.[20] A more nuanced view of Schlieffen and his ideas is now developing.

However, regardless of their differences, almost all recent interpretations have assumed that Schlieffen and his ideas had a large, if not dominating, impact on the army of Kaiser Wilhelm II. Many have seen in this the seeds of Germany's defeat in 1918, and some have even gone so far as to argue that Schlieffen's influence led to defeat in 1945. This viewpoint stands in contrast to that of the writers of the Schlieffen School, who argued that Schlieffen's influence had not been strong enough in the *Kaiserheer* (Imperial German army), and that this led to Germany's defeat in the First World War. The truth of the matter is that each side has exaggerated its position. Schlieffen's influence and impact was not all-pervasive, nor was it negligible. In fact, the nature and organization of the Imperial German army combined to make his influence more subtle and his impact more discreet than has generally been assumed.

SCHLIEFFEN AS CHIEF OF THE GENERAL STAFF

On 7 February 1891, *Generalleutnant* Alfred Graf von Schlieffen succeeded his mentor Alfred Graf von Waldersee as Chief of the General Staff when Waldersee's political intrigues finally brought him on the

INTRODUCTION

wrong side of Kaiser Wilhelm II. The selection of Schlieffen for this, one of the top positions within the Imperial German army, was not a surprise, as Schlieffen was well suited to replace the objectionable Waldersee. First, he had the requisite military experience, both in the line and in the staff. As a young *Rittmeister*, he had commanded a squadron in the 2nd Dragoon Regiment, and as an *Oberst*, he had commanded a regiment, the prestigious 1st Guard Uhlans, for eight years. He had served for a number of years in the *Truppengeneralstab* (Troop General Staff), the body of General Staff officers assigned to individual divisions or army corps, and had also served as a section chief in the *Großer Generalstab* (Great General Staff), the body of General Staff officers responsible for Germany's strategic planning. Moreover, Schlieffen had seen service in the Wars of Unification, even winning the Iron Cross, 1st Class, for his efforts in the Franco-German War of 1870/71.[21]

In addition to his military experience, Schlieffen was also seen as a politically reliable choice. He was firmly rooted in the Prussian establishment, coming from a good family and being well connected in the Prussian army and Court. His time as a young officer in Berlin and as commander of a prestigious cavalry regiment in nearby Potsdam had allowed him to build upon family connections and to strengthen ties with leading figures within the Reich's bureaucracy.[22] Moreover, Schlieffen was known to have a narrow set of interests outside the army and army life.[23] Thus, despite his closeness to Waldersee, Schlieffen's past and his connections to the establishment made him appear to Kaiser Wilhelm II and his advisers as a safe, more malleable alternative to the politically active Waldersee.[24]

Indeed, the political activities of Schlieffen's mentor were to have a large impact on Schlieffen's tenure as Chief of the General Staff. Waldersee's long-standing attempt to gain more influence over the foreign policy of the German Reich had upset the delicate balance of power that had grown up between the bureaucracies in the Prussian/German government. His intrigues had caused him to run afoul of the Foreign Ministry, the Chancellory, other institutions within the Army and, ultimately, the Kaiser himself.[25] Reaction to these activities would shape how Schlieffen and the rest of the German government and military saw the role of the General Staff and its Chief. Thus, they would have an impact on the direction in which Schlieffen steered the organization throughout his 15 years at its head.

Schlieffen took over one of the German Empire's most important institutions.[26] Originally a minor department within the Prussian Ministry of War, the General Staff had, under the leadership of one of Germany's and the nineteenth century's greatest military minds, extended its influence within the German government and had established its bureaucratic independence within the German army in the years following the German Wars of Unification. With the man largely seen as the architect of the Prussian victories in these wars against Austria and France, Helmuth Graf von Moltke, also known as Moltke the Elder, at its head, the General Staff took over more and more functions of the German army. It had already been responsible for plans for the deployment of the Prussian army. However, after the experiences of the Danish War of 1864 and the Austro-Prussian War of 1866, Moltke became the King's prime adviser on military operations, with the authority to issue orders in the King's name during wartime. Thus, the General Staff Chief became the *de facto* commander of the Prussian, and later German army in time of war. The central role played by Moltke and his organization in the Wars of Unification ensured that it would have a more important role in peacetime. In 1872, the *Kriegsakademie*, the War Academy responsible for providing higher education to German officers, fell under the control of the General Staff and slowly began to focus on providing training in the tasks of General Staff officers. Finally, in 1883, the General Staff achieved formal bureaucratic independence from the Ministry of War; it was created as an independent office within the Prussian government roughly on a par with organizations such as the Foreign Office. With this, the General Staff Chief was granted right of access to the Kaiser, an important right in Imperial Germany.[27] The General Staff had become a major player within the bureaucracy of the ever-growing German Empire, with central roles in war planning and military education as well as at least an indirect impact on German foreign policy.

However, it is important to remember that the General Staff was merely one of many actors in the German government. Hans-Ulrich Wehler has used the term 'authoritarian polycracy' to describe the government of Wilhelmine Germany with its many different centres of authority under the Kaiser competing with each other for influence and power.[28] This was mirrored within the army as well. Although under Moltke the General Staff had gained independence from the Ministry of War, this organization still carried out many functions in the army and represented it in financial matters and in the Reichstag. Moreover, the Kaiser's Military Cabinet had authority over promotions and assignments and the commanding generals of the Reich's various corps districts had important powers of their own.[29] Thus, not only did the General Staff have to contend for influence with other bureaucracies within the Reich, it faced rivalry from within the army.[30] While Waldersee had bridled at these restrictions on the influence of the

INTRODUCTION

General Staff, ultimately it was these institutions in the army that profited from Waldersee's failed attempts at gaining more political power for himself and his organization.

Symbolically, one of Schlieffen's first acts as Chief of the General Staff was to punish, on the orders of the Military Cabinet, Waldersee's former adjutant, Major Zahn, for his role in Waldersee's intrigues.[31] Although Schlieffen was able to negotiate a less humiliating assignment for Zahn, the message was clear to Schlieffen and all other observers: the General Staff Chief and his officers were ultimately answerable to the Military Cabinet for their actions. The wings of the General Staff had been publicly clipped.

In place of Waldersee's attempt to gain more power and influence for the General Staff, Schlieffen concentrated on its consolidation and inward development. In contrast to Waldersee's attempts to engage in and to shape German foreign policy, during his time as Chief of the General Staff Schlieffen would quietly influence or passively accept changes. In the post-Waldersee period, Schlieffen would rise again within the General Staff and take as his own Moltke the Elder's expression 'Viel leisten, wenig hervortreten – mehr sein als scheinen' ('Do much, but stand out little – be more than you appear').[32]

Thus rebuffed from playing an active role in German policymaking, Schlieffen fell back on his natural inclination and refocused the General Staff on its core activities – the technicalities of war planning and war fighting. This inward focus of the General Staff Chief, ostensibly Germany's top strategic planner, would have important and long-lasting negative consequences for Germany. First, just as Schlieffen was bedding into his position, German foreign policy was changing course radically. Under the influence of his new Chancellor, Leo von Caprivi, in late 1890 Kaiser Wilhelm II had allowed Otto von Bismarck's Reinsurance Treaty with Russia to lapse. With this treaty no longer tying Russia to Germany, France could come to terms with the Russian Empire, and further German diplomatic blundering allowed this to happen.[33] In 1892, France and Russia signed a military convention that called for 1.3 million French and between 700,000 and 800,000 Russian soldiers to be launched against Germany in case either of the signatories was attacked.[34] A scenario that had been every German strategic planner's nightmare since the wars of Friedrich II (the Great) had come true – Germany now faced a war on two fronts against enemies with far superior manpower.

One would expect such a scenario to bring the General Staff Chief, Germany's top strategic planner, to the fore. However, this was not the case. Imperial Germany possessed no means for bringing together all agencies with an interest in foreign policy and strategic planning.

Instead, such coordination relied upon individuals to seek each other out to discuss issues.[35] As we have seen, Waldersee's meddling had dealt a blow to the General Staff's bureaucratic prestige and Schlieffen's narrow focus had reinforced the General Staff's withdrawal from the policy realm. One factor could have off-set this. In Wilhelmine Germany, the Kaiser played a central role in policy formulation.[36] Moltke the Elder was able to bend the ear of Kaiser Wilhelm I, and Waldersee had been close to his grandson, Wilhelm II. Thus, the two were able to have some influence over the course of German foreign policy. However, Schlieffen did not enjoy a similarly close relationship with Wilhelm II. While Schlieffen regularly met the Kaiser, the two were at best on cordial terms and there is no evidence to suggest that Schlieffen was able to exercise any significant influence over Wilhelm's thinking.[37] Despite some interaction with the Foreign Office, Schlieffen neither was consulted by nor attempted to influence those who set the foreign policy of the *Kaiserreich*.[38]

As the foreign policy of successive Chancellors worsened Germany's diplomatic position in Europe by alienating not only France and Russia but also Great Britain, Schlieffen was able only to react. Rather than attempt to alter German foreign policy by discussing its poor strategic situation with Germany's foreign policymakers, Schlieffen remained focused on his military role. During his time as General Staff Chief, all his energies went into developing a plan and an army that would be capable of meeting the challenge of a two-front war. However, even in this important task, he was to have mixed results. Once again Waldersee's actions and the polycratic structure of the *Kaiserreich* and the *Kaiserheer* would limit Schlieffen's ability to carry out even this core function of the General Staff.

Faced with the certainty of a two-front war, Schlieffen responded by attempting to fall back on what he saw as Germany's advantages – interior lines and a good railroad system. From early in his tenure as Chief of the General Staff, Schlieffen hoped to take advantage of Germany's geographic position between its two enemies to defeat one quickly and then make use of Germany's excellent rail system to turn on the other; he hoped to be able to defeat France and Russia piecemeal before they were capable of taking concerted action that would overwhelm a German army inferior in manpower. Almost as soon as he took over his position, Schlieffen focused on first defeating France, the enemy capable of taking the field first and the one he believed to be most dangerous to Germany.[39] However, in order to do this in the manner he believed would give Germany the best possible chance of success, Schlieffen required a German army that was larger, better equipped and better trained. This would bring the General Staff into conflict with other bureaucracies within the *Kaiserheer*.

INTRODUCTION

For Schlieffen, probably the most pressing issue in his planning for a two-front war was manpower. The Franco-Russian Military Convention of 1892 called for the two nations to attack Germany simultaneously with around 2 million men. In 1891 when Schlieffen became Chief of the General Staff, Germany could field an army of around 1.2 million and could rely on its Austro-Hungarian ally for additional support.[40] However, rough parity would not ensure victory. To defeat France and at the same time provide enough protection against a Russian advance in eastern Germany, Schlieffen needed more manpower.

Most galling for Schlieffen, and indeed for many of his contemporaries, was that Germany did not need to be so deficient in manpower. Since its defeat in the Franco-German War of 1870/71, France had copied Germany and introduced universal conscription. However, although it had been a German strength before 1870, France applied conscription more rigorously than Germany or any other European power. By the early twentieth century, France was conscripting around 80 per cent of its eligible young men, as opposed to around 50 per cent of eligible German males.[41] Thus, a France with a declining birth rate and around 20 million fewer inhabitants than Germany could field an army as large, if not larger, than the German. For Schlieffen, as for many of his contemporaries, the solution to Germany's manpower problems, and hence to Germany's strategic situation, was to increase the number of German men conscripted and with this the size of its army.[42]

Although additional manpower was crucial to Schlieffen's plan to fight a two-front war, as Chief of the General Staff, he was not in a position to bring about the army expansion he required. The responsibility for the organization of the army fell to the Prussian Ministry of War.[43] In order to get his army increases, Schlieffen needed to convince the Minister of War that they were necessary. The Minister of War, in turn, needed to convince the Chancellor and the Reichstag that the increases were essential and that it was worth the additional strain on the Reich's finances and on society. However, in Imperial Germany, army increases were not that simple. Just as there was no unified strategic organization within the *Kaiserreich*, so there was no unified Ministry of War. Although the Prussian Ministry of War was the most important and issued some orders to the other national contingents of the *Kaiserheer*, the Kingdoms of Bavaria, Saxony and Württemberg each maintained independent ministries of war, making army increases more difficult. Moreover, any changes to Germany's conscription law would have led to constitutional changes, and this would have involved negotiation with other states within the German Empire. The plans of Julius Verdy du Vernois, the Prussian Minister of War from 1889 to 1890, to increase the numbers of German males conscripted resulted in a political storm and ultimately in his dismissal.[44] Thus, despite its undoubted appeal, Schlieffen and each of Verdy's successors were reluctant to take up the idea again.[45]

Instead, Schlieffen pressed for steady growth in the size of the army and for increased combat power within the army. In some areas, he was successful in getting what he wanted from a Prussian Ministry of War reluctant to increase an already high defence budget. Convinced of the need for and the efficacy of mobile heavy artillery, Schlieffen pressured not only the Ministry of War but the Kaiser. With Wilhelm's personal intervention, the heavy guns Schlieffen believed necessary to break into the French fortress line were forthcoming and, by 1914, the German army was the only army equipped with large numbers of mobile howitzer batteries.[46] However, in other areas, Schlieffen was less successful. In each army law, Schlieffen pushed for greater numbers than the Ministry of War was willing to support, and in every case his advice was ignored.[47] The General Staff Chief also pushed for the creation of greater numbers of army corps in order to create a larger number of manoeuvre units. These, Schlieffen believed, were essential to fighting the fluid, mobile battle he planned. Here, he met with limited success; between 1891 and 1905 the German army added three new army corps to its peacetime order of battle. None the less, Schlieffen always had to make do with less than he believed he required to carry out his plans.[48]

Rebuffed by a parsimonious Ministry of War, Schlieffen turned to training to make the German army more tactically proficient than its numerically superior foes. Once again, Schlieffen ran into opposition from other institutions within his own army. As Chief of the General Staff, Schlieffen had no formal role in either the formation of German army doctrine or in the training of the bulk of the army's officers. Responsibility for the former fell to the Ministry of War and responsibility for the latter to commanding generals of Germany's peacetime army corps districts. Indeed, Schlieffen found these men to be his most potent enemies in his quest to influence how the German army fought.

Perhaps because they were not a bureaucratic institution like the Ministry of War or the General Staff, the authority and the power of the corps commanders have been largely forgotten by historians. However, as the highest peacetime commanders within the Empire, these men had considerable powers and had considerable influence over the army. As Schlieffen took over as Chief of the General Staff, there were 20 such commands throughout the Reich. By the time he retired in 1905, this number had increased to 23. These generals had responsibility for recommending promotions and advancement for the troops under their command. They had the right of access to the Kaiser, and Wilhelm II

INTRODUCTION

liked to think of these men as being under his personal command. Crucially for Schlieffen's desire to influence the army's training and doctrine, these generals were solely responsible for the training of their troops, and this was a task that most took very seriously.[49]

A significant number of corps commanders were military intellectuals in their own right, who had very definite ideas as to how they wanted their men to fight. Indeed, it was in the corps that some of the most innovative tactical and operational ideas were formed within the *Kaiserheer*. Some of Germany's best-known military theorists held corps commands, men such a Friedrich von Bernhardi, the author of numerous works of military theory; Sigismund von Schlichting, the author of the *Drill Regulations* of 1888; Colmar Freiherr von der Goltz, a noted author and famous for reorganizing the Ottoman army; Gottlieb Graf von Haeseler, one of Germany's longest serving and most respected corps commanders. Generals such as these stamped their personality on their command and developed subordinates who carried on their ideas after they retired.[50] With self-confident and able men such as these at the head of Germany's army corps districts, Schlieffen stood little chance of having his operational ideas accepted in the way he wanted, and, indeed, these men offered the most vocal opposition to Schlieffen's tactical and operational ideas.[51]

Thus, Schlieffen was blocked by the bureaucratic structure of the *Kaiserheer* from carrying out a number of tasks he believed necessary to prepare Germany for the difficulties of a two-front war. The Prussian Ministry of War thwarted his efforts to increase the size and change the structure of the army.[52] At the same time, the commanding generals of Germany's 20-odd army corps districts offered serious resistance to his tactical and operational ideas. However, while Schlieffen might have had a limited ability to influence the German army as a whole, his ability to do so within his own organization was much greater, and it was his influence over the General Staff that was to be of the greatest significance and his lasting legacy.

In the 15 years that Schlieffen led the Great General Staff, he was able to build upon the foundations laid by Moltke the Elder and Waldersee. Under his leadership, the General Staff, those serving in the Great General Staff in Berlin and those serving as General Staff officers in the army's divisions and army corps, expanded from less than 300 officers and men to more than 800. When Schlieffen took over as Chief of the General Staff in 1891, the Great General Staff in Berlin, the portion of the organization responsible for strategic planning, consisted of five sections, with the chief of each being equivalent to a regimental commander in rank (*Oberst*), grouped under three *Oberquartiermeisters*, each being equivalent in rank to a brigade commander

(*Generalmajor*). By the time Schlieffen retired in 1905, the Great General Staff had expanded to nine sections under five *Oberquartiermeisters* with remit to cover a much larger area of work than previously.[53] Moreover, the General Staff increasingly became seen as a means of gaining added responsibility and accelerated promotion. Completion of the *Kriegsakademie* and acceptance to the General Staff was believed to translate into eight years' seniority on the promotion list for the lieutenant skilled enough to make it. As such, it attracted some of the best minds and most ambitious officers within the army. Competition for entry was fierce, with only about 30 per cent of those who began the course of study at the *Kriegsakademie* being accepted for the organization.[54]

The relatively junior rank of most General Staff officers and their small number belied their authority within the army. As mentioned, Moltke the Elder built the Great General Staff into Germany's peacetime strategic planning body. In time of war, it was designed to form the core of the Royal Headquarters and to assist in the direction of the war's operations. During wartime, the Chief of the General Staff was the Kaiser's prime military adviser and had the authority to issue orders in his name. In addition to the Great General Staff, each division and army corps had a number of General Staff officers attached to it, the so-called *Truppengeneralstab*. As the Chief of the Great General Staff was the Kaiser's primary military adviser, so the Chief of the General Staff of a division or an army corps would be the prime adviser to the commanders of these units. Over time, this system developed into a unique system of 'dual command':

> The essence of this system lies in the fact that under it the chief of the staff officers attached to a commander is his commander's 'junior partner' and not a mere subordinate in the direction of operations. The ultimate decisions remain in the hands of the commander himself, but his chief of staff is not relieved thereby of his full responsibility for the results ... [N]ormally the relationship between the commander and his chief of staff is expected to conform to that prevailing in a happy marriage. The two men are expected to form a unity rather than two distinct personalities, supplementing each other, composing any differences that may arise without distinguishing the share which each of them contributes to the common good; if to the commander falls the glory as well as the blame, his chief of staff is expected to find his reward in the confidence of his chief.[55]

Such was the importance of this dual command system that in August 1914 Kaiser Wilhelm II told his son, Kronprinz Wilhelm: 'I have

INTRODUCTION

entrusted you with the command of the 5th Army. You will have *Generalleutnant* Schmidt von Knobelsdorf as chief of staff. *What he advises you to do, you must do*.'[56] As the war progressed, staff officers increasingly ran the show and when things went wrong, it was not the commanders who were replaced, but their chiefs of staff.

As Chief of the General Staff, Schlieffen played a central role in the careers of these officers. He recommended officers for assignments and for promotions and, importantly, he was responsible for their professional education. This was a role that Schlieffen took very seriously and one that would ensure his influence over the army until long after his retirement.[57]

Unable to change army doctrine because of the power of the Ministry of War and the corps commanders, Schlieffen turned instead to influencing how the army fought by means of educating his subordinates in the General Staff. Throughout his time as Chief of the General Staff, Schlieffen worked hard to develop within his subordinates the skills he believed necessary for modern mass warfare in the knowledge that at least some of these men would one day be in the position to influence how their troops fought.[58] To do this, he employed the traditional German army wargaming methods – staff problems, staff rides and *Kriegsspiele* – to get across his ideas about the value of flank attacks and envelopments, the need for high-tempo operations, the need for subordinates to understand and work within the framework of a superior's plan and the importance of destroying the enemy's force completely – in short, his ideas about how a commander should conduct his force on the modern battlefield.[59]

There can be no doubt about the success of Schlieffen's stratagem. Hundreds of officers passed through his school throughout his 15 years at the head of the General Staff. Of course, not all of these men agreed with their Chief's ideas about modern warfare. While Friedrich von Bernhardi, the future corps commander and military theorist, was serving in the Historical Section of the General Staff, he clashed with Schlieffen over his ideas about the lessons to be drawn from history. As a result, he was transferred out of the General Staff.[60] Berthold von Deimling, later the commanding general of the XV Army Corps, suffered a similar fate when he clashed with Schlieffen over strategic matters.[61] However, in part by culling those who disagreed greatly with him, Schlieffen was very successful in creating a following within the General Staff, and these men, as the best and the brightest of the German army, went on to high command and to important staff positions. Thus, at the outbreak of the First World War in August 1914, the majority of Chiefs of General Staff of the army's higher commands and a number of the commanders of these units had served under Schlieffen. Moreover, those who emerged as Imperial Germany's best soldiers during the war more often than not had gone through the Schlieffen school – Erich Ludendorff, Hans von Seeckt, Hermann von Kuhl, Wilhelm Groener and August von Mackensen all later acknowledged their intellectual debt to Schlieffen.

Indeed, it was these men who would ensure that the relatively obscure Schlieffen would be remembered long after the First World War. Ironically, although the Versailles Treaty was meant to limit the influence of the General Staff within the interwar German army, it had the opposite effect. By reducing the German army to just 96,000 men and 4,000 officers, it ensured that only the brightest officers remained, and these were generally men who had undergone General Staff training before 1914. Moreover, the army's limited size allowed men such as Hans von Seeckt and Wilhelm Groener, students of Schlieffen and strident proponents of his ideas, to have much more influence over the *Reichswehr* than Schlieffen had ever possessed within the *Kaiserheer*. These men put this influence to good use, laying the foundation for mobile war in the fashion of Schlieffen, but this time with the use of technology in the form of the tank and aircraft. The concepts underpinning the so-called 'Blitzkrieg' of 1939–41 would have been recognizable to any officer who accompanied Schlieffen on one of his staff rides between 1891 and 1905.[62]

Thus, that which was denied to Schlieffen by his contemporaries within the German army – the ability to create an institution imbued with his concepts of a mobile war – was granted to his subordinates by the victorious allies in 1918. However, along with this came Schlieffen's narrow military focus – as Schlieffen had concentrated throughout his time as Chief of the General Staff completely on providing battlefield success, on the operational level of war, so his disciples focused their attentions almost solely on the same thing. While they were successful in the short term, conquering France where the Imperial army had failed, the lack of long-term, strategic planning ensured that such operational successes were not translated into permanent gains.[63]

Note on Equivalent Military Ranks

Portepee-Fähnrich	Cadet
Leutnant/Sekondleutnant	Second Lieutenant
Oberleutnant/Premierleutnant	First Lieutenant
Hauptmann/Rittmeister	Captain
Major	Major
Oberstleutnant	Lieutenant-Colonel
Oberst	Colonel
Generalmajor	Brigadier-General/ Brigadier
Generalleutnant	Major-General
General der Infanterie/Kavallerie/Artillerie	Lieutenant-General
Generaloberst	General
Generalfeldmarschall	General of the Army/ Field Marshal

Part I:

WARGAMES

Introduction

Between 23 and 31 August 1914, the four corps of the German 8th Army under the command of Paul von Hindenburg, with Erich Ludendorff as chief of staff, halted the Russian invasion of Germany and all but annihilated the Russian 2nd Army near the East Prussian village of Tannenberg. By the battle's end, three Russian army corps lay shattered, nearly 200,000 Russians lay dead (including the 2nd Army's commander), wounded or had been taken prisoner, and Germany had itself a new hero – Hindenburg.[1] Indeed, as the Hindenburg legend grew in early 1915, rumours and exaggerations inevitably began to spread about the taciturn new field marshal. One such rumour was that Hindenburg had spent the years between his retirement in 1911 and his recall in 1914 wandering the countryside in East Prussia preparing a trap for the invading Russians and that he merely had to dust off his plans when he took over command of the 8th Army in August 1914.[2] Members of his staff, however, were not content to allow the field marshal to take all the credit for planning the battle; both his chief of staff, Erich Ludendorff, and his first General Staff officer, Max Hoffmann, and even the commanding general of the I Corps, Hermann von François, claimed the honour, and each pressed his case after the war's end.[3] Despite all that has been written, we will probably never know from whose head the idea for the encirclement at Tannenberg sprang, precisely because almost any General Staff officer in the German army could have, and would have, done almost the same thing faced with such a situation.

TRAINING IN THE *KAISERHEER* AND THE GENERAL STAFF

Throughout the ages, the training of military officers in peacetime has always been difficult. This problem became more challenging as armies became larger and more complex in the wake of the Industrial Revolution. With the advent of comprehensive conscription by the end of the nineteenth century, most European armies amounted to several million men when fully mobilized, equipped with complicated weapons and supplied by sophisticated logistical systems. It became impossible to mobilize these armies completely for training purposes, and even partial mobilization was extremely disruptive to civil life. Indeed, most armies were only able to carry out one large-scale manoeuvre per year.[4] Therefore, other training methods had to be found.

Despite this, the Imperial German army prided itself on the tactical and operational skill of its officers. In order to develop in its officers this high level of skill and to keep it honed, each officer participated in a rigorous education system, which did not end with the completion of formal schooling. German officers continued their professional education once they had reached their units. The task of providing for this fell, in the first instance, to the regimental commanders, who were, by regulation, to develop a programme for professional education that ran the whole year through.[5] In the summer and in good weather, commanding officers exercised their troops and officers through manoeuvres and staff rides. In winter and inclement weather, other means of instruction were found – *Kriegsspiele* (war games), tactical problems, and lectures, the so-called *Winterarbeit* (winter-work).

Although *Winterarbeit* is little known today, it was far from unimportant. It had the goal of 'providing the officers the occasion for serious, scientific study' of their field. Indeed, its place was enshrined in the *Field Service Regulations* of 1888, which read *Winterarbeiten* 'offer an abundance of suggestions for the study of our regulations, tactical principles, and experiences and, at the same time, the opportunity [for officers] to make rapid decisions [*schnelle Entschlüsse*]'[6] and again in 1908: '*Kriegsspiele* and tactical problems offer the opportunity to make decisions based on specific circumstances and to articulate them quickly in the form of orders. At the same time, they provide stimulation for the study of the regulations and of tactical principles.'[7] In order to facilitate such training, books of *Kriegsspiele* and tactical problems were published.[8] In addition to *Kriegsspiele* and problems, lectures offered officers the opportunity to study military topics at an even deeper level, and military societies were run in most garrisons to provide a forum for such research. These lectures provided many articles for the large number of professional military journals published in the *Kaiserreich*.[9]

For the vast bulk of the German officers corps, professional education took place under the direction of their regimental commanders. For the officers of the General Staff, however, the Chief of the General Staff provided educational guidance, and this was a role that Alfred von Schlieffen took very seriously. Indeed, Schlieffen was often referred to by his subordinates as the 'master teacher of modern war',[10] and many important commanders and staff officers from the First World War,

INTRODUCTION

such as Erich Ludendorff, Hans von Seeckt and August von Mackensen, later spoke of their intellectual debt to Schlieffen.

The General Staff Chief generally used the same methods as regimental commanders – staff rides, tactical problems, *Kriegspiele* and lectures – to instruct the members of the General Staff, both those serving in the Great General Staff in Berlin and those serving with the troops in the so-called *Truppengeneralstab*. Indeed, such exercises offered almost the only opportunity for Schlieffen to propagate his ideas to a wider audience in peacetime. Although the Chief of the General Staff is often seen as a crucial figure in the formation of 'doctrine' within the German Army, in fact, he had little means of influencing training outside of the Great General Staff. The *Drill Regulations* and the *Field Service Regulations* were written by a commission under the direction of the Ministry of War, and it was the commanding officers of the army's units, in particular the commanding generals of the German army's 25 army corps, who had the responsibility for general training.[11]

Following the First World War, the Reichsarchiv, the successor to the Historical Section of the General Staff, began publishing Schlieffen's 'lessons' – his staff rides and staff problems. By the outbreak of the Second World War, two volumes had been published – one containing his staff problems and one containing a number of his eastern staff rides.[12] A final volume covering his western staff rides was under way when the Second World War began, but this was lost in the destruction of the German archives by British bombers in April 1945.[13]

Every spring, Schlieffen handed out his famed 'tactical-strategic problems' to junior officers in the Great General Staff. These, instituted by Helmuth von Moltke the Elder in 1857, served as the last part of the first stage in a young General Staff officer's training and as such were nicknamed, *Schlußaufgaben* or 'final tasks'.[14] They were designed to test an officer's problem-solving skills and his ability to articulate his ideas clearly and efficiently – both essentials for a good staff officer. The scenarios for these problems were drawn from a number of sources; some came from wargames, others from history, but many were drawn from contemporary situations.[15]

However, it was not only young General Staff officers who had to complete these problems. Even the more experienced amongst Schlieffen's subordinates could not avoid them. Hermann von Kuhl, in the First World War the Chief of the General Staff of the 1st Army and later of *Heeresgruppe Kronprinz Rupprecht*, recalled how he spent one Christmas:

> Many long years ago, the bell to my flat rang on Christmas Eve. A special messenger brought me [Schlieffen's] Christmas gift – a

5

scenario, drawn up by him, of a large-scale war along with the task of drawing up a plan of operations. It would have been absolutely astounding if the final solution had not been in his hands by the evening on Christmas Day. On Boxing Day, there arrived the continuation of the problem, again composed by Schlieffen, with additional tasks. In [Schlieffen's] opinion, Sundays and holidays were ideal for bigger tasks, as one required quiet, continuous work, undisturbed by the routine of everyday life.[16]

The *Schlußaufgaben* were only part of a staff officer's continuing education. Perhaps a more important vehicle for training was the staff ride. During his tenure as Chief of the General Staff, Schlieffen generally conducted two General Staff rides per year, one in June and another in October, and in all, he led 16 rides to Germany's western border and 15 to its eastern border. Each ride lasted from 10 to 14 days and pitted two teams of 25 to 35 General Staff officers of all grades against one another.[17] These rides were far from a pleasant jaunt in the countryside. Officers spent long hours in the saddle and bent over maps, locked in fictitious combat. Karl von Einem, Minister of War from 1903 to 1909 and commander of the 3rd Army during the First World War, described the pace at which they ran. Typically, the day began at 0430 with several hours of map study being followed by up to nine hours on horseback issuing orders as the ride made its way across country along Germany's borders. After a short break in the evening, Schlieffen would provide a critique of the day's events, and participants would retire around midnight.[18]

Like the *Schlußaufgaben*, staff rides served several training purposes.[19] First, they familiarized officers with the terrain along Germany's borders – terrain over which they would likely fight any future war. Further, they provided officers normally cooped up indoors with an opportunity to get a renewed appreciation for some of the consequences of their orders. Thus, the staff officers of the 8th Army issuing orders at the battle of Tannenberg knew the terrain over which their units had to march and had some appreciation for what could be achieved in a specific space of time. Additionally, staff rides gave some opportunity for officers inexperienced in war to make tactical- and, increasingly, operational-level decisions against a reactive opponent and with incomplete knowledge – conditions they would face during wartime.[20] As can be seen from Schlieffen's critiques of these rides translated below, he held this last point to be one of the ride's most important functions,[21] and he had these critiques distributed to each of Prussia's 23 army corps so that those officers who had not participated could still gain a clear view of 'the systematic conduct of war and battles, the influence of higher commanders, issuing of orders, co-

INTRODUCTION

operation of all arms, and the mutual support of divisions and army corps fighting together in battle'.[22]

During the winter when outdoor activity was curtailed, lectures at the famed *Militärische Gesellschaft* and at the nearby Friedrich-Wilhelms-Universität allowed General Staff officers stationed in Berlin to continue their military studies.[23] However, another type of *Winterarbeit* was crucial for General Staff officers – the *Kriegsspiel*. Schlieffen held a *Kriegsspiel* during the winter months every year between 1896 and 1905, and from 1899 to 1904 the Kaiser took part. These exercises had many of the same goals as the General Staff rides and the *Schlußaufgaben*. However, *Kriegsspiele* had several great advantages over these other forms of instruction: combat on both the eastern and the western fronts could be played simultaneously and, thus, the close connection between the two could be clearly demonstrated. Moreover, *Kriegsspiele* gave officers the opportunity to command larger-scale units and 'fight' larger-scale battles.[24] Unlike the *Schlußaufgaben* and General Staff rides, however, Schlieffen's critiques of these games were not distributed throughout the army. While this attests to the importance, and the sensitivity, of these games, it also means that only one critique has survived – that of 1905 (reproduced below, pp. 119–39).

SCHLIEFFEN'S TACTICAL AND OPERATIONAL IDEAS

Clearly, staff rides, staff problems and *Kriegsspiele* were designed to be methods of instruction for staff officers. What, then, was Schlieffen teaching his subordinates? The short answer is that he was teaching them to fight intelligently. Schlieffen, as the person responsible for Germany's war plans, was perhaps more than any other officer of his day cognisant that in a future war the German army would be outnumbered by its enemies. On the eve of the debate over the military law of 1892, Schlieffen wrote about the difficult strategic situation in which Germany found itself; the situation for which he would have to find a solution as Chief of the General Staff. Sandwiched between France and Russia, both potential enemies, Germany faced a 'stronger' and 'younger' French Aarmy and 'the greater part' of the huge Russian army. The General Staff Chief calculated that the strength of Germany's enemies was almost twice the strength of the German army (a ratio of 5:3, to be precise).[25] One way around this problem was to increase the size of the German army, and Schlieffen worked towards this end for most of his tenure as Chief of the General Staff.[26] However, there were limits to the extent to which the

German army could be expanded, and, regardless of this, Germany's potential enemies with their larger populations could always easily match any German increase. Thus, Schlieffen turned to another solution to this problem – the creation of an army that was far superior in quality to its enemies. Schlieffen aimed to create an educated, thinking corps of staff officers who would be able to outfight their enemies even when outnumbered. In his view, quality should replace quantity.

However, Schlieffen had a very specific quality in mind that was sometimes at odds with what his contemporaries desired. Schlieffen aimed to create officers who were adept at what we would today call the operational art. In 1899, Schlieffen and the then Minister of War, Heinrich von Goßler, exchanged a number of letters arguing over army increases. Goßler argued that the German army had reached, or perhaps even surpassed, the limits of possible expansion. The War Minister was concerned that the quality of the units had not kept pace with the army's expansion and had, in his opinion, even fallen. He bemoaned the fact that line units had disproportionately high levels of reservists and that these troops were not capable of combat under 'modern' conditions.[27] It was these highly trained and efficient line units that Goßler believed formed the basis for a future German victory:

> The decisive victories of our last wars were won exclusively by active army corps, and we would do well, I believe, to depend essentially upon the solid fighting ability of our active army corps to win the decisive battles expected soon after the outbreak of a future war.[28]

Thus, for the Minister of War, the tactical quality of these units was decisive.

However, Schlieffen had a slightly different view of what was crucial for success in a future war. While he acknowledged the importance of tactical quality, the General Staff Chief was more interested in *numbers of units* in the field at the beginning of a war than their tactical quality. Living in the period of mass armies, Schlieffen understood that the dynamics of battle had shifted. While during the Austro-Prussian War of 1866, the Prussian army could field 335,700 troops, by the time Schlieffen became Chief of Staff in 1892 this had risen to around 1.2 million. By the time he retired in 1905, Germany intended to deploy a field army of 1.95 million troops in wartime.[29] Schlieffen believed that the size of modern armies had made success of small units on the battlefield less important than success in the overall battle, the *Gesamtschlacht*.[30] This success was to be achieved by superior planning and by a force articulated by numerous sub-units

INTRODUCTION

capable of independent action and manoeuvre. The more of these units available, the more possibilities for deployment and the more flexibility in combat. In order to fight the type of war he wanted – a rapid campaign, the overall success of which would be derived from the victories achieved in numerous smaller encounters, Schlieffen required as many of these manoeuvre units as possible. During the German Wars of Unification, the army corps was the basic Prussian unit capable of fighting independently, and this had remained so during Schlieffen's time as Chief of the General Staff. Thus, in his exchange with Goßler, he called for the creation of greater numbers of corps-level formations to serve as his manoeuver units.[31]

The increase in the size of the army meant that a commander in chief could no longer control his entire army, as had generals of the past, and in order for these increased manoeuvre units to be effective, his subordinates needed more skill at fighting independent corps and army-level actions. Through the media of General Staff training – staff problems, staff rides, *Kriegsspiele* and so on – Schlieffen attempted to form a body of officers within the army capable of fighting the rapid, mobile war he desired. Thus, Schlieffen said to his subordinates in 1903,

> I do not see any reason why the future should not see a few of you gentlemen at the head of an army. None the less, I hope that you are at least called to lead an army corps or a division or to stand by the side of a commander as a chief of staff or as a general staff officer. Then you will have to understand how to judge the manoeuvres of an army. Only then, and this will happen frequently in war, will you be in a position when you, together with your army corps or division, are given an independent task and have to make a decision that will redound to the advantage of the whole army.[32]

Throughout his time as Chief of the General Staff, Schlieffen attempted to teach his subordinates how to fight more effectively by teaching them to think for themselves. Staff problems and wargames did not have 'school solutions'. Those officers set staff problems had to justify and discuss their answers with Schlieffen and their colleagues. Wargame players were forced to develop their own courses of action and make their own decisions against reactive enemies. Such training tools were made as realistic as possible, with players being forced to make decisions quickly and with limited information. Schlieffen's games demanded that its players develop the ability to plan and issue orders rapidly, thus teaching how to issue clear orders and also how to follow the commander's intentions.

This command style was also central to Schlieffen's vision of how the German army should fight. Moltke the Elder had bequeathed to the army his idea of 'mission command'. Under this system, higher commanders were to issue 'directives' to subordinates, which would outline for them the higher commander's intentions and set them tasks to perform to meet these intentions. Higher commanders were to give subordinates the greatest possible latitude for accomplishing the tasks assigned to them.[33] Like Moltke and most other German soldiers, Schlieffen believed that only through this style of command could the large mass armies of the modern era be controlled. However, Schlieffen placed great emphasis on the importance of the commander's intentions. First, he believed that the higher commander had to elaborate clearly his plan and what goals were to be achieved. Second, and importantly given Moltke's difficulties in getting his subordinates to follow his directives, Schlieffen believed it was the responsibility of the subordinate commander to understand his commander's intentions and firmly subordinate his own actions to these intentions.[34] Schlieffen's goal was for 'the army commanders to make as their own the plan of the highest commander, and that *one* idea ... run through the entire army'.[35]

Schlieffen also had his ideas about how his subordinates should conduct their battles. In response to the increased lethality of modern weapons, his critiques and his writings continually stressed the efficacy of flank or encircling attacks.[36] Indeed, Schlieffen was criticized for his over-emphasis on these forms of attack and accused of developing a *Umfassungssucht*, or 'encirclement mania', within the General Staff.[37] However, a close examination of his critiques shows that, although he viewed flank attacks and encirclements as offering the best possible success for the least numbers of casualties, the method of attack would depend upon the tactical circumstances and Schlieffen did not rule out the use of a breakthrough. Indeed, the lessons taught by Schlieffen about the role played by terrain features and fortresses for blocking and channelling enemy forces often made breakthrough operations more likely in his games, and he did not hesitate to recommend such tactics.[38] The key lesson offered by Schlieffen was not the value of encirclements or flank attacks, but the necessity of destroying one's enemy as quickly and as thoroughly as possible by the method most appropriate to the situation.[39]

Despite having supposedly inculcated the officers under his command with an 'encirclement mania', the officers of Schlieffen's staff did not hesitate to employ other forms of combat when the situation demanded. Throughout the wargames conducted under Schlieffen's direction, a combination of breakthrough, envelopment and encir-

INTRODUCTION

clement operations was employed by the players. If Schlieffen had been able to reduce German tactics to a dogma, this would have been reflected in the conduct of his closest staff.[40]

SCHLIEFFEN'S STRATEGIC IDEAS

While staff rides, staff problems and *Kriegsspiele* were integral to training Schlieffen's subordinates in the ways of modern war, they also played another important role – that of planning.[41] Schlieffen used these media as means of trying out ideas for his war plans and for testing strategic concepts. Indeed, Schlieffen often went so far that he was at times criticized for using his wargames more for his own uses than for teaching, and hence for diminishing the usefulness of such teaching tools. One of Schlieffen's subordinates, Egon Freiherr von Gayl, wrote: '[The rides] more and more have the character of a study for the Chief himself, rather than for the participants ... One was only the instrument of an unspoken higher goal.'[42] However, it was not only Schlieffen's critics who recognized how Schlieffen manipulated his wargames for his own ends. Even one of Schlieffen's staunchest supporters, Hermann von Kuhl, had to admit:

> It is no lie that Graf Schlieffen usually altered now and then the course of the General Staff rides and *Kriegsspiele*. For him, it was less about the free play of two parties against one another, than the carrying out of a particular operational idea. He tested how an operation would take shape under particular circumstances, which courses of action a commander could find against the actions of his enemy. To this goal, he often deliberately put difficulties before one commander, while he made the situation easier for the other. It was, therefore, mainly a study for himself.[43]

Regardless of these criticisms, the fact that Schlieffen's wargames were often based upon German war plans was important. It ensured that Schlieffen's subordinates were thoroughly familiar with their commander's strategic ideas and that each General Staff officer knew how Schlieffen judged Germany's strategic situation. This allowed each General Staff officer to have a common approach once war broke out, regardless of whether or not he was privy to the exact details of Germany's deployment plan.

Despite having only a limited number of examples upon which to draw, it is possible to reconstruct some of Schlieffen's key strategic concepts.[44] First, all of Schlieffen's wargames involved Germany fighting a two-front war against at least France and Russia, and sometimes also against Great Britain. Thus, Schlieffen assumed the German army would be fighting against an enemy superior in numbers. It was also apparent from Schlieffen's wargames that he planned to utilize Germany's position between the two main enemies and to defeat each in detail. Thus, the bulk of the army would be deployed first against one enemy and then against the other after the first had been defeated.[45] Each of Schlieffen's pupils knew the importance of winning the initial victories rapidly, as the weak forces deployed to the other front would be under severe pressure until they could be reinforced.

The necessity for a rapid victory and a quick end to the war was a recurring theme throughout Schlieffen's games. Schlieffen was convinced that Germany's only chance against enemies with larger populations and economies was an early 'decisive' victory on the battlefield. Thus, Schlieffen proclaimed in his final *Kriegsspiele*:

> In western Europe ... the military machine with its thousands of wheels, costing millions to maintain, cannot stand still for long. One cannot fight a war for one or two years from position to position in 12-day-long battles until both combatants are completely exhausted and weakened and are forced to sue for peace. We must attempt to defeat our enemies quickly and decisively.[46]

Thus, when war broke out in the summer of 1914, Germany's corps of General Staff officers were well prepared by Schlieffen's training to fight a mobile war on two fronts. His staff problems, General Staff rides and *Kriegsspiele* had created officers adept at the operational level of war and inculcated with the key ideas of Germany's war plan. With a General Staff officer at the side of each corps and army commander and with many of these commanders having trained under Schlieffen, Kaiser Wilhelm II's army was generally able to outfight its opponents unit for unit. In the encounter battles along the Franco-German border, conscious of the need for a rapid victory to relieve their hard-fighting comrades in the east, German forces generally rapidly and soundly defeated their French opponents.[47] In the east, imbued with the knowledge that they were fighting a desperate holding action, the well-led 8th Army won their spectacular success against the slow-moving Russians. However, despite these early operational-level victories, German General Staff officers would soon learn that all their excellence at this level of war and all the operational-level victories in the world would not add up to strategic success.

1

General Staff Ride (East), 1894

In this ride, a weak German Ostheer *faced two Russian armies, one of which, the Niemen Army, advanced against East Prussia from the north and the other of which, the Narev Army, advanced against West Prussia from the south, from Congress Poland. Each Russian army initially disposed of four army corps and two cavalry divisions.*[1] *The Germans faced the Russians with five army corps, six reserve divisions and four cavalry divisions. This force level is close to what was intended in the German deployment plan for 1893/94. This plan called for four army corps, six reserve divisions, and four cavalry divisions to be deployed to the east, while the remaining three-quarters of the German army deployed on the western border with France. However, while the force levels are similar, the operational intention of the deployment plan was different from the ride. The German plan called for an offensive from Posen in cooperation with the Austro-Hungarians, for which three army corps, four reserve divisions and three cavalry divisions were earmarked.*[2] *That said, this ride is notable for the fact that it resulted in a similar battle to that fought by the German 8th Army in late August 1914, the so-called battle of Tannenberg.*

An army's deployment [*Aufmarsch*] is determined by the peacetime location of its troops, the nation's railroad network, and the border of the country against which the deployment is directed.[3] From these three factors, the deployment of any army can, for the most part, be calculated. This goes in particular for Russia, where the railroad network is simple and wide spread. Therefore, on the basis of not very complicated calculations, we can say with reasonable certainty that Russia will deploy against Germany one army on the Niemen River and another on the Narev River. If it is assumed in this ride that one army corps will assemble in the south of the Baltic Sea provinces and two others at Bialystok, it is not important. The essential point is that the Russian army will appear in two main groups far from each other on the Niemen and Narev Rivers.

Yet another detail is of significance. In the last 15 years, Russia has accomplished a great deal in preparing for war and in the advancement of her mobilization [*Mobilmachung*].⁴ However, the expanse of her country, the great distances of Russia, cannot be defeated. The reserve divisions with weak manpower pools [*mit schwachen Stämmen*], which have to take in men from the eastern provinces, will always be late in getting ready to march [*marschfähig*] and will appear even later on our borders.⁵ Therefore, if we allow the Russians to take the initiative, all the forces directed against us will be very late in taking the offensive. However, consideration for its ally may induce Russia to take the offensive before all its strength is assembled.⁶

This case was assumed here. Russia took the offensive with two armies (all together 10 army corps), while one army and seven reserve divisions remained behind. During the advance, detachments from the main forces were necessary, so that the 30 divisions at the start of the ride were quickly reduced to 16.

Very unfavourable conditions were assumed for the Germans. The Russian cavalry rendered almost unusable all the railroads on the right bank of the Vistula River and mobilization was essentially destroyed and brought to a halt in the corps districts of not only the German I and XVII Army Corps, but also of the II, V and VI Army Corps.⁷

In the face of this Russian advance, initially the Germans could only withdraw behind the Vistula River. It is not difficult to defend this river barrier from Thorn to the river's mouth with 16 divisions against an enemy of equal strength. Possibly, the Russians could be prevented from forcing the crossing. They were marching to cross the river above Thorn. This would give a favourable moment for the Germans to launch a counterattack, and this would win the Germans a respite. However, a respite would only defer the battle for the Germans. They could not look forward to substantial reinforcement, while the Russians could look forward to unifying their armies and coming up to full strength. The Germans would then have to deal with a unified army, while at this point they only faced two separated, smaller armies, whose communications could be repeatedly hindered by the cutting of the telegraph lines by German *Landsturm* troops.⁸

Obviously, the Germans had to exploit this situation. They had to attempt to strike one Russian army decisively and then turn against the other. There could be no doubt against which army the first attack should be directed. The direction of its advance made the Narev Army the more dangerous. It was also the army against which the greater part of the German strength could be assembled most easily. Once the German commander decided to attack the Narev Army, he had to bring together against the Russian army as many troops as were in his power. Not one division could be employed in another task, unless that task was essential. The only approvable course of action, therefore, was to unite all German strength, with the exception of the I Army Corps, the 1st Reserve Division and the 1st Cavalry Division, against the Narev Army. This would yield 13 infantry and reserve divisions, as well as three cavalry divisions. If these were assembled along the Deutsch Eylau–Strasburg line, the enemy would be forced, in the event of a successful attack, to retreat in an easterly direction, i.e., in the direction whence he could hope for the earliest meeting with the Niemen Army. This would hardly serve the Germans. The Narev Army had to be decisively struck and separated completely from the Niemen Army. This was only to be accomplished by enveloping the Russian right wing. The only approvable course, therefore, was for the German leader to advance with the III and V Army Corps in a southern direction by way of Osterode–Bergfriede, move the two reserve corps to Deutsch Eylau and south of there, and the II Army Corps to Strasburg. However, the XVII Army Corps was to withdraw to Neumark, avoiding contact with the advancing Narev Army.

As determined by their initial deployment, the two Russian armies advanced separately. They remained separated since they knew that they faced only weak enemy forces, whose annihilation could easily be brought about so long as they both continued their advance in the direction of Marienburg. However, the intelligence delivered to both army commanders up to 15 June should have convinced the two men that the Germans intended to take the offensive with the reported reinforcements, some of which were already over the Vistula. Under these circumstances, the unification of the two Russian armies should have been brought about without delay. This unification could not be attempted in the centre, since one would end up in the lake region, or to the north since the defiles between Preußisch Holland and Saalfeld allow no room for a large army to operate. It could only take place to the south, where the enemy's attack was to fall and where the enemy could be encountered to the greatest effect. The Niemen Army, therefore, had to march to the south. This is not to say that the Narev Army could remain idle; inactivity would abandon the Niemen Army to its fate. The Narev Army had to march to close with the Niemen Army, but before this could be done, it had to throw back the enemy facing it [the reinforced German XVII Army Corps] back behind the Gilgenburg–Lautenburg line.

Indeed, this was the initial intention of the Narev Army's commander. However, he did not continue with this course of action as the commander of the Niemen Army felt the German offensive was impossible and wanted to advance rapidly on the Vistula. Thus, there remained nothing for the Narev Army to do but to advance as before. Operations began on the 16th, when the Narev Army advanced over the Soldau and Niede. The German XVII Army Corps evaded the enemy's thrust, as per directive. The continuation of these operations on the 17th brought the Narev Army to the Gilgenburg–Lautenburg line and the German XVII Army Corps east of Neumark.

In the meantime, the remaining German corps had carried out their intended march. Given the position of the two armies, the Narev Army could continue its advance and face annihilation; come to a halt and avert the disaster; or it could evade to the east and, if the Niemen Army advanced in a southwestern direction, could place the Germans in the worst of all possible positions.

The commander of the Narev Army had, however, become convinced that the German offensive was directed against the Niemen Army and, therefore, that his task remained the same – to hold the enemy troops before him in Schach with a portion of his command and to advance with the rest to the right to support the Niemen Army. He held firm to this intention, despite knowing that the German II Army Corps was advancing from Thorn to Strasburg and despite being able to deduce that another enemy corps was drawing near from Graudenz. On the 18th, he decided to attack the German XVII Army Corps and, if possible, to defeat it before it was able to withdraw across the Drewenz and before the advancing German corps could reach it. If he were successful in this, he then wanted to advance with the greater part of his army to support the Niemen Army. With this decision, which was based on false assumptions but was at least decisive and energetic, he appeared to have overcome his certain defeat. Indeed, he nearly won the day brilliantly, for various circumstances aided his undertaking.

On the 17th, the combined German 2nd and 3rd Cavalry Divisions were successful in defeating the 4th Russian Cavalry Division before it could receive support from the 5th Cavalry Division. To stiffen the shaken cavalry of their right wing, a brigade of the Russian VII Army Corps was advanced. Although there could be no doubt about the strength of this brigade from the arriving intelligence, it was mistaken as a whole corps. Therefore, the attentions of the German III and V Army Corps, which were to carry out the decisive manoeuvre in the coming battle, were directed completely against the supposed enemy corps east of the Gilgenburger Lake. To allow the Russian corps to advance closer, the two German corps remained at first halted on the morning of the 18th, and with this the true battle more or less took place.

GENERAL STAFF RIDE (EAST), 1894

The German XVII Army Corps remained east of the Drewenz on the evening of the 17th. One can see here an error, since the remaining corps of the German right wing were to cross this river only on the 18th. Moreover, the 35th Infantry Division on the left wing of this corps was too far forward and remained in this exposed position until the Russians attacked early in the morning of the 18th. The situation certainly did not warrant holding such a forward position. On the contrary, the Russians seemed all the more dangerous the further they advanced. So it occurred that the 35th Division met the full force of the Russian X Army Corps, which possessed an almost three times greater weight of artillery, and was forced to retreat. The German II Reserve Corps, which now faced not only the victorious Russian X Corps but also the Russian VII Corps, would have had great difficulty restoring the situation had not the German I Reserve Corps deviated from its original march goal and advanced against the right flank of the Russians. Both Russian corps were forced to withdraw, since in the meantime the German V Army Corps had also finally arrived. In the process, the Russians, in particular their VII Army Corps, suffered a serious defeat.

On the left wing, the Russian corps advanced in two columns behind one another. The forward-most army corps (the IX) struck the German XVII (36th and 35th Infantry Divisions), but could not overcome the German resistance. The opportunity to hold the German II Army Corps, which had to cross the Drewenz in a single column, by means of the artillery of the Russian 6th Cavalry Division was missed. Therefore, as the Russian VIII Army Corps advanced, it found before it resistance from the already strong enemy force. In the artillery battle that followed, the Russians were not successful in gaining superiority, but they could have held their position had not their right wing withdrawn, causing the left to pull back also. It might have been possible perhaps to contrive to withdraw the infantry under the cover of the withdrawn guns, but they had certainly suffered severe losses. If the commander of the Narev Army did not yet feel himself completely defeated, the army's situation on the evening of the 18th left no doubt that the 19th must end with a fateful Russian defeat. On the German side, it was necessary to advance all their corps in the direction of the Soldau and to allow the cavalry divisions and the II Army Corps to cross the Soldau, and thereby to enmesh the Russians in a catastrophe on the river's few crossings. However, only a small portion of the German forces could conduct further pursuit; the main force had to turn against the Niemen Army, which had already drawn near.

Initially, the Niemen Army had intended to push the German forces facing it against the Frisches Haff by advancing its left wing. This plan was, however, thwarted when the enemy concentrated precisely against this same Russian left wing. Thus, during the course of the operations, the corps of the Russian right became the enveloping wing. The Germans pushed forward on the Russian left wing in the numerous defiles and broken ground, but were induced to withdraw by the advance of the Russian right wing. The Germans retreated, whether intentionally or not, in a southwestern direction. The Russians pursued; at first interested in the enemy, then, as the advance of the main German strength to the south became known, with the intention of coming to the assistance of the hard-pressed Narev Army.

The difficult retreat of the German I Army Corps was executed with great skill. With hindsight, it might be said that it would have been better to withdraw not in the direction of the main army, but rather for the I Corps to take to Marienburg and from there to be withdrawn not pushed forward again. There were sufficient *Landwehr* and *Landsturm* units on hand to block the defiles between the Narien, Mahrung and Eising Lakes. Cavalry could not advance so easily there, and communication between the two enemy armies was effectively broken. If this area could not be held, there was a second and a third position that could be held by even unseasoned troops against cavalry. If the I Army Corps withdrew gradually in the direction of Maldeuten–Preußisch Holland, it would have been very likely that the Russian army would have followed. All German communications would then have been covered. The Russian cavalry would have been given no insight into the German manoeuvre. The enemy would have followed in a direction that for him was unfavourable. If he had then marched to the south, he would have found the German I Army Corps standing on his flank, binding a considerable portion of his forces: the remainder would have reached the area of Osterode later, rather than earlier as actually happened.

After the main German army had thrown the Narev Army over the Soldau with great losses on the 19th, a small portion took up the pursuit on the 20th. In general, however, the day had to be used to bring order to the mixed-up units and to the supply trains and columns.[9]

It was obvious that the defeat of the Narev Army could not remain hidden from the Niemen Army after the 20th, and it was predictable that the Niemen Army would not enter into a battle with the victorious and doubly superior German army. The Niemen Army would neither advance further nor would it halt; it would have no other recourse but to withdraw and await reinforcement. Since the German and Niemen armies stood at least two days' march from one another, a simple pursuit would have been pointless. If the Germans were successful in reaching the enemy through forced marches, rear guard actions would have prevented a decisive battle from taking place.

Fortunately, however, the Niemen Army could not retreat in a normal direction. It did not have its homeland or its reinforcements to its rear, but rather the Haff and Königsberg. Therefore, it had to make a wheel, either a half wheel to make the border by way of Wehlau and Tilsit or a complete wheel between Insterburg and Angerburg to regain the great army route [*die große Heerestrasse*] by which it had earlier advanced. Both courses would be difficult. The first led over two formidable rivers and through swampy forests; the second was especially constrained by the Drengfurth–Astrawischen Forest (southwest of Insterburg, east of Allenburg). An army corps could escape through either route, but an army of 160,000 men with a march length of 60 kilometres and a breadth of around 30 kilometres could barely do so. There, the Germans had to seek out the Niemen Army in order to bring it to battle. Therefore, the corps of the German right wing, which stood at this time at Niedenburg, had to be moved to the line Passenheim–Rastenburg–Drengfurth. The other corps had to follow to the left and the I Army Corps had to pursue the enemy directly. If the enemy stopped before the northern tip of the Mauer Lake (east of Drengfurth) was reached, the German forces would only need to wheel to the left in order to attack the enemy from a fatal direction. This wheel would not have been difficult, since the army would have been arrayed in a sort of echelon formation. The right wing was already forward on the 20th, and the left was further back. In order not to lose any time, this situation would have remained the same during the march.

Indeed, it is worth mentioning that one would not have to deal only with the four-corps-strong Niemen Army alone under all circumstances. The Niemen Army could receive reinforcements from the rear or from across the Narev River. The Germans could hope to meet the latter before they united with the Niemen Army, and the former alone could not bring the Russians superiority.

This is indeed what the German commander intended to do. He wanted to catch the enemy, force him to do battle and to retreat in a northern direction. However, I believe that the march goals set to achieve this aim (Allenstein with the outermost right wing at around Wartenburg) were too close. It was impossible to catch the retreating Niemen Army at Allenstein–Wartenburg, even with the fastest marches. Therefore, it could only come to battle if the enemy voluntarily halted there or if he was blocked from marching out of Allenstein. Fortuitously, both conditions were met to a certain extent. The commander of the Niemen Army intended to halt at Allenstein–Wartenburg and the commander of the German 2nd *Armeeabteilung* decided to attack the enemy under any circumstances in order to hold him as long as necessary for the 1st *Armeeabteilung* to reach Allenstein and appear in his rear.[10] If, however, the Germans had no success, the failure lay in the fact that, first, a considerable error took place in the execution of the commander's correct ideas and second, neither in the entire operations plan nor in any subsequent directions was any consideration given to the fact that the enemy could receive reinforcements.

On the 21st, the Niemen Army, as has been said already, could not advance and could not stay in place, as it was not in a position to engage the doubly superior, victorious German army in battle. The Russians had to secure reinforcements, and these were on the way: on the evening of the 20th, the Russian VI Army Corps stood at Sensburg and Bischofsburg and the XI Army Corps at Friedrichshof. The former could join the Niemen Army without difficulty by means of a withdrawal in a northeastern direction; the latter only when it set out immediately in a northern direction. However, such a withdrawal did not lie within the intentions of the commander of the Niemen Army. He wanted to face the enemy again. To do this, he intended to take up position with the II, III, IV and V Corps at Allenstein, east of the Alle and north of Wadang. He wanted the VI and XI Corps to draw near and take the offensive as soon as possible against the German right wing. This chosen position did not seem favourable, as one would have to form a front to the south, whence the main attack was expected, and to the west, against the German I Army Corps. Regardless of this, it was questionable whether or not the overall situation [*Kriegslage*] warranted taking up a defensive position. As was well known, on the 19th and 20th the German right wing stood not far from Neidenburg, while the left was south of Lautenburg. Therefore, the latter was far behind, while the right-wing was exposed by its advance. If the Niemen Army halted and awaited the enemy, it would give the Germans time to concentrate their disorganized corps. It would appear more appropriate to have attacked the enemy right-wing with as much strength as possible, while staying on the defensive against the approaching weak German left. For such an operation, the Russian VI and XI Army Corps were already prepared. It was necessary only that the remaining corps of the previous Niemen Army be applied to this same goal.

On the 21st, both armies reached their prescribed march goals, the Germans largely by means of forced marches [*Doppelmarsches*]. Since the German 2nd *Armeeabteilung*, with the I Army Corps and the 1st Reserve Division, wanted to attack the enemy positioned behind the lake line and since the Russians, or at least the Russian right-wing, were unable to carry out a rapid withdrawal due to the location of their trains, it had to result in a clash here on the 22nd.

The column of the German wing farthest to the left (the 1st Reserve Division) was set in march against Locken. No care was paid to effective flanking cover or reconnaissance against the Russian II Corps (at Horn) and the Russian 2nd Cavalry Division (southwest of Mohrungen). Therefore, these Russian units could intervene very effectively in the battle that developed at Locken between the German 1st Reserve Division and the rearguard of the Russian III Corps. The 1st Reserve Division was thrown back against the I Army Corps' 2nd Infantry Division, and the entire I Corps soon found itself entangled in a battle in the forests north of Osterode. Its left flank repeatedly turned, the I Corps only found a solution to its problem on the southern edge of the forest.

It may appear questionable whether or not the Russian II Corps was properly employed, as despite direct orders to withdraw, it took the offensive. Without a doubt this offensive would have been a severe error if the Niemen Army had been limited to its original four army corps. A defeat on the 23rd easily could have followed the victory on the 22nd. However, since the enemy could not be avoided and since, in fact, the Russian commander wanted to strike the enemy, and since the doggedly following German I Army Corps would have to be dealt with in any case, it was more expedient to deal with the I Corps on the 22nd under especially favourable conditions than on the 23rd under perhaps worse conditions.

Poor reconnaissance had led here to a German defeat, and the same error would bring a similar calamity on the opposite wing.

Already at mid-day on the 21st, Russian cavalry had shown itself at Omulef on the Passenheim–Niedenburg road. This enemy, who appeared from a direction from which no enemy had been seen previously, did not, however, disturb the German 2nd and 3rd Cavalry Divisions. They hurried on towards the general goal of the army – Allenstein. The Russian cavalry retreated before the advance guard of the III Army Corps. However, the commander of the Russian XI Army Corps at Ortensburg was now accurately informed by this cavalry as well as by a detachment of the 7th Cavalry Division that had crossed the Omulef further upstream, as to the position of the outermost formations of the German right wing. Early the next day, the advance of the German corps in the direction of Passenheim was reported to him. Since he had already reached the western rim of the forest west of the Great Schoben Lake and the Schoben River, he set his own corps marching on Passenheim and allowed it to deploy there.

In the meantime, the Germans entered completely unsurveyed terrain. Their patrols were prevented from advancing by the Russian cavalry, so that they continued their march without knowing what was happening in their immediate surroundings. When the Russian commander believed that the enemy had advanced far enough, he attacked with his deployed corps. The Germans attempted to deploy for battle and to defend themselves as best they could. However, the German defeat was completed when a division of the Russian VI Army Corps, which bordered the XI Corps, hurried its march from Bischofsburg and entered the battle and when the 7th Cavalry Division flanked the German right wing and pushed on from the south. A division from the V Army Corps, which was dispatched to the battlefield as support, arrived too late.

Thus, the two corps of the German flanks were defeated, and with this, the entire operation was diverted from its goal. However, the German commander would not give up his undertaking. He withdrew his right wing (III and V Corps) behind the strong Alle sector (Lansker Lake [south of Allenstein] – Kurken). He wanted to take the offensive with his left wing (seven divisions) between the Schilling Lake and the Wulping Lake in the early morning hours of the 23rd. The three divisions of the centre between Alle and Wulping Lake were to await the results of the left wing's attack. These attacks would not have been carried out uniformly under the commands of the subordinates [*Unterführer*] and would have succeeded only with great difficulty in the face of the enemy's field positions. Not to mention that it was barely possible for the units to carry out the marches required to reach their positions by the attack hour (0300). Before the *Feldherr* could have adequately informed himself about the conditions on a 50–60 kilometres wide front, at least night would have fallen. Coming up with decisions for the next day and the composition and delivery of the orders would have also taken time. In order to reach the march goals at the specified time, one corps would have to decamp at 2100 on the 22nd. When one also considers that on the 21st a forced march was conducted and on the 22nd a further march was made, and now another, a night march, was to be undertaken, all in order to enter into a battle the next morning, one sees that it would be completely impossible for a march to be started before the orders for it could arrive. Although the German commander's idea was interesting and laudable, his orders for the 23rd were beyond the realm of the possible. Since there was no time to develop a new concept, the pursuit had to be broken off.

Some general comments are added: for reconnaissance, some commanders were satisfied with sending a great number of patrols and detachments in every conceivable direction whenever possible. The result of this is the entry of countless, insignificant reports, among which the most important are lost. Others sought reconnaissance by sending out patrols to the farthest possible points, which are often not reached or from which often there is no returning. Good reconnaissance requires above all exact knowledge of the overall situation [*allgemeine Kriegslage*] and of the intentions of the supreme commander [*Oberfeldherr*]. With this knowledge, the cavalry commanders can conduct reconnaissance principally in the direction about which one must be informed, where one has to avoid danger, or where one wants to produce results.[11]

One can say that between the fronts of the two armies a large number of patrols were always to be found, and that [both sides] were generally well informed as to what was occurring there. However, reconnaissance on the flanks was, in part, ignored. Thus, the Narev Army sent no one to determine what was happening in Osterode. When everything depended upon whether or not the Narev Army would continue to advance from the position Gilgenburg–Lautenburg toward the Drewenz on the 18th, barely a patrol was sent out from the German III and V Army Corps to determine whether the enemy advanced or not. In the crucial moment when this fact alone was in question, a fact that would determine whether the Russians could be dealt an effective blow, the available cavalry was repeatedly used to secure villages against surprises. On the 22nd, three and a half German cavalry divisions were assembled around Allenstein. They reported unanimously that the enemy stood south of the city. On the wing around Ortelsburg and Horn–Mohrungen, no cavalry remained, and because of this, the campaign was lost.

In other cases, strong cavalry forces deployed on the wings were used to advantage. If the 2nd and 3rd Cavalry Divisions on the German left wing had not screened the march of the III and V Army Corps, then the entire German operations plan would have been unworkable. The manoeuvre of the Russian 2nd Cavalry Division against the flank and rear of the German I Army Corps and the manoeuvre of the German 4th Cavalry Division against the left flank of the Narev Army were of the greatest significance.

A deployment of the cavalry to the front of an army has to cease when the armies come closer to one another. The choice is then whether to transfer the cavalry to the wings, i.e., where they can accomplish something effective during and after the battle, or behind the front, i.e., where they will remain inactive and will only be a hindrance to their own troops.

The art of commanding an army has changed fundamentally since earlier times. The commander can no longer direct the battle solely with the assistance of adjutants and orderlies. The expansion of armies has become too great. Moreover, a special order for battle cannot always be issued. Often a march order will have to replace the attack order, and indeed not a march order that leads directly to the battlefield, but rather a march order that sets the army in motion immediately after deployment has been completed and that finally leads to a clash with the enemy. If everything comes off smoothly and normally, the army corps will have nothing to do but deploy and attack when they finally clash with the enemy. The direction of an army corps' approach will determine whether it envelops an enemy wing, whether it breaks through the enemy line, etc. – in short, the form of battle that the *Feldherr* intended to be fought.[12] However, it is difficult to see everything turning out as easily as planned. Countless difficulties can arise that will make necessary sudden alterations to the original plan in one place or another. It will not always be possible to get new orders from the *Feldherr* in such cases. Further, telegraph and relay lines will fail. The necessity of issuing an order on his own authority will fall to a commanding general [*Kommandierender General*],[13] a subordinate. The commanding general must ensure that his decision falls within the sense of the supreme commander's intentions. Accordingly, he must take great pains to keep up to date on the picture of the larger operation [*Gesamtoperation*], and he must take great pains to understand the supreme commander's ideas.[14]

Since a commander cannot realistically handle a battle directly, the bringing about of a decision by means of a reserve held back from the battle is also barely possible. The battle lines are too long to bring reserves to the decisive point in good time, and the battlefield is too large to know where this decisive point will be when it is not predetermined by the general operation plan. The reserves in a modern battle (a battle of envelopment) belong on the enveloping wing. At the battle of Königgrätz, the 2nd Army can be seen performing the role of a decisive reserve; at Gravelotte, the XII Army Corps; in this ride on the 18th, the German III and V Army Corps.[15] It is beyond the ability of the supreme commander to direct this reserve. He must give up his claim to command these forces. As a rule, this task falls today to the general who commands at the appropriate spot. The day's decision, therefore, depends upon this commander knowing the overall situation and, thus, correctly determining the right spot and time to bring his troops.

GENERAL STAFF RIDE (EAST), 1894

RIDE PARTICIPANTS

(a) Directors

Generalleutnant Oberhoffer
Generalmajor Freiherr von Falkenhausen (from the evening of 19 June, commander of the German Vistula Army)
Oberst Freiherr von Rechenberg
Major von Unger
Hauptmann Chales de Beaulieu
Hauptmann Wegner

(b) German Side

Higher Commanders

Generalleutnant von Mikusch-Buchberg (commander of the Vistula Army until the evening of 19 June)
Generalmajor Freiherr von Hausen (commander of the reinforced XVII Army Corps until the evening of 19 June, then commander of the 2nd *Armeeabteilung*)
Generalmajor Meckel (commander of the reinforced I Army Corps until the evening of 19 June, then commander of the 1st *Armeeabteilung*)

Commanding Generals and Divisional Commanders

Oberst Sommer
Oberst Linde
Major von der Goeben
Major Deines
Major von Bagenski
Major Dittlinger
Major von Witzleben
Hauptmann Klingender
Hauptmann Koenig
Hauptmann Wangemann
Hauptmann von Basedow
Hauptmann von Alten
Hauptmann von Kraewel
Hauptmann von Henk

(c) Russian Side

Higher Commanders

Generalmajor von Sick (commander of the Narev Army)
Oberst Freiherr von Gayl (commander of the Niemen Army)

Commanding Generals and Divisional Commanders

Oberstleutnant von Heeringen
Oberstleutnant Rasmus
Oberstleutnant Gronau
Major von Twardowski II
Major Freiherr von Mauchenheim gen. Bechtolsheim
Major von Pritzelwitz
Major von Lochow
Major von Gründell
Major von Hartmann II
Hauptmann von Boehn
Rittmeister Freiherr von Reitzenstein
Hauptmann Leuthold

(d) Additional Participant

Major Herzog Albrecht von Württemberg

2

General Staff Ride (East), 1897

In this staff ride, eastern Germany faced invasion by overwhelmingly superior Russian forces advancing in four armies concentrically into East and West Prussia.[1] To face the Russian army of 'around a million men' organized into 36 divisions, the Ostheer *initially consisted of only five army corps, five reserve divisions and four cavalry divisions. However, Schlieffen assumed that the* Westheer *had successfully defeated the French and forced them back behind their fortress belt by the 25th mobilization day. Thus, the weak* Ostheer *received reinforcement of four army corps and four reserve divisions beginning on the 30th mobilization day. The German forces used in this ride differ somewhat from those earmarked for the east in the actual deployment plan for 1897/98. In this plan, the Germans intended to deploy six army corps, two reserve corps, four reserve divisions and five cavalry divisions. Like the preceding deployment year, Schlieffen intended to operate offensively in conjunction with the Habsburg army.[2]*

It was assumed during this year's General Staff ride that great numbers of Russian cavalry had fallen on the Prussian provinces east of the Vistula on the first mobilization day and that they had done considerable damage at various places to the railways there.[3] While the mass of this Russian cavalry was thrown back over the border again by the I and XVII Army Corps and by the rapidly transferred German cavalry divisions, the condition of the railways made their effective use impossible for a long period. Therefore, the Germans believed that they had to forgo offensive action in the east and restrict themselves to the defensive. They employed the greater portion of their armed forces against France, directing only three additional corps and three reserve divisions to the Vistula to support the I and XVII Army Corps.

In the meantime, the Russians carried out their deployment with two reserve divisions at Schawli (halfway between Riga and Tilsit), an army west of the Niemen, one at Bialystok and one on the Narev from Lomza to Warsaw. One reserve army was assembled at Wilna and a smaller one at Bielsk. In all, 36 divisions were deployed against Germany, an army of around a million men, the size of which, at least in modern times, has never been seen. The Russian army, deployed in a wide arc along the border from Schawli to Warsaw, advanced concentrically into the Prussian provinces. The Russian commander was given the task of pushing back all German forces that appeared and then to cross the Vistula between Thorn and Danzig. Since the left wing stood much closer to this goal than the right, it was held back somewhat, and this pause was used to move a number of the army corps and divisions deployed behind the front line to the area of Warsaw, reinforcing this wing. However, it was not possible to transfer all the reserve divisions; six, most of which had been earmarked for duties on the lines of communication, had to remain behind. Since an additional six were claimed by the encirclement of Königsberg and another to besiege Lötzen, the advance could only be continued from Königsberg with 23 divisions. These were divided into four armies, each of three army corps.

In the face of this general offensive, the German I Army Corps retired to Königsberg and the XVII Army Corps withdrew in the direction of Deutsch Eylau–Marienburg. Active, reserve, *Landwehr* and *Landsturm* units alike retired on a wide front. None entered into an encounter of any significance. Instead, they exerted themselves only in holding back the Russian cavalry and in preventing them from gaining any knowledge of circumstances on the German side.

On the 32nd mobilization day, the Russians had reached the Frauendorf–Guttstadt–Allenstein–Niedenburg–Mlawa–Sierpc–Wloclawek line. The Russian commander had anticipated that the Germans would give battle early with their few corps. Since this did not occur and since the reports arriving spoke only of weak forces east of the Vistula, he believed he could not continue his advance along the same line and that he would not be in a position to force the Vistula between Thorn and Danzig if the enemy still occupied, even if with only eight divisions, the river's right bank. This fear could only grow, as it was highly probable that the Germans would have received reinforcements.

On the 25th day, German arms won a victory in the western theatre of war that forced the French to retreat behind their fortress line. In the following days, first rumours and then definite reports reached Russian headquarters that German army corps were being transported from the west to the Vistula. Therefore, the Russian commander decided to envelop the reported Vistula position, cross the river at Plock, Wloclawek and Nieszawa, and to attack the enemy on the left bank of the river. The army of the left wing (the 4th) was to begin the crossing at Plock, then the 3rd Army was to cross at Wloclawek, and the 2nd

Army, which together with the 1st was to take over the role of covering the two other armies, was to follow at Nieszawa. Finally, the sole remaining army, the 1st, was to advance via Deutsch Elyau on Thorn and Graudenz.

However, this plan was not without grave faults. At Plock, one could cross with relative security, but Wloclawek and Nieszawa lay not far from the enemy's right wing at Thorn, and a destruction of the river crossings leading from Thorn would not have been possible. During the crossing, the Russian forces would be divided in the immediate vicinity of the enemy and would give the Germans the opportunity to win, through an advance on the left or the right of the Vistula, a victory over a half of the Russian army. Without a doubt, the advance and the crossing could be covered. However, the 1st Army, which was to advance via Deutsch Eylau on Thorn, was barely enough for this task. The 1st Army itself was more endangered the more decisively it set to fulfilling its task, as this would necessarily bring it closer to the defended areas. Therefore, as the circumstances were on the 32nd, there was nothing else for the Russians to do but to stick to their original intention of going straight for the Vistula and forcing a crossing.

As chance would have it, the prospects of the planned outflanking manoeuvre [*Umgehung*] were improved by the dispositions taken by the Germans. The German commander had refrained from deploying his weak forces along the Vistula. He had sent a reserve division to Graudenz and another to Thorn and intended with the rest (three army corps and a reserve division) to operate offensively against the flank of the enemy in co-operation with the XVII Army Corps as soon as this unit was brought up to the Vistula. All intelligence arriving about the Russians indicated that their left wing was advancing directly on the Vistula from Warsaw. Therefore, there did not appear to be a favourable opportunity to attack this wing. On the other hand, the Russian right wing was not secured in the same way; it was not marching right along the coast of the Frisches Haff and had weakened itself by leaving detachments at Königsberg. Therefore, the German commander directed his attentions to this wing and assembled his small army on the Nogat. The additional units that would reach him from the Rhine reinforced him in his plan. However, four complete army corps with their accompanying reserve divisions could not all be brought to the Nogat – if for no other reason than that the rail lines running from the west to the east forced a deployment of the German forces on the Elbing–Thorn line.

Therefore, the attack on the Russian right wing could only be carried out with part of the German forces. The nearer to the Vistula this took place, the more effective it would be. However, now the enemy left wing also drew near. The Russian column, originally almost 500 kilometres long, now shortened to around 200 kilometres and became denser every day. The more the Russian line shortened, the less opportunity to attack the flank of a long column. Therefore, the German commander decided not to hold off his attack any longer, even if the Russian wing to be attacked was still fairly far from the Nogat and the Vistula.

The execution of this plan occurred simultaneously with the beginning of the Russian crossing of the Vistula. Thus, the German undertaking was not initially threatened. An offensive from the Thorn–Bromberg line or from the lower Drewenz could not stop it, since the main German forces were assembled far away on the opposite wing. If now the Russian right wing was refused somewhat and marched in a southern direction to take up cover behind the Passarge, the German offensive from the Nogat would turn out to be fairly harmless.

From the positions of the two opponents on the evening of the 33rd day, it was to be seen that the 2nd, 3rd and 4th Cavalry Divisions were assembled on the German left wing. This force was going be joined by another division formed from the cavalry regiments of the infantry divisions.[4] On the 34th, these four divisions were to advance from east of the Elbing and push back the cavalry of the Russian right wing, which had pushed forward to the Oberländer Canal. Additionally, they were to determine the position or the march direction of the corps of the enemy's wing. The attack of the superior German cavalry succeeded. The Russian cavalry was beaten and sought cover from the infantry who were located between Mohrungen and Liebstadt.

The report from here brought a disappointment for the German commander. He had hoped that the Russian march columns would have already advanced farther, so that an effective attack could be launched. The hope that the Russians would continue their march on the next day and that they might thereby place themselves in an unfavourable position was natural. From this hope, however, arose the belief that the enemy would, in fact, advance. Therefore, the V and VI Army Corps received the order to await the enemy at Liebemühl and Alt-Bestendorf, respectively, and allow themselves to be attacked. While the Russians were attacking there, the VII and VIII Army Corps were to fall on their flank and rear.

Such a plan, to allow the enemy to attack a force in a good defensive position and then to fall upon the flank and rear of the exhausted enemy and finish him off, appears very tempting. One can hardly think of a better way of annihilating an enemy. However, the enemy rarely enters into such a well-laid trap. Indeed, this was shown here. To find out exactly why, one has to put oneself in the place of the Russian 1st Army.

The on rush [*Vorbrechen*] of the German cavalry in such noteworthy numbers could only be the introduction of a large-scale undertaking.

After all, the Germans would not amass almost all their cavalry in one place and thereby weaken the rest of their line to gain a worthless victory over the Russian cavalry. It was to be expected that the cavalry would be followed by infantry or that the infantry would appear from another direction. Indeed, this is how it was seen by the Russian 1st Army. If they continued their advance on Liebesmühl, they would find there an enemy force, while another followed in the difficult, lake-broken terrain. Therefore, it is understandable that the Russians halted. That they did not begin a withdrawal in the face of enemy cavalry was also justified.

Under these circumstances, only a rapid, energetic attack by the Germans, an intervention by all available forces, could lead to their goal. Every delay and every halt could only impede the result. From the German left wing, the VII Army Corps was sent to Mohrungen and the VIII Army Corps to Great Hermenau–Liebstadt. From the cavalry corps, one division held the beaten Russian cavalry in check at Sportehnen and two divisions crossed the Passarge and sought to come upon the enemy's rear.

On the 35th, the Russian I Army Corps was set upon widely along the Mohrungen–Great Hermenau–Liebstadt line and in the evening the 1st Army had to begin a retreat.

The Germans were unable to record a decisive victory. Their commander believed that such a victory was no longer to be found here and decided to march the corps of the left wing to the right to meet the enemy he believed to be approaching from the south.

However, this was impossible to carry out. These corps still faced the enemy nearby. The Russians would have followed the departing corps and a battle under disadvantageous circumstances would have developed. Before seeking out a new enemy, you must first defeat the enemy standing before you. Moreover, events proved themselves more powerful than the given orders. On the 35th, the German XVII Army Corps advanced from the area of Burgfriede and beat an enemy division at Great Schmueckwalde pushing it back on Wittigwalde.

If he had been free in his decisions, the commanding general [*der Kommandierende General*] could not have decided for anything other than an advance. A defeated enemy stood before him, an enemy which he had to pursue. He knew that in the next days cannon fire would be heard and that he had to march to this fire. A battle was ahead of him and, in this battle, the Germans could not be strong enough. The enemy could evade to the south and shun any defeat. None other than the XVII Army Corps could prevent this retreat. Perhaps the enemy would retire on Allenstein, and no German corps stood closer to Allenstein than the XVII Corps. Therefore, it was regrettable that the commanding general decided instead to follow his original order [*Befehl*] and march off to the south.[5] In the end, the enemy was beaten on the Alle by the three army corps of the German left wing, and his position from Guttstadt to south of Allenstein was threatened. The Germans were successful in breaking through and finally in inflicting on the Russians a decisive defeat.

With this, the Russian 1st Army was the first to withdraw from the act. It owed its fate to an overwhelming desire to stay in close contact with the enemy. If it had held off from this overwhelming enemy somewhat more, it would have achieved its goal of drawing the enemy upon itself and occupying him without exposing itself to a decisive defeat.

On the Russian left flank, the crossing of the Vistula was in progress. On the 36th, four corps stood on the left bank and had begun to march to the west. Then, the report of the battle of the 1st Army at Mohrungen on the 35th arrived. These and other reports left no doubt that the German army had taken the offensive on the Vistula's right bank.

The Russian commander now had to bear the consequences of his decision to cross the Vistula. If he continued to cross over, he would have no enemy before him, but one behind. He would not have won the left bank without considerable losses. The Germans stood closer to the bridges at Nieszawa and Wloclawek than the corps of the 2nd Army, and to the defeat of the 1st Army another partial defeat could be added. There was the possibility that he could continue operations on the Vistula's left bank with only two-thirds of his force. And these operations would have proved to be without any purpose [*gegenstandslos*]. If he marched on Berlin, he would certainly be pursued by the Germans. The battle that would come sooner or later would be fought under bad circumstances for the Russians.

On the other hand, a withdrawal to the right bank of the Vistula was not without its problems. Implicit in an order given to the corps already across the river to turn around and re-cross the river is the idea that the supreme commander has made an error that now has to be rectified. This would have to result in the troops' trust in their leadership being considerably shaken. And, aside from this negative effect on morale, to carry out a new deployment in the face of the enemy would not be without danger, and it would be difficult to end up in a favourable position. Therefore, the question arose whether it would have been more desirable to assemble the army farther to the rear, somewhere behind the Przasnysz–Plock line or at Warsaw and behind the Narev and use this as a base from which to launch anew the campaign, which now had no good outcome in sight. This withdrawal certainly would not be very heroic, but it definitely would have been the most unwelcome step for the Germans. They could not deprive the western theatre of war of nine army corps for long. For the Germans, everything depended upon quickly bringing the campaign in the east to a decisive end. They had no time left. Therefore, the time that would have been lost by needing to follow the retreating, unbeaten Russians would have been sorely felt.[6]

However, the Russian commander decided on the 36th to withdraw with all his forces only to the right bank of the Vistula and to restore the earlier conditions as quickly as possible. He could carry this out unmolested, because the Germans did not make use of the Russians' poor situation. They faced strong Russian cavalry and, owing to their own deficiency in this arm, were unable to locate the Russian corps. None the less, deduction allowed them to gain a fairly accurate picture of the Russian situation.

The Germans knew that the Russians would be busy for some time with the crossing. Some corps would already be on the left bank and others would be drawn up ready to cross on the right bank. In short, the bulk of the Russian army was to be found near the river. However, if only the Russian right wing (the 2nd Army) was located at Lautenburg, it would follow that strong enemy forces could be at hand in the area between Lautenburg and the Vistula. However, although three German army corps were in the area of Allenstein, there still remained on the Drewenz sufficient troops to take up the offensive and have a good chance of success. The German commander rejected such a risky offensive, because he did not believe he had a clear enough picture of the situation. Instead, he wanted to assemble all his forces before undertaking anything. Without a doubt, this gave the enemy the time to extract himself from a poor position and with reassembled, even reinforced, forces to set forth again. If the Germans were resolved to assemble all their strength before going on to the offensive, then their plan of operation was set: they had to march against the enemy's rearward lines of communication in the hope of forcing him, in the case of a victory, against the Vistula. The corps of the left wing were set in march from Allenstein on Niedenburg–Mlawa. The other corps had to follow to the right, and the right wing could be made comparatively weak and be refused somewhat. Accordingly, the idea was executed not, however, with the intention of pushing the enemy on to the Vistula, but rather to break through his line at the place where he was believed to be weak.

The progress of the march was disturbed by two episodes that would have been better left undone. An undertaking was directed at Hohenstein on the 38th day and another at Lautenburg on the 39th day. The presence of the enemy was reported at both places. A number of German columns were concentrated on these villages, but found them deserted. The Russians had employed the same method as the Germans:

they were marching. The German columns enveloped one another. From this one can learn that in an envelopment the columns should not be directed to converge on *one* point, but instead must advance in parallel until the enemy is found and then wheel in according to need.

On the 41st, both armies had completed their deployment and stood parallel to each other. This is a picture usually depicted at the conclusion of *Kriegsspiele* and General Staff rides. It is a sign of trouble when both, or at least one of the commanders, allow for no possibility of enveloping the enemy. Indeed, such a deployment certainly promises no decisive defeat, but equally promises no decisive victory.

To win the parallel front, the Russian 2nd Army also had to withdraw. As the decision was made to bring the 2nd Army back to the Vistula's right bank and the right wing of the 2nd Army had begun the march from Gilgenburg to Lautenburg, it received the order to stay where it was in order to cover the flank of the Russian army. In this position, it was extremely exposed; indeed, seldom has a force covering a flank needed its own flank covered like the two corps of the 2nd Army. This army was subsequently withdrawn behind the Soldau to a position south of Lautenburg, and, finally, it was moved somewhat east from its Lautenburg position. Even here, the 2nd Army still stood in an exposed position, but was not initially withdrawn any further. Before this could occur, there needed to be an outside stimulus, and this stimulus was to be given by the German cavalry. As soon as the head of the German cavalry showed itself, the army order would be given, the content of which should run something like: 'Enemy cavalry has shown itself before the army's front. In order to avoid all encounters, the army will retire, etc.' However, it would be difficult to call for great feats of arms from an army that has been given such an order and invited to march off at the mere appearance of an enemy.

Until the 41st day, the Russians had intended to envelop the German right wing. They would barely have succeeded in this, as it is very difficult to carry out an envelopment from a parallel front. As a rule, in order to carry out such an envelopment, a long sideward movement would have to be executed to win the enemy flank. This would encounter great difficulty in the present situation. On the western wing, the Russians were confined by the Vistula. They would have to cover themselves from Thorn, and this would leave only limited forces available for the envelopment. Indeed, the Russians themselves faced envelopment on the opposite wing before they could carry out their own envelopment by an enemy who was somewhat closer.

Reports arriving on the 41st put strong enemy strength on the lower Drewenz. This created a fear that the Germans were likewise intending an envelopment with their western wing and that the Russian envelopment would not be equal to the German one. To avoid a battle under unfavourable conditions, the Russian left wing (three corps) was to make a rearward wheel [*Rückwärtsschwenkung*] on the 42nd day and form a defensive position [*Defensivhaken*] behind the Skrwa. This would have been a dubious step even if a general defensive was intended, but when the centre was to advance, as was actually ordered here, the formation of a defensive position was extremely dangerous. The defensive position could offer no cover and no protection. Contrary to intention, the left wing of the Russian centre was now more exposed to an attack than before; the left wing of the advancing army was laid bare, rather than covered.

The right wing faced similar fears. Since the Russians had given up the idea of an envelopment on the left because of the strong German force on the lower Drewenz, the decision was now to fall on the right. However, the Germans might also intend an envelopment there. The Russians believed that they had first to deprive them of this envelopment. Therefore, the right wing received the directive to remain in position, but in case of enemy attack to withdraw to Ciechanow immediately.

On the 42nd day, the Russian side was formed thus: in the centre, five army corps were advancing; on the left wing, three corps were wheeling rearward; and on the right wing, two and a half corps were standing their ground. Since on the German side similarly strong armies advanced, the outcome could not be in doubt. The Russian situation was improved somewhat when the right wing (2nd Army) joined the advance of the centre. However, a success could not be obtained here, as the Germans held back in order to impose a strenuous march upon their not much stronger enemy and because the three divisions intended for an envelopment were held up by the swampy banks of the overflowing Orzyc.

The Russian centre, six army corps strong after the transfer of a corps from the 2nd Army, had set upon the advance along a 60 kilometre wide front, although its left wing (XXII Army Corps) was far behind. It was obvious that on such a wide front gaps between the separate corps and divisions were bound to form and that the enemy, who advanced in great strength and in close order, was sure to find the opportunity to break through the Russian line and to envelop individual portions of the Russian force. Additionally, the Germans were assisted by the terrain and occupied a position that was, in general, better for deployment at the initial encounter. Although the Russians would meet almost everywhere an enemy who was stronger or at least as strong, they were faced always with the choice of either attacking or turning around due to the nature of the terrain. In the various skirmishes, the

Germans were subsequently victorious or at least came away with no disadvantages. The final decision was brought by the German right wing, which found no enemy before it (the Russians were occupied with their rearward wheel) and could advance unhindered against the enemy's left flank.

The somewhat strange Russian manoeuvres on the 42nd therefore indicated that the Russian leader intended to do battle only on the 43rd. The march on the 42nd was only to serve as preparation for this battle. The original plan, held to until the 41st, was made null and void by the cavalry reports, which placed a very strong enemy on the lower Drewenz. Under these circumstances, there could be no chance of enveloping the enemy's western wing, but rather there was the very real fear of being enveloped there by the Germans. Accordingly, the attack plan had to be altered and the offensive transferred to the eastern wing. To accomplish this, however, it would have been necessary to reorganize the front and in particular to remove the threatened left wing from the influence of the enemy.

However, this does not explain all, let alone excuse all. There still exists a contradiction: one has set the battle for the 43rd, i.e., has acted as the master, but has at the same time left one's own actions fully dependent upon those of the enemy. Another contradiction lies in the fact that the left wing has been refused and the centre has moved forward. That the right wing is to provide the decision, but has received orders to withdraw in the event of an enemy attack, cannot be seen as a sign of decisive action. Fear of the enemy, concern for one's own forces, was clearly stronger than the desire to beat the enemy. Without a doubt, one wanted to beat the enemy, but thoughts turned even more to not being beaten by the enemy.

These cautious steps, which the Russian commander believed he had to take, were not respected by the enemy. The Germans did not keep the appointment set by the Russians, and instead struck their enemy mercilessly.

The position of the Russians was in no way good after the decision was taken to return to the right bank of the Vistula. Additionally, one could not easily demand to re-cross the Vistula, even if it offered a brilliant victory. That the deployment on the right bank of the Vistula was successful had already been proved. If the Russians had advanced on the 42nd with all available strength, they would in all likelihood have brought the Germans to a halt. If they wanted to accomplish more than this, they would have to reckon with another crossing of the Vistula and another campaign [*Feldzug*].

It was the task of the Germans after the victorious battle to begin an immediate pursuit. No harm would come from the Russian right wing.

It could retreat harmlessly back to Putusk and Rozan, but one could hinder the retreat to Zegre and Nowo Georgiewsk. However, one must above all attempt to push the Russian left wing and the greater part of the Russian centre against the Vistula. Along the river, many bridges had already been destroyed, and the Russians could here destroy and there build more bridges according to need. While this is easily and brilliantly done on paper, it is doubtful whether in reality the issuing of orders or the execution of the task would have gone perfectly. In army headquarters, certainly, each corps was intended to have its own bridge across the Vistula, but soon after the order was issued, intentionally and unintentionally, some bridges would be used by more than one corps. This would happen regardless of the correct functioning of the order system. Moreover, what *Feldherr* would have been in a position on the 42nd to gain a clear picture as to what had happened 100 kilometres distant. What staff, given the available intelligence, would have been able to assign individual corps lines of retreat and bridges to cross and influence just where each unit, down to the individual divisions and baggage trains, would be along during the retreat? In reality, the impression would quickly be gained that each corps, each division, and perhaps even each brigade would have to seek out the best and closest roads and bridges for itself. The unavoidable result would be confusion and a crossing of paths. In order to take advantage of and to increase this certain confusion, the Germans had to advance south against the Vistula immediately and without pause.

The task of possibly hindering the German operation fell to the intact Russian right wing. Standing on the left flank of the Germans, it could effectively bring the pursuit to a halt and give the beaten Russian corps the opportunity and time to reach security.

RIDE PARTICIPANTS

(a) Directors

General der Infanterie Oberhoffer
Generalmajor Freiherr von Rechenberg
Major von Unger
Hauptmann von Volkmann

(b) German Side

Higher Commander
Generalmajor Rothe (commander of the German *Ostheer*)

Commanding Generals and Divisional Commanders
Oberst von Wittken
Major Mattiaß
Major Claasen
Major Freiherr von der Goltz
Major von Hutier
Major Rogge
Major Staabs
Hauptmann Wangemann
Hauptmann Wundt
Hauptmann von Studnitz

(c) Russian Side

Higher Commanders
Generalmajor Freiherr von Gayl (commander of the Russian Northwestern Army)
Oberst Gronau (commander of the 4th Army)
Oberstleutnant Graf Yorck von Wartenburg (commander of the 3rd Army)
Oberstleutnant Waenker von Dankenschweil (commander of the 2nd Army)
Major Dittlinger (commander of the 1st Army)

Commanding Generals and Divisional Commanders
Major von Krosigk
Major Roos
Major von Trossel
Major Prinz Friedrich von Sachsen-Meiningen
Hauptmann Fuchs
Hauptmann Schwarte
Hauptmann von der Esch
Hauptmann von Bülow-Stolle

3

General Staff Ride (East), 1899

The Ostheer *in this staff ride faced the entire Russian army without the assistance of Austro-Hungarian forces.*[1] *The four original army corps of the* Ostheer *were quickly reinforced by three additional army corps. By the 30th mobilization day, the Germans could muster seven army corps, eight reserve divisions and four cavalry divisions. However, this German force faced 12 Russian army corps, four rifle brigades, ten reserve divisions and 14 cavalry divisions advancing in four armies from Congress Poland and northern Russia. On the German side, the forces used here were roughly equal to those assigned to the east in the deployment plan (variant II) for 1899/1900. For the first time in this mobilization year, the Germans developed two deployment plans, one that called for the entire German army to be deployed against France and another that would have deployed two-thirds of the army against France and the remainder against Russia. In this second plan, seven army corps, two reserve corps, four reserve divisions and five cavalry divisions were due to be deployed along the Russo-German border.*[2]

As the basis for this staff ride, it was assumed that Germany found itself at war with France and Russia, while Austria maintained a neutral attitude. Russia kept a portion of its army deployed against Austria and turned with the rest against Germany. It advanced with 12 army corps, 12 cavalry divisions and three rifle brigades – around half a million combatants [*Streiter*] – arrayed in four armies against the middle Vistula, while at the same time a reserve army (the Niemen Army) of ten reserve divisions, two cavalry divisions and a rifle brigade was to fall upon East Prussia from the Niemen River in order to guard the Russian right flank.

The Russian deployment on the Vistula took a considerable amount of time since only two rail lines were available and around half the troops were ordered to march by foot. It was only completed on the 26th mobilization day. Initially, the 4th Army crossed the Vistula at Iwangorod. It was followed in succession by the 3rd Army at Warsaw, the 2nd at Nowo Georgiewsk, and on the 30th day, the 1st Army at Plock. On the 27th and 28th days, the Niemen Army entered East Prussia.

The Russian commander knew that the Germans had left only around four army corps and a few cavalry divisions on the eastern border. The rest of the German armed forces were in motion against France. By the 32nd, he also became aware that two or three German corps were dispatched from the west to reinforce the eastern border. Where the Germans would assemble was uncertain. Therefore, the Russian commander decided to march on Berlin, on the assumption that the enemy would make a stand somewhere before him. He also assumed that the Germans would not meet him in front, but would operate on his flanks, i.e., out of the south from Silesia or out of the north from the Netze River sector. The Russian commander did not believe an offensive from the south was likely, since there was not a great deal of space on the left bank of the Oder, and, therefore, the Germans would be forced to violate Austrian territory in the case of a defeat. An operation against his left flank appeared to him to be far more advantageous for the Germans, since then the fortress of Thorn would really come into play and, particularly, since the Germans would remain closer to their troops on the lower Vistula in such an operation. Therefore, he believed with some certainty that he would find the main German forces assembled in the Netze River sector. Accordingly, he let the two lead armies of the right wing (the 1st and 2nd) turn against the Netze sector at the border. The results of this reconnaissance would determine whether the whole Russian army [*Heer*] or at least the greater part of it would be deployed on this side or whether the originally intended march on Berlin would be taken up again. His luck, as well as German counter-measures, convinced the Russian commander of the necessity of abandoning his scheme of marching on Berlin. As it was planned – the 3rd Army was to advance directly on the fortress of Posen and the 1st and 2nd Armies were to march into the angle between Posen, Thorn, the Netze and the Warthe, while the 4th Army was to advance south of Posen, isolated and threatened from Silesia – it could not have led to a happy end. If one were dead set on marching on to Berlin, despite the conviction that the enemy was not to be found in this direction but rather on the left or the right flank, it would have been advisable to advance to the south of Posen, rather than marching directly towards Posen even if this was the most obvious route, as this would avoid splitting up the armies right from the start [*von Hause aus*].

Initially, the Germans had left on the eastern border only the I, XVII, V and VI Army Corps, along with their attached cavalry, reserve divisions and *Landwehr* brigades, and the 4th Infantry Division. These units withdrew behind the Vistula before the advance of the Russian Niemen Army from East Prussia.

At this point, the German *Ostheer* received reinforcement – the II and III Army Corps along with part of the IX Corps and the Guard Cavalry and the 4th Cavalry Divisions were transported by rail from the west. Due to the differences in their peacetime organization, the six army corps now available had very different strengths.[3] Subsequently, they were reorganized into eight corps of equal strength, each of two divisions and one reserve division, or 37 or 38 battalions and 25 batteries. Each regiment was re-formed with three battalions. In this way, the Russian army's 408 battalions, 312 squadrons and 1,560 guns could be met by the German *Ostheer*'s 299 battalions, 148 squadrons and 1,260 guns. The German infantry amounted to three-quarters of the Russian, the German cavalry around a half, while their artillery came to nearly four-fifths of the Russian.

On the 30th, the *Ostheer* was deployed thus: on the heavily fortified stretch of the Vistula from Thorn to Danzig stood the I, XVII and XX Army Corps with the 1st, 35th and 6th Reserve Divisions; at Schneidemuhl–Bromberg stood the XXI Army Corps with the 3rd Reserve Division; between Posen and Glogau, the V Army Corps with the 9th Reserve Division; and between Breslau and Oppeln, the VI Corps with the 11th Reserve Division.[4] The 1st and 2nd Cavalry Divisions were still east of the lower Vistula in contact with the cavalry of the Niemen Army. The 5th Cavalry Division was in upper Silesia. As support for the cavalry divisions and to cover the border, 14 *Landwehr* brigades and *Landsturm* from six army corps, to which were joined a number of cavalry regiments, were deployed on the lower Vistula, the Netze, the Warthe and the Obra and pushed forward to the Prosna. The fortresses of the eastern border were fully alert and provided with full garrisons.

The II and III Army Corps with the 17th and 5th Reserve Divisions and the Guard Cavalry and 4th Cavalry Divisions were in transit.

The German commander believed himself unable to meet the overwhelmingly superior enemy frontally at Posen on the direct route to Berlin. He feared that he would be completely enveloped and crushed by the superior enemy. Instead, he wanted to operate against one of the enemy wings in order to secure superiority at a particular point. Since, in regard for the concentric Russian advance against the lower Vistula, the left German wing could no longer advance over this river, superiority had to be striven for on the right wing. To this end, he decided to remain on the defensive on the lower Vistula with three reserve divisions and to draw the Russian army upon a German army of three corps and two reserve divisions deployed on the upper Netze between the Warthe and the Vistula. The main German strength (five army corps and four reserve divisions), however, he decided to assemble in Silesia. This force would be temporarily held back, but then launched in an attack on the Russian wing.

Various criticisms can be made about this plan. The deployment of the forces resulted in a division of the comparatively small army, which could be fatal. Only around half the total strength remained available for the decisive battle. The pushing forward of the northern army (Netze Army) to the border would bring the enemy's advance to a halt sooner, although it was in the interest of the Germans to allow the Russians to come into German territory as far as possible to meet the Russian left wing with greater certainty. Finally, everything depended on concealing the presence of the southern (Silesian) army from the enemy for as long as possible. While the Germans could certainly calculate on their movements being kept secret in their own countryside, the presence of such a large army on their flank could not remain a secret for long, especially as the Russians had twice as much cavalry available.

None the less, the German plan was based on a correct idea. Since a breakthrough is ruled out, the only possibility a weaker army has of defeating a stronger, and therefore less mobile, army is to set upon the stronger enemy's wing while keeping his front engaged. There is no rule as to how this is to be accomplished; the method is dependent upon the skill of the commander and the circumstances of the action. It will not always be necessary or expedient to deploy in 'close order' the units earmarked for use in the decisive action beforehand; a separation of the units will generally be necessary due to the preceding strategic situation [*die vorhergegangene Kriegslage*]. However, proper manoeuvring must assemble all available forces at the decisive point. The prospects of accomplishing this here were lacking.

While the Netze Army had assembled its forces on the Argenau–Gnesen line by the 36th and the Silesian Army was still deciding to transport its corps by rail to the Gleiwitz–Oppeln–Breslau line, the Russian army [*Heer*] continued its advance and came into contact with the Netze Army with its reinforced cavalry. In order to draw the attention of the Russians towards themselves and cause them to advance in a northeastern direction, the commander of the Netze Army gave the order to advance along the whole line against the lead Russian detachments to the defiles of the Goplo and Powidz Lakes.

This undertaking by the Netze Army on the 37th was successful. The Russian advance troops were pushed back. The Russian commander, under the impression that he had considerable enemy troops before him, held back the six corps that faced the three German corps and advanced with his 3rd and 4th Armies. He intended to envelop the enemy's right flank with the 3rd Army, while the 4th Army was to be kept back as protection for the left flank.

The Netze Army felt itself too weak to continue to play the roll of bait and to continue to draw the enemy upon itself in the same manner. Instead, they believed it would be possible to induce the enemy to follow their withdrawal on the 39th. However, this stratagem, like all such stratagems, failed to lock the enemy in an unfavourable position.

It must be granted that the Netze Army, as it had been assembled, was exposed to danger. The three army corps stood in close order, but separated from one another in rough, broken terrain. If one corps was attacked by the superior enemy, the others could come to its aid only with great difficulty, and the necessary retreat through the area's defiles threatened to become fatal. Since the objective here was not to defeat the enemy, but rather to show the enemy numerous troops, who could then be withdrawn quickly, perhaps it would have been better to deploy the three corps in smaller (brigade-sized) detachments along a wide front. These could then have been withdrawn without much difficulty. Better, though, would have been to give the front to *Landwehr* and *Landsturm* troops, while the three army corps were concentrated on the right wing. These three corps could then fall upon the flank of the enemy advancing between Posen and Thorn.

The Netze Army's evasion on the 39th made it clear to the Russians that they were not facing the main German army here.

In the meantime, the assembly of the Silesian Army was almost complete. In order to hide their position on the Oder from the enemy for as long as possible, the German commander ordered that the cavalry show themselves to the considerably superior Russian cavalry as little as possible and that the advanced *Landwehr* brigades press the Russian reconnaissance detachments and prevent their advance. Although the concealment of the cavalry worked well, the concealment of the army could not last long. From the beginning, belief in the operation was lacking. The *Landwehr* brigades did not press the Russians, but retreated instead. This allowed the three strong Russian cavalry corps, supported by rifle brigades, to reconnoitre the land between Posen and Breslau to the Golgau. Thus, on the 39th, the Russians received the decisive intelligence that there were German infantry posts on the Bartsch.

This report, together with the retreat of the German Netze Army, let the veil fall from the German plan of operations and alerted the Russian commander that his left flank was threatened by the main German forces coming from Silesia. At this point, he decided to turn against this new enemy with the bulk of his army. He did not allow the 4th Army to continue its initial march. From the 41st to the 43rd, it withdrew over the Prosna to the Kalisz–Sieradz line, while the 3rd Army turned sharply left and advanced to the Neustadt–Jarotchin line. The XX Army Corps from the 2nd Army was to follow the movement of the 3rd Army via Wulka–Wrechen from Kochowo. Three corps from the 2nd and 1st Armies were to push the German Netze Army back by yet another day's march.

From these orders it is obvious that the corps of the right wing (the 3rd Army and the XX Army Corps) offer the German Netze Army first their flank and then their rear; that the Netze Army's pursuit begins in a sluggish manner; and that the left wing of the 4th Army stop and wheel. It appears very questionable whether an army would be in a condition to carry out such a manoeuvre without its trains and rearward communications falling into complete disarray, especially here, where there were few places to cross the Prosna.

In addition, the moral factors have to be considered. That armies must sometimes put off fighting a decisive action cannot be avoided; further, when there are sufficiently good grounds for postponing a decisive encounter, it may not have an adverse influence on the morale of the troops. For example, every Prussian soldier knew in 1813 that they held off fighting Napoleon until there was a certain probability of success (Trachenberg operations plan).[5] Here, however, the case was different: the Russian troops had been mobilized and had reached the Vistula after strenuous marching. Finally, the army's advance begins, the Prussian border is crossed in high spirits, everyone is anticipating the first clash with the Germans. Suddenly, based on reports that cavalry far head has come to blows with enemy infantry, everyone turns about and hurries, in part by way of night marches, back across the border. Such an event would certainly lower the morale of the troops and cause them to doubt their leaders.

The directives [*Anordnungen*] of the Russian commander led to a partial clash with the Germans on the 40th. While the Silesian Army set out from the Oder in a northeastern direction, in order to turn on the Russian left wing (assumed to be on or east of the Prosna), on the 40th the Netze Army received the order to take the offensive with a strong right wing toward Pyzdry–Slupca.

This manoeuvre by the XXI and part of the XVII Army Corps of the Netze Army met the flank of the Russian XX Army Corps, which had marched from Kochowo to Wreschen via Wulka. The Russians wheeled on Mieltschin, but were beaten there and forced back on Pyzdry after having suffered considerable losses. At Pyzdry, the XX Corps found refuge with a division of the Guard Corps that had just arrived.

On the same day, the Russian II Army Corps attempted to advance from Wilczyn to Tremessen. However, it was unable to force the defiles between the lakes there. By the evening, it stood in Orochowo.

Encouraged by the comparatively easy victory at Mieltschin, the commander of the Netze Army ordered the continuation of the offensive against Pyzdry for the following day. This was a very risky decision [*Entschluss*]. The strength of the Netze Army was thereby divided, and its right wing struck the superior Russian masses, which, as was known, were to be found on the Warthe. A much more secure result would have been a concentric advance against the Russian II Corps, which, completely isolated and surrounded by lakes at Orochowo, had only one escape route and could have hardly avoided annihilation. Moreover, a concentric advance against the Russian II Army Corps would have had the advantage of unifying the Netze Army and of cutting off the Russian corps standing still on the Goplo Lake from the main Russian army.

However, the Germans did not consider a tactical success against the II Corps enough. Consequently, the XXI and XVII Army Corps moved forward on the 41st, were halted by the Russian Guard and XVI Army Corps at Wreschen, attacked in the flank and rear by the Russian II Corps, and pushed back on Gnesen in disorder.

Thus, the relatively favourable position won by the Netze Army by its encounter at Mieltschin was made considerably less favourable by the failure of their action at Wreschen, and the Netze Army's role in the expected decisive encounter was called into question. Indeed, the German commander now had to concern himself with reinforcing the Netze Army. Accordingly, he transferred the 1st and 35th Reserve Divisions by rail from Marienburg over the Netze to Graudenz and from there to Posen. Additionally, he transferred the main reserve of the fortress of Posen to the army. However, instead of also sending the XX Corps, he formed a special *Armeeabteilung* out of it and two reserve divisions (6th Reserve Division and the main reserve from Thorn), which remained at first inactive at Kruschwitz.

With their victory at Wreschen, the Russians gained the advantage from having their 2nd and 3rd Armies relieved and of thus having the opportunity to send three army corps from the area of Radiejow–Stulsk toward the Prosna as reinforcement for the left wing. This was made all the easier because there was no threat from East Prussia. There, the Niemen Army had formed a front against Königsberg with a portion of its strength and with the remainder had reached the area of Preußich Eylau–Bartenstein by the 40th. Further, in addition to its cavalry, it had also pushed infantry units forward to the Passarge.

The same day on which the Netze Army was beaten at Wreschen, the Silesian Army had reached the Morawin–Schildberg–Jutroschin line.

The German commander correctly concluded from the arriving reports that the enemy army had decided to form a new front against the Silesian Army and believed that its right wing could be assumed to be at Schirmm and its left somewhere in the area of Stawisyzn (north of Kalisz). He understood that under the present circumstances, he could not continue with his original intention of enveloping the Russian left wing. Therefore, he decided to attack the enemy's newly formed right wing. To this end, on the evening of the 41st, the Silesian Army was ordered to make a 'left march' into the Jutroschin–Schmiegel line. The Netze Army was to 'support' the Silesian Army by moving from Posen and Gnesen to Schirmm and Schroda.

In view of the situation as it now stood after the Russians had discovered the existence of the Silesian Army and had taken appropriate counter-measures, the decision of the German commander can be approved of. Though even he had to admit that the decisive action could only be achieved with the assistance of the beaten Netze Army.

Through our considerable numerical superiority in the battles of 1870 and, in part, in those of 1871, we were almost always in the position of being able to keep the French front completely occupied and, at the same time, to envelop one or both of their wings, to threaten the French lines of retreat, and thus to achieve a really decisive result. This procedure found its most brilliant expression in the battle of Sedan. However, the strength of our adversaries makes the possibility of such battles in a future war unlikely.[6] Therefore, we must operate with our smaller army in such a way that we not only attack the enemy's wings with as much strength as possible, but we must also seriously endanger his lines of retreat, which will become more sensitive due to the great size of the enemy army. Only in this way can we win a truly decisive result that will bring the campaign quickly to an end, and in a war on two fronts such a rapid campaign is absolutely necessary for us.

The left march of the Silesian Army was no longer easily carried out, as the enemy had drawn very near. The Silesian Army kept the enemy occupied with mixed detachments with strong artillery [*gemischte Abteilungen mit starker Artillerie*], through *Landwehr* brigades, *Landsturm* units and cavalry divisions, which had the task of hiding the army's march from the Russians and making the Russians fear for their left wing. Despite this, the Silesian Army's movement would have been discovered by the strong Russian cavalry, which had by this point enveloped the left wing of the Silesian Army in the area of Gostyn–Guhrau, if the Russians, concerned about their left wing, had not taken the bulk of their cavalry from the decisive point and transferred it to the right bank of the Prosna. This allowed the left wing of the Silesian Army to reach the area of Dolzig, between the Obra and the

Warthe, on the 44th. From there, its front stretched to Krotoschin and to Adelnau. On this 60-kilometre line, four German army corps, altogether 14 infantry and reserve divisions, were assembled.

Closely facing the Silesian Army stood the Russians, whose right wing had reached the area of Jarotschewo–Borek, south of the Obra, i.e., outreaching [*überragt*] the left-wing corps (V) of the Silesian Army which stood north of the Obra. The Russians were successful in forming the new front with eight army corps and a rifle division, and a ninth corps, the VI, was in march from Turek. However, five of these corps were still to be found east of the Prosna, so far from the German right wing that they could not possibly intervene on the 45th.

Thus, on the 45th, the day for which the German commander had ordered the attack, two forces of almost equal strength clashed with one another. Since the German left wing was outreached, but not yet enveloped by the enemy, a decisive tactical result was not expected there. Such a result could have been achieved if the Netze Army had recklessly taken up the offensive. The orders from the Supreme Headquarters, however, directed the Netze Army to maintain its advance on the Schroda–Wreschen line, since an effective intervention by the so-long held back *Armeeabteilung Vistula* could only be reckoned on to occur on the 46th. Thus, the Netze Army contented itself with pushing back the weak enemy detachments at Schroda, while the campaign's decisive battle was fought south of the Warthe.

There, the German left wing enveloped a division of the enemy's right wing at Jaratschewo and, mainly through their superior artillery fire, forced the Russian right wing back to Jaotschin and then to Zerkow. Although the Russian XX Army Corps, no longer held back by the Netze Army, attempted to intervene at Neustadt (south of the Warthe), it had been considerably weakened during the earlier encounter at Mieltschin and it was likewise pulled into the retreat to Zerkow. With the remaining portion of their front, the Russians attempted to rescue their right wing by means of an offensive. However, since they generally struck against German units of equal strength and since their right flank – laid bare by the retreat of the XVI Army Corps to Jarotschin – was continually enveloped, the Russians soon had to give up their counterattack and retreat behind the Lutynia. On the outermost point on the Russian left flank, the Russian 4th Army crossed the Prosna on this same day and pushed back the weak German detachments and *Landwehr* units before it, but could not take part in the decisive action.

The Germans had doubtless won a success. However, they had not won a decisive victory. Behind the Lutynia, the Russians formed another front and brought the II Army Corps over the Warthe to Zerkow on their right flank. On their left wing, strong elements of the 4th Army arrived on the Olobok at Raschkow–Ostrowo. The Russian army stood ready to defend against a renewed German attack, which they expected to meet with equal strength (630 Russian guns to 660 German). Everything depended upon the Russian 4th Army.

The German commander believed that little resistance was likely from the Russians. Therefore, he ordered a frontal advance on the Lutynia for the 46th, without enough concern for the threatening danger on his right flank. The Netze Army was now set in motion against the Warthe above Pogorzelice, but there it met an enemy of similar strength. Therefore, the encounters that developed on the Warthe and the Lutynia had to be judged as indecisive.

Perhaps the course of the battle would have played out thus: the III and the IV Army Corps from the Russian 4th Army would have intervened on the 46th and would have become involved in such a heated battle that, despite the fact that the XIV Corps could intervene at Raschow, no decision would have come about on this day. For the following day, then, the Russians would have had three army corps (III, IV and XIV) available on their left wing to take the offensive. However, the thick forests and poor road network in this area would not have been favourable for this offensive manoeuvre, and the Germans would have been able to bend back their right wing. If this operation had been pursued further, the considerable superiority of the Russians might possibly have come into play and caused the Germans to retreat. However, neither side would have achieved an effective tactical success; the operations would have been bogged down.

The success that had stood within close sight as the fruit of the German operations on the 45th slipped from their grasp, since the Netze Army was not employed vigorously enough in the decisive blow.

On the other side, the Russians, despite their considerable superiority, were unable to gain a decisive victory because they held their 4th Army too far back and were thereby robbed of the necessary superiority at the decisive moment.

In general, the following observation can be made: during General Staff rides and *Kriegsspiele*, it is obvious that the reports that are being sent from all the points on a widely separated theatre of war are known by the supreme commander at all times and that he will direct the movements of all of his units [*Heeresteile*] according to this knowledge by means of calm orders. However, this peacetime procedure should not lead to unrealistic notions. In war, issuing orders in such a manner is impossible. Due to the great distances, intelligence arrives too late, and orders will commonly be overtaken by events. The conduct of manoeuvres in wartime, therefore, generally lies in the hands of subordinates, and based on this fact subordinates have the duty to understand completely and fully the intentions of the supreme commander. They must not have eyes merely for the roles of their own units, but must also understand the whole situation [*die gesamte Lage*] and conform and subordinate their decisions and orders to this. Only when subordinates know how to bring their necessary independent decisions and actions in line with the intentions of the higher commander can they correctly carry out their missions.

RIDE PARTICIPANTS

(a) **Directors**

General der Infanterie Oberhoffer
Oberst Freiherr von Manteuffel
Major Freiherr von der Goltz
Hauptmann von Volkmann
Hauptmann von Haxthausen

(b) **German Side**

Higher Commanders
Generalmajor von Lessel (commander of the German *Ostheer*)
Oberstleutnant von Oven (commander of the Silesian Army)
Major von Zitzewitz (commander of the Netze Army)
Major Graf von Bredow (commander of the Vistula *Armeeabteilung* and of an army corps)

Commanding Generals and Divisional Commanders
Major Dorrer
Major Fuchs
Major Kinzelbach
Major Freiherr Treusch von Buttlar-Brandenfels

(c) **Russian Side**

Generalmajor von Blankenburg (commander of the Russian Northwestern Army)
Oberstleutnant Dittlinger (commander of the 4th Army from the 39th to the 45th day)
Major Schmidt (commander of the 1st Army and the 6th Cavalry Division)

Major von Basedow (commander of the I Cavalry Corps from the 39th to the 45th day, thereafter of the II Cavalry Corps)
Major Messing (commander of the 2nd Army and of a cavalry corps)
Major von Wussow (commander of the 3rd Army and a cavalry corps)
Major Kuhl (commander of the 4th Army from the 36th to the 38th day, thereafter of two cavalry corps)

Additional Participants

Vizeadmiral von Diederichs
Generalleutnant von Alten

4

General Staff Ride (East), 1901

Once again in this ride, the German forces in the east were initially outnumbered by their Russian opponent.[1] *At the war's outbreak, the* Ostheer *consisted of only six army corps, four reserve divisions and four cavalry divisions facing the Russian's 11 army corps, eight reserve divisions, one rifle brigade and eight cavalry divisions. The Russian forces, divided into two armies and an* Armeeabteilung, *advanced from Congress Poland and northwestern Russia. Again Schlieffen allowed for the* Ostheer *to be reinforced from the* Westheer, *assuming that a 'decisive' victory had been won over the French on the 23rd mobilization day. The* Ostheer *was reinforced by nine army corps and three cavalry divisions by early on the 35th day. This appears to be in keeping with the operational idea at the centre of the first variant of Schlieffen's deployment plan for the years 1900/1 and 1901/2. In these plans, Schlieffen called for the bulk of the German army to be employed against France, leaving only token forces (two or three army corps and four or five reserve divisions) to protect the east against the Russians.*[2] *These plans and this ride differ from those preceding – Schlieffen assumes that it would be possible to achieve a 'decisive' victory over the French quickly and that sufficient forces would thereby be free to deal the Russians a serious blow. This is a significant indicator of his strategic planning – by this date, Schlieffen had come to believe that, under the right circumstances, Germany could defeat France decisively and quickly.*

In a war between the Dual Alliance and the Triple Alliance, the numerical superiority of the former will be of great concern to the latter. Austria-Hungary has great difficulties to overcome before it can complete its deployment [*Aufmarsch*] and will only be ready for operations [*operationsfähig*] late. The Italians will only bind a small amount of the French strength along their border.[3] Only Germany has an advantage: it lies between France and Russia, separating these two allies from one another. However, it would surrender this advantage if it divided the army, each part of which would then be inferior in numbers to each of her enemies. Germany must, therefore, endeavour to defeat one enemy, while keeping the other at arm's length. Once the first enemy has been defeated, it must employ the railroads to build up a superiority fatal to the other enemy in the other theatre of war. The first stroke must be carried out with full strength, and it must result in a truly decisive battle [*ein wirkliche Entscheidungsschlacht*]. We have no use for a Solferino; it must result in a Sedan, or at the very least a Königgrätz.[4]

A German advance against the French fortresses appears inadvisable in a two-front war. Instead, the Germans must await the French, who will finally advance from their fortified position.[5] This scenario has been assumed for this ride, and it was assumed that the Germans had won a decisive victory over the French. With this victory, the ride began. Immediately, nine German army corps, which had stood close to the railroad stations in the west, were transported to the eastern theatre of war.[6] There, the Germans had left six army corps and two reserve corps; somewhat much considering the military strength of France, but not too many when one considers the Russian army deployed against Germany.

The Russian deployment was executed in four groups, of which the Niemen and Narev Armies were directed against Germany and the Bug and Southwest Armies were directed against Austria-Hungary. The German forces deployed in East and West Prussia faced a difficult task, despite finding themselves between the two Russian armies with the benefit of interior lines. They faced the danger of having their rearward communications cut if they turned against the Narev Army, and they could only await being pushed against the Frisches Haff if they tangled with the Niemen Army. They would always have one Russian army before them and another on their flank. Based on this, it appeared necessary to have another base of operations aside from the Vistula and that base was Königsberg – which may or may not be suitable.

This ride assumed that the German 1st Army withdrew from the Angerapp River to Königsberg and that the German 2nd Army evaded from the Neide and the Soldau to the Vistula, conscious of the danger of being pushed against the Haff by the Narev Army. While the armies carried out the manoeuvres (to the 33rd day), the nine army corps and the three cavalry divisions that had stood ready near the railroad stations in the west arrived on the Vistula and were arrayed on their assigned routes of advance [*Vormarschstraßen*].

The question was now what would the Russians, who could not be kept ignorant of the arrival of the German forces from the west for long, do? By this point (the 33rd day), they had encircled Königsberg with part of the Niemen Army and had reached the line Bartinstein–

Gallingen–Bischofstein–Sensburg with the remainder of this army (though their cavalry had come into contact with the German 2nd Army at Mehlfack and Wormditt). The Niemen Army stood in the line Allenstein–Biessellen–Osterode–Bergfriede–Rosenberg with its advance guards a day's march apart from the rear guards of the German army. The cavalry corps covering its left flank had reached Riesenburg.

The notion that the Russians would initially exploit their advantage over the German 2nd Army and push this army on to the Haff certainly has much going for it; yet this would place the Russians in a very poor position, since they could be attacked in the rear by the German corps coming from over the Vistula and themselves be pushed against the Haff. There remained nothing else but for the Narev Army to wheel to face the defended river line. Even this would not be easy, for the army has to make a very difficult turning movement. Different recommendations were made for this manoeuvre, but in reality the transfer of the army's columns and trains would barely have been possible. The simplest appears to be a wheel with the pivot at Deutsch Eylau, whereby the outermost corps on the left wing (the V) would have to take up a rearward movement. In this way, the V Army Corps could be withdrawn from its exposed position, and the left wing could form a new front.

On the 33rd, the Russian commander ordered the Narev Army to form a front as quickly as possible on the Rosenberg–Lautenburg line against the Vistula line Graudenz–Thorn in order to deal offensively with whatever force the Germans pushed across the river. The Niemen Army's *Abteilung Königsberg* was left behind to encircle the fortress more closely and to guard the flanks and rear from the German units found in and around Königsberg. The remainder of the Niemen Army was to take the offensive against the lower Vistula, resting its left wing on Mohrungen.

On the German side, a recommendation was made that the 2nd Army be pushed to the left bank of the Vistula. There, it would await the Russian attack in conjunction with five corps brought up from the west, while the four corps of the right wing took the offensive on the right bank. This did not appear favourable. The Russians could have formed a front against this offensive with only a portion of their strength, while the German side could have expected no further support. The idea of threatening the enemy's lines of retreat is completely correct, but one does not do this with four army corps, but rather with everything one has.

On the 33rd, the German army headquarters [*Heeres-Hauptquartier*] ordered the advance for the following day: the 4th Army with its left wing to Janowko, the 3rd Army with its right wing to Goral and its left wing to Deutsch Eylau. The 2nd Army was given the task of using its right wing to prevent the enemy reported at Bergfriede and Osterode from intervening in any battle west of the Geserich Lake. If necessary, they were to withdraw by way of Elbing, Preußisch Holland–Hirschfeld and Christburg. The 1st Army was directed to try to advance against the rear of the Niemen Army and thereby break through the encirclement.

On the 34th, the advance of the German 3rd and 4th Armies was carried out without hindrance, and it was discovered that Riesenberg was occupied by enemy infantry and that strong cavalry was deployed southward from there. The 2nd Army pushed forward a division of its right-wing corps (V) to the defiles from Sumpf and Liebemühl and took its remaining corps somewhat back. Further, it attempted with cavalry to connect with the 1st Army and to determine the condition of the enemy. The 1st Army decided to gather reports about the enemy's position before going on to the attack. Against it, the enemy's siege troops remained in their earlier positions. The Niemen Army entered into its advance and the Narev Army began its left wheel, veiled by its cavalry divisions, and its right flank covered by detachments at Liebemühl and Sumpf.

The 35th brought the first encounters. The 1st Army attempted a breakthrough to the south. However, the Russian III and XX Army Corps, reinforced by heavy artillery of the field army [*Feldheer*][7] and by the 70th and 77th Reserve Divisions and supported by favourable terrain, was able to ward off the German attack.

The German V Army Corps deployed its artillery against the detachment from the Russian XVIII Army Corps at Liebemühl and Sumpf. The German fire was only weakly returned, but the Russians did not give up their positions. The V Army Corps later gave up the battle and remained north of Liebemühl. The improper handling of this corps was a great error – an energetic strike through the defiles against the right wing of the Narev Army would have brought about a catastrophe. The remaining corps of the 2nd Army formed a front on the Preußisch Holland–Schlobitten–Huehlhausen line.

The Russian commander, operating on the false assumption that the Germans would not employ all available rail lines to transfer their troops to the Vistula, believed himself threatened above all from the Graudenz–Thorn line. Upon receiving reports that the Narev Army had encountered German troops at Riesenburg and Jablonow on the 34th, he ordered the lead corps to advance on Graudenz on the 35th. Early on the morning of the 35th, the 1st Rifle Brigade at Riesenburg and the other detachments of the V Army Corps sent to guard the flank at Rosenberg and southwest of Reisenburg were taken by surprise by the attack of the German Guard and XXII Army Corps and pushed back.

The Rifle Brigade and the other detachments were absorbed into the V Army Corps north of Freystadt, against which the German IV and X Army Corps advanced. This Russian force faced total annihilation in which even the XVIII Army Corps took part.

The ride directors [Leitung] intervened at this point in the scenario and ordered the Germans to halt on the 36th to enable the Russians to escape from this hopeless position. For the German 3rd Army, this halt was welcome, as they had been pushed together during the preceding days' fighting and had to assemble themselves again on the various march routes. For the 4th Army, this halt had perhaps not been necessary.[8]

The Russians won time to re-order themselves. However, it would have been more correct to have drawn in the beaten and more forward-standing corps rather than pushing forward the rearward corps. The Niemen Army received orders to set in march two corps on Kraplau–Hohenstein to support the Narev Army, to block the Oberländer Canal between Preußisch Holland and Liebemühl, and to withdraw the XX Army Corps and the 3rd Cavalry Division from the siege of Königsberg, but to send the 73rd and 76th Reserve Divisions as replacement.

On the German side, the continuation of the advance of the 4th and 3rd Army against the Narev Army and the beginning of the offensive by the 2nd Army against the Niemen Army was ordered. Further, the 1st Army was directed to renew its advance and envelop the enemy on the right. The 4th Army, which was advancing with a powerful right wing, was directed to echelon a corps of this wing to the right in order to provide flank protection. It would have been better to refuse the 4th Army's right wing to the south, directed towards Mlawa. The 3rd Army wanted to avoid the defiles around Deutsch Eylau, which could have been easily cleared by an energetic thrust by the V Army Corps. This, however, would only result in the 3rd and 4th Armies being pushed together in the centre and marching along poor roads so close together that a deployment would have been impossible. Instead of an offensive with the German 2nd Army against the Niemen Army, about whose strength nothing was known on the German side, it would have been more advisable for the 2nd Army, the German left wing, to stop and for the 4th Army to envelop the Russians from the right, while the 3rd Army advanced against the Russian center.

While the relief of the Russian XX Army Corps by the 77th Reserve Division was under way early on the 37th, the German 1st Army at Königsberg attacked along the whole line under the cover of heavy artillery. Under these circumstances, the commander of the Russian siege army [Einschliessungsarmee] decided to hold the XX Army Corps and the 3rd Cavalry Division in place and thus succeeded in defeating the German attack. The German 1st Army was forced to withdraw to the Seepothen–Wickbold–Weissenstein line, and it required many days to re-form its units and re-stock its munitions and supplies.

The commander of the German 1st Army must have known that the weakest point of the enemy was their left flank, where only a single cavalry division stood. If he attacked energetically there and merely kept the remaining parts of the siege army occupied, he could roll up the enemy's left flank and establish immediate contact with the 2nd Army. Instead, he relied solely upon the superiority of his artillery, when it must be observed that the real breakthrough had to be carried out by the infantry and that they had to traverse extraordinarily difficult swampy terrain.

The German 2nd Army, which was denied any glimpse of the enemy's position by the Russian cavalry, believed the Niemen Army to be right behind the cavalry encountered on the Passarge and calculated from this, since the enemy detachments at Liebemühl and Sumpf had also maintained their positions, that it would come to a clash along the entire line on the 37th. It began to advance on Deutschendorf, Borchertsdorf, and Tiedmannsdorf with the intention of enveloping the enemy's right wing. At Tiedmannsdorf, the corps of the wing was to wheel towards the southeast by way of Lindenau. The cavalry corps covering the 2nd Army's left wing reported a Russian advance on the Passarge via Mehlsack, but then reported that the enemy made an about face at Mehlsack and was now awaiting an attack behind the Walsch. Since another report arrived indicating that strong enemy forces at and around Wormditt threatened the flank of the reserve corps if it advanced further, the 2nd Army's attack was abandoned.

The 9th Infantry Division, from the corps given the task of covering the right flank (V Army Corps), advanced by way of Liebemühl and Sumpf and, since it met only some of the enemy's trains on the Deutsch Eylau–Osterode road, it marched on further on to Kraplau–Osterode and occupied the crossings there. The 10th Infantry Division had blocked the defiles at Horn with a composite brigade [*gemischte Brigade*] and successfully defended against the attack of the Russian II Army Corps. Its other brigade reached Liebstadt.

Early on the morning of the 38th, the 2nd Army deployed and attacked, expecting the enemy to be in the approximate line Wormditt–Mehlsack. However, they only encountered enemy rearguards. The Niemen Army had already begun to withdraw to the Wangnick–Drewenz line, from which it was to advance again after receiving reinforcement. The 2nd Army's advance, however, caused it to form a front before it had reached this position and to accept the

German attack in the Walchsee (south of Plauten)–Lichtenau line. When during the course of the day the Russian 73rd and 76th Reserve Divisions and later the XX and II Army Corps intervened and enveloped the Germans, the 2nd Army's fate was sealed. The Germans attempted to withdraw the remnants of their forces behind the Passarge, but were pursued immediately by the Niemen Army. On the 39th, the Russians continued their pursuit with the 2nd and 4th Cavalry Divisions and the XX and II Army Corps, which inflicted further casualties upon the Germans retreating behind the Baude.

The 2nd Army had begun with generally the correct disposition and, as the Niemen Army was widely dispersed, it had been quite likely that Germans would be successful. That the Russians still remained victorious comes first from the fact that the 2nd Army did not bring in the V Army Corps and further from the fact that the 1st Army encircled in Königsberg was forced to end its break-out attempt because of inept handling. With the failure of the 1st Army to break out, the Russians were able to remove forces from the siege line to take part in the decision against the 2nd Army.

The German 3rd and 4th Armies had continued their offensives on the 38th and 39th without hindrance. Initially, they pushed the Narev Army back to the Niedenburg–Soldau line, while the German XVIII Army Corps occupied the Alle crossings from Bertung to Kurken. However, the success of the Niemen Army on the 37th allowed it to send, after a reorganization of its formations, the 76th Reserve Division and the XVI and I Army Corps to the Narev Army. The Russian commander wanted to await the arrival of these forces as well as the arrival of the 54th and 57th Reserve Divisions, which were a day's march away, before he sought a decision [*Entscheidung*] against the German armies. To reach this decision, the Narev Army was assembled on the 39th on the Allenstein–Niedenburg line. The I Guard Corps and the Cavalry Corps took over the task of covering the army's left flank.

On the 40th, the German 1st Army finally succeeded in breaking through on the right wing of the Russian siege line after their superior heavy artillery had shaken the enemy at and to the west of Kobbelbude. However, the Russians maintained their right wing in reinforced positions, and at Zinten the 73rd Reserve Division and the 3rd Cavalry Division were able to bring the German advance to a halt.

The portion of the Niemen Army pursuing the German 2nd Army was unable to prevent it from retreating behind the Elbing River.

In their attack on the Russian Niedenburg–Allenstein position on the 40th, the German 4th Army only encountered weak resistance, but the 3rd Army found a good deal more. The German X and XXII Army Corps had to break off the attack in the evening without success and, in the case of the XXII Corps, having suffered heavy casualties. Only the IV and Guard Corps succeeded in pushing back the enemy somewhat. The V Army Corps could not participate; it had to form a front to the north, since the advance of a strong enemy column of all arms was reported marching by way of Peterswalde on Heiligenthal and by way of Mohrungen. To meet this threatening envelopment and in consideration of the heavy losses of the XXII Army Corps, the 3rd Army was withdrawn to the Hohenstein–Geierswalde–Peterswalde line on the following day (41st). The vanguard of the X Army Corps remained in close contact with the enemy at Schwedrich and the IV Army Corps faced strong enemy forces northeast of Lahma after its indecisive encounter. The Russians followed the 3rd Army with two and a half army corps of the Niemen Army and two army corps of the Narev Army, while their cavalry drove before them in a southwestern direction.

The German 4th Army had its left wing resting on Niedenburg and its right on Mlawa. Now, the question was whether the Russians could actually be enveloped and whether it would be possible to advance against their lines of retreat. In essence, the fronts of the 4th Army and the Niemen Army struck at one another. The Russian position, as well as the position taken up by the Germans when they occupied Niedenburg, was very strong. Accordingly, the German commander wanted to await the effects of the envelopment before he attacked. Such a delay, however, will never lead to an action when one already stands so close to an enemy; this only allows the enemy time to reinforce his threatened wing. *The enemy front must always be attacked in order to permit and make effective an envelopment.*[9] In the end, the Narev Army bent its left wing further back, thus forcing the German right wing to extend further its turning movement. A decision would be reached here within two days.

During this time, fate decided against the German left wing.

The 3rd Army had occupied a 12-kilometre line from east of Hohenstein to Drewenztal with two army corps. This position was not very favourable and could be outflanked on the left at Droebnitz. Therefore, two army corps (one and a half divisions strong) were sent to the left. The Russians advanced against the German 3rd Army with a front of four divisions and with an envelopment of five divisions. They would have won a victory only with great difficulty, if the German left wing had not advanced. With this, the Russian columns echeloned further behind could also participate in the battle and bring their superiority to bear. It was quite right of the commander of the Russian forces to turn against the weak German corps with everything he had on hand and to annihilate them. Since the two corps would have been forced to retreat into the German front, a catastrophe of the greatest proportions would have occurred for the Germans.

Events here show clearly the unsuitability of setting up a defensive flank at a right angle. Such a flank must always be formed obliquely so that in the case of a defeat, the lines of retreat of one's other corps will not be crossed and a catastrophe will be avoided.

The operations during this ride did not progress along their desired course. It was hoped that the Germans would be successful in their envelopment with the right wing and that the 1st Army would break through its encirclement at Königsberg. Then, it would have been quite possible to push the Russians back against the lake line and there to bring them into a difficult situation [*eine schlimme Lage*].

We must adhere to the principle of advancing by way of envelopment against the enemy's lines of retreat, for in a war on two fronts we need a *complete victory*!

RIDE PARTICIPANTS

(a) Directors

General der Infanterie von Oberhoffer
Royal Saxon Generalmajor Graf Bitzthum von Eckstädt
Oberstleutnant von Eberhardt
Major Graf von Schmettow
Hauptmann Graf von Lambsdorf

(b) German Side

Higher Commanders

Generalleutnant Freiherr von Rechenberg (commander of the German *Ostheer*)
Oberst Dienes (commander of the 1st Army)
Major Freiherr von Freytag-Loringhoven (commander of the 4th Army)
Major Dickhuth (commander of the 2nd Army)
Major Jochmus (commander of the 3rd Army)

Commanding Generals and Divisional Commanders

Royal Bavarian Major Freiherr von Speidel
Major Hahndorff
Royal Württemberg Major Hofacker
Hauptmann von Studnitz

(c) Russian Side

Higher Commanders

Generalmajor von Goßler (commander of the Russian Northwestern Army from the 36th to the 41st day)
Oberstleutnant Deimling (commander of the Russian Northwestern Army from the 33rd to the 36th day, thereafter commander of *Armeeabteilung Königsberg*)
Oberstleutnant von Steuben (commander of the Narev Army)
Major von Knoerzer (commander of the Niemen Army)
Major Freiherr von Hirschberg (commander of the *Armeeabteilung Königsberg* from the 33rd to the 35th day)

Commanding Generals and Divisional Commanders

Major Stengel
Major Schwarte
Major von der Esch
Oberleutnant Sydow

5

General Staff Ride (East), 1903

In this year's ride, Schlieffen has arranged once again that the Ostheer *be reinforced from a victorious* Westheer; *to the* Ostheer's *seven original army corps (which included two corps formed from excess and reserve units) were added 11 army corps from the western border.*[1] *However, unlike the 1901 ride, Schlieffen returned to his earlier belief that the French could not be beaten decisively in the early days of the war, and that they could only be forced to withdraw behind their fortifications. Troops would have to be shipped back to the west after the Russians had been dealt a mortal blow. The reinforced* Ostheer *faced a Russian force of 12 army corps and 12 reserve divisions arrayed in two armies. Additionally, in the ride, Schlieffen has factored in Austro-Hungarian forces. To the south, two Austro-Hungarian armies of six army corps face a Russian army of four army corps. Information on the German deployment plan for 1903/4 is incomplete, but Schlieffen's force levels for this ride do not seem to relate to what is available. For deployment plan (variant I), Schlieffen envisioned the bulk of the field army (25 army corps and 15 reserve divisions) being employed against France, leaving only three corps and four reserve divisions to face the Russians. For deployment plan (variant II), it appears that Schlieffen would deploy roughly half of the field army against France, leaving around 14 army corps in the east.*[2]

For this ride, a war between Germany and Austria-Hungary on one side and Russia and France on the other was assumed. Germany initially employed the greater part of its armed forces against France; it left only the eastern border corps (the I, II, V, VI, XVII, XX and XXII Army Corps) and an appropriate number of reserve divisions and *Landwehr* and *Landsturm* formations facing Russia. These were to protect German territory as much as possible and to hold the railroads for later troop movements.

The Russians, on the other hand, took the offensive as soon as they could, and started their advance. The Niemen Army (six army corps and four reserve divisions) pushed forward against the fortified Vistula front from Thorn to Marienburg. The Narev Army deployed with a number of rifle brigades, six army corps and four reserve divisions, two of which were to cross the Vistula at and downstream from Warsaw in order to move around Thorn and envelop the right flank of the enemy forces presumed to be behind the river.

However, this deployment plan was later altered. Three reserve divisions from the Niemen Army were sent by rail to the Narev Army, and this force, now eight and three-quarters army corps (including a rifle brigade), formed into two separate *Armeeabteilungen* (the Narev and Vistula). The Niemen Army received the 1st Guard Infantry Division, and now comprised six corps, two divisions and a rifle brigade. Additionally, both armies received a number of border guard brigades.

On the 29th mobilization day, the Russians were arrayed in very long and widely dispersed columns. The Niemen Army had cut off Königsberg with a reserve division, two cavalry divisions and a rifle brigade. Its advance units had reached the Liebstadt–Osterode–Tannenberg–Willenberg–Kolno line. The advance units of the Narev Army had reached the Dobrzyn–Lubien–Dombrowice–Kutno–Bielawy line. The long Russo-German border to the south was guarded by border guard brigades (11th–16th). To cover the flank of the Narev Army, the Bug Army had taken up position to the south of Brest Litowsk along the Lublin–Cholm line. On this day, the news arrived that on the 27th the French army had been pushed back, with great losses, behind the fortified Moselle and Meuse lines. The possibility, later proved right, that the Germans would redeploy a portion of their forces from the western theatre of war to the eastern loomed large. It was calculated that the redeployed German corps could arrive in the east by the 34th day. This calculation proved too optimistic; realistically, they could not arrive before the 35th day.

The Russians determined to advance quickly with the Niemen and Narev Armies in order to achieve a success before the enemy reinforcements could arrive. The Narev Army was given the goal of reaching the area of Hohensalza and the Niemen Army the lower Drewenz. At both positions, enemy troops were reported. At Hohensalza these were a number of reserve divisions and on the Drewenz, *Landsturm* units.

The question was now what would Germany do. If it acted here in the east as it had in the west and threw the enemy back behind the Narev, the Vistula or some other sector, it would be forced to see at least a portion of its corps sent back to the west in order to deal with the French who were advancing again. The Russians would have exploited this transfer. In time, troops would again have to be sent from the west to the east. This back-and-forth transfer of German forces and pushing the enemy back here and there would have been repeatedly played out – a strategy that must ultimately lead to the exhaustion [*Aufreibung*] of the entire German army.

Such a two-front war is not to be waged by the pushing back [*Zurückwerfen*] of one or the other enemy, but rather by annihilating, as soon as possible, one and then the other enemy. Military history has shown us the means of achieving such an annihilation. Friedrich the Great strove for it repeatedly. Napoleon applied it in 1800, 1805, 1806 and 1807 and would have employed it in 1809 if Berthier or, as one can certainly say, his own arrogance had not spoiled it. The Alliance broke Napoleon's domination in October 1813 in the same way. The immortal Field Marshal Graf von Moltke built his successes in August and September 1870 with the same method.

This method consists of throwing all of one's strength, or at least the greatest part of it, against the enemy's flanks or rear in order to force him to fight with a reversed front or to push him in an unfavourable direction. This can occur if the attack leads to success on two sides, as it did at Leipzig, Gravelotte and Sedan.[3] At the very least, it can lead to the encirclement [*Einschließung*] of the enemy army.

With this in mind, the Germans quickly brought up to Marienburg and Elbing the four corps that were on the left bank of the Vistula River (the II, V, VI and XXII Army Corps). The three corps on the river's right bank were ordered to withdraw before the advancing enemy – the I Army Corps was to withdraw to Königsberg, the XVII to the area of Marienburg, the XX to the area of Thorn. Four reserve divisions, assembled into two reserve corps, had been brought to Königsberg at the beginning of the war. Of the 11 corps brought from the west, five were deployed on the Vistula between Marienburg and Thorn. Of the nine reserve divisions that had been assembled at Thorn, Bromberg and Hohensalza, two were formed into a corps and brought to the right bank of the Vistula. When the deployment of the left wing's five corps between Elbing and the Passarge was complete, the Germans could attack with 15 corps from the line Thorn–Königsberg.

Certainly, one could have asked for more forces, but this did not appear possible. That four corps (the II, V, VI and XXII) could be deployed around Elbing had been made possible only at a cost to the army still facing the French, and this transfer could certainly be seen as a serious mistake [*schwerwiegender Fehler*]. The railroads did not suffice to transport more than five corps to the lower Vistula, since one had to assume that the Moglino–Thorn line was destroyed. The remaining six army corps that could be sent from the west had to be unloaded on the Polish border to be used against the flank of the Narev Army. Seven reserve divisions at Thorn–Hohensalza formed a reserve for both lines of attack, as they could be employed on either side of the Vistula as needed. *Landwehr* and *Landsturm* units covered the long Russo-German border south of Hohensalza.

The Russian armies had advanced so far forward by the 32nd day that they had come into contact with German forces at various points before the German reinforcements from the west could complete their redeployment. First, a Russian cavalry division, which together with the 1st Cossack Division and the 5th Rifle Brigade was observing the southern front of Königsberg, was sent forward on the 30th day to reconnoitre the area around Elbing. This unit struck against a German cavalry division on the Passarge, evaded it, and withdrew to the 5th Rifle Brigade.

On the 31st day, the German 5th Army – the three corps from Königsberg – had begun their advance and had, in conjunction with the I Cavalry Corps, pushed back this weak Russian detachment. Under the cover of this manoeuvre, the German 4th Army could deploy and advance in the direction of Guttstadt with its left wing, so that it quickly made contact with the 5th Army.

This manoeuvre went unobserved by the Russians, who had absolutely no cavalry there. The right wing of the Niemen Army, upon which the 2nd Cavalry Division was to be found, could not escape the fact that enemy troops were to be found in the Christburg–Stuhm–Marienwerder line. The Russian XX Army Corps was detailed to guard against this force.

On the 32nd day, the Narev Army drew near to the German reserve units on the left bank of the Vistula. A clash here appeared to be inevitable. The Germans had not planned to fight here, but as the Field Marshal once said, 'one thankfully accepts a victory wherever it is offered'. The seven reserve divisions found an excellent position at Hohensalza, one which could not be enveloped or turned on its right wing. Further, if the enemy attempted to turn the Germans' left flank, he would have brought presumably an annihilating defeat down upon himself, so long as the German forces on the right bank of the Vistula at Thorn crossed the river in good time. Nevertheless, the German commander did not want to allow this battle to take place. Instead, he wanted to withdraw in the night, work around behind the Russians, and lock them tight in the grip of an envelopment.

However, this night march undertaken by the seven reserve divisions was around 30 kilometres long and took place along terrible roads. It brought the troops, who been in fine shape as they awaited an enemy attack in a good defensive position, close to physical and moral collapse, a state one would rather have spared them. The goal of marching after the enemy was unsuccessful, and in the end only a few units were able to pursue. For the most part, the Russian units chose to withdraw and avoid the flank attacks that they had been awaiting since the 34th day.

Away to the north, reports of German troops on the right flank of the Niemen Army had increased on the 33rd day. The Germans had advanced to Saalfeld, Preußisch Mark and Riesenburg. Further, Russian reconnaissance patrols clashed with enemy outposts at Marienburg and Graudenz, and they found the enemy in defensive positions between Briefen and Gollub. Under these circumstances, a further advance of the Niemen Army appeared impossible. They determined to withdraw the XX, III and II Army Corps across the Drewenz between Strasburg and Neumark, to extend their left wing to Gollub with the 1st Guard Infantry Division, and to answer the impending envelopment of their right wing with a counter-envelopment.

With this, the Russians took up the offensive on both sides of the Vistula. To carry out the two offensives, the Russian army remained divided. There would seem to have been no reasonable basis to maintain the division. It appears it would have been better to have united the divided force on one side of the Vistula, and then to turn first against one and then the other divided enemy forces. Nothing appears simpler than carrying out such a plan. The right wing of the Niemen Army needed to be not only brought back behind the Drewenz, but also behind the Soldau. The army corps following to the rear (the I and XVI) needed only to have made a right wheel to fall in rank in the battle line. The 79th Reserve Division, the Guard Corps and the III Reserve Corps, which found bridges across the Vistula at Nowo Georgiewsk, Wyszogrod and Plock, could have done the same. The Narev Army had the bridges at Nieszawa and Wloclawek right behind it, which would facilitate a crossing. In three or four days, the Russian army would stand against the Germans equal in number. It would have taken no time at all to determine along which routes the northern corps would have to withdraw and along which lines the southern corps would have to advance. The Germans would certainly have brought their 2nd Army across the Vistula, but the greater part of the 1st Army would remain behind. It would come to a battle, the outcome of which could not be predetermined, but in which the Russians would have even odds.

However, the Russian commander could not arrive at this decision, and such a decision is rarely taken in similar circumstances. Only one who has the initiative carries out such a rapid and decisive manoeuvre. The other, who sits back, is too often surprised and finds the situation too clouded. Moreover, a general who had crossed the Vistula with an army of 200,000 to 300,000 would not want to withdraw back behind this river empty handed and without striking a blow, even when a new enemy was to be found there. Vacillating between the two possibilities – to attack or to retreat – one falls into the unpalatable decision [*unheilvollen Ausweg*] merely to dig in and await the enemy.

So it was that the Niemen Army only assembled to meet the threatening enemy attack. From the beginning, it was lost to the advance of the powerful German masses. To avoid this defeat, it remained only to begin the retreat as quickly as possible. However, there was not yet enough motive to carry out this retreat – the honour of arms [*Waffenehre*] would not allow the Russians to take to their heels at the appearance of the enemy's advance guard.

On the 35th day, the first contact occurred. At Neumark, the German IX Army Corps struck the Russian XX, which was not even able to deploy, and the German XVII struck the Russian I. The appearance of the German VI Army Corps from the north forced the Russian I Army Corps to form a front in this direction as well. Darkness fell before a decision was reached here. To bring about a decision on the next day, the Russian XVI Army Corps was to come up. However, this offensive was not enough for the Russian commander. The Russian IV and III Army Corps were to carry out a further offensive. In the close terrain between the Drewenz and the forested area north of Strasburg, with its lakes and defiles, the IV Corps was to advance in a northern direction and to arrive in the close, strongly defended area between the Skarlinersee and the Drewenz. The III Army Corps, which followed to the left, could give no support since its left flank was attacked and held by the German III Army Corps coming from the forested area north of Strasburg. Further north, on the heights of Löbau stood the greater part of the German IX and XVII Army Corps in adequate strength to beat off any attack by their opponents – the Russian XX Army Corps and a division of the I Army Corps. Less secure, however, was the position of the German VI Army Corps in the area of Marwalde, which had the other division of the I Corps and the whole XVI Army Corps facing it. Since the Gilgenburger Lake prevented an envelopment of their left wing and since a breakthrough between the German VI and XVII Army Corps could not have occurred before being suppressed by the strong German artillery, the Germans [VI Army Corps] faced no real danger here.

South of Strassburg, the Russian II Corps offered a successful resistance to the German Guard Corps. Further south, the outermost unit of the Russian left flank, the 1st Guard Division, was withdrawn from the Drewenz to behind the Rypinitz. Aside from this corps, claim was laid to the rest of the Russian units. Three German army corps launched attacks against both Russian flanks. When the batteries of the German V Corps appeared west of the Gilgenburger Lake, the Russian commander gave up the fight. The attempt to counter-attack with the XVI Corps between Gilgenburg and Tautschken broke up on the defences of the German V Corps, while the German VI Corps pursued hotly and cut off every retreat. The Russian I, XX, IV and III Corps received the order to retreat behind Lautenburg. However, they could not hold here long, as the Germans pursued closely the next day. As they withdrew in great confusion along the single route left to them (the Lautenburg–Zuromin road), they were taken under fire by the German II Army Corps and I Cavalry Corps, which had come up from across the Soldau. The attempt to evade to the west led them directly into a fatal circle of fire created by the II Cavalry Corps, the IV and the XX Army Corps, and the Guard Reserve and Guard Corps. With this, the Niemen Army was annihilated, despite its heroism.

The Narev Army and the *Armeeabteilung Vistula* had, in the meantime, as already mentioned, decided to dig in somewhere between the southern end of the Soplo Lake and Klodawa. They later advanced their left wing to the Ner. When the reports of the Niemen Army's defeat arrived, the decision was made to retreat to Warsaw. Since the German 1st Army was further behind than necessary, this retreat could be conducted without great difficulty as long as it was carried out without pause and as long as the bridges across the Vistula below Nowo Georgiewsk were destroyed. Of course, the columns would have to have been very crowded together before Warsaw.

In contrast to this, the Germans had to direct all their efforts to barring the retreat of the Narev Army and to annihilating it before it reached the comparative safety of the Vistula bridges. After all, the Germans had to send strong forces back to the western theatre of war as soon as possible, and this would not be possible if they were forced to besiege a powerful Russian army in Warsaw. The Narev Army had to follow the Niemen Army and capitulate in open battle [*auf freiem Felde*].

Accordingly, on the 38th day, the German 3rd Army had set the IV Army Corps and the II Cavalry Corps immediately to march on Wyszogrod, while the XX Army Corps was thrown in the direction of Plock by way of Sierpc. The remaining corps were to follow the IV Corps.

Into the hands of these corps fell the Russian XIII Army Corps, which had been sent to support the Niemen Army and had reached Skempe on the 37th and now on the 38th wanted to retreat to Warsaw. Forced against the Vistula, it had to surrender. The German XX and IV Army Corps renewed their advance on Wyszogrod. The III Reserve Corps remained at Plock in order to cross the Vistula there.

The Narev Army's retreat did not take place at the desired speed. The II Reserve Corps, which had been left far behind to secure the

Russian left wing, was caught by the German 2nd Army near Brzesc. The Narev Army's commander did not want to leave this threatened corps in the lurch, so he ordered the XVIII, XV and VI Army Corps to build a front again to the north. This forced the Narev Army to pause and created a complete separation between it and the neighbouring *Armeeabteilung Vistula*.

By the 39th, the Narev Army could continue its retreat, but in the meantime the Germans had already advanced between the two armies. To facilitate the Narev Army's retreat, the *Armeeabteilung Vistula* wanted to throw back the enemy's right wing, while the Narev Army's left wing (the VI Army Corps) held back the German left wing. This led to a general engagement with the *Armeeabteilung Vistula*, which was struck across its entire front by the Germans and held fast. The attack of the Russian VI Army Corps led it into a very difficult situation, as the reserve corps of the German 2nd Army pressed into it from the rear. To free this corps from its threatening position and to throw back the pursuing enemy, the Russian XV and XVIII Army Corps, the II Reserve Corps and the 1st Rifle Brigade had to once again form a front.

Thus, on the 40th day the situation was as follows: the front of the Narev Army stood in battle with the German 2nd Army and its left flank was embraced by the German XI Army Corps. *Armeeabteilung Vistula* stood against the German 11th Reserve Division, the XXI and the XIX Army Corps. Three German corps, the X, XII and XVII, had broken in between the two armies and were able to turn against the rear of one or the other according to their will.

At Plock, a bridge was thrown up within 48 hours and the German III Corps with the main reserve from Thorn stood ready to begin its advance on Gombin on the 41st day. The German IV Army Corps had crossed at Wyszogrod, where the Russian order to destroy the bridges had arrived too late. This corps, together with the II Cavalry Corps, had reached Sochaczew. The German XX Army Corps intended to follow.

In the meantime, to the south, the Austro-Hungarian reserve army advanced over the Pilica. On the 41st day, its left wing was to take up position at Rawa, and its right wing was to continue to advance.

The ring around the Russian armies, from which they could only escape with great difficulty, was closed. With this the fate of the Narev Army and *Armeeabteilung Vistula* was decided, and the German goal of forcing their capitulation before they reached the safety of Warsaw was accomplished.

Now there remained only *a third Russian army* (the Bug Army) facing the Austro-Hungarian 1st Army and the Austro-Hungarian Bug Army.

The Austro-Hungarians, who had deployed in Galicia, faced three Russian armies: the Russian Bug Army between Lublin and Cholm, a second in the Wolhynisch Festungsdreieck and a third at Proskurow. If the Austrians advanced against one army, they would have the others on their flanks and in their rear. Therefore, it is assumed here that they would break through between the two main armies and envelop the northern Russian army to the left and the southern to the right. The strength of their army would permit them to conduct such a manoeuvre.

The left wing of the Austrian army found itself in the following situation: the Russian Bug Army had the task of covering the rear of the Niemen and Narev Armies against the Austrians. They could most easily carry out their task by attacking the Austrian left wing, despite the numerical superiority of the Austrian army. None the less, the commander of the Russian Bug Army decided to forgo the offensive and instead withdrew behind the Bug River, resting his left wing on Brest Litovsk. This manoeuvre made the intended Austrian right-wing envelopment impossible, especially since the terrain on the right bank of the upper Bug is very difficult and since the crossing of the Muchawiec was blocked by artillery and *Reichswehr* units. Therefore, the Austrians brought their right wing back across the Bug, made a half-left movement, and attacked instead the Russian right wing. To meet this manoeuvre, the Russians concentrated the units of their right wing, and went over to the attack on the 38th. The Russian attack was supported by the I Reserve Corps, which was detached from *Armeeabteilung Vistula*. The attack struck against difficult terrain and a strong Austrian defensive position, and it soon came to a halt. While this was taking place, greatly superior Austrian forces advanced against the Russian Bug Army's left wing, which had not advanced. However, because of the distance, the Austrians could not proceed with their attack that day.

The Russians manoeuvred their left wing to the northwest to evade the Austrian attack expected on the 39th day, but they soon heard that the Germans had already crossed the Narev in their rear. (This was the German 5th Army, which had broken out of Königsberg on the 31st day and had advanced on the Bug in unbroken marches by way of Pultusk and Rozan.) To give themselves room, the Russian Bug Army formed a front again and wanted to renew their attack on the Austrians. After the exertions of the previous days, however, any attack against the greatly superior enemy was hopeless. The decision to attack was merely an act of despair, and the outcome was determined beforehand. The attack would be repulsed and, in the meantime, the Germans would have come up in the rear.

The not inconsiderable result achieved during this ride was due essentially to the advance of the 3rd, 4th and 5th German Armies against the flanks and rear of the enemy. The 3rd and 4th Army had encircled the Niemen Army, while the 3rd Army had cut off the Narev Army from any retreat. The 5th Army had done the same for the Russian Bug Army.

The advance of the German 4th and 5th Armies would have been hindered if the Russians had covered Königsberg properly in the south and if the Russians had advanced with their right wing near the Frisches Haff. However, the Germans would then have made the same attack they had made from the north with their left wing from Thorn in the south. To block this attack, it would have been necessary to cover the entire line from the Haff north of Elbing to the Vistula at Nieszawa. Such a covering force would demand such forces, however, that an envelopment on the left bank of the Vistula around Thorn would have been ruled out. The entire Russian advance would have been limited to an attack against the Thorn–Haff line. How such an attack would be met is too much to go into here. However, one should always attack the enemy's flanks and rear with great strength. Examples from history have shown us that this is the only way not only to resist our enemy, but also to annihilate him.

RIDE PARTICIPANTS

(a) Directors

Major Chales de Beaulieu
Hauptmann von Hahnke (Wilhelm)
Hauptmann von Meiß
Royal Saxon Generalmajor Barth

(b) German Side

Generalmajor von Scheffer (commander of the German *Ostheer*)
Oberst von Loos (commander of the Austro-Hungarian *Westheer* and
 Reserve Army)
Oberstleutnant Eben (commander of the 4th Army)
Oberstleutnent Stein (commander of the 3rd Army)
Oberstleutnant Staabs (commander of the 1st Army)
Major von der Esch (commander of the 2nd Army)
Royal Saxon Major Lucius (Governor of Thorn from 33rd to 40th day)
Royal Saxon Major Leuthold (Governor of Thorn on 32nd day)
Major Sauberzweig (commander of the 5th Army)
Hauptmann von Rath (attached to the commander of the 4th Army)
Hauptmann Heye (attached to the commander of the 3rd Army)

(c) Russian Side

Generalmajor Freiherr von Gayl (commander of the Russian Northwestern Army)
Oberst von François (commander of the Niemen Army)
Royal Württemberg Oberstleutnant von Knoerzer (commander of the Narev Army)
Major Jochmus (commander of the Bug Army)
Major Hoeppner (commander of the *Armeeabteilung Vistula*)
Major Balck (commander of the *Armeeabteilung Königsberg*)
Major von Kobbe (attached to the commander of the Niemen Army)
Major Freiherr von Tettau (attached to the commander of the Narev Army)
Major Lequis (attached to the commander of the Northwestern Army)
Royal Württemberg Major Strölin (attached to the commander of the Narev Army, at the same time, commander of the border guard with Silesia)
Major von Uckermann (attached to the commander of the Northwestern Army)

6

Tactical-Strategic Problems, 1892

In these problems, Schlieffen required his subordinates to address the problem of covering the deployment of the Westheer *from a French attack.*[1] *They are asked to play the role of the Commanding General of the XVI Army Corps (based in Metz) and are given reinforcement from the II Bavarian Corps and the VIII Army Corps. From these problems, it is clear how important Schlieffen felt the railways were for flexibility in the deployment of the German army. The problems are also notable for the fact that they are based upon the assumption that the French opened the war with an invasion of Luxemburg, demonstrating the potential threat posed to the German deployment from the direction of the neutral countries along the western border.*

FIRST PROBLEM

On the evening of 31 July, the mobilization order was issued in Germany as well as in France. The Commanding General of the XVI Army Corps is detailed with covering the German deployment west of the Vosges. This means he needs to keep open the railways north and east of the Diedenhofen–Metz–Bensdorf–Saarburg line. In order to accomplish this, additional troops from the VIII Army Corps in Trier, Saarlouis and Saarbrücken; troops from the XV Army Corps in Saarburg and Dieuze; and troops from the Bavarian II Army Corps in Metz, Dieuze and Saargemünd are placed under the command of the XVI Army Corps. In general, these troops have remained in the garrisons. Only small detachments keep the border under surveillance.

It has been learned that before 1 August the French have neither called up reservists nor transferred units, but since the 1st, the 11th Infantry Division in Nancy has received reinforcements. Allegedly, the entire VI Army Corps is to be assembled there. The 2nd Cavalry Division is to be assembled at Lunéville.[2] No enemy units of any meaningful size are said to have crossed the Meuse along the river from Commercy to Verdun. According to a report from Vixton (Belgium), since 3 August, military trains have been moving continually through the station at Montmédy in the direction of Longuyon.

On the evening of 4 August, France delivered its declaration of war. During the course of the afternoon of 5 August, a long line of reports arrived in Metz according to which the French have crossed the border with troops of all arms and can be found advancing on Luxemburg. From the direction of Nancy and Lunéville, only cavalry patrols were to be found up until afternoon.

The German units, including the two reserve battalions forming in Trier and Saarlouis, are ready to march, even if they have not received their full compliment of manpower. A directive to hold themselves at the ready was given to them in the early morning, but they have not yet formed columns and trains.

Railway Administration Saarbrücken declared itself ready to supply a train of 100 axels at the Saarbrücken station from 0200 on 5 August. Additional railway material for seemingly necessary troop movements is not available.

The tunnel west of Audun le Roman (Longuyon–Diedenhofen line) has been destroyed, as has the railway bridge at Conslans.

The first German deployment transports [*Aufmarschtransporte*] are to cross the Saar early on 7 August.

> *Problem:* What directives does the Commanding General of the XVI Army Corps give on the afternoon of 5 August?
>
> *Note: To secure against a* coup de main *and to observe the approaches to the fortresses, nine infantry battalions are required for Metz and two for Diedenhofen.*

SECOND PROBLEM

By order of the Commanding General of the XVI Army Corps, the following movements were carried out during the course of 5 August:

(1) From Trier: the staff of the 16th Infantry Division, the 31st Infantry Brigade of the same division and three squadrons of Hussar Regiment 9 were advanced by way of Conz and Tawern to Helsant. Two reserve battalions occupied the bridges at Ecternach, Wasserbillig and Grevenmacher. One squadron of Hussar Regiment 9 reconnoitred towards Luxemburg.

(2) From Saarlouis: Infantry Regiment 30, one reserve battalion and the 1st Battalion, Foot Artillery Regiment 8 were moved by way of Wallerfangen and Niedaltdorf to Halsdorf, Kirchnaumen and Obersterck. The remainder of the Foot Artillery Regiment 8 was deployed along the Meuse to Mettlach and from there it was joined by the staff of the 32nd Infantry Brigade and the 1st Battalion, Infantry Regiment 70, which had arrived by rail that very same evening at 1815 from Saarbrücken and extended to Orschholz and Oberleucken. This force fell under the command of the 16th Infantry Division. The staff and the 2nd Battalion, Infantry Regiment 70 were to depart Saarbrücken at 0034 on 6 August and arrive at Mettlach at 0245. A train stood ready in Saarbrücken to transport the 3rd Battalion, Infantry Regiment 70 at 0904 on 6 August.

(3) From Diedenhofen: 1st Battalion, Infantry Regiment 135 and three squadrons of Dragoon Regiment 6 were moved to Rüttgen and conducted reconnaissance towards Luxemburg. One squadron of Dragoon Regiment 6 was moved to Wollmeringen and conducted reconnaissance towards Esch.

(4) From Metz: the staff of the 34th Infantry Division, the 66th and 67th Infantry Brigades, 33rd Cavalry Brigade (without one squadron from each regiment), staff of the 1st Brigade and the 3rd Battalion, Foot Artillery Regiment 33, Foot Artillery Regiment 34, two pioneer companies, and the divisional bridging train moved in two columns along both banks of the Moselle. The infantry vanguards reached Diedenhofen and the cavalry pushed forward from there. The pioneer companies and the bridging train are to be found at the head of the right-hand column.

(5) Uhlan Regiment 14 moved to Mörchingen; battalions from Forbach and Saargemünd, Dragoon Regiment 7 and Chevauleger Regiment 5 as well as the 2nd Battalion, Foot Artillery Regiment 33 moved to Hellimer–Gross Tänchen.

The corps staff remained temporarily in Metz. A train to transport the corps staff stands ready at Metz station.

According to available reports, the French occupied the city of Luxemburg on the afternoon of 5 August, but appear only to have advanced weak detachments from there. The French have crossed the border along the Avricourt–Cheminot stretch and have pushed back our observation detachments. By nightfall, Marsal, Château-Salins, Delme and Buchy were in the hands of the enemy.

> *Problem:* What orders [*Befehle*] does the Commanding General of the XVI Army Corps issue for 6 August?

TACTICAL-STRATEGIC PROBLEMS, 1892
DISCUSSION OF THE PROBLEMS

From the first problem it can be seen that the deployment of the German army west of the Vosges is threatened from two sides – from Nancy–Lunéville and from Longwy. It must be assumed that a full army corps and a cavalry division that have almost completed their mobilization are advancing from Nancy–Lunéville. There is absolutely no sure intelligence about the strength of the enemy that has crossed the border from Longwy. Moreover, exact information about this force is neither to be awaited nor is it required. In reality, an abundance of exaggerated and contradictory reports will arrive, more likely to obscure the facts of the case than to clear them up. However, one can reckon that by full use of the given time and the efficiency of the rail line, an army corps, obviously without its columns and trains, could be set in march from Longwy on the morning of the 5th. That an army corps may be here, however, does not permit one to conclude that there is definitely a corps here, since we know neither when the rail transport was begun or ended, nor in what intervals the trains followed one another. It is known that we are only dealing with units that have not yet fully mobilized, therefore, in the worst case, with an army corps that is not of full war strength, i.e., without its full compliment of guns and without its full fighting power. Certainly one must not forget that our units have not yet completed their mobilization and that they are also in some respects not up to their full fighting power. None the less, however weak the enemy reported at Longwy may be, he certainly intends more than a demonstration, for one only violates the neutrality of a country, thereby allowing the enemy to do the same, with good reason.

An invasion from Nancy can threaten the Metz–Saarburg rail line, while an attack from Longwy can easily threaten the Diedenhofen and Ecternach stretch and further on along the Sauer. The around 75-kilometre Metz–Saarburg line is fairly open and is only difficult to cross at the western end. The 60-kilometre Diedenhofen–Ecternach line is covered by the heavily defended sector between the Mosel and the Sauer. If the Commanding General wants to hold both lines purely defensively, he will defend the long, open southern line against the stronger enemy with two of the three divisions available to him and defend the shorter, more easily defended northern line against the weaker enemy with the last division available to him. However, two divisions are barely sufficient to cover the southern line, and even less so considering that the extremely limited Metz garrison can only have a very limited effect outside the fortress. As during any defence of a long line, if the defender details his units to cover every available road, the attacker can amass superior forces at a favourable point and break through the thinly stretched defence without difficulty. On the other hand, if one holds his force together, he runs the risk of being bypassed. Even more difficult is to defend such a long line by deploying just in front of it. A corps concentrated around Mörchingen can easily secure the Bensdorf–Saaralben line, but can hardly prevent the rail line from being broken between Rémilly and Forbach or Courcelles and Bolchen or some other point. One must advance as far as possible. Only on the heights between Delme and Château-Salins will one be able to defend the line in a far more effective manner than from a defence based on Mörschingen.

To secure the northern rail line, the 16th Infantry Division could be concentrated generally between Remich and Sierck. This would result in surrender of the Trier–Diedenhofen railway, as the French can take the line under fire from the left bank of the Moselle and this line will only be kept in operation with great difficulty. Some Gentlemen mentioned this grievance, but did think it very important to lose this stretch of line as it is only single track. I would like to recommend that these Gentlemen look at a railway map and count the number of lines available to both France and Germany for deployment [*Aufmarsch*]. Perhaps then they will be convinced that we cannot do without a single line, be it single tracked or not.

However, even if one is willing to accept the loss of this stretch of line, the defence of the 60-kilometre Moselle and Sauer line is not as easy as it first appears. In what makes this position strong – the difficulty of the crossing, the impassibility of the banks and the steepness of the valleys – lies its very weakness; the defender also has difficulty overcoming the terrain. Therefore, reconnaissance against the French-occupied left bank can only be spotty and insufficient. The movements taking place on the French side will remain unknown. The attacker will not attack where the defender is located, and the defender cannot be everywhere at once. The attacker will demonstrate here and there and finally cross at some point unseen and unopposed. At least, this has happened often enough in the past. It may be better to throw back the advancing enemy, than to wait and worry day and night for him to advance into some path left open!

To be sure, one cannot take the offensive on both lines at once. One must launch the offensive in the direction where a result can be obtained and where as much strength as possible can be deployed. On the other line, the weak forces left behind must evade the blow of the superior enemy.

In the south, it would be impossible to go over to the offensive. The advancing troops, who are ill-equipped for a siege, would be brought to a halt by Nancy. Much better would be an advance against the enemy troops moving through Luxemburg, since their march can be flanked from Metz and Diedenhofen. An offensive here is also more important, as greater danger comes from this direction. If the French advance south from Nancy on the Metz–Saarburg line, they will only push in somewhat the front of the German deployment [*Aufmarsch*]. However, if the French are successful with their invasion of Luxemburg in crossing the Moselle and reaching the Saar, the deploying German army would be divided into two parts. Only the centre and the left wing of the German army would be successful in reaching Lorraine. The right wing, which would be transported via the Eifel and Moselle rail lines, would be forced to unload in Trier at best. There would eventually be two groups, one which would attempt to deploy on the Han line between the Nied and Saarburg and the other which would assemble north of Trier.

However, one does not need to assume such a French result. Perhaps the enemy advancing in Luxemburg does not have the intention of advancing as far as the Trier–Saarlouis rail line and perhaps it does not have the strength necessary for such an undertaking. Perhaps their initial thoughts do not reach beyond the Moselle and the Sauer. Perhaps one is only dealing with a small force [*Truppenkörper*] that has been rapidly advanced merely to secure Luxemburg and the railways therein, and additional divisions and army corps will follow when mobilization has been completed. One cannot wait inactive on the right bank of the Moselle for such an event to take place.

According to the given problems, a deployment of the German army along the Diedenhofen–Metz–Saarburg line can be assumed. This deployment can only be designed with the assumption that the German right wing could rest securely on a neutral Luxemburg. If this assumption is proved wrong and, in fact, an enemy army corps is assembled on the right bank of the Moselle on our flank and in our rear, the planned deployment is no longer viable. We would either have to refuse our right wing or drive the French from Luxemburg.

Under these circumstances, an offensive into Luxemburg appears to me to be not only recommended, but absolutely necessary. The question can only be whether the Commanding General carries out the undertaking immediately with the troops at his disposal or whether he should await the arrival of reinforcements. However, the German position can hardly be improved by waiting for reinforcements. On the contrary, German reinforcements can be met and even surpassed by the French. Moreover, the German deployment can only take place according to plan when the French are driven quickly out of Luxemburg. Therefore, the Commanding General's decision on the

5th to assemble the 16th Infantry Division as far as possible east of Remich–Sierck and to march all available troops from Metz to Diedenhofen meets with approval. Certainly with this decision the Metz–Saarburg rail line and behind cannot be held under all circumstances, but a general retirement from here would hardly be a great disadvantage for us. On the other hand, so long as the question of Luxemburg is not solved, we cannot deploy further forward than the Saar.

The directives issued to the border guard detachments in 1870 called for the advancing enemy to be held back as much as possible, but for the detachments to evade superior enemy forces until enough strength could be assembled to overcome the enemy. Similar directives should be issued by the Commanding General here to the troops left behind in Lorraine. One must visualize the advance of the French VI Army Corps from Nancy. If this corps wants to achieve a meaningful result, it must advance as far as possible into German territory, to somewhere around Saargemünd or Saarbrücken. While this corps advances in constant battle with the retiring German border guard detachments, German troop transports are arriving on the Saar. In Saarburg, Saaralben, Saargemünd and Saarbrücken, the advance guards of various army corps are being formed and are being reinforced hour by hour. If these units are too weak to offer enough resistance to the advancing French, in the worst case they merely have to retire along the rail line and cover the detraining taking place at station after station. The further the French corps advances, the more enemies it finds on its front, on its flanks and in its rear. It is a hopeless undertaking that will perish under its own weight.

In the second problem, the Commanding General had sent the 16th Infantry Division to assemble in the general area of Remich and Sierck, while the 34th Infantry Division, with reinforced artillery, marched to Diedenhofen. The choice was now either to take the offensive into Luxemburg or to remain in a somewhat tighter concentration on the right bank of the Moselle. The latter would allow any enemy attempt to cross the river to be met with powerful German forces and, by means of a few marches, to reach the Saar to be in place if the enemy force from Nancy advanced against this river. The task of removing the French from Luxemburg would hereby be left to the army corps arriving as part of the general deployment.

Most Gentlemen decided, however, for an offensive. Before an officer launches an offensive, it would serve him well to be as clear as he can be about the enemy's intentions. On the morning of the 5th the French had broken out of Longwy and reached Luxemburg with their advance guards after a march of 30 kilometres. From here, they sent out only weak detachments. From this, one can conclude that the French corps only has very little cavalry or does not have very active cavalry. A sign as to future steps has not been given. However, one can assume that the French, by way of their good friends in Metz, Diedenhofen and the Grand Duchy of Luxemburg, will be supplied with a great deal of intelligence. Through this, they will know that an enemy stands before them and that they have another on their right flank. If they are not very strong or do not feel themselves confident enough, they will give up their march on Trier, Remich or Sierck, if this was indeed their intention. The position in which they would find themselves by such an advance is too unfavourable. They might perhaps turn against the German force waiting at Diedenhofen, west of the Alzette or, as is most likely, they might remain in Luxemburg. From here, they can undertake a guerrilla war [*kleiner Krieg*] against the Eifel and Moselle rail lines much more easily since they control the Luxemburg railways.

I do not believe that those Gentlemen who wish the 16th Infantry Division to take up an entrenched position west of Remich and there allow the French to attack them frontally while the 34th Infantry Division annihilates the French through a flank attack would have a great prospect of success. I fear that the enemy would not come and if he, in fact, takes the path up to Remich, he will not advance far enough for the net to be thrown around him. A day will have passed uselessly and the only lesson will have been that one should not make plans on the basis of a single case.

Those Gentlemen would also have wasted a day who would have the 16th Infantry Division march southwest of Remich and the 34th Division march northeast of Diedenhofen closer to the Moselle and concentrate far from Luxemburg in order to advance united against the enemy. It is laudable to concentrate one's forces, but it is not advisable to do so in this manner. One should imagine how the battle of Königgrätz would have turned out if this means of concentrating forces had been employed. The Prussian 1st and 2nd Armies would have united somewhere around Horsitz and only on the 4th would they have advanced together frontally against a position that had in the meantime been considerably strengthened. Unification of one's forces is to be found in the march forward, and on the battlefield early enough. In this case, if reports arriving during the course of the day make a change of march necessary, the individual march columns will be given new goals. Those march columns that have encountered the enemy put up resistance until the other columns arrive.[3]

In most cases, for a direct march against the enemy in Luxemburg, Gentlemen have chosen the roads via Fristingen and Filsdorf and via

Ötringen and Trintingen. All of these routes, however, lead through easily defended sectors and, courageously, against the enemy's front. This will lead to a costly frontal assault and to a direct pursuit at best. The occasion does not demand such a difficult and fruitless exercise.

In some answers, it was suggested that the entire French undertaking in Luxemburg would fail. So much the better for us! An error committed by the enemy must be exploited by us. This cannot happen if I entrench my forces at Remich or concentrate my forces further to the rear or if I take up a position of readiness. We must march against the lines of communication of this exposed, isolated enemy force, and this is easily done. The earlier march route of the 34th Infantry Division from Metz to Diedenhofen continues along in a straight line via Great Hettingen and Bettemburg into the rearward communications (Dippach to Luxemburg) of the enemy. Certainly part of the way is difficult, but one cannot allow poor roads to force the postponement of a battle. In any case, the two other columns will be given their march goals based on Bettemburg. This is not to say that all three columns would cross the Alzette at Bettemburg, but rather this place would be the general goal, from which no further goals can initially be assigned. The northern column would follow the good road via Dalheim when possible. If this route appears too dangerous, the worse route via Mondorf–Ewringen could be taken.

If the Germans advance beyond Bettemburg and if the French remain in the city of Luxemburg, the Germans would force the French to fight a battle west of the city with a turned front [*mit verkehrter Front*]. If the French march southward to meet the Germans, they will fall between our supply columns. However, if they set out on a march toward Remich, Trier, etc., they will find us in their rear.

Thus, the German strategic position is as good as it can be. Some might now ask whether or not the Germans have enough superiority to attack. The strength of the enemy is unknown. However, that nothing certain is known about this should not make the problems more difficult. Rather, this uncertainty should be accepted as the normal condition during wartime. We no longer live in an age of cabinet wars where one knows exactly how many battalions and squadrons each general has under him. We find ourselves today in an age of peoples' armies and, indeed, not yet even at the apex of this age. Behind the army corps that are already formed in peacetime and that can be counted, there emerge time and again, new reserve corps and reserve armies. How is one to know which part of such a million-man army one faces? Actions are directed by puzzles, estimates, conjectures and, I might say, hunches. The general who marches against an enemy must be inwardly convinced of the superiority, either in numbers or in quality, of his army. He will rarely ever be given mathematical certainty that his is the stronger. According to the calculations made earlier, the French could barely be stronger than the Germans. However, the reports received were too inexact to allow one to rely definitely upon such calculations. The French could have received reinforcement. Doubts and fears, which can make decisions difficult, are normal. However, the Commanding General has done all he can do. He has brought together as much combat strength as he could. The rest must be left to fortune, which, as is well known, favours the bold. If he is to have success and great success, he must always leave something to chance.

7

Tactical-Strategic Problems, 1896

These problems addressed a notional invasion of Germany from Denmark and the possibility of an amphibious landing by a British corps somewhere along the northern coast of Germany – the only time such a scenario was addressed in Schlieffen's games.[1] The involvement of the Royal Navy was assumed to have forced the German fleet into its ports. Schlieffen's subordinates were placed in the role of the Deputy Commanding General of the IX Army Corps (based in Altona). They were set the challenging task of defeating the invading forces using only the reserve troops at hand – no active duty troops could be spared to deal with what Schlieffen clearly considered a sideshow to the main battle elsewhere.

FIRST PROBLEM

Germany finds itself at war with a great power [*Großmacht*]. It is necessary for the bulk of the German fleet to withdraw to Kiel and for the rest to withdraw to Wilhelmshaven. Both ports have been blockaded. A Danish corps, the strength of which is estimated at 30 battalions, 12 squadrons and 96 guns, has advanced from Kolding, by way of Christiansfeld, and crossed the German border.[2] Arriving intelligence indicates that the landing of another enemy corps on the coast of Holstein or Mecklenburg is imminent.

The Deputy Commanding General [*der stellvertretende Kommandierende General*] of the German IX Army Corps has received the directive [*Weisung*] to hold, if possible, the Kaiser-Wilhelm Canal, but at least to cover Kiel and Hamburg against the advancing enemy. He has assembled the 1st Reserve Brigade, which had been dispersed around the Province of Schleswig, and has withdrawn it to Rendsburg. At Kiel, provisional fortifications have been constructed on the land side, based on the port forts, and all possible exertions have been made to reinforce

TACTICAL-STRATEGIC PROBLEMS, 1896

these. The complete armament of the west front with naval artillery should be complete early on the 7th. To cover Hamburg, [construction of defensive] works have been quickly begun. Reinforcements are on their way to both cities.

On 6 June, the Deputy Commanding General has at his disposal the following units, including fortress garrisons:

Rendsburg: 1st Reserve Brigade (8 battalions, 4 squadrons, 5 batteries)
Holtenau–Levensau: 1 *Landwehr* battalion
Grünenthal: 1 *Landwehr* battalion
Brunsbüttel: 1 *Landwehr* battalion
Kiel: 2nd Reserve Brigade (8 battalions, 4 squadrons, 5 batteries); 5 *Landwehr* battalions, 2 *Landsturm* battalions
Hamburg-Altona: 2nd Reserve Division (16 battalions, 8 squadrons, 10 batteries) 6 *Ersatz* battalions, 2 *Ersatz* squadrons, 2 *Ersatz* batteries, 2 *Landwehr* battalions, 2 *Landsturm* batteries
Lübeck: 1 *Landwehr* battalion
Wismar: 1 *Landwehr* battalion
Rostock: 1 *Landwehr* battalion, 1 *Ersatz* battalion
Schwerin: 1 *Ersatz* battalion, 2 *Ersatz* squadrons, 2 *Ersatz* batteries.

At 1900 on the evening of the 6th, the following message arrived in Altona from the 1st Reserve Brigade: *Attack on Rendsburg this afternoon successfully repulsed. None the less, enemy successful in bridging the canal southwest of Schirnau and in advancing units to Rade. Therefore, withdrawing tonight to Jevenstadt.*

Problem: Deputy Commanding General's orders and actions for the 7th, with reasons.

DISCUSSION OF THE FIRST PROBLEM

The Deputy Commanding General could not fulfil one of his missions. The enemy has not only reached the Kaiser-Wilhelm Canal, which was to be defended, he has crossed it. To fulfil the assigned mission, the enemy must now at least be thrown back. If this is successful, the remaining missions take care of themselves: Kiel and Hamburg remain free of the enemy.

However, one has to deal not only with the enemy that is advancing on Rendsburg and Rade – any day can bring a second enemy corps on the coast of Holstein or Mecklenburg, which can be soon on the field of battle. The Deputy Commanding General does not have enough forces to deal with both enemies simultaneously. Therefore, he must endeavour to be completely finished with the Danish corps before the second enemy corps arrives, and, in order to have a free hand against this landing corps, it is not enough simply to push the Danish corps back, it must be worn down [*aufgerieben*] as soon as possible and annihilated.

For such a task, forces must be assembled that are superior to the Danish corps. Available for this initially are the 1st and 2nd Reserve Brigades and the 2nd Reserve Division, which together add up to 32 battalions, 16 squadrons and 20 batteries. This gives a slight superiority over the enemy force that had crossed the German border at Christiansfeld on 1 May with 30 battalions, 12 squadrons and 16 batteries. However, it gives a greater superiority against the enemy that is expected in the morning of 7 June, as the Danish corps has had to make some detachments since its advance into Schleswig to cover its lines of communication and Rendsburg. Moreover, the bridges at Schirnau must certainly be occupied on the 7th. If the Danish corps turns to march on Kiel, it would surely have to leave behind a force to cover the German 1st Reserve Brigade. If it marches to the south, it would need to leave at least an observation force to cover itself from whatever force could advance from Kiel. Thus, the Danish corps would hardly be able to continue its operations on the 7th with its original 30 battalions, 12 squadrons and 16 batteries.

The Germans can therefore expect a not inconsiderable superiority. Such a superiority is absolutely necessary, and it is inexcusable to lose a victory because the 2nd Reserve Brigade has been left behind supposedly as to not endanger Kiel. Kiel is not endangered without this brigade, so long as the German corps is not beaten. The danger of defeat, however, is certainly greater if the German corps has to enter battle with only three, rather than four brigades. The best security for Kiel, therefore, lay in sending the 2nd Reserve Brigade into the field. For the time being, the battalions left behind and the numerous sailors of the fleet are enough to defend the port's improvised fortifications.

While some Gentlemen renounced the use of the 2nd Reserve Brigade, still many more wanted nothing to do with the numerous *Ersatz* and *Landwehr* units at hand in the corps region. Some find the superiority won by the addition of the 2nd Reserve Brigade enough. However, these Gentlemen stand in opposition to the elementary principle that one can never be strong enough in battle. Others believe that these troops have only a limited combat capability and would rather leave them behind. It is certain that line troops would be preferable if they were available. However, one has to be satisfied with what one can get. It is in no way excusable to leave troops in their garrisons to carry out peacetime exercises [*Friedensübungen*] while a few miles away a battle is being fought. The individual battalions in the coastal cities are superfluous there under the threatening circumstances. While they serve to defend the citizens of these cities from the raids of sailors put ashore by boat, they are insufficient to defend against the landing of a corps or against the bombardment of an enemy fleet. Therefore, I would put in all the units that could be obtained and that the railway could carry into the field in order to seek a decisive action.

The question of where all the available troops are to be concentrated answers itself as soon as the decision is made to utilize the railways. The difficulty in transporting the 2nd Reserve Division from Hamburg to Neumünster lies in the fact that the double-track rail line by way of Elmshorn can be broken by enemy cavalry, and therefore only the single-track line via Oldesloe is available if this were to happen. However, the Elmshorn line could be secured easily by the first unloaded troops. Regardless, the arriving intelligence indicated that the transport would have to go via Elmshorn or Oldesloe. The 1st Reserve Brigade, which was retiring on Nortorf, would naturally take up the covering of the detrainment at Neumünster, while the 2nd Reserve Brigade was to be brought to the right flank by means of a foot march. In which place the latter spent the night could be of no real significance. It was only important that this unit, and indeed the remainder of the units, be accommodated on the 7th as close to the front as possible, but that no real contact be made yet with the enemy.

If one chooses not to use rail transport, the corps' concentration not only takes more time, but must take place further to the rear – around Segeberg or Bramstedt. One would not then be ready for any eventuality and would find oneself in a comparatively worse off position. In whatever manner the concentration of the corps is accomplished, all available forces must nevertheless be brought together. With every grouping of two or three forces distant from one another, the danger increases that the enemy will be encountered with only a part of the total German force and that the Germans will then be defeated.

Initially, on the 6th, no particulars can be given about the course of events after the concentration at Neumünster and Nortorf. At most, one could say, the object was to seek out the enemy and beat him. Many Gentlemen already designed a detailed plan of operations while still in Altona, since they believed they knew with certainty what the enemy would do and must do. I believe that if these Gentlemen had sought out the Danish commanding general in his headquarters in Rendsburg, they would have found him greatly embarrassed by what he had to do. This general could not know whether a further advance would strike an enemy as strong as his force or whether an attack was to be expected from Kiel or from Neumünster or from Itzehoe. He was directed to unite with a corps which was still at sea, the time and place of the landing of which was dependent upon the wind and the weather and innumerable other acts of chance. Whichever way he turned, his flanks were threatened and to his rear lay an obstacle difficult to cross – the Canal. Out of the difficulty of the Danish position came the simplicity of what the Germans had to do as soon as the enemy had made an advance on the 7th. The Danes had to be pushed back from the Rendsburg bridges and thrown back against the Canal, regardless of whether they turned to the east against the Rendsburg–Holtenau stretch or to the south against the Rendsburg–Brunsbüttel stretch.

SECOND PROBLEM

The 2nd Reserve Division was transported by rail from Hamburg to Neumünster via Oldesloe and was concentrated north of Neumünster by 1600 on the 7th. Likewise, the 2nd Reserve Brigade marched from Kiel to Neumünster. This force was billeted for the night of the 8th in Schönbek, Hohenhorst and Mühbrook. The 1st Reserve Brigade retired on Nortorf. When, however, the enemy columns which had crossed the Canal at Schirnau advanced on Nortorf via Bokelholm, Bokel and Papenkamp, the 1st Brigade withdrew to Krogaspe. On the evening of the 7th, the advance guards of the two sides were separated by the Rehmsbek at Timmaspe. The right-hand enemy column succeeded in advancing through Jevenstedt; its vanguard reached Heinkenborstel and its main body Oldenhütten.

Troops were arriving in Neumünster from the garrisons in Mecklenburg and from Hamburg from the evening of the 7th.

Problem: Orders for the German troops on the evening of the 7th.

DISCUSSION OF THE SECOND PROBLEM

The plan sketched above to throw the Danes back against the Canal after they had advanced on the 7th to Nortorf–Oldenhütten was made more difficult by the terrain. The Brahm and Warder Lakes limited an envelopment [*Umfassung*] of the Danish left wing. This made it all the more important not to hold back with the attack, but to win the commanding heights of Borgdorf and Eisendorf quickly with the enveloping wing, before the Danes could occupy them and bring the whole German attack to a frontal assault. Notwithstanding, a not inconsiderable number of orders were issued to the troops that did not call for an immediate attack. Misjudging the situation [*Gefechtslage*], again many Gentlemen wanted to await the enemy's attack and many wanted initially only to take up positions of readiness.

If the attack is to be carried out quickly, it must be laid out simply. Three brigades should not be bound up together on one road so that they can only deploy for battle slowly. Moreover, any troop movements away from their basis of operation, even if they are designed to improve the order of battle [*Kriegsgliederung*], must be avoided. If the attack against the enemy front at Timmaspe–Schülp and against the enemy left flank at Borgdorf–Eisendorf succeeded completely, the Danish corps would be forced to the southwest, i.e., in a direction unfavourable to it. A German pursuit would have undoubtedly led to its disintegration.

THIRD PROBLEM

Against the enemy reported at Nortorf, the Germans advanced on the 8th with two reserve brigades by way of Timmaspe, with one by way of Schülp and one via Springwedel and Borgdorf. A brigade formed mainly from *Ersatz* battalions and batteries advanced from Neumünster via Prehnsfelde and extended the German left wing. A combined cavalry brigade, to which an artillery battery was attached, received the order to take part in the battle at Eisendorf. Individual squadrons occupied the defiles from Bokel and Jevenstedt.

The Danes had also concentrated at Nortorf, in order, as it appeared, to take the offensive. However, neither of the two sides came to a decision on this day. After many vain attacks from both sides, by the evening the two forces maintained just about the same positions they had occupied that afternoon. The Germans and the Danes faced each other separated by the Rehmsbek and by the river north of Nortorf and Theinbüttel. Until 0300 of the 9th, the following reports and intelligence had arrived:

(1) The *Landwehr* Battalion Grünenthal believes itself to be enveloped by the enemy from Rendsberg. It was retiring to Itzehoe.
(2) The cavalry squadron in Bokel reports that patrols sent out to Brammer have heard the continuous sound of wagon wheels on the Nortorf to Bargstedt road [*Chausée*].
(3) The cavalry squadron at Jevenstedt reports that only enemy patrols occupy the front.
(4) The Hohenwestedt station reports long columns of troops marching from Nindorf to Remmels at 0200.

(5) The Beringstedt station, which was in connection with Grünenthal earlier in the evening, reports at 0300 that it is no longer able to raise the town.
6) The advance posts report nothing new.

Problem: Intentions and actions of the Deputy Commanding General for the 9th.

DISCUSSION OF THE THIRD PROBLEM

It was assumed in the third problem that the enemy would be successful in holding fast until the coming of darkness, but that darkness would not prevent him from withdrawing from his poor position; in fact, this would be unstoppable. Operating completely according to its directives, the Danish corps had found before it an enemy force so overwhelming that it appeared impossible to advance further. Indeed, it had held its position only with difficulty, but it could not hope to hold on for another whole day. Moreover, it was perhaps lacking in munitions. In the best case, they carried one munitions column along on the 7th, and one could only fear that no more was to be had since the routes to Rendsburg were occupied by German cavalry. The Danish corps could not advance and it could not stay where it was. Moreover, the Danes could also not retreat back to Rendsburg, not, as was postulated by some Gentlemen, because a German squadron stood in Jevenstedt, which could be easily defeated, but because the march back to Rendsburg could not remain undiscovered and because the corps would then be forced into a battle south of Rendsburg under unfavourable circumstances. Rapid assistance from the landing corps was not to be hoped for. On the contrary, it was feared that the Germans would grow stronger by the hour and that the Danish corps would be completely encircled.

Thus, the Danish commanding general decided to avail himself, under the cover of darkness, of the only way remaining open to him and, thanks to the misjudgement of a *Landwehr* battalion, take off via Grünenthal unhindered.

With this exit came the conclusion of the battle; a step was taken that has been taken repeatedly in all wars, even in 1870/71. On 6 August 1870, General Frossard left his position with the coming of darkness, as did General Bazaine on 16 August 1870, and only with the coming of morning on the next day were the Germans convinced that the battle would not be taken up again and that they, in fact, were victors. Similar events also occurred repeatedly during the Loire campaign and in the northern theatre of war.[3]

TACTICAL-STRATEGIC PROBLEMS, 1896

The Danish general's decision was already taken in the afternoon of the 8th, and the marching away of the baggage and of the trains and columns that were in Jevenstedt had already begun. The combat units followed in the evening. At 0200, columns of troops, which did not need to be marched off initially, could be found between Nindorf and Remmels – a distance of at least 14 kilometres from Nortorf. At 0400, the earliest time at which the Germans could hope to attack the former Danish position, the observed portions of the march columns had to be at least 24 kilometres from Nortorf. Since the entire corps needs only a march length of 24 kilometres, one could calculate, even under the best of circumstances, that it would be impossible to meet considerable enemy forces in yesterday's position. A direct pursuit, no matter how energetically carried out, offered therefore little prospect of success. The pursuing infantry could not march faster than the retreating. If no special destruction or blocking had taken place, the pursuer could hope only to hinder seriously the retreat of a rearguard, which could offer considerable resistance behind the numerous bends in the road. Not much could be expected of the cavalry, whether one leaves their batteries behind or not, due to the unfavorable roads and the broken terrain. Therefore, the Germans would perhaps have encountered a fair number of marauders and have captured considerable numbers of rifles, rucksacks, baggage wagons, etc. However, they would not force the enemy to deploy for battle again and a full-scale disintegration of the enemy corps would not take place. Regardless, the pursuit would come to a halt at the Canal on the 10th. Behind this obstacle, the Danish corps would find comparative safety and would have the time to reform its units after the considerable exertions of the previous days and to restore its lost communications with the north.

If the German force now stood, as was repeatedly advised, east of the Canal at a greater or lesser distance to await the landing of the second enemy corps somewhere on the coast, it could soon find itself between two enemies. It would then possess the advantage of inner lines, but one of the two enemy forces, the one it has relinquished, is covered by the Canal and the Germans must leave behind considerable forces in order to turn against the landed corps. As a consequence, they would not be strong enough to fight the new enemy.

A victory such as was won on the 8th can in no way be enough under the pressing circumstances. Further, it is not sufficient for a corps in an operation against two, separated enemies merely to push one back; rather one enemy must be completely beaten before turning on the other enemy force. In 1757, Friedrich the Great could only turn back against the Austrians in Silesia after a victory like the one at Rossbach.[4] Napoleon's attack against Blücher's isolated corps in February 1814 did not have the desired result because he turned away from the Silesian Army too soon.[5] Also, one only has to think back to Ligny and Waterloo.[6]

Therefore, the incomplete victory of the 8th must be finished before all else. This cannot be accomplished through a direct pursuit. All possible results from a direct pursuit of the Danes could be accomplished merely with a brigade; pursuit with the entire corps would be superfluous. The corps has to be directed via Rendsburg against the enemy's lines of retreat or all that had been accomplished would be in vain. Such an undertaking is not, as has been often said, something exceptionally daring or risky, but rather it is necessary that one has to do it if one wants to end the campaign favourably. On the contrary, a risky undertaking would be to remain east of the Canal.

The situation on the 9th would have been as follows: the Danish corps has succeeded in slipping through Grünenthal and in gaining a rest after being completely exhausted by a day's fighting and a night march. A Danish rear guard has possibly been left at Hademarschen and a pursuing German brigade has made a halt at Beringstedt. The remainder of the German force (four brigades) stands at and west of Rendsburg. German cavalry has occupied the crossings of the Eiler, or at least those along the stretch between Friedrichstadt and Lexfähr. The Danish trains and supply columns have been pushed to the north. Troops from Germany will be advanced to the Canal as soon as possible via Hamburg and Itzehoe. If the bridges at Rendsburg have been destroyed by the Danes, they must obviously be rebuilt before the troops, possibly as early as the morning of the 10th, can be advanced over the Eiler in a western direction.

The experience of the coming days cannot be predicted, but the Germans must exploit the advantage of their position. However, it can be asked whether the Germans still have the time for further operations against the Danish corps and whether they might in fact be surprised by an attack by the second enemy corps that has landed in the meantime. To this must be said: a large transport fleet of 60 to 70 ships [*Dampfern*] cannot anchor off the coast of Holstein secretly without being noticed. Until the 9th, no reports of the enemy fleet had arrived. Thus, it is to be calculated that the enemy fleet has not yet shown itself on the coast. Moreover, according to the examples given by military history (the landing of the English and French at Eupatoria in 1854, the English and the French at Peh-Tang in 1860, the English at Ismaïlia in 1882 and the Japanese at Port Arthur and Wei-Hai-Wei in 1895), at least five days pass between the landing and the marching off from the landing site. Even if, considering recent improvements in landing procedures in European navies, one cuts down this time considerably, it is still doubtful whether an enemy corps landed at Hochwachter Bay at Lütjenburg or at Neustädtler Bay can be in Rendsburg quickly, especially since it must secure the landing area, receive intelligence and orientate itself, and complete three or four marches before reaching Rendsburg. Thus, more than enough time would remain for the Germans to turn their incomplete victory of the 8th into a real victory. So long as this is accomplished, the corps landed by the enemy, which must secure its landing site and logistical base against Kiel, loses all its threat.

The peculiarities of the Schleswig theatre of war are known to us, taught to us by four campaigns. Essentially, the Danes have always moved only on one main road, the one running from Kolding via Flensburg and Schleswig to Rendsburg. Thus, they had their main communication on their left flank. However, this left flank could not be taken from them, as deep bays and fjords reached into the land to the immediate vicinity of the main road from the eastern coast at almost regular intervals and frustrated every German attempt to envelop or to outflank the Danish left wing. Thus, the Danes, when pushed back, could fall back on Alsen, Fredericia, Aarhus and finally over the Limfjord in comparative safety in order to break out again at the appropriate time or to be loaded onto ships and to appear by surprise on a favourable point along the long coast. As long as the German fleet controls the sea, this would be impossible. However, if, as was assumed in these problems, the German fleet was forced into inactivity, the Danes have more opportunities. We would then be forced to conduct a war requiring far more strength than the simple size of the enemy requires, especially if Germany finds itself at war with a great power [*Großmacht*] like Great Britain.

The advantages of the theatre of war will be less for the Danes once they pass the Schleswig–Eckernförde line and they cease altogether when the advancing attacker undertakes to cross the Kaiser-Wilhelm Canal. They then have a bridge behind them that can be cut and, which ever way they turn, a hard-to-bridge canal on one of their flanks. The Germans, on the other hand, can base themselves, according to their wish, on Kiel, Lübeck or Hamburg and can possibly call upon the navy for assistance on the Canal. Under these favourable circumstances, the Germans must set as a goal the annihilation of the enemy.

8

Tactical-Strategic Problems, 1903

*These problems were based upon Helmuth von Moltke's initial plans for the early phase of the Franco-German War of 1870/71.[1] Here, Schlieffen has asked his subordinates to outline the orders of the German armies in their invasion of France. Although the size of armies had changed considerably in the intervening 33 years, Schlieffen clearly felt the underlying lessons remained the same and could provide useful instruction to officers who had never seen combat. As such, it is a good example of how historical events were used for training by the Kaiserheer. Moreover, these problems demonstrate Schlieffen's commitment to preparing his officers for bigger and better things – despite the fact that most of those solving these problems were junior officers (*Oberleutnants *and* Hauptleute*), they were asked to develop plans for directing armies.*

FIRST PROBLEM

On the evening of 2 August 1870, the troops of the German 2nd and 3rd Armies stood in their assigned billeting areas near the French border. Both army commands [*Oberkommandos*] had reported their armies ready for operations on 3 August to the Supreme Headquarters [*Große Hauptquartier*].

From the 1st Army, the VII Army Corps is expected in Losheim by way of Trier, the VIII Army Corps in Wadern via Bernkastel, and the 3rd Cavalry Division in Saarburg on 3 August.

According to the latest reports received on the French, the following deployment has to be assumed:

Guard Corps (two infantry divisions and one cavalry division) in Metz

I Army Corps (four infantry divisions and one cavalry division) in and south of Hagenau

TACTICAL-STRATEGIC PROBLEMS, 1903

II Army Corps (three infantry divisions and one cavalry division) at Saarbrücken and Forbach

III Army Corp (four infantry divisions and one cavalry division) at St Avold and Buschborn

IV Army Corps (three infantry divisions and one cavalry division) at Bolchen and Busendorf with an advance guard at Saarlouis, one brigade or division at Sierck

V Army Corps (three infantry divisions and one cavalry division) at Saargemünd, one infantry division at Bitsch

VI Army Corps (four infantry divisions and one cavalry division) encamped at Châlons

VIII Army Corps (three infantry divisions and one cavalry division) in southern Alsace.

On 2 August, the French II Army Corps had attacked *Oberstleutnant* von Pestel's weak detachment at Saarbrücken and forced him to retreat to south of Heusweiler.[2] It was possible that this attack meant the commencement of an offensive against the German 2nd Army. For this possibility, General von Moltke suggested to the command of the 2nd Army that they meet the French attack behind the Lauter.

> *Problem:* What directives, later shelved, should have been given for the execution of this proposal:
> (1) By the command of the 2nd Army?
> (2) In agreement with the Supreme Command and the 1st and 3rd Armies?

DISCUSSION OF THE FIRST PROBLEM

On the evening of 2 August, the Germans were ready for operations, but their armies had not yet deployed. The report arrived that the weak garrison of Saarbrücken was forced by the French to retreat. There was a very real possibility that this encounter with the French represented the beginning of a French offensive over the Saar against the German 2nd Army. The present state of the 2nd Army prevented it from going at once to meet the advancing French; it could only strike at him with individual corps. First, it had to deploy, and this had to be covered. Therefore, the Field Marshal recommended that the 2nd Army initially take up a defensive position behind the Lauter.

We know that it did not lie within the Field Marshal's intentions to await the enemy exclusively in this defensive position. At most, only a repulse of an enemy attack could be accomplished from this position. On the contrary, the goal has to be to give the French the rapid decision they appear to be seeking and to inflict upon them an annihilating defeat. Therefore, not all troops should be placed in the Lauter position; instead, as large a number as possible must be employed against the enemy's flanks and rear. This could be accomplished all the more easily, as three or four army corps (Guard, IV, IX and XII) appeared to be sufficient to cover the proposed Lauterecken–Kaiserlautern line. The question was then how should the remaining two corps (III and X Army Corps) be employed?

By many Gentlemen, they were merely used to lengthen the front to the Kirn–Oberstein road, with the right wing at Fischbach or Oberstein. Little would be achieved by this. The enemy, even if he is weaker, could advance against this lengthened front in about the same breadth. His frontal attack was presumably repulsed frontally. His annihilation was not accomplished.

In order to outflank the enemy, other Gentlemen wanted to lead the two corps in a wide curve through Hunsrück, to place them in readiness at an apparently suitable point, and then wanted to break forth, as if in an ambush, at a given moment, against the enemy's flank and rear. This manoeuvre would demand great exertions from the troops and it would require a great deal of time, but whether a timely intervention would succeed, is entirely doubtful.

It is easier for a flank attack to be carried out with the support of the 1st Army, which is to march from Trier and Bernkastel to Losheim and Wadern on 3 August. Certainly the two armies would be separated by a great distance. To fill this gap, the X and III Army Corps would have to advance via Kirn–Oberstein and via Baumholder. If the Bavarian II Corps were now to be assembled at Pirmasens, a semicircle would be formed within two days, in which the advancing enemy must be smothered.

Two objections have been raised against these dispositions. First, the enemy will not march into this semicircle. To this, it must be replied that the semicircle would not exist before the French offensive, but rather it is only formed during the enemy's advance.

As a second objection, it has been pointed out that the 1st Army, so long as it is isolated, could be attacked and annihilated and that this would result in the whole fine formation being rolled up from the right to the left wing. Therefore, the 1st Army should by no means be brought forward to Losheim and Wadern, but rather it should be held back on the Moselle or, at most, advance to Zerf and Thalfang. I believe that, upon closer examination, the danger to which the 1st Army appears to be exposed will be considerably decreased.

To determine this, I asked a number of Gentlemen just how would the French launch an attack on 3 August. It was assumed in this case that during the course of the 2nd, or perhaps already on the 1st, the French IV, III and Guard Corps had been brought up on the Saar. Most of the solutions that dealt with this have the French advancing against the German right wing, i.e., against the 1st Army. However, they disregard the nucleus of the question, namely, just how the 1st Army is to be annihilated. They accept the defeat of the VII and VIII Army Corps as an accomplished fact and wheel to the right toward Lauterecken, where they assume the 2nd Army's right wing to be waiting patiently. It is necessary, however, to take up the preceding encounter with the 1st Army in greater detail.

The French could not be directly at the Saar bridges on the evening of 2 August. In order to appear by surprise, they had to hold themselves back on their side of the border. On the morning of 3 August, one column could advance by way of Merzig and another towards Trier by way of Beckingen. After marches of around 18 and 25 kilometres, both columns could strike the enemy in the area of Losheim. The deployment of two divisions each would have demanded a great deal of time, and it is doubtful whether it would have come to an attack on the same day. Regardless, this attack would have turned out badly against the stronger enemy. A better situation would only have been expected if a third column had been successful in advancing the 30 kilometres from Dillingen. Since a French division was only around two-thirds the strength of a German division, the two sides would have stood facing one another in equal strength. For the Germans, the danger of defeat would not have been great. On the contrary, the Germans could very well have used their initial superiority to beat back the French. Only during the course of the 4th, when a fourth French column could advance from Bous, could a French superiority and a pushing back of the Germans on Hochwald be assumed. However, the victorious French would then have the head of the X Army Corps at Nohlfelden and the III Army Corps, which had advanced to Tholey by way of Friesen, on their right flank and in their rear. To fend off the Germans on the next day, new columns would have to be drawn up, so that now almost the entire French army would soon have to wheel to the north and the four corps behind the Lauter would barely find any further resistance.

In whatever formation the French might have started their advance, they would have been forced by the appearance of the German 1st Army at Losheim and Wadern on the 3rd and by the appearance of the German X and III Army Corps at Lohfelden and Freisen on the 4th to wheel in that direction. With this, they would have so weakened their front that their annihilation would have been accomplished without difficulty by the Guard, IV, IX and XII Army Corps.

ALFRED VON SCHLIEFFEN'S MILITARY WRITINGS

Some Gentlemen attempted an outflanking [*Umgehung*] of the German right wing between the Moselle and the Saar by way of Saarburg or Trier with a French corps or division. The latter would have required at least three days to reach and would only be reached too late on the evening of the 5th. The former could have been defended at the difficult crossings at Saarburg by the side detachment with which the VII Army Corps was defending itself.

I come to the result: the VII and VIII Army Corps should not be held back either at Trier and Bernkastel or in the middle of the mountains. They must advance and seek to unite their forces and to join with the 2nd Army. The positions of Losheim and Wadern that the Field Marshal designated to the 1st Army for the unification could not have been more suitably chosen. All units had to advance. If the French had taken the offensive on 3 August, the war would have been ended by the 8th.

This result would have been accomplished with 10 German army corps. If the French did not advance, it would have been better for future operations that, as the Field Marshal originally intended, not only the II, but also the I Bavarian Corps, had been brought through the Hardtwald and the offensive against the French troops in Alsace had been left to the three army corps remaining to the 3rd Army.

SECOND PROBLEM

On the evening of 2 August, the 2nd Army ordered the XII, IX, IV and Guard Corps to withdraw behind the Lauter between Lauterecken and Kaiserlautern by the evening of the 4th. The X and III Army Corps, in cooperation with the 1st Army, were to form a flank to the Lauter position on the Nohfelden–Freisen line. In agreement with this order, the Supreme Headquarters ordered that the 1st Army remain in the Losheim–Wadern line, which had been reached on 3 August, on the 4th.

Since the reports that arrived until the evening of the 3rd showed that the French had not advanced, on the 4th, the XII, IX, IV and Guard Corps were pushed forward to Eisenbach, Matzenbach, Meisenbach and Landstuhl. The 3rd Cavalry Division was to cover this formation on the right, the Guard Cavalry Division was to cover the left, and the 5th and 6th Cavalry Divisions the front.

The 3rd Army was to keep its initial task of advancing in the direction of Hagenau. However, it had to give up the II Bavarian Corps, which was to have been drawn together by the 4th at Pirmasens, to the 2nd Army.

By the evening of the 4th, the 1st Cavalry Division was to be detrained at Birkenfeld, where the I Army Corps was also to be detrained by the evening of the 5th. Both were assigned to the 1st Army.

From the 4th to the 5th, the 12th Infantry Division would be detraining in Landau. This division would be followed by the 11th Infantry Division from the 5th to 6th and the first formations of the VI Army Corps.

As of the evening of the 4th, the French had not crossed the Saar. On the 4th, the German 3rd Army crossed the Lauter and beat a division of the French 1st Army Corps at Weissenburg.

The Supreme Headquarters had the following picture of the French dispositions on the evening of 4 August:

Guard Corps: east of Metz in the area of Kurzel
I Army Corps: on the Sauer
II Army Corps: at Saarbrücken–Forbach
III Army Corps: at Püttingen–St Avold
IV Army Corps: at Bolchen–Busendorf
V Army Corps: at Saargemünd and Bitsch
VI Army Corps: in camp at Châlons
VII Army Corps: one division entrained at Hagenau, the remainder in Upper Alsace
1st Reserve Cavalry Division: with I Army Corps
2nd Reserve Cavalry Division: at Lunéville
3rd Reserve Cavalry Division: at Falkenberg
Main artillery reserve in Nancy.

Problem: How are the operations of the German army to be continued?

DISCUSSION OF THE SECOND PROBLEM

The general outcome of a French offensive could already be seen on 2 August, and the French therefore avoided any such undertaking. The question now was how the German operations should be conducted. The answer could only be: march forward and seek out the enemy. If one accepted this answer and if the corps followed the roads leading to the Saar, upon which they already stood, then they would arrive, almost by themselves, in the following position by the evening of the 6th: the 1st Army would have crossed the Saar, the right wing of the 2nd Army would have been advanced to the Saar, its left wing would have found itself further behind with the XII Army Corps and the Guard Corps on the Blies and with the II Bavarian Corps and the VI Army Corps at Hornbach and Pirmasens.

Most Gentlemen assumed that the French wanted to defend the Saar.

However, according to the reports received about the enemy, this was in doubt; only the refused right wing of the French II Army Corps and one division of the V Army Corps stood on the Saar between Saarbrücken and Saargemünd. The IV Army Corps at Busendorf; the III Army Corps somewhat further back in the space between the IV and the II Army Corps; and the Guard Corps held back on the left wing, all principally had north-facing fronts. Against these fronts, the German right wing had to advance, obviously with the intention of enveloping the French left wing, only conscious of the fact that this manoeuvre could be prevented by the Moselle fortresses of Metz and Diedenhofen and by a reinforcement of the French left wing.

In order to bring about a decision, an envelopment of the French right wing therefore had to commence. This would have been the natural task of the 3rd Army. However, it was still too far to the rear, faced the enemy, and could not know whether it would still be able to come up in time to intervene in the operations of the other two armies. Therefore, the 2nd Army had to carry the responsibility for this envelopment. Consequently, the XII Army Corps and the Guard Corps were pushed out to the II Bavarian Corps along the Saargemünd–Bitsch line and the recently arrived VI Army Corps was brought up over the mountains. This wing had to be made particularly powerful, not only for the envelopment, but also to cover Bitsch.

Many Gentlemen proceeded in this sense. However, some merely limited themselves to general suggestions [*Andeutungen*]. They gave directives [*Direktiven*] whereas the armies had already drawn so near and the decision was so imminent that, as the Field Marshal said explicitly in a similar situation, 'it was admissible and advisable to direct the movements of the large army units [*Heeresteile*] by means of definite orders [*bestimmte Befehle*] from the highest headquarters, even though the independence of the army commanders was thereby temporarily restricted'.[3]

Many Gentlemen did not content themselves with the most immediate task of attacking the enemy where he happens to be and where he happens to be found. Their gazes wandered further. Some already thought of forcing the enemy back on Paris. Conversely, others thought of cutting him off from his capital city. The one wanted to see him forced to the south, the other to the Belgian border in the north. Through such considerations, they came to one of the worst errors that can be committed in operations: awaiting the effect of the envelopment before advancing against the front. In strategy and in tactics, the same rule applies: he who wants to envelop, must attack the front firmly in order to prevent the enemy there from making any movement, thus enabling the enveloping wing to be effective.

Therefore, the 2nd Army could not remain in the Pfalz, even if one wanted to omit the envelopment by the 3rd Army. The 2nd Army had to advance to the Saar. Its right wing had to cross the river in conjunction with the 1st Army to immobilize the front so unfavourably chosen by the enemy. The enemy had to be forced to reinforce his front, thus enabling the left wing of the 2nd Army to cross the Saar at Saargemünd and Saarunion and envelop the French right wing.

THIRD PROBLEM

On 6 August, the French army stood with its
- I Army Corps, VII Army Corps and 1st Reserve Cavalry Division behind the Sauer at Wörth;
- V Army Corps at Bitsch;
- II Army Corps south of Saarbrücken;
- III Army Corps: 1st Infantry Division at Saargemünd,
  2nd Infantry Division at Püttingen,
  3rd Infantry Division at Marienthal,
  4th Infantry Division at St Avold,
  3rd Reserve Cavalry Division at Falkenberg;
- Guard Corps at Spangen;
- IV Army Corps: 2nd Infantry Division at Hargarten,
  1st and 3rd Infantry Divisions at Busendorf,
  2nd Reserve Cavalry Division at Bolchen;
- VI Army Corps at Metz, pushed forward on the road to Busendorf.

The German army has penetrated across the Lauter into Alsace, defeated an isolated division of the I Army Corps at Weissenburg on the 4th, and is advancing on the Sauer with four or five army corps and a cavalry division. An attack against the position of the I and VII Army Corps is expected on the 7th.

The main German army has reached the Saar at Saarbrücken with its advance guards, if it has not already crossed with its right wing. Its manoeuvres are veiled by strong cavalry, which has pushed forward against the IV Army Corps and around it by way of Vigy to the area of Metz.

An enemy army corps and strong cavalry face the V Army Corps at Wolmünster–Hornbach.

Problem: Intentions of the French Supreme Headquarters and the dispositions [*Anordnungen*] taken for their execution.

ALFRED VON SCHLIEFFEN'S MILITARY WRITINGS
DISCUSSION OF THE THIRD PROBLEM

In all river crossings, a critical moment occurs during which a small portion of the army has reached the opposite bank but the mass still remains on the other. The Germans found themselves in such a dangerous position on the evening of 6 August. A rapid offensive by the French on the morning of the 7th against the lead elements of the German army corps could have brought great results. However, the French army corps were too unfortunately grouped to have made possible such a rapid attack with forces of any consequence. The 7th had to pass before the units to the rear could be brought into the front line. While this was taking place, however, the Germans won the time to place themselves completely on the left bank of the Saar. The French leadership tried to make good their earlier error by conducting a night march. This, though, has to be seen as futile. After a night march of 20–30 kilometres, a feat of arms [*Waffentat*] can hardly be expected from the troops. Besides this, orders can rarely be given early enough and reach their destinations early enough to make possible such a night march.

Of those Gentlemen who used 7 August to deploy, the vast majority pushed the VI Army Corps and the Guard Corps between the IV Army Corps and the Moselle. They wanted to take up the offensive here on the 8th, if they were not attacked by the Germans before then. This decision is certainly to be approved, but it is doubtful whether this attack with the left wing could be combined with an attack by the right.

An offensive there with the V Army Corps alone would encounter a greatly superior enemy. Even if the III Army Corps was sent forward to support this attack, the seven French divisions still faced three and a half German corps and little prospect of success. Worse is that such a combination would leave the space between the IV and the II Army Corps completely open. Three German corps can penetrate here without resistance and put a quick end to the French right or left wing attack. If one wants to attack with the left wing, the space between Busendorf and Saarbrücken must at least be filled with enough [forces] that a breakthrough by the enemy can be defended against. To guard against an envelopment of the right wing, the left bank of the Saar has to be defended at least as far as Saargemünd. If the V Army Corps remained at Bitsch, an envelopment by the right wing of the enemy would at least be made very difficult.

It is noteworthy that some Gentlemen wanted to give up this hopeless battle and retire behind the Moselle. I do not consider this possible. A nation [*Volk*] that has entered into war with such eagerness for victory [*Siegesfreude*] and such a vivacious expression of premature victory as the French in 1870, cannot take to flight at the first approach of the enemy. The battle has to be taken up as best it may. Besides, it is doubtful whether a retreat behind the Moselle was possible without a fight and without a defeat and whether the prospects there were much better than behind the Saar.

Other Gentlemen did not want to extend their retreat to the left bank of the Moselle, but rather limited themselves to retiring to a position behind the French Nied or Rotte, supporting their left wing with Metz. This means merely a postponement of defeat, since the right wing could be enveloped after some time in any case and then the catastrophe would be all the more serious as the Moselle would lie close behind the French army.

FOURTH PROBLEM

On 6 August, the Germans have reached with their vanguards:
1st Army:
 VII Army Corps: Kreuz, by way of Merzig and Halsdorf
 I Army Corps: (had on the 5th pushed forward its troops at Nonnweiler as they arrived in Birkenfeld) Bachem, via Losheim
 VIII Army Corps: Niedaltdorf, by way of Beckingen
 X Army Corps: Felsberg, via Tholey, Lebach and Saarlouis
 III Army Corps: Lisdorf, by way of St Wendel, Dirmingen, Eiweiler, Heusweiler, Schwarzenholz and Ensdorf
 I Cavalry Corps (3rd, 1st, 5th Cavalry Divisions): the area north and northeast of Vigy with reconnaissance toward Metz–Bolchen and also on the left bank of the Moselle.

2nd Army:
 IX Army Corps: Engelfangen, via Ottweiler and Holz
 IV Army Corps: Saarbrücken, via Waldmohr, Wiebelskirchen, Neukirchen and Dudweiler
 Guard Corps: Assweiler, by way of Homburg and Blieskastel
 XII Army Corps: Neuhaeusel, by way of Wolfstein, Kollweiler, Kottweiler, Spesbach, Ober Miesau and Homburg
 II Bavarian Corps: Hornbach
 VI Army Corps: 12th Infantry Division: Pirmasens; 11th Infantry Division: Wilgartswiesen
 II Cavalry Corps (Guard and 6th Cavalry Divisions): area of Wolmünster with reconnaissance at Bitsch and the Saar.

The 5th Cavalry Division reported from Bettsdorf (north of Vigy):
 Malroy, Charly, Vremy and St Barbe are occupied by the enemy.

ALFRED VON SCHLIEFFEN'S MILITARY WRITINGS

Patrols that crossed the Moselle at Busz yesterday (5 August) observed long columns of all arms from the area of St Marcel on the Mars-la-Tour–Vionville–Rezonville road in march from Verdun to Metz, but were prevented from gaining further information.

The 1st Cavalry Division north of Busendorf and the 3rd at Hargarten have encountered the enemy.
The IV Army Corps has found enemy advance posts at Spichern and the Guard Corps has found them at Klein Blittersdorf and Saargemünd. The II Cavalry Corps reported that Hanweiler, Schorbach, Hottweiler, Siersthal and Enchenberg are occupied by the enemy, but the Saar line from Settingen up to Saarunion is free of enemy troops.
On the afternoon of the 7th, the detraining of the II Army corps begins in Homburg and Zweibrücken. On the 8th, the last troops of the 3rd Infantry Division will be detrained in Zweibrücken. The command of the 3rd Army has reported that they intend to attack the enemy located behind the Sauer (estimated to be six or seven divisions) on 7 August. The 4th Cavalry Division has advanced south of the Hagenauer Forest and has cut the Strassburg–Hagenau railway in the area of Bitschweiler on the 6th; a military train from Strassburg had to turn around.

Problem: How did the German Supreme Headquarters judge the situation and what directives does it give?

DISCUSSION OF THE FOURTH PROBLEM

When one considers the position of the French army on the evening of the 6th, the German task on the 7th seems to be uncommonly simple. However, everything could be called into question if a further march was entered into. The corps had conducted very long marches from the 3rd to the 6th. They had become very strung out, and only weak lead elements were initially available. An advance by the 1st Army would have culminated presumably in an attack on the strong position of the French IV Army Corps at Busendorf. An attempt to envelop this position with the VII Army Corps on the right would in all likelihood have been met with a counterattack by the French VI and Guard Corps. An envelopment of the French right wing by the X and III Army Corps, which are still further behind, would have been parried likewise by a division of the French IV Corps and three divisions of the III Army Corps. It is not advisable to expose oneself with inadequate forces to the possibility of defeat at the point where the enemy could most quickly assemble his main forces. The delay of a single day would not permit the enemy to better his situation [*Lage*]. The further northward he advanced towards the 1st Army, the worse the retreat for him in the case of a defeat, while 24 hours would allow the Germans to reinforce their two wings considerably and they could bring their left wing still closer. Under these circumstances, on the 7th, the VII and VIII Army corps remained generally in position and only brought up their rearward divisions. The X and III Army Corps pushed their vanguards forward up to the Bist in order to deploy behind it. The IX Army Corps crossed the Saar at Völkingen with at least one division to take up position on the other side. Then, one division of the IX Army Corps and the entire IV Army corps were still available for an attack on the Spichern Heights. The XII Army Corps advanced north of the Blies in the direction of Saargemünd about as far as Babelsheim. The Guard Corps advanced to Bliesbrücken and Brandelsingen, the II Bavarian Corps to Gistingen and Urbach, the 12th Infantry Division to Wohlmünster, and the 11th Infantry Division to Eppenbrunn.

On the 8th, it was intended that the enemy be held along his entire front and an envelopment of his right wing be attempted. The holding action could not simply consist of waiting, however – it had to be an attack along the entire line with all strength. Only an attack would have shown where the weaknesses of the enemy lay and only then could they be exploited and the enemy prevented from turning to face the envelopment. Possibly, the decisive battle would have taken place at Saargemünd. In order to leave the XII Army Corps as strong as possible for the battle, it would have to be assisted at the difficult crossings at Blittersdorf.

The battle would have been of no significance if the French left wing had been merely held fast and prevented from evading behind the Moselle. The French had to be forced to retreat in a southern direction. Then, if the left wing of the German 2nd Army pushed forward quickly, the French could be forced once again to give battle on the right bank of the Moselle, unless they meant to seek the left bank in total disarray. From this, it can be seen just how important it was that the left wing of the 2nd Army be pushed forward as quickly as possible and in the greatest possible strength in the direction of Saaralben and Saarunion on the Moselle. However, such a manoeuvre was hindered by the French V Army Corps, assumed to be at Bitsch.

FIFTH PROBLEM

(A) On 7 August, the right wing of the German 2nd Army has advanced thus:

XII Army Corps: from Neuhäusel via Lautzkirchen and Nieder Würzbach to Bebelsheim (its cavalry found Gross Blittersdorf and Saargemünd occupied by the enemy)

Guard Corps: from Blieskastel to Bliesbrücken and Brandelsingen (bridges at Saareinsmingen occupied by weak enemy)

II Bavarian Corps: from Hornbach 3rd Infantry division to Gisingen, 4th Infantry Division to Bettweiler (encountered enemy at Hottweiler and Holbach)

VI Army Corps: 12th Infantry Division to Weisskirchen, by way of Vinningen and Wolmünster (found Schorbach and Hanweiler occupied); 11th Infantry Division from Wilgartswiesen to Eppenbrunn via Langmühle (found Haspelschied occupied and observed the march of a column of all arms from Ziegelscheuer to Strürzelbronn).

The II Cavalry Corps (Guard and 6th Cavalry Divisions) stands at Rahlingen and has occupied Herbitzheim, Saaralben and Saarunion with detachments. Patrols have run into the enemy at Enchenberg and Mombronn.

According to the army order of 8 August, the IV Army Corps is to attack the enemy position at Spichern from the Saarbrücken–Brebach line. The XII Army corps, the Guard Corps and the II Cavalry Corps are to support this attack as much as possible by an envelopment of the enemy's right wing. The II Bavarian and the VI Army Corps, under the command of the senior commanding general, are to cover the army's left flank. The 3rd Infantry Division, which has pushed its vanguard forward from Zweibrücken to Mittelbach, is to follow via Altheim as reserve.

Problem (A): Orders [*Befehle*] for the II Bavarian and the VI Army Corps.

(B) From the area of Weissenburg, the German 3rd Army has advanced thus:

I Bavarian Corps to Lembach with a right side detachment to Frönsburg

V Army Corps to Preuschdorf

XI Army Corps to Sulz.

The Württemberg Division has marched from Lautenburg to Nieder Roedern and the Baden Division has advanced to Selz.

The 4th Cavalry Division has cut the railway at Bischweiler on the 6th, forced one troop train to return to Strassburg, and has taken this fortress under observation, as well as Brumath and Hagenau. From Hagenau, the patrols have recieved fire.

TACTICAL-STRATEGIC PROBLEMS, 1903

During the advance, the 3rd Army command received repeated reports that the enemy had given up the Sauer. According to later reports received up until noon, the enemy was assumed to be behind the Nördliche Zinsel between Zinsweiler and Merzweiler. The I Bavarian Corps has reported that the Frönsburg detachment in Nieder Steinbach is in contact with the enemy at Ober Steinbach.

Problem (B): Any directives from the 3rd Army command on 7 August, noon, for that afternoon.

Problem (C): Army order for the 8th, under the assumption that reports received by evening have confirmed the enemy's supposed position.

DISCUSSION OF FIFTH PROBLEM

(A) The II Bavarian and the VI Army Corps were charged with covering against the French V Army Corps. If this corps were still in Bitsch, the attack upon this corps would presumably have been the task of the two German corps. Arriving reports, however, made it probable that the French V Corps had been moved to Alsace. If this was so, the two corps were relieved of their task and could join the advance over the Saar without delay to take part in the expected annihilation of the enemy main army. However, it was to be borne in mind that, on one hand, it was not certain that the French V Corps had moved off completely and, on the other hand, if it appeared in Alsace, it could intervene in the expected battle there to the disadvantage of the German 3rd Army.

Under these circumstances, the decision of those Gentlemen who continued the march toward the Saar because they recognised it as the most important thing to defeat the enemy's main army could only be approved, even though the 3rd Army was exposed thereby to possible danger. Of course, these Gentlemen ran the risk that the enemy still stood at Bitsch and could fall against the marching columns. However, even in this case, the two army corps, with a degree of attention, would have been in a position to wheel left and to advance and envelop the enemy.

Many Gentlemen believed it advisable to rush to the aid of the 3rd Army. In view of the length of the march to be made, the difficulties offered by the mountain routes, and the delay that even small enemy detachments could cause, one ran the risk of neither helping the 3rd Army nor being present for the main decision [*Hauptentscheidung*].

Those who wanted to try to determine by an attack into the mountain valleys whether the enemy who was reported to be on all the roads

ALFRED VON SCHLIEFFEN'S MILITARY WRITINGS

in the area of Bitsch consisted of merely weak vanguards or whether strong units were still to be sought behind them would have fared equally as badly. As soon as the departure of the French V Army Corps had been determined, they then wanted to follow the 2nd Army to the Saar. In all probability they would not have found out the true state of things during the entire day and would have been stopped from any active intervention in either way.

(B) and (C): The 3rd Army probably faced two enemies. The first was descending from the mountain valleys from Bitsch into the Rhine Valley. The second should stand in a nook behind the Nördliche Zinsel. It appeared advisable to cover against an attack by the former and against an attack on the right wing by the latter enemy. It was not likely that the latter would have awaited the attack threatening his right flank; he would have taken a front more toward the east, thereby making an envelopment more difficult. There remained nothing else for the Germans but to attack principally the right wing.

In consideration of these circumstances, the I Bavarian Corps would have been assembled at Wörth, with a detachment at Lembach–Frönsburg. The V Army Corps would have been deployed between the Gunstedt–Gundershofen road and the Walburg–Merzweiler road. The XI Army Corps and the Württemberg and Baden Divisions should have advanced on Hagenau and south of there. The 4th Cavalry Division was to have reconnoitred towards Strassburg.

To conduct these manoeuvres on 8 August, relatively difficult marches still had to be made on the afternoon of the 7th. It was doubtful that the 3rd Army would, despite its not inconsiderable superiority in numbers, gain a victory. Regardless, it was certain that the French would have to retreat from Alsace in an unfavourable direction when the left wing of the 2nd Army reached the Saarunion on the next day.

None the less, an attack had to be made on the 8th to prevent the French from escaping unharmed and in order to prevent them from intervening in the approaching or still awaited battle with the main army. The two enemy forces had to be kept apart.

The part of the operations of 1870 from which this task was formed was not, for sufficiently well-known reasons, carried out according to the Field Marshal's intentions. According to his plan, the 2nd Army was to advance on the Saar, behind which the enemy was assumed to be. To the right of the 2nd Army, the 1st Army was to cross the river as soon as the 2nd Army approached, somewhat in the manner in which it happened here. The 3rd Army should have penetrated Alsace sooner, if possible on 1 August, thrown back the enemy there, pursued him with a corps to Strassburg, and have gone with the rest over the Vosges to appear on the Saar at about the same time as the 2nd Army. A battle with envelopment [*Umfassung*] of both wings was planned.

The Field Marshal's plan was deviated from in these problems – the 3rd Army was held back so that the problems would not be too easy. If, in spite of the great superiority in numbers of the German forces, difficulties have been found in Problems 1 and 2 as well as 4 and 5, it should be understood that these would have been considerably increased if faced with an equally strong, or even superior, enemy.

The armies with which we have had to deal in these problems were very large, too large, it is said. Some say it is not the task of young officers to lead armies [*Armeen*] and combinations of armies [*Heere*].[4] I do not see any reason why the future should not see a few of you Gentlemen at the head of an army. None the less, I hope that you are at least called on to lead an army corps or a division or to stand by the side of a commander [*Truppenführer*] as a chief of staff or as a General Staff officer. Then you will have to understand how to judge the manoeuvres of an army. Only then, and this will happen frequently in war, will you be in a position, when, together with your army corps or division, you are given an independent task and have to make a decision [*einen Entschluß zu fassen*] that will redound to the advantage of the whole army. I do not see any reason why the future should not set quite a few of you, Gentlemen, at the head of an army.

9

Tactical-Strategic Problems, 1905

Schlieffen has based these problems on a Kriegsspiel *that he believed needed further elaboration.*[1] *Played mostly from the Russian (here referred to as the Red Army) perspective, these problems indicate some of the difficulties with a German invasion of Russian Poland.*

FIRST PROBLEM

A Red Army assembled in Poland turned to the south against an enemy force that had penetrated between the Vistula and the Bug Rivers. To defend against an attack from the north, only the following fortress garrisons were left behind:

Nowo Georgiewsk (Modlin): 16 infantry battalions, 5 battalions of foot artillery, 4 mobile sortie [*Ausfall*] batteries

Warsaw: 18 infantry battalions, 5 foot artillery battalions, 6 mobile sortie batteries

Zegrze: 8 infantry battalions, 1 foot artillery battalion, 4 mobile sortie batteries

Pultusk: 4 infantry battalions, half a battalion of foot artillery

Rozan: 4 infantry battalions, half a battalion of foot artillery

Ostrolenka: 75th Reserve Division (16 infantry battalions, 1 cavalry squadron, 6 batteries (48 guns))

Lomza and Nowogrod: 58th Reserve Division.

There were also the following border guard brigades (each of four companies and four squadrons):

The 4th at Grajewo
The 5th at Kolno
The 6th at Rypin
The 7th at Woclawek.

The 6th Cavalry Division (24 squadrons, 12 guns) stood at Myszyniec and the 15th Cavalry Division at Chorzele and Mlawa.

TACTICAL-STRATEGIC PROBLEMS, 1905

Upon receiving reports that a Blue Army in many columns was advancing on the border between Thorn and the Soldau, a Red Army (II, III and XX Army Corps (each corps possessed 32 infantry battalions, 2 cavalry squadrons and 12 batteries (96 guns)) was sent and given the task of throwing back the Blue Army over the border when it crossed it. The above fortress garrisons, border guard brigades, and reserve and cavalry divisions were placed under the Red Army's command. On 1 May, the Red Army's infantry advance guards had reached:
   The II Army Corps, by way of Serok: Pultusk and Przewodowo
   The III Army Corps, by way of Dembe: Kalenczyn and Nowe Miasto
   The XX Army Corps, by way of Nowo Georgiewsk, Plonst and Nacpolsk.
The intelligence which had arrived by this time reported that the enemy infantry advance guards had advanced to Plock, Bielsk, Drobin, Racionz, Glinojeck, Opinogora, Chorzele and Parciaki. The 5th Border Guard Brigade had withdrawn behind the Pissa crossing at Ptaki and reported facing enemy cavalry at Kolno. The 6th Cavalry Division had withdrawn to Ostrolenka and reported enemy cavalry at Chudek. The 15th Cavalry stood at Krasnosielc. The 6th Border Guard Brigade stood at Sochocin and the 7th at Bodzanow, reporting enemy cavalry at Gora. The 4th Border Guard Brigade at Grajewo reported nothing of the enemy.

Problem: What are the intentions of the Red Army's commander and what are his reasons for the orders he gives and the dispositions he makes on the night of 1 May?

SECOND PROBLEM

A Red Army assembled in Poland has turned to the south against an enemy force that penetrated between the Vistula and the Bug Rivers. A Blue army coming out of East Prussia from the north has the task of cutting off Warsaw, which including Nowo Georgiewsk and Zegrze, was said to have a garrison of around 40 battalions and 15 field batteries, from the right bank of the Vistula to the Bug. On 1 May, the Blue 1st Army had reached:
   3rd Reserve Division – Plock
   5th Reserve Division – Bielsk, via Goleszyn
   6th Reserve Division – Jezweo–Drobin
   2nd Cavalry Division – Gora
   VI Army Corps: 11th Infantry Division – Wolany–Racionz; 12th Infantry Division – Glinozeck, via Radzanowo

XVII Army Corps: in a column from the train station at Mlawa to Konopki

V Army Corps: 9th Infantry Division – Lipa–Opinogora; 10th Infantry Division – Turowo to Miliewo

XX Army Corps: 37th Infantry Division – from Willenburg to Chorzele; 41st Infantry Division – from Zawady to Paraciaki

4th Cavalry Division – Chudek

1st Cavalry Division – Kolno.

Arriving reports indicate that there are weak units, infantry and cavalry, in front of the Blue columns between the Vistula and the Wenigierka, a cavalry division is in front of the XX Army Corps between the Wenigierka and the Orzyc, and another has retired before the 4th Cavalry Division on Ostrolenka. Ostrolenka will be kept under observation. The 1st Cavalry Division is being delayed by weak enemy units on the Pissa at Ptaki. Lomza and Nowogrod are occupied by a reserve division, Ostrolenka is occupied by a second reserve division, and Pultusk is reportedly lightly held. Fresh troops seem to be arriving from the south. In the evening, Przewodowo, Kalencyn, Plonsk and Nacpolsk are found to be strongly held.

Problem: What are the intentions of the 1st Army's commander and what are his reasons for the orders he gives and the dispositions he makes on the night of 1 May?

THIRD PROBLEM

On the evening of 2 May, the Red Army is disposed thus:

58th Reserve Division – head at Golanka

75th Reserve Division – Ostrolenka, advance guard at Nowo Wies

6th Cavalry Division – Wydmusy

15th Cavalry Division – Dylewo (north of Ostrolenka)

II Army Corps – on the Pultusk–Zambiski–Lubiel road with its advance guard at Ostrykol

III Army Corps – on the Wyszkow–Pultusk road with its advance guard at Pniewo

Division Zegrze – Serok

Division Warsaw – Dembe

Division Nowo Georgiewsk – Nowo Georgiewsk.

Preparations for the transport of the XX Army Corps have been made – the first train can leave at midnight on 2/3 May.

Advance guards and border patrol brigades have remained in their initial deployment positions or have retired step by step before the advancing enemy.

TACTICAL-STRATEGIC PROBLEMS, 1905

The following is known of the enemy: A column of all arms has marched over the Orzyc at Paraciaki and cavalry has crossed at Chudek. They have dismantled the bridges over this river and have occupied bridgeheads on the right bank. In the evening, enemy infantry was in Krasnosielc. The enemy at Milewo has not advanced. However, another enemy force has advanced against the Sochin–Bienki road by way of Ciechanow and between there and the Wkra. Sochin is threatened from both sides of the Wkra. Gora and Bodzanow are occupied.

> *Problem*: How does the commander of the Red Army judge the situation on the evening of 2 May and what directives and orders does he give?

FOURTH PROBLEM

On the evening of 3 May, the Red Army is deployed thus:
  4th Border Patrol Brigade – Grajewo
  5th Border Patrol Brigade – Ptaki
  6th Cavalry Division – Willenburg
  15th Cavalry Division – Zaremby
  58th Reserve Division – on the Omulev at Zelazna (southwest of Berdowe)
  75th Reserve Division – Paraciaki
  XX Army Corps – the greater part at Ostrolenka, advance guards at Nowo Wies
  II Army Corps – Chelsty and Rozan
  III Army Corps – Szelkow and Gnojno
  Division Zegrze – Winnica
  Division Warsaw – Nasielsk
  Division Nowo Georgiewsk – Borkowo.

The enemy has not left his position on the Orzyc between Krasnosielc and Mlodzianowo. Makow has been occupied, and from there he has pushed forward his advance guards via Gzy and Strzegocin to north of Borkowo. He has advanced between the Wrka and the Vistula to Michalinek, Strzembowo and Radzikowo. Enemy cavalry at Kolno has been pushed off in a southwestern direction.

> *Problem*: How does the commander of the Red Army judge the situation on the evening of 3 May and what directives and orders does he give?

ALFRED VON SCHLIEFFEN'S MILITARY WRITINGS
DISCUSSION OF THE PROBLEMS

The scenario from which the first task was drawn was taken from a *Kriegsspiel*. Thus, it is not artificially constructed, but rather is the result of naturally developed operations. In this *Kriegsspiel*, Red attacked Blue and was beaten back. I was given the impression that the players of the Red Army had the feeling of being set in front of an insoluble problem, whereas I was of the opinion that Blue's position was the more unfavourable. To clear this question up, I posed these problems.

In the first task, most Gentlemen have likewise proceeded immediately with an attack in a northern direction. For this, certainly no reproach can be made. However, they proceeded from false assumptions. They believed that the reports they had received were complete. However, this is never the case in war. Something is always left to speculation and conjecture.[2] Here, it was only to be expected that the enemy would advance not only on the side roads, but also on the main Mlawa–Warsaw road. According to the incomplete reports that arrived, they wrongly believed themselves to be facing several enemy groups, whereas in reality they only had one long line before them, which was followed by an army corps behind the left wing. With the part of their forces immediately to hand, they wanted to throw themselves on a corps that they thought to be pushed forward. They would have thus suffered a defeat at the hands of the superior enemy.

This matter has a special importance. The French intend to have one corps advance ahead of their armies as a vanguard believing, among other things, that an offensively minded enemy would throw himself concentrically upon this vanguard. They then intend to thrust into this concentrated crowd [*in den zusammengeballten Knäuel hineinstoßen*] with the corps of their main body.[3]

I have regarded this French intention as fairly harmless, but I see that I have been mistaken and that they could quite well succeed. When one wants to attack a corps that is pushed forward, one should not attack concentrically, but rather advance in numerous parallel columns and only wheel when one is certain what follows the vulnerable corps.

Other Gentlemen have recognized the difficulties of the attack and have tried to eliminate them by changing the task. They have placed the chessmen as it best suited them. To win time, they have started in the afternoon rather than in the evening of 1 May, and this based on intelligence that could only arrive the next evening. I do not find this method very respectable. It gives a questionable appearance to the reliability and accuracy of work expected of a General Staff officer. Aside from this, they would hardly have reached their goal. Even if the reserve corps has already advanced to Krasnosielc and the XX Army Corps to

Sochin on the evening of the 1st, a short withdrawal by the Blue V Army Corps can frustrate the whole plan.

A smaller number of Gentlemen have likewise recognized the difficulties of an attack and said to themselves, 'if the enemy can only be attacked with difficulty on the front turned toward us, I will attack him from another side'. This side could not be the left, which was supported by the Vistula. Only a right-flank march could be considered.

Yet a smaller number have said to themselves: 'This attack is not only difficult, but even if it is successful, it will not have any great effect. Therefore, I will attack the enemy on another side and force him to assume another front. I will attempt to beat him and then force him back against the Vistula. I want to annihilate him.'

This idea of annihilation, which emanates from all the battles of Friedrich the Great, which permeates all of Napoleon's operations, and which served as the basis for all of Field Marshal von Moltke's unparalleled successes, is seemingly being gradually lost. In all the works that have been handed in, I have found the intention 'I want to annihilate the enemy', expressed only twice. On the other hand, one meets again and again the intention to make energetic advances, to echelon the front strongly, and to take up positions of readiness [*Bereitschaftstellungen*].

Not long ago, the Japanese Minister of War, or some other high dignitary, had a discussion with the German Ambassador in Tokyo and said something along the lines of: 'We have now taken Port Arthur, but we are still looking in vain for a Metz and a Sedan. You Germans have the secret. You have taught us tactics; now you must also teach us strategy.' Perhaps one of you Gentlemen will go to the far-off island empire to give the Japanese Minister of War the desired instruction and will say: 'Make energetic advances, echelon your flanks strongly, and take up positions of readiness.' To which he would reply: 'But we constantly make energetic advances, not only we, but also the Russians. With echeloned flanks, as I believe, your *Oberst* Leutwein has had bad experiences, and as for positions of readiness, we have been in positions of readiness for months on end. However, we have yet to find a Metz or a Sedan.' The Japanese would have taught you, not you the Japanese. You would now know that not much is to be accomplished with energetic advances, flanking positions and positions of readiness. Why do you not want to follow the noble examples that have been handed down to you by the history of your Fatherland? All great captains have done fundamentally the same thing. When Friedrich the Great marched around the Austrian flank on that foggy December day, when Napoleon marched down the Saale in that fateful October 1806, and when the Field Marshal crossed the Moselle in the August days of 1870,[4] these events appear very different, but fundamentally all three manoeuvres rely upon the same idea: the enemy was to be forced onto another front, was to be beaten, and was to be forced back in the most unfavourable direction.

Here was an opportunity to carry out this idea, and a better opportunity could hardly be found. The most endangered part of all these operations is always the refused wing. Here, this wing was secured absolutely by the fortifications of Warsaw. The Narev River could serve as a cover and a veil behind which desired manoeuvres could be made. Two reserve and two cavalry divisions stood already prepared to lengthen the right wing. The three army corps should have deployed between Rozan and Pultusk, and the 75th Reserve Division should have advanced to Nowo Wies, the 58th to Kadzidlo, the 6th Cavalry Division to Dylewo and the 15th to Myszyniec. These marches could in no way be prevented by the enemy, until the 15th Cavalry Division's advance on Myszyniec. If this had been prevented, the division would go back to Demby, and little would be altered. The divisions formed from the fortress troops would be concentrated on the left wing.

(I hold it as obvious that, if a battle is being fought before the gates of Warsaw, the fortress troops will not merely observe the fight from the ramparts, as if from the walls of Troy, and simply fill the spectators' stands. They must climb down and participate. However, this is not to say that these troops will, by preference, be taken, put on a train, and sent to the most remote regions.)

This was, approximately, the content of the first problem. It was variously judged. Some said it was infinitely easy and ridiculously simple. Some found the desired solution so absurd that they complained about those who had found it, because they believed this would not have been possible without illegal help. I shall content myself with placing these two views next to one another.

Since the intention of Blue remained fairly unclear in the first problem, I gave the second problem with the intention of facilitating for you the question that every commander must ask himself before he undertakes a battle: 'What will my enemy do?' While very few were to be found ready to carry out an envelopment in the first task, in the second almost everyone was ready to do so. However, the circumstances were now completely different. Here, the refused wing was in no way covered, rather it was extremely threatened. Here, there was no Narev River to cover the manoeuvre, rather just the opposite, every manoeuvre would be seen immediately. In the first case, the front became shorter rather than longer; here, it was extended endlessly. If all the difficulties had been successfully overcome and the extreme right wing had advanced on Lomza, it would have met a fortress, which was not impregnable, but none the less would have caused trouble and cost time. If the Narev had now been crossed, one would still by no means be on the enemy's flank and in the enemy's rear. The enemy might be in a completely different place and would have to be sought out. One would barely have crossed the river before probably finding oneself faced with a stronger enemy.

Two cases could occur. Either the Red Army would remain north of Warsaw, and, if the Blue columns of the left wing marched off, the Red Army would advance and beat the refused Blue right wing; or the two enveloping manoeuvres would meet each other, in which case the Blue army corps would have been held up by the Red Army's reserve and cavalry divisions on one of the numerous rivers flowing into the Narev. Then, nine divisions (including the fortress divisions) would advance in close order between the Rozan and Pultusk on 4 May. In all cases, I believe there would be every prospect of a first-rate catastrophe for Blue.

It is hardly possible to march leftwards out of the Blue Army's long front. Initially there remains nothing for this army to do but draw its line to the left and then attack the enemy's front and right flank appearing north of Warsaw. In the meantime, however, one or two days must elapse. Nothing can be said on 1 May as to how far this attack is to be extended. One has to wait and see where the enemy will be on 3 May.

The third problem gave the intelligence that the enemy had advanced to Krasnosielc and had occupied both crossings, at Dronzdzewo and Jednorozec. It was clear from this that an envelopment over these crossings would hardly be successful. If one looked at a somewhat larger-scale map, one would find that these Orzyc crossings are very easily defended. The question is then whether or not one should extend still farther. For a long stretch north of Jednorozec, there are no crossings. Therefore, one has to decide whether or not to go as far as Chorzele, where there is still a second and third crossing to be found above and below the town. Many Gentlemen were unable to decide to do this, as they feared that a very superior enemy could then advance across the Narev between Rozan and Pultusk. I believe that there can be no question of a 'very superior enemy'. All that could be brought up to the Orzyc by the evening of 3 May was the XX, V and XVII Army Corps. It was difficult for the VI Army Corps to come up, and an intervention by the three reserve corps was out of the question. This would have amounted to 72 battalions, and the Russians would have had – aside from the fortress troops – 128 battalions. Therefore, one could not speak of a 'large superiority'. The Red Army's advantage consisted precisely in that it was on the flank of the Blue Army, which was stretched out in a long line. As soon as the Blue Army observed the Red Army's envelopment, it would have deployed to the threatened side. However, their line was far too long to carry this out quickly. Therefore, the Red Army had sufficient strength to attack the Blue front and, at the same time, envelop a wing.

A not inconsiderable number of Gentlemen wanted to continue the offensive but not further to the right. They felt too weak in the front. There was no basis for this belief. Others wanted to give up the manoeuvre to the right and envelop the left instead. This is an extremely awkward manoeuvre – the II and III Army Corps had already been set to marching and were now to face about again. It is hard to say whether or not this manoeuvre would have been successful, and whether or not Blue would then have carried out an eastward envelopment depends upon many circumstances. Regardless, a great result would not have been achieved, and the intention of annihilating the enemy would have had to be completely abandoned.

Others wanted to give up the attack completely and retire to a flanking position between the Narev and the Bug (approximately between Ostrolenka and Ostrow) in order to fall upon the enemy when he crossed the Narev and force him back upon Warsaw. This scheme appears very fine and looks very good, and has often been attempted in a more or less similar fashion, but it always fails. The enemy will not condescend to fall into the trap laid for him and do us the favour of letting himself be attacked. He will undertake something different. It is a rule that no battle is won by taking up a position, but only by manoeuvring. Therefore, if one wants a result, one has to reach out by way of Chorzele, and not with weak forces but with at least two reserve divisions or, if possible, with even stronger units.

If the two reserve divisions move via Chorzele, a large gap will be formed between Chorzele and Rozan. Therefore, many decided to transport the XX Army Corps by rail to Ostrolenka. This rail transport has provoked numerous objections. It is said that the capacity of this rail line is not sufficient. However, the three rail lines that come together at Ostrolenka were in no way built for trading purposes – the products of the Orient and the Occident will not be exchanged here. These rail lines were built solely for military purposes. Therefore, I cannot imagine that they would not be capable of such a transport. Regardless, the Russians have set up ramps here. They have prepared the Polish battlefield well. They await a German advance on the Narev and an Austrian advance between the Bug and the Vistula, and they want to be able to reinforce one or the other front according to need.[5] For this purpose, they have established a rail and road system between the Narev, Vistula and Bug Rivers that facilitates transfers in any direction. Two lines can be employed to transport the XX Army Corps from Warsaw to Ostrolenka, the first via Nowo Minsk and Wyskow and the other via

Malkin. The empty rolling stock can be run off via Lapy. It is reckoned, without exaggerated assumptions, that the first train could depart around midnight on 2/3 May. For the combat troops, 48 trains [*Züge*] are necessary. The majority of these could have arrived in Ostrolenka and at a station near Kamionka by the morning of the 4th, and the rest would follow during the course of the morning. Only the entrainment would cause any difficulties, as the line from Nowo Georgiewsk to Warsaw is only single track. The troops would have to march to Warsaw. This, however, is possible without great exertion. By the evening of the 3rd or the morning of the 5th, the two cavalry divisions would stand at Willenberg and east of Chorzele, the two reserve divisions would be east of Chorzele, the first elements of the XX Army Corps would be before Ostrolenka and Kamionka, the II Army Corps at Chelsty and Rozan, and the III Army Corps at Szelkow and Gnojno. The following could then advance: the two reserve divisions on Chorzele; one division of the XX Corps on the crossings at Jednorozec and Dronzdzewo and the other on Krasnosielc; the II Army Corps and one division of the III on the stretch of the Orzyc between Krasnosielc and Makow; and the other division of the III Army Corps and the Division Zegrze between the Orzyc and Pultusk. Then, only the two divisions from Warsaw and Nowo Georgiewsk remain on the left wing south of Pultusk. This will result, primarily, in a battle on the Orzyc between Krasnosielc and Pultusk, with secondary encounters at Jednorozec and Dronzdezewo as well as south of Pultusk. Should the Blue Army advance across the Orzyc, this would facilitate success for the Red Army.

For this battle, it is of the utmost importance that the entire force, without exception, attack, and not, as some Gentlemen have done, leave a portion on the defensive or in waiting. This is the only way to hold the enemy and prevent him from manoeuvring, for the only dangers are that Chorzele is still occupied or will be occupied and that the enemy marches away. However, these dangers will be lessened by the fact that the Blue Army cannot know the movements of its enemy until the evening of the 3rd and up to this point the intelligence received can only be very vague. None the less, these dangers must be faced. There is no remedy against them other than rapidity of movement and the quickest general attack. On the 5th this will be too late. It has to take place on the 4th. Still, it is possible that Chorzele will be found to be occupied. However, since there are three crossings, it is to be hoped that the southern bank will be won. If this is accomplished, the question arises, as some Gentlemen have recognized, as to how one should advance further. I feel it is not good to hold to the Orzyc and to open crossings there; rather, one has to march further to the west. The direction of

Przasnysz should be the right one. The cavalry divisions should cross the river still further west, at Janowo, etc. It is obvious that these divisions should be made up of troops who not only understand how to fight from horseback, but who also do not hesitate to hurl the fire of their carbines, machineguns and batteries at the enemy. With the crossing of the Orzyc, nothing is won of course unless the enemy is pursued relentlessly and unless every effort is made to throw him against the Vistula.

10

Kriegsspiel, 1905

This is Schlieffen's critique of the final Kriegsspiel *conducted while he was Chief of the General Staff and the only one of Schlieffen's* Kriegsspiele *to have survived.*[1] *It was played in late November/early December 1905, i.e., just as Schlieffen was writing his famous memorandum on war with France. Its scope is much wider than either the tactical-strategic problems or the General Staff rides, dealing as it does with war on two fronts, and must surely be part of the planning process that resulted in the memorandum later in December. However, the conduct of the game is significantly different from that envisioned by the Schlieffen plan. In this game, Schlieffen first knocked Russia out of the war, before turning against and defeating an Anglo-French force that had advanced on Germany through Belgium. Moreover, rather than begin the war offensively, Schlieffen allowed both the Russians and French to attack Germany.*

Several important conclusions can be drawn from this game. First, it demonstrates that Schlieffen's strategic ideas had not yet hardened into dogma. He was willing to entertain the notion of remaining on the strategic defensive in the event of a two-front war and that a decision could be reached quickly against Russia. Second, this Kriegsspiel *offers a piece of evidence to show the doubts Schlieffen felt about how Germany should fight a two-front war. He would not have tried this scenario if he had been firmly convinced in the efficacy of the strategic offensive. Third, Schlieffen recognized the political consequences of a violation of Belgian or Dutch neutrality (though he misjudged the British attitude towards these countries). Although in this game he does not value highly the fighting potential of their troops, Belgian and Dutch troops none the less play a role in the ultimate defeat of the Anglo-French forces.*

The scenario upon which this *Kriegsspiel* is based – a war between Germany and England, France and Russia – is the same as assumed several months ago by *France Militaire* and later by *Le Matin* and which has now become accepted by all newspapers. While the realization of such a scenario is unlikely or, better said, impossible, it none the less offers enough interest for us to occupy ourselves with it. Basically the scenario entails nothing new, as we have anticipated a war on two fronts for almost 20 years. For the last 40 years it has been repeatedly asserted also that in addition to fronts in the east and the west, Germany might be faced with a third front to the north as well. For a long time now, we have not believed that Italy would live up to its treaty obligations and provide us with support by holding down significant French forces in the Alps. On the other hand, we can assume that Austria will take on a part of the Russian army. Consequently, the German army will have to fight the whole strength of the French and British armies without Italian support, as well as a considerable part of the Russian army.

Not the most important, but certainly the most interesting question is how Great Britain will take part in the war. Some people say its army will land in Jutland, though there it would feel somewhat lonely, while others would have it landing in a Channel port, playing the unenviable role of French auxiliaries. In this *Kriegsspiel*, we have assumed that they will land at Dunkirk and Calais. The three British corps, therefore, will form only a reinforcement to the French army. This limits our enemies to two – the French and British, who will deploy between them 1,300,000 men in active and immediate reserve formations, and the Russians, who intend to deploy against Germany a force of 500,000 men.

To turn against both opponents offensively – with one army driving on Moscow and another on Paris – would, even in the best of cases, bring about a condition that Clausewitz called 'strategic consumption' [*strategischer Schwindsucht*]. Additionally, an all-out offensive directed against only one of our enemies, be it in the swamps and forests of Lithuania or in the confusion [*Wirrsal*] of the French fortresses, would require so much strength and so much time that we would have too little strength left to defend ourselves against our other enemy. Instead, it is advisable to await the approach of our enemies and to fall at once upon the enemy who crosses our border first and then to turn against the other enemy. Even this plan could fail, however, as our enemies would most likely cross the eastern and western borders simultaneously. The question then becomes, should one first fall with all possible strength against the weaker or the stronger of our enemies? Either choice has its advantages and disadvantages.

In this case, the choice fell on the Russians in the east because of the greater prospect of not only defeating the Russian force but of annihilating it completely. With the Russian threat removed, we could then proceed with greater freedom against France. However, even the success of this plan initially appeared doubtful: the number of corps that could be transported in the narrow strip of German land on either side of the Vistula River with the available railroads is limited. Aside from fortress garrisons, *Landwehr* and *Landsturm* troops, only 13 army corps and 12 reserve divisions (456,000 infantry in all) could be made available for operations in the east.[2] This force was inferior to the Russian force (11 ½ army corps and 10 reserve divisions, or 500,000 rifles) in number of rifles, but possessed a limited superiority in the numbers of corps, divisions and artillery. However, this superiority would not suffice to destroy the Russian force completely, and a decisive victory against the Russians was deemed absolutely necessary. We cannot afford to fight a war as in Manchuria, driving the enemy from position to position, lying inactive for months at a time until both sides are worn down enough to seek peace. Rather, we must dispose of one enemy in the shortest possible time to win a free hand against the other. To this end, the eastern theatre offers two advantages.

The first advantage arises from the Masurian Lakes. They extend from Angerburg to south of Johannisburg and create an obstacle around 75 kilometres in length. The main road leading through this area of lakes is blocked by Fort Boyen at Lötzen. The remaining east–west roads can be blocked easily with field fortifications. In this way, two new fortresses between the Löwentin Lake and the Spirding Lake and between the Spirdling Lake and the Nieder Lake take shape, which can be occupied by *Landwehr* and *Landsturm* troops and possibly armed with heavy guns as well.

The Russians, who in this *Kriegsspiel* send one army from across the Niemen River (18 divisions strong) and another from across the Narev River, can only unite west of the Masurian Lakes. This provides the opportunity for the German forces to advance with one army through the narrow passages between the Lakes and attack from the eastern bank either the Russian Niemen or the Narev Army in the flank. Alternatively, the Germans could approach the western side of the lake and attack one Russian army with great superiority before it can unite with the other.

In a future war, the fortress of Königsberg will form the second advantage of the eastern theatre. However, as the fortress can be rendered harmless by a small number of reserve troops, it offers no advantage in its current state. Even a Königsberg with the planned *enceinte* north of the Lakes is not worth mentioning. For this *Kriegsspiel*, a fortress will be required in which a German army can be assembled and from which this army can break out easily. The natural perimeter of the fortress follows the course of the Deime to the Pregel, and then to the Frisching. It is not necessary for the engineers to reinforce this 80-kilometre line with detached fortifications [*Panzerfort*]. In the space of four weeks, as we have in this *Kriegsspiel*, we can improve upon Nature, who has already done most of the work, to such an extent that the Russians will not be able to get into the fortress without great reinforcement. In this fortified area, an army can be assembled to fall upon the flank of the Niemen Army from either over the Dieme or over the Frisching.

Almost everyone who led the Russian forces in earlier *Kriegsspiele* has done so in the following manner: the Niemen Army advanced with its main body between Insterburg and Angerburg heading in the direction of Friedland–Rastenburg while the Narev Army advanced south of the Masurian Lakes in a northerly or northwesternly direction. The Russians, who believed the Germans to be assembling their forces either behind the Lakes or behind the Alle, hoped to crush the assembling Germans through the concentric advance of their two armies. They have been regularly mistaken. The German force in the past has not waited for this manoeuvre. Instead, they have usually retired but have taken the opportunity to attack the left wing of the Narev Army vigorously.

In this game, apart from the obvious option of a frontal attack, the German commander had the following options:

(1) advance against the right flank of the Niemen Army;
(2) advance against the left flank of the Narev Army;
(3) advance against the inner flanks of one or both the armies west of the Lakes before they could unite. (There was not enough time for a similar attack east of the Lakes.)

To cover the German deployment, the following units stood to the right of the Vistula River:

The I Reserve Corps (1st and 35th Reserve Divisions) at Tilsit
The *Landsturm* of the I Army Corps behind the Inster River
The I Army Corps behind the Angerapp River
The Guard Cavalry and the 1st Cavalry Division pushed forward to the border
The *Landwehr* of the I Army Corps in the fortifications between the lakes
The XX, XVII and VI Army Corps along the line between the lakes and Lautenburg
The *Landwehr* and *Landsturm* of the XVII Army Corps as well as the 2nd, 5th and 8th Cavalry Divisions behind the Drewenz
The 7th, 9th and 11th Reserve Divisions south of Königsberg (independent of the garrison troops)
The II Army Corps on the left bank of the Vistula by Fordon–Graudenz
The V Army Corps by Thorn.

As soon as the Russian route of advance was discovered, the following forces were brought up by rail:

The Guard Corps to Labiau

The X Army Corps to Königsberg to deploy to Tapiau north of the Pregel

The 2nd Guard Reserve Division and the 19th Division to Löwenhagen and Tapiau

The Guard Reserve Corps to Mehlsack

The IV Army Corps to Allenstein

The IXX Army Corps to Osterode

The III Army Corps to Deutsch Eylau

The 5th and 6th Reserve Divisions behind the III Corps at Deutsch Eylau

The XII Corps with the 23rd and 24th Reserve Divisions behind Strassburg

The II and V Army Corps and the 3rd Reserve Division were set marching to the east.

The Russian Niemen Army advanced by six roads in the direction of Friedland with its right wing along the Pregel. Its left wing rested on Angerburg and was advancing generally in the direction of Rastenburg.

The Narev Army sought to unify with the Niemen Army with its right wing advancing towards Sensburg. It covered its left wing from a western envelopment with a powerful leftward echelon, with which it moved in a sort of 'half-column' [*Halbkolonne*] in a northerly direction. To the deputy of the temporarily absent commander of the Narev Army, the left wing appeared to be too far back. Consequently, he pushed it forward, exposing thereby the Narev Army's left wing to the right wing of the German forces advancing from Mlawa and Soldau (XII, V and VI German Army Corps). The Narev Army would certainly have been defeated then and there if its commander had not returned in time to countermand his deputy's order. The steps he took were definitely justified. However, the swinging back behind the Orzyc River of the three corps that made up the army's left wing was too cautious. With this movement, the army's whole forward movement came to a halt. The few crossings of the overflowing Orzyc could easily have been blocked by relatively few troops and the left flank of the Narev Army sufficiently covered. Instead, the result was that the connection between the Narev and the Niemen Armies could not be effected. This movement also allowed the German force to penetrate between the two armies, forcing the Narev Army to retreat.

Through this retreat, any envelopment of the Narev Army by the Germans was made impossible – only an envelopment from the north or a breakthrough was now possible. If either course was to be successful, the German forces would have to attack the Russian front. However, before this could occur, the Germans had to build a front themselves, which at this point did not exist. Accordingly, the Germans attempted to construct a front as quickly as possible along the approximate line Mlawa–Allenstein–Heilsberg–Friedland. The retiring I, XVII and XX Army Corps, the corps unloading to the west, and the reserve divisions from south of Königsberg were to make up this front. Despite the difficulty of this manoeuvre, it nevertheless succeeded, due to the slow advance of the Niemen Army and the inaction of the Narev Army. By the 30th day, this manoeuvre was complete.

On the 31st day, the two opponents met. The Niemen Army left the whole area north of the Pregel to the Germans, so its right wing remained almost completely unprotected. Originally, the Niemen Army's commander had intended to cover his right flank with three reserve divisions. These divisions could either have blocked the Dieme line or they could have, as Napoleon would have done, followed the army in deep echelon. The commander of the Niemen Army chose instead another course of action. He sent these three reserve divisions piecemeal into an area where German forces had already been reported. In short order, one and a half of these divisions had been partly destroyed and one division had been pushed back onto the army's main body. Only a brigade's worth of troops was left to cover the Narev Army's 40-kilometre long flank.

The German troops advancing from the north to the Pregel and Inster (I Reserve Corps, Guard Corps, X Army Corps and a *Landwehr* division) faced no serious Russian obstacle. The few Russian troops left to guard the bridges across the Pregel could offer no meaningful resistance.

On the 32nd day, the Niemen Army stood in battle with German forces of roughly equal strength. Its commander learned early in the morning that the Germans had crossed the Pregel at numerous locations and he believed his rear to be threatened. In my opinion, there remained nothing else for him to do under the circumstances than to pull significant numbers of troops from his front to face the German forces to his rear. The original front should have then been held purely defensively. The Niemen Army's commander chose another course. He sent only two and a half divisions against the German units to his rear (while holding two brigades in reserve), too small a force to achieve a complete victory. With the weakened main body of his army, he intended to maintain his battle with the now-stronger Germans to his front. However, he soon felt that his main body was too weak to carry out his intentions, so he assembled his remaining units into three or four groups, which were so far from one another that they could be easily enveloped and destroyed piecemeal by the Germans.

In reality, no commander would have carried out such a plan. The truth is, if one weakens one's front by transferring units to cover the flanks, as did General Kuropatkin, the enemy can easily break through the weakened front and the battle is lost.[3]

Accordingly, the Niemen Army's now separated groups were forced to fall back by German counterattacks on the evening of the 32nd day. Its commander now intended to take up a position behind the Alle and Omst during the night in order to continue resistance. At the same time, he intended to deploy more units to combat the Germans to his rear. Although this position behind the Alle and Omst appeared to be good, the plan could not be accomplished with a beaten and exhausted army in the few hours left of night. This decision showed again quite convincingly that such a hastily taken position can always be outflanked or even completely encircled. Further, it shows that units that have been shuttled around the battlefield pell-mell do not have the strength either to mount a successful attack or to conduct a successful defence. In two long lines, one facing east and the other west, the Russians tried to bring the Germans to a halt. However, the Niemen Army did not possess enough strength to man both lines, and into the lines' breaches came the Germans. The Russian troops began to waver and any way out for the Niemen Army was now closed.

On the 31st, the Narev Army was also encountered and taken into battle, which continued into the next day. The Russians stood in a long line from approximately Przasnysscz–Chorzele–Willenberg–Ortelsburg to the Great Schoben Lake and from the northern tip of this lake outwards with a front facing Krummendorf to the northwest. The army's right flank, built from the Russian XVIII and VI Corps, was attacked by superior German forces and pushed back. This made the Russian position untenable. The army's main body, however, had to hold its position long enough for the VI and XVIII Corps to reach the heights around Ortelsburg. This made the retirement very difficult. Nevertheless, the orders were competently issued and the retirement carried out without heavy losses initially. However, despite all the care taken, the crossing points over the Orzyc remained unoccupied through the negligence of subordinate officers. The Germans advanced over these crossing points on the 32nd and 33rd days and on the 34th day were able to bar the Narev Army's route of retreat by placing brigades to cover the numerous defiles through the swamp- and stream-ridden terrain. The German blocking forces were able to delay the remnants of the Narev Army long enough for more German forces to come up.

On the eastern flank, the German 24th Division reached the crossing points of the Skrwa at Dudy-Pussczanskie before the Russian XVIII Corps and was able to deny these points to the Russians. Four Russian corps were completely cut off from the main body of the Narev Army through this manoeuvre.

The Russian VI Corps, while marching through Kolno, was met by the IV German Corps, which had advanced through Johannisburg, as well as by the 40th Division. It could only continue its retreat with great losses and harried by German pursuit.

In all, one corps, three reserve divisions, and four cavalry divisions escaped reasonably intact over the Narev at Ostrolenka and Rozan. The greater part of the Narev Army was destroyed. The surviving part was in no condition to undertake any significant operations against the victorious Germans and would have sought refuge in Warsaw.

By the 35th day, a few German corps, which stood close to railway stations, could begin transportation to the west. Some units were needed to transport Russian prisoners and to clear the battlefields. The remainder began marching to the nearest train station to follow the initial corps to the west.

There is no obvious reason why the aforesaid operation against the Niemen Army should not succeed in reality, as long as the envelopment is carried out with the necessary strength and to the greatest possible depth. For such an encirclement of the enemy's army, certainly, an obstacle like the Masurian Lakes is imperative. It is more doubtful whether an encirclement of a greater part of the Narev Army would have been successful and whether the German commanders, who had by crossing the Orzyc at Budki strayed into the swamps and rivers north of Narev, would ever have met up. However, even if they never managed to meet, the individual units would have been able to cause heavy casualties on the Russians retreating through this area. The Narev Army would only have managed to re-cross the Narev River with great losses, which would have left it incapable of further offensive action.

In a future war we will have to deal with armies arrayed in long positions [*Stellungen*]. The possibility of holding off a superior enemy from even somewhat strengthened field fortifications will result in more instances of trench warfare [*Positionskrieg*]. The Russo-Japanese War has shown this. Far away in Manchuria, it is possible for both sides to fight for months at a time from unassailable positions. In western Europe, however, one cannot allow oneself the luxury of such a strategy. The military machine with its thousands of wheels, costing millions to maintain, cannot stand still for long. One cannot fight a war for one or two years from position to position in 12-day-long battles until both combatants are completely exhausted and weakened and are forced to sue for peace.[4] We must attempt to defeat our enemies quickly and decisively.

Long fronts of modern armies offer the possibility that gaps can be found through which an attacker can break. Although it did not result in a sweeping success, the battle of Shaho gives an example of this.[5] This *Kriegsspiel* has also shown that a breakthrough is completely possible

1. *Generalfeldmarschall* Alfred Graf von Schlieffen. (IWM HU HU1777)

2. Kaiser Wilhelm II with his staff at the 1899 manoeuvres. Wilhelm is at the front of the group and Schlieffen third from the left wearing the uniform of a Guard Uhlan. (IWM HU68707)

3. Kaiser Wilhelm II strikes a dramatic pose at the 1906 manoeuvres. To the right of the photo can be seen a mounted soldier flying the Imperial Standard. (IWM HU53847)

4. *Generalfeldmarschall* Gottlieb Graf von Haeseler (right), shown here in the field during the First World War, was one of Schlieffen's intellectual opponents. (IWM Q45568)

5. Kaiser Wilhelm II (third from left on horseback) shakes hands with Graf von Haeseler at the 1905 manoeuvres. Schlieffen's successor as Chief of the General Staff, Helmuth von Moltke the Younger, can be seen on horseback at the far right of the photograph. (IWM HU68475)

6. One of Schlieffen's fiercest critics was *General der Kavallerie* Friedrich von Bernhardi (second from left), shown here during the First World War. (IWM Q52782)

7. An artillery team fires a field gun at the 1902 manoeuvres. (IWM HU68446)

8. Airships like these were increasingly seen by Schlieffen as crucial for the gathering of intelligence in wartime. (IWM HU68469)

9. As modern weapons became more effective, German infantry increasingly resorted to field entrenchments such as these for protection. (IWM HU68452)

10. Despite the evidence of the lethality of modern weapons, European soldiers were loath to give up their faith in the effectiveness of massed cavalry attacks. Here, Bavarian cavalrymen advance during the 1906 manoeuvres. (IWM HU53862)

11. Schlieffen expected modern communications, such as the field telephone pictured here, to make it easier for a 'modern Alexander' to command his widely spread forces in a future war. (IWM HU68485)

12. Machine guns, such as these firing at the 1905 manoeuvres, gave infantry units a vast increase in firepower. (IWM HU68478)

13. Postscard showing one of Imperial Germany's most prolific military writers, Hugo Freiherr von Freytag-Loringhoven, one of Schlieffen's staunchest supporters.

(when the unoccupied Orzyc River crossing at Budki was exploited by the German forces). It also shows that a breakthrough can result in a meaningful success.

In general, however, we will always turn again to the use of envelopment – not an enveloping manoeuvre, however, with only one division or merely a pushing back of the enemy's wing but rather a well-prepared, far-reaching envelopment with great strength. We must build a Napoleonic *bataillon carré* of 100,000 men or more and advance with this formation in such as way as to threaten not just the enemy's flank but also his rear.

The envelopment of the Niemen Army in this *Kriegsspiel* by a German force of around three corps provides us with an example of how such an operation can be done. This manoeuvre only turned out poorly because the available strength was definitely too weak.

However, it would be a great mistake if one were to rely totally on an enveloping manoeuvre. The envelopment must be combined with a powerful frontal attack even if the required number of men are unavailable. Further, once an envelopment has been successful, it must be combined with an unbroken pursuit of the enemy.

In this *Kriegsspiel*, the encirclement of the Russians was made easier by the Masurian Lakes. Though other such obstacles can be found on other battlefields, they might not be as effective as the Masurian Lakes and it is better not to rely on them. It is more important to execute a powerful envelopment with sufficient forces and to exert all possible strength to close every route through which the enemy might escape.

In the west, there remained no alternative but for the small German army to await where the more than doubly superior enemy would direct his attack.

First, the border, or more importantly the railway lines running close to the border, had to be secured. To this end, *Landwehr* brigades and cavalry divisions were pushed forward to the Belgian–German border from the Meuse to the Moselle.

In the widened fortress of Metz stood, in addition to the fortress' normal wartime garrison, the XVI Army Corps, the 43rd Division and nine *Landwehr* brigades.

The main front between Metz and Saarburg was covered by two army corps, two reserve divisions and a cavalry division.

The XV Army Corps stood in Strassburg.

The XIV Army Corps and the 28th Reserve Division stood in Upper Alsace.

A number of *Landwehr* brigades covered the upper Rhine.

The three northern army corps with their reserve corps were assembled behind the right wing of this covering force at Cologne and Aachen.

The XXI and XIII Army Corps, together with the three Bavarian Army Corps and a number of reserve divisions, were held in their corps regions [*Korpsbezirken*] ready for transportation.

Already during the army's initial deployment [*Aufmarsch*], the observation stations [*Beobachtungsstationen*] on the Franco-Belgian border discovered that the French intended to assemble a strong army around Lille and that this French force would be joined by the three British army corps which had landed at Dunkirk and Calais. Additional French armies deployed along the Franco-Belgian border between Verdun and Maubeuge. The French also deployed not inconsiderable forces [*Streitkräfte*] across the upper Moselle and in the Vosges.

Based on this information, it was therefore highly likely that the French intended to march through Belgium along both sides of the Meuse.

Fifty years ago, the Field Marshal[6] discussed the advantages of this manoeuvre: the French cannot advance over the Rhine on a wide front, instead they must wheel right against the Moselle. If they are not destroyed during this manoeuvre, the exact time at which they will arrive at the line Verdun–Coblenz can be calculated. If the French succeed in crossing the Moselle, they will find themselves in an unpleasant situation – enclosed on two sides by the Rhine and on another by the Moselle between Metz, Strassburg and Mainz.

The advance through Belgium, as it was planned by the French, was subject to many difficulties without the prospect of a great result as recompense. The prospect of success, then, only appeared likely when another French army crossed the upper Moselle and supported the advance of the main French army with a left wheel against and across the line Metz-Saarburg. With the reports of French troops pushed over the Moselle and to the Vosges it appeared that the French intended to carry out such a manoeuvre.

This manoeuvre had to be thrown back. The right bank of the Moselle had to be kept free and secure for use as a base of operations and as a base for the assembly of the German forces which would come from the east as reinforcement. Therefore, those corps left behind, other than those in Cologne and Aachen, were brought forward:

the VIII and XXI Army Corps to Strassburg,
the II Bavarian Corps to Saarburg,
the XVI Army Corps and the 43rd Infantry Division to south of Metz,
the I and III Bavarian Corps to Hüningen and its environs, where they united with the retiring XIV Army Corps.

With this deployment the German commander intended to set out upon an encircling attack [*umfassender Angriff*] when the French stole a march on him and advanced with numerous columns through the Vosges from Belfort as well as against Strassburg. The Germans would be able to advance with a part of their force from Strassburg upstream through the Rhine Valley and with another part advance downstream after crossing the Rhine at Hüningen and Istein, where bridgeheads were constructed.

The enemy force, which was composed mostly of territorial and reserve divisions, was compressed from north and south in the narrow valley and destroyed within a few days. Although the troops were only of minimal quality, this action diminished the French strength by 12 divisions right at the beginning of the campaign. The Germans had won in a splendid manner the *première victoire*, which the French had always wanted for themselves. This victory would have raised morale in Germany while lowering morale in France.

The whole right bank of the Moselle fell into German hands when the German right wing threw the French forces between Saarburg and Metz back over the river.

The question was then whether or not the Germans should exploit this victory by pursuing the French between Toul and Épinal. Probably an attempt to cross the Moselle would not have succeeded because of the strong French defensive position. If the attempt had succeeded, however, the Germans could have advanced on Paris without encountering any significant obstacles. The Germans would then have had the whole Anglo-French army against them under extremely unfavourable conditions and with very unfavourable means of retreat [*Rückzugsverhältnissen*].

It appeared from earlier events that the Germans could assume with confidence that the French intended to carry out an envelopment [*Umgehung*] from the north and that their entry into Belgium would soon be confirmed.

Under these circumstances, the question was whether the Germans should have awaited the attack from behind the Moselle. The defence of the river seemed to be not unfavourable since it could be combined with an attack upon the French left wing from across the Rhine. However, it was impracticable to abandon the entire left bank of the Rhine and the whole left bank of the Moselle to the enemy and to stand by while a large area of German land was laid waste by the enemy.

Despite the limited forces available to the Germans, they had to attack, as an attack offered many opportunities. The left flank of the advancing French army was threatened by Antwerp, from both banks of the Meuse, and from the Rhine between Cologne and Coblenz during its entire advance and during its entire right wheel. Therefore, the German attack had to fall against this exposed flank. The further west this attack fell, the more effective it would be, as it would threaten not only the enemy's flanks, but also his rear.

The German commander therefore resolved to transport by rail as many army corps as possible to Antwerp. The remainder would be transported to Cologne to reinforce the force already there (the VII, VIII and IX Army Corps). By the 33rd day, three army corps were transported to Antwerp using the three available single-track rail lines. By the 37th day, three further corps were transported to Antwerp.

This transport had to be covered, so the Belgians were asked to occupy the line of the Dyle and the Demer between Mechelen and Diest with their five divisions. The four Dutch divisions were to continue this position from Hasselt onwards and be joined by a number of German reserve corps, so that the whole stretch between Mechelen and Liège was closed.

The question was, however, would Belgium and the Netherlands comply with these demands [*Forderungen*].

The French had violated the neutrality of their northern neighbour when they crossed the Belgian border. In order to uphold their independence, the Belgians had to defend their neutrality. They found in France's enemy their natural ally, as did the Dutch. Although Dutch neutrality had not yet been violated, if the French continued their advance it was sure to be. It would certainly be advisable for them to employ their strength early in conjunction with the Belgians and Germans to safeguard their independence. There could be no doubt that, if the French and British emerged as victors in the war with Germany, both small states would form a part of their booty. The Belgians and Dutch could, however, expect considerably better terms from a victorious Germany. Self-interest called Belgium and the Netherlands to the side of Germany. It is by no means certain, however, that these states would follow this call. The question of which of the two sides had the greatest prospects of victory had to lie with the choice of the party in power, and, given the number of enemies, Germany's prospects did not appear very good. Yet, one can accept that the two threatened states would have made the good and right decision.

The value of the Belgian and Dutch troops has been estimated as very low by the enemy. Indeed, the armed forces [*Wehrsystem*] of both states have a very 'militia' tinge [*milizartigen Anstrich*] about them. Nevertheless, the Belgian officer corps enjoys the best reputation, and, as for the Dutch soldiers, they bring with them the temperament to persevere in the defence. Initially, the two were earmarked for easy tasks.

It was later shown that their enemy was also not of especially high military value. Initially their enemy consisted of French reserve divisions, composed of older classes recalled to the colours, who appeared to be little suited to especially heroic deeds. As for the British, one who should know, Field Marshal Lord Roberts, said in a public speech that they are poorly prepared for battle and it would be the 'height of madness' if they were employed in a Continental war. Therefore, not much could be said for either enemy force.

The position the Belgian and Dutch troops were to occupy beside the German troops was sufficiently strong. The Dyle and the Demer upstream from Diest are navigable rivers and form a considerable barrier, while the heights of the northern bank help the fire of the defenders. The Demer above Diest is not as deep, but will, like the Herck, delay the enemy considerably. Also, the spot where the Herck flows into the Demer appears to offer the attacker considerable difficulties. Only a small area of the front near Tongres possessed no natural obstacles. There, creativity and hard work had to correct this failing. Worse for the attacker was that the wings of this position were fully secured by the fortresses of Antwerp and Liège.

Accordingly, this position could not be outflanked. On the contrary, the attacker himself risked envelopment. He advanced into an envelopment [*Umfassung*], into a cul-de-sac. The difficulties offered by the location and the properties of the position were increased by the Allies themselves through the manner of their attack. They advanced in close order with five French corps, three British corps, six reserve divisions and a territorial division, with little regard for the danger which threatened on both flanks. In disregard for the lessons of past wars, which have been reinforced by the experiences in South Africa and East Asia, they believed that mass attacks [*Massenangriffen*] and superiority in numbers would allow them to overcome the murderous fire of an entrenched enemy [*das verheerende Feuer des gedeckten Gegners*]. They had to draw the short straw. Gradually, it became clear to them that the operation with the 26 divisions of their left wing (4th French Army, the English army and the 2nd Reserve Army) could not be conducted as planned.

In the meantime, the French 1st, 2nd and 3rd Armies had carried out a right wheel and on the 30th and 31st day had reached a line running from Liège to Verdun. A further advance meant splitting the whole army in two. One either wheeled with the 1st, 2nd and 3rd Armies further south, which would leave only the left wing north of the Meuse, or the 2nd and 3rd Armies could wheel leftwards, going around Liège to the east, in order to open the way over the Meuse south of Maastricht. This would leave the 1st Army and the 1st Reserve Army with a completely new task, namely, to cover the Moselle. There would then remain only the clearing of the northern bank of the Meuse. However, by doing so the situation would barely be bettered. The enemy would be pursued to the line Liège–Namur and would have extended his right wing from the latter fortress outwards to the Meuse.

The French commander initially decided to advance northwards with the 3rd and 2nd Army, secure Liège, and thus open the way over the Meuse for the 4th Army and the English army. The 1st Army and the 1st Reserve Army were to take over covering the Moselle. With this movement, a gap between the northern and southern halves of the army would come about, into which the enemy advancing from the Rhine could penetrate. To prevent this, a 5th Army would be created out of drafts from the 1st and 4th Armies.

In the meantime, three German army corps and two German cavalry divisions had concentrated by way of rail movements and forced marches behind Antwerp's fortifications. Upon the completion of deployment, this force was to advance against the left wing of the 2nd French Reserve Army, which had been discovered in the area of Mechelen.

One can question whether or not this movement would be countered by the enemy. Experience has shown that in war a multitude of reports come in and that an even greater number of rumours spread. Also in this case, a large number of reports and rumours would have spread concerning the whereabouts of the enemy army, which could have placed it on the right bank of the Moselle. One would have heard that they stood on the other side of the Moselle; that they had been transported to the east; that they were concentrating on Cologne; that they were transporting to the Netherlands; and, finally, that they were transported to Antwerp. It would have been impossible to make further decisions with any certainty based upon these reports, even if the Field Marshal himself had ordered his army north based only upon the first newspaper reports of MacMahon's movements.[7] Before one takes such a step, one wants to have certainty so that one does not undertake an operation which is doomed from the start. Every commander builds for himself a picture of possible enemy operations. He initially rejects reports which do not confirm this picture and holds on to his own view for a long as possible. That German troops would be transported to Antwerp was so unlikely that the French commander did not yet believe the report, especially when the entry of 100,000 troops into Brussels had already been reported to him.

The commander of the German force in Antwerp did not believe that he could await the arrival of the three corps of the second echelon and still maintain surprise. If the French discovered his intentions, they could take sufficient steps to prevent his break out from Antwerp. However, if he began his operation with only three German corps, even supported by a part of the Belgian army, there was the danger that the

French would advance from around the south of Namur and counter-attack with overwhelming strength, which they could draw from their 4th, 3rd and 2nd Armies. Since the Germans could know nothing of a French 5th Army, which was in the process of formation, and believed the French 4th Army to be sufficiently tied down, they saw a real danger in the French 2nd and 3rd Armies. These armies had been reported by the *Landwehr* brigades and cavalry divisions that had been pushed forward to the Belgian border. As soon as the reports of the German advance from Antwerp reached these armies, they turned on the weak German forces. It appeared very important to the Germans, therefore, to hold the 2nd and 3rd French Armies fast. Despite their weakness, the German commander [*Oberfeldherr*] ordered the three corps which had assembled southwest of Cologne (the VII, VIII and IX Army Corps) to advance against the two French armies. The three corps which were being transported to Cologne after the battle to the south (the XIII, XIV and XXI Army Corps) were to deploy to the left of this advancing force as soon as possible. On the 32nd day, the first three corps came into contact with the French between Montjoie and Prüm. The next day, this would develop into a full-scale attack.

By chance, then, on this day (the 33rd), three events took place in sequence: (1) the French 2nd and 3rd Armies attacked the VII, VIII and IX Army Corps of the German 4th Army; (2) three corps (the XIV, XV and XIX Army Corps) detached from the French 4th Army on the Meuse to form the French 5th Army; (3) the German 1st Army advanced with three corps (the XI, XV and XVI Army Corps) and three Belgian divisions against the left wing of the French 2nd Reserve Army. In the first event, the appearance of the Germans caused the French to fail completely. Although they attacked with seven and a half corps, the French units advanced so closely together that they could outflank the three German corps on neither the right nor the left flank. This force saw its goal of attracting the French upon them fulfilled and could retire almost unmolested. This withdrawal brought the Germans into a sector of terrain at the mouth of the Urft in the Roer which was very good for the defender but poor for the attacker. Four and a half French corps were compressed here by two German corps before their front between the two rivers and the heights of Venn almost to the point where they could not manoeuvre. By means of a deep flanking movement with the two corps of their right wing, the French attempted to outflank the Germans. This was halted by the three corps of the German second echelon (XIV, XV and XXI Army Corps) which had arrived in the meantime. A little more time and seven and a half French corps would have been, if not encircled, as good as completely smashed by the numerically far inferior German 4th Army. Only the advance of the French 5th

Army rescued them (36th day) by causing the Germans to abandon their encircling manoeuvre. It is absolutely necessary, in such cases, that the parts of the two armies do not advance under different commanders, but rather that they fall under a unified command.

The advance of the three corps of the 4th French Army (the XIV, XV and XXI) did not succeed completely. The blocking off [*Abschliessung*] of Liège was given up by the 3rd Army on the right bank of the Meuse. They had fulfilled this task in the sector between the Vesdre and the Ourthe in a proper manner but not in the area between the Ourthe and the Meuse. A German reserve corps advanced into this sector. This forced the French XIX Corps to swing left, but allowed the two other corps (the XIV and XV) to continue their march across the Meuse.

The Germans had calculated that it would be in some way possible for them to advance from Antwerp. The encirclement of this powerful fortress requires so much strength that it would in all likelihood show gaps. However, no one could have foreseen how easy the break out from Antwerp would actually be. The French 2nd Reserve Army, which was given the task of encircling Antwerp, had conceived of their task in such a way that they closed not the front door, not the great gate, not the main exit, but rather a side door, which was difficult to use anyhow. Moreover, they had so chosen their position that their flanks were exposed to attacks from Antwerp and that, if such an attack succeeded, their rear was exposed to every danger from the start. It was hardly surprising then that merely the appearance of three Belgian divisions caused the flank divisions of the 2nd Reserve Army to vacate their dangerous positions. Under the prevailing circumstances, the withdrawal could have changed into a bloody defeat or a panic-filled flight, if the Belgians, who possessed two cavalry divisions, had even tried to pursue. Therefore, it was assumed that three reserve divisions (52nd, 60th and the Zuave), who had their left flank on Louvain, were thrown back behind the Dyle in confusion and disarray, and that the Belgians pursued immediately. It would have been advisable for the French to withdraw their reserve divisions from immediate contact with the enemy, to reinforce considerably their front to the west from rearwards, and then to go over to the offensive. It is questionable whether or not these steps would have resulted in success, given the superiority of the enemy and the support which he could find from Namur. However, it would have been appropriate to the situation to vacate the left bank of the Meuse, which could indeed barely be held, if one wanted to avoid being encircled.

The steps actually taken by the French commander were in part impracticable, in part completely insufficient. The defeated and disorganized aforementioned reserve divisions were to execute a flank march along the enemy front in order to extend the French front and prevent a further outflanking. Individual units were brought up from the rear to reinforce the threatened wing. Since in order to fulfil their mission, these units had to execute long marches, up to 40 kilometres, they obviously arrived late. This procedure repeated itself in the following days. The Germans and Belgians extended their front steadily, sending the free divisions behind the Dyle and Demer to their left wing, while simultaneously extending their right wing to the south. In this manner, the Germans steadily extended their front considerably further than the French. The French observed always the same process [*Verfahren*]. They attempted, without result, to extend their front through flank marches and the movement of individual divisions. They saw themselves continually outflanked. After the French had thoroughly weakened their eastern front through drafts, the Germans advanced also against this front from Liège. The two French wings were forced continually back and gradually came closer together, as the northern wing also retired before the enemy flanking fire. The circle became ever tighter. By the 36th day, the encirclement was complete.

Until then, the commander of the French side had not seen the situation north of the Meuse as serious. He believed that there he only had to deal with an inconsiderable enemy, who could be thrown back without difficulty. The reports that he received on the 36th forced him to recognise the seriousness of the situation. A decision had to be made. Previously, he had underestimated the enemy. Now, according to the laws of psychology, he proceeded to overestimate the enemy. He resolved to withdraw to the French Meuse (essentially with the 2nd Army); the 3rd and the 5th Armies were to cover the Belgian Meuse and the 1st Army was to cover the Moselle. When one examines the conditions closely, this withdrawal would have been very difficult to execute. It did not offer itself under the current conditions. Indeed, the French had twice sustained considerable losses on the Upper Rhine and north of the Meuse, which was for the most part restricted to units of limited worth, to reserve and territorial divisions as well as the English army. As for active French units [*Truppenkörpern*], only two divisions on the Upper Rhine and two corps north of the Meuse were lost. The French still possessed 19 complete army corps – considerably more than the Germans could possibly reckon on even under their best assumptions. In addition, the French enjoyed the advantages of interior lines, even if they could not go too far in concentrating their forces. Too great a concentration would have opened them up to the most extreme consequence: encirclement on the battlefield.

However, this situation need not have arisen. One option was to have a strong army deploy with its front facing west to throw back the enemy who had had success north of the Meuse and who now seemed to have the intention of advancing over the Meuse and through Namur. This would relieve the 4th Army as well as the English. Additionally, the 2nd Army and the right wing of the 3rd Army had to be extricated from their poor position and they themselves had to go over to the offensive with the goal of at least preventing the enemy standing before them from advancing any further. The 1st Army had to be made to throw the inconsiderable enemy before them back over the Meuse. Then, they should be so deployed that no enemy could again cross this river or advance from Metz.

The French possessed more than sufficient strength to carry out all these tasks, especially, if one did not feel bound by the original order of battle [*Armee-Enteilung*].

The steps ordered by the French commander corresponded to these tasks in so far as the 3rd Army and the 5th Army were to be assembled against the main enemy and the 1st Army was given the task of covering the Moselle. However, the withdrawal that the 2nd Army was ordered to make made the success of the other undertakings doubtful. Their success was made even more doubtful when a change of command took place and the new commander laid the main weight of the withdrawal in a southwestern direction and when other unpleasant circumstances came about.

The neglected section of the front covering Liège between the Meuse and the Ourthe had been secured since the 34th day by two corps (the III and the XIX). To support this force, the command of the 4th Army had sent one division (the 37th) over the Meuse, which did nothing to avert the fate that had befallen this force. The other division of the XIX Army Corps (the 38th), which faced the German army advancing from Namur, succumbed to superiority in numbers. The III Corps, instead of retreating behind the Ourthe in good time, remained standing with its front facing Liège and awaited the appearance of the Germans (XI and XVI Army Corps) in its rear. Its annihilation was unavoidable. Thus, the number of army corps available to the French was reduced from 19 to 17 and the attack to stop the German advance over the Meuse was made more difficult.

Yet, the German position was by no means brilliant. Their 2nd and 3rd Armies were for the most part victorious north of the Meuse, but were still held up by the encirclement of the enemy. The 4th Army stood against superior enemy forces. The units by Metz and on the Moselle were so weak that they could accomplish nothing. Reinforcement from the east could only arrive in several days time. On the 37th day, the 1st Army was still far away. Indeed, the three corps of the second echelon, which were being transported from Antwerp to Brussels, were brought forward by train right to Namur and Charleroi. However, the army (five army corps and one reserve corps) had first to be assembled before it could advance. This was certainly the minimum strength necessary for the army to carry out its assigned mission of advancing against a far superior enemy, especially when one did not know the enemy's dispositions. When this army set about its task, it would also have the whole of France to its rear and would have to reckon on being attacked from there by, at least, some hastily assembled territorial units.

Originally, on the German side, after the six corps had completed their journey, they hoped to be able to transport some reserve divisions by rail to cover the rear of the army. However, the pressing transports from the eastern theatre of war had hindered this plan, and the detachment of one or two corps from the army's main body to cover the flanks would have made it too weak to carry out its main mission. Therefore, there remained only a cavalry division available to secure, to some degree or other, the rear from surprises. Gradually, as many units as possible were withdrawn from the army encircling the French forces north of the Meuse, which were to follow the 1st Army later. Already on the 38th day, the XV Reserve Corps, the XI and the XVI Army Corps ran into the enemy, who had taken up position on the right bank of the Ourthe from the Ambleve to beyond Durbuy and then further to Marche. The French could not be thrown out of their positions without the greatest effort. The deployment of the 1st German Army was continued with the intention of the right wing reaching, if possible, the area of the Semois, there to take up position to await the enemy attack on comparatively good ground (avoiding the forest as much as possible). Cavalry divisions tried further to block the few and difficult crossing points over the Semois with their machineguns. The 1st Army pressed the retreating French 2nd Army until it was brought to a halt by the barrier formed on the Semois. There, they were forced to defend themselves against their pursuers. At this point, the encirclement was complete.

In the meantime, the French 4th Army, the English army and the 2nd Reserve Army had surrendered. The four German and Belgian divisions thus freed could advance first on the Meuse and then onwards. It was high time that this support was brought to the 1st German Army. The French had mobilized their final reserve. The *chasseur* detachments, which had guarded the highest Alpine passes on the Italian border, were assembled into a corps, transported to Maubeuge, and from there set to marching, by way of Givet, against the rear of the 1st Army. Two divisions of the two corps of the right wing (II Army Corps and III Bavarian Corps) had to turn around and turn against the newly arrived enemy, who offered resistance until the four divisions advancing from the north completed the French defeat.

The French 1st Army perceived its mission to be to offer determined resistance on the Alzette and west of Diedenhofen. They would have done better to begin a retreat as soon as the 2nd Army had reached the heights on their left wing. As they stood their ground, their left wing was encircled by the I Bavarian Corps and their left was encircled by a number of corps arriving from the eastern theatre. Thus, their situation became, to say the very least, difficult.

This portion of the *Kriegsspiel* offers the opportunity to show that a smaller army [*Heer*] can also defeat a larger enemy force. The smaller force will have great difficulty succeeding if it directly attacks its strongest opponent. It will simply be swallowed up. The smaller army must advance against the enemy's most sensitive points, seek to attack the flanks and rear, and force the surprised enemy to carry out a change of front [*Frontveränderung*]. If it does this, the smaller army takes upon itself the greatest of dangers and takes a significant risk, for its own flanks and rear are thereby seriously threatened. Such an action requires a focused leader [*zielbewusster Führer*], who has an iron character and who possesses a determined will to win, and troops who understand the gravity of the undertaking. However, these factors alone do not bring victory. Victory requires that the enemy, surprised by the suddenness of the attacks, makes more or less confused decisions and that his rash decisions are spoiled by hasty execution.

At Leuthen, the Austrians believed that they would be attacked on their right wing, but the attack fell against their left. However, there was still sufficient time to carry out a left wheel in accordance with the instructions of their drill regulations. Had the Austrians done this, with their great superiority they would have certainly defeated the *Potsdamer Wachtparade*. The turning [*Schwenkung*], however, did not succeed. In the hustle and bustle, the result was only a deep, confused crowd, into which the thin Prussian line unceasingly fired regularly and on command. The wild crowd succumbed to the thin, ordered line.[8] So it was in all similar cases and if one were to review the maps for the individual days of this *Kriegsspiel*, one would be forced to say that similar conditions prevailed.

I would like to mention one last thing. It has often been said that these *Kriegsspiele* are too grandly laid out and that first lieutenants are not called upon to lead armies. So long as they are lieutenants, certainly not. However, it is hoped, they will have the honour at some point to command an army, or if they are more modest in their goals, to serve as the commanding general of an army corps or to stand by the side of a commanding general as his chief of the staff. In wars, these army corps would hardly operate alone. These corps are part of an army and the army [*Armee*] is part of the nation's army [*Heer*]. From this relationship arise their missions, of which the individual corps often know nothing. The difficulties grow with the size of the army. In part, Napoleon failed in this, as his marshals did not operate according to his ideas. If one follows the events of 1870, one meets at every step the failures of the subordinate commanders [Unterführer].[9] It is reported from the Manchurian war that the Russian commanders [Führer] understand no better than the Russian General Staff how to lead armies or the army corps within these armies.[10] If you, Gentlemen, were to question, in confidence, the leaders of the various sides of this *Kriegsspiel*, you would hear that this or that subordinate had misunderstood me completely and had acted entirely differently to my wishes. Another will have corrupted all my ideas. It is an art form [Kunst] for the supreme commander [Oberbefehlshaber] to make his ideas and intentions clear to his subordinates; it is an art form for the subordinate to grasp the overall situation [Kriegslage], to understand the intentions of the supreme commander, and to translate these in a purposeful manner [zweckmässige Weise] into deeds. These arts must be learned. One means of accomplishing this is such a *Kriegsspiel*. This method is imperfect, but it offers the possibility of delving deeply into how a large army and its army corps fulfil their tasks. It also offers the possibility of learning how to act according to the ideas of the supreme commander and how to act according to the interests of the overall situation.

In such *Kriegsspiele*, petty annoyances and arguments are hardly to be avoided. The players, though, will get over them as long as they keep the main goals before their eyes – to train as commanders and to prepare for war. Thus, it is unimportant whether one or the other of the players is the victor. It is more important that each was forced to make as many difficult and swift decisions [schwierige und entscheidende Entschlüsse] as possible.

Part II:
MEMORANDA

Introduction

While training his subordinates was a crucial function of Schlieffen's role as Chief of the Great General Staff, planning for any future war had been the *raison d'être* of the General Staff since Gerhard von Scharnhorst had presided over the first beginnings of the modern General Staff in the early nineteenth century.[1] It was this function that occupied most of Schlieffen's time and energy. Indeed, the lives of almost all those officers assigned to Schlieffen in the *Rote Bude* on the Königsplatz in Berlin revolved around the production of the annual *Aufmarschplan* (deployment plan). Under the tutelage of Helmuth von Moltke the Elder, this planning process had become regularized and bureaucratized, and each year the Chief of the General Staff would preside over the writing of a detailed deployment plan that would form the basis for the deployment of the German army at the beginning of any future war.[2]

The construction of this plan began in October of each year. This massive project would be guided by a memorandum produced by the Chief of the General Staff outlining Germany's initial deployment and basic strategy for the subsequent year,[3] and it was the task of Schlieffen's subordinates to translate this rough sketch into concrete plans.[4] For each individual army, the General Staff drew up 'deployment portfolios', containing the army's initial wartime directives, information on enemy formations, the wartime order of battle of the German army, and the borders between the individual armies, among other information. The Railway Section added to these portfolios the crucial 'deployment transport lists', which determined by which route and when particular formations would be deployed. For each army corps and reserve corps, summaries of the army portfolios were written, and the border army corps received special orders concerning border protection.[5] This work was to be completed and sent out each year by 1 April, when the new mobilization year began. The summer months would be spent testing the plan's various components through staff rides and wargames.[6]

Schlieffen created his deployment plans in the face of certain strategic challenges and with certain assumptions that remained reasonably constant throughout his time as Chief of the General Staff. First, he, like his predecessors, assumed that any future war for Germany would be fought on two fronts. The outcome of the Franco-German War of 1870/71 had created a permanent foe in France, and ham-fisted diplomacy under Kaiser Wilhelm II had thrown away Russia as an ally and allowed it to form an alliance with France against Germany and Austria-Hungary.[7] Thus, Schlieffen assumed that any future war would entail fighting enemies on two sides – France to the west and Russia to the east. The Franco-Russian Military Convention of 1892, signed shortly after Schlieffen took up his post as Chief of the General Staff, also ensured that Germany would be fighting opponents superior in numbers, even if Germany could count on the support of its Triple Alliance allies – Austria-Hungary and Italy.[8] Schlieffen assumed that the Franco-Russian forces would outnumber those of the Triple Alliance by five to three.[9] The General Staff Chief also assumed France was Germany's most a dangerous enemy. He knew that the modern French army could deploy far faster than the backward Russian army. Within the space of a few short weeks, Germany would have to face a fully mobilized French army on its western border, an army that would always be larger than the Germans could field. Germany's enemies not only had larger armies, they also possessed strongly fortified defensive positions, making any offensive against them difficult. However, Schlieffen saw opportunities as well as dangers in this strategic situation.

SCHLIEFFEN'S NEW STRATEGIC PRIORITIES

While Schlieffen's predecessors, Helmuth von Moltke the Elder and Alfred Graf von Waldersee, had resolved to meet any future two-front war with an initial offensive against Russia, Schlieffen had other ideas.[10] In the summer of 1892, Schlieffen began exploring the possibility of shifting the main German deployment to the west against France. He argued that Germany needed to defeat its enemies rapidly, as Germany did not possess enough strength to fight a long war against enemies overwhelmingly superior in numbers.[11] He felt the only way to do this was to defeat them piecemeal, and here Germany had the strategic advantage of laying between its enemies. As the French army would take to the field earliest, Schlieffen felt it should be defeated first.[12]

By December 1892, his early ideas had solidified. Schlieffen felt that an offensive against Russia was unlikely to result in the rapid and decisive victory he felt Germany needed. First, Russia had been strengthening its border fortresses, making a German offensive more difficult. He

INTRODUCTION

argued that even if German forces managed to by-pass the Russian fortifications, the offensive would not bring the desired decisive victory. Moreover, the distance between the German and Austrian offensives was too great (375–450 kilometres) for them to be mutually supporting. He wrote:

> Should a German attack ... be successful, the enemy would certainly not withdraw to the south into Austrian hands, but rather to the east, where the terminus of the railways upon which he is withdrawing are to be found. We would not succeed in fighting a decisive battle and in smashing the Russian army, but instead fighting a series of frontal battles against an enemy who is offered respite by a retreat into the heart of a powerful empire, while our own lines of communication would be poor and greatly endangered.[13]

Instead, Schlieffen envisioned the main battle being fought in the west, where not only Germany's most immediate and most dangerous foe was to be found, but also where the prospects of a speedy victory were the greatest. Schlieffen hoped to be able to defeat the French quickly and decisively enough to be able to shift German forces east on Germany's excellent rail system before the Russians had even finished deploying.[14] This idea was reflected in the *Aufmarschplan* for 1893/94, which called for the deployment of three-quarters of the German field army in the west, or in total 16 army corps, 15 reserve divisions and 6 cavalry divisions arrayed in four armies. These 54 divisions were to be joined by 12½ *Landwehr* brigades. This force was to deploy from Diedenhofen in the north down to Metz and Contchen, from there along the course of the German Nied to Falkenberg and Lörchingen and Wasselheim, finally ending at Rosheim, west of Strassburg. A weak detachment was to be deployed in Upper Alsace.[15] In the east, only 4 army corps, 6 reserve divisions and 14 *Landwehr* brigades were to be deployed. Eleven of these 15 divisions were to conduct a much-pared-down offensive in cooperation with the Austro-Hungarian army from Silesia and the southern end of the province of Posen.[16]

The initial eastern offensive favoured by Moltke and Waldersee was finished. With some variations, the *Aufmarschplan* of 1893/94 was to remain the basis for Germany's war plans until the turn of the century, but the assumptions upon which it was based and the objectives it sought to meet would remain for the rest of Schlieffen's time as Chief of the General Staff. A future war was to be won first in the west, in Schlieffen's view the most important theatre. The east would have to make do with limited forces and wait until sufficient forces were released by a hopefully speedy western victory to conduct a large-scale offensive.[17]

THE FRONTAL ASSAULT ON FRANCE

The question was then how should the desired rapid and decisive victory in the west be brought about? Schlieffen's outline for the next year's deployment plan gives a good idea of how he envisioned the battle in the west would be fought. Clearly, a French offensive into German territory would offer the best prospects for a German success, and this assumption had formed the basis for Moltke's and Waldersee's plans. However, Schlieffen feared that France would not take up the offensive as had previously been assumed. He held it for certain that 'for many years the French have held strongly to defensive intentions in a possible war against Germany'.[18] Moreover, Schlieffen feared that even if France took up an offensive, the German army would not be well placed to meet the French in defensive positions and, crucially, would be unable to achieve the rapid, decisive victory Germany needed. Schlieffen concluded that the Germans needed to retain the initiative and that only by the means of a German offensive would his goals be met. In the case of a French attack, Schlieffen determined to meet the French offensive with one of his own in the hopes of bringing about an encounter battle on German terms. This is reflected in his initial deployment plan, with its relatively strong wings designed to protect against any possible French outflanking movement. However, if the French did not attack immediately, which was the true French plan and Schlieffen's fear, then he intended to go after them.[19]

Any German offensive against France was substantially hindered by the line of fortresses constructed by France in the aftermath of its defeat in 1871. This system created, in Moltke's words, an almost 'hermetically sealed' border[20] by heavily fortifying a line from Belfort in the south to Épinal and then, after a gap, another line from Toul to Verdun.[21] Schlieffen's memorandum of July 1894 explored a number of possible attack routes through this obstacle. Schlieffen held the most favourable route to be across the Maas below Verdun, i.e., an attack around the north of the French border fortress line. It was there that 'the fewest fortifications and fewest troops are to be found', and a successful attack there would allow German forces to envelop the French army deployed in its fortress line. However, this attack could not be a simple outflanking manoeuvre. Schlieffen felt that for it to succeed, it would have to be supported by a breakthrough attempt by other armies between Toul and Verdun. This, Schlieffen believed, would itself have to be supported by an offensive against Nancy. Thus, for the first time, Schlieffen had raised the prospect of outflanking the French fortified line from the north. This appears to be the genesis of what would become the powerful right wing of the 'Schlieffen Plan'. Schlieffen's continual return to this idea over the next 11 years indicates that, if the conditions were right, he believed this offered the best prospects for a rapid German victory in the west.[22] However, the time was not yet ripe for such a plan. Schlieffen did not feel that the strength of the German army was great enough to conduct three simultaneous offensives, while at the same time sending forces to the east.[23]

Instead, Schlieffen concluded that there were two remaining possibilities – either a breakthrough along the Maas between Toul and Verdun or a breakthrough along the Moselle above Épinal. However, the conduct of either was predicated upon the capture of Nancy. Schlieffen wrote: 'If one is in possession of the plateau west of Nancy, it then only depends upon creating difficulties for Fort Pt. St. Vincent [the French fortification south of Nancy] to make the entire stretch of the Moselle above Nancy untenable and thus to spring open the French defensive line.'[24] This attack on Nancy was to be carried out by the centre army (the 2nd) of the *Westheer*, which was to be deployed initially behind the German Nied. Its advance was to be supported by offensives carried out by its neighbouring armies. Additionally, this breakthrough army was to be supported by a special *Fußartillerie* (heavy artillery) force of 120 to 144 guns. How Schlieffen intended to continue operations after the breakthrough was not specified.[25] This frontal attack against the French fortress line was to remain the basis of the German war plan until the turn of the century when new factors prompted Schlieffen to alter it.

Schlieffen's immediate predecessor, Waldersee, reportedly reacted with horror when he learned of Schlieffen's intention to conduct a frontal assault against the French fortress line. 'We are doing', he wrote in his diary, 'exactly what the French have hoped and prepared for.'[26] Indeed, Waldersee was not alone in pointing out the plan's weaknesses. In August 1895, *Generalmajor* Ernst Köpke, one of the General Staff's *Oberquartiermeister*, completed a report on the prospects for an offensive against France. Köpke warned that, although he believed Nancy could be taken, the operation could only be carried out by means of 'a step-by-step, laborious, and bloody working forward – here and there by the means of a formal siege-warfare attack – gradually gaining advantages'. Furthermore, even as Germany developed more powerful artillery, France developed stronger fortifications. He concluded his report with the gloomy prediction: 'war of the future will have a very different face from that of 1870/71. We cannot expect rapid victories of decisive significance.' Instead of the war of movement the German army had been preparing to fight since 1871, Köpke predicted a people's war characterized by position warfare.[27]

With the benefit of hindsight, it is possible to give these warnings greater significance than they might have had at the time.[28] Schlieffen had been aware of the difficulties and the unsatisfactory nature of his planned undertaking before Köpke's report. However, Schlieffen continually found himself in a dilemma created by the strategic situation and his own strategic assumptions. Germany was stuck between its two enemies. To the west lay France with a modern army capable of rapid mobilization. To the east lay the enormous, but backward, Russian army, which would require significant time to mobilize and deploy. To Schlieffen, this seemed to offer the opportunity to achieve that which he believed Germany needed to win a future war – a rapid victory. If France could be beaten before the Russians were ready for offensive operations, German forces could be shifted to the east in time to fight the Russians. However, in order to do this, he needed to defeat the French army decisively, and this meant a battle in the open field. While he hoped that the French army would come out of its fortresses and invade Germany, thus offering the prospects for the crucial rapid, decisive victory, he doubted whether the French would be so obliging. Therefore, as Schlieffen believed a rapid victory was essential in the west, he was forced to plan for a German offensive to bring about such a victory.

Thus, even before Köpke's damning report, Schlieffen was taking steps to rectify the situation. Immediately after his decision to attack Nancy, Schlieffen began pushing for the creation of mobile *Fußartillerie* batteries to be used with the field army in its attack on the French fortified line. Prior to this date only a limited number of *Fußartillerie* batteries had been capable of operating with the field army. In cooperation with the Inspector-General of *Fußartillerie*, *General der Artillerie* Elder von der Planitz, and with the personal intervention of the Kaiser, in 1896, Schlieffen was successful in overcoming the objections of the corps commanders and in gaining approval for the creation of a mobile 15cm howitzer battalion in each army corps. Moreover, the numbers of very heavy batteries (21cm and above) were increased.[29] Schlieffen hoped that these heavy guns would provide the concentrated firepower needed to break through France's fortifications quickly.

It must also be remembered that the attack on Nancy was not Schlieffen's preferred option. His 1894 memorandum had expressed the belief that an envelopment around the north of Verdun offered the best prospects for success. Schlieffen had only ruled out this option due to lack of sufficient manpower. In addition to pushing for increased heavy artillery, the General Staff Chief also worked hard to increase the strength of the German army and to rectify this deficiency. The army had been strengthened with the Army Bill of 1893. The time recruits spent on active duty was cut from three to two years, thus raising the numbers available during wartime. However, as a means of introducing these increased numbers into the ranks, each of the 173 infantry regiments stood up a half battalion of two companies. These half battalions were to take over a good deal of the training normally done in the full-strength battalions.[30] However, these rapidly proved themselves to be unworkable and Schlieffen, among others, pushed for their amalgamation into full-strength units. Schlieffen hoped to convince the Minister of War, Heinrich von Goßler, to agree to form additional army corps, the manoeuvre units he needed to conduct a war against France offensively, from the new units thus created. He was unable to gain approval for the creation of new peacetime corps, but in 1896 was able to get Goßler to agree that from 1898, five new army corps would be formed from excess units upon the outbreak of war. Schlieffen would have to make do with a total of 25 active army corps in his wartime army, five of which would be formed only at the beginning of a war.[31]

Still not convinced that the French would begin a future war with an offensive and uneasy about the prospects of a breakthrough along the French fortress line, with more heavy artillery and units becoming available, Schlieffen soon began to examine other possibilities for a German offensive against France. In a memorandum of August 1897, he returned to the idea of a manoeuvre around the French fortifications to the north. He wrote:

> The circumstances north of Verdun are the most favourable. The Maas will certainly be occupied, but not with considerable strength. Here, at least the right wing is free and there is the possibility of crossing the river by means of an envelopment. If this is successful, one can direct one's march against the rearward communications of the enemy and thus force the French army away from Paris.[32]

However, Schlieffen still felt there were problems with such a course of action. First, the five march routes that existed south of the Belgian border were insufficient for an army of any meaningful size. Therefore, Schlieffen concluded that the advancing army would have to use routes in the south of Belgium as well. In other words, the German army would have to violate Belgian neutrality, a neutrality of which Germany was a guarantor. This, however, was not for Schlieffen the plan's fatal flaw. While the German violation of Belgian neutrality certainly made it easier for the British Cabinet to decide for war in 1914, much subsequent historiography seems to have been coloured by the propaganda of the period.[33] The violation could hardly have shocked the Entente leaders, considering they had discussed the idea and it was openly spoken about in the press.[34] Indeed, the question of using Belgium as a pawn was not new. Only some 30 years before, France under Napoleon III had hatched plans to annex parts of Belgium and all of Luxemburg.[35] Even Bismarck, the master of *Realpolitik*, had enquired whether the German army might not wish to make use of Belgian territory on its way to Paris.[36] Schlieffen had always considered the possibility that the French would invade Germany by the same route.[37] Nevertheless, Schlieffen was well aware that the violation of Belgian territory might bring Britain into the war against Germany.[38] However, given Britain's small and ineffective army at the time, this intervention would be of significance only in a long, protracted war. Schlieffen was clearly determined to prevent such a war and was convinced that the early battles would put an end to the war, one way or the other, quickly. Given the time necessary to assemble troops and cross the Channel, Schlieffen believed the war in the west would be over before British troops even arrived on the Continent.

It was practical military matters, rather than political concerns, that made such a German offensive around the north of the French defensive line impossible. Once again, Germany lacked the necessary troop numbers. By Schlieffen's calculation, Germany would need to deploy against France 25 army corps, two armies formed from reserve divisions, and numerous *Landwehr* units to secure communications, etc., in order for such an operation to have a chance of success. Even with the wartime reinforcement agreed upon with Goßler, this amounted to the entire strength of the field army and left no forces available to defend in the east. As much as Schlieffen would have liked to ignore the war in the east, he could not and, thus, he was forced once again to shelve his plans for outflanking the French and rely upon his earlier plans.[39]

Schlieffen turned in another direction to come up with the troops necessary for an offensive in the west. In late 1896, Schlieffen began pushing for a strengthening of the fortress of Metz. A strengthened fortress of Metz could play a number of roles. In the case of a French invasion, it would split the advancing French forces, thus making easier their defeat in detail. In the case of a German offensive, it could provide a fortified point upon which a German right wing could pivot. Moreover, this fortified hinge would prevent French forces from hitting the advancing wing where it was weakest – its connection with the other German armies. After some debate, Kaiser Wilhelm II finally authorized the construction of a number of modern fortified outer-works on the

INTRODUCTION

left bank of the Moselle on the northwest and southwestern fronts of Metz and the building of some additional works on the southern and eastern fronts of the fortress in March and April 1899.[40]

Moreover, Schlieffen again began to press for additional forces in the run-up to the Army Bill of 1899. The General Staff Chief demanded of the Minister of War seven new army corps in order to carry out his desired war plan. However, in view of the large expenditures on the navy, Goßler was determined to keep costs down, and in the end, only agreed to create three new army corps.[41] These were to be formed by readjusting existing formations and with an increase of only 23,377 new personnel. No amount of argument from Schlieffen could sway the Minister of War, and the Reichstag even forced him to reduce the expansion by some 7,000 men. However, Schlieffen was successful in gaining approval for the creation of five additional army corps upon the outbreak of war, giving him a total of 27 active corps during wartime.[42]

THE CONDITIONAL ENVELOPMENT PLAN

Shortly after beginning construction on the new Metz fortifications, Schlieffen again returned to his idea of a northern envelopment of the French fortifications. This time, perhaps anticipating additional troops that would have been deployed at Metz and additional units formed by the Army Bill of 1899, Schlieffen felt confident enough to incorporate it into German war plans. In a memorandum of October 1898, Schlieffen outlined his ideas for the *Aufmarschplan* of 1899/1900. Indeed, for this year for the first time, two separate plans were devised to deal with various scenarios. *Aufmarschplan I* was designed for a war primarily in the west and *Aufmarschplan II* for a simultaneous war in both the east and west.

There remains some doubt as to when each *Aufmarschpläne* was to be used. *Aufmarschplan II* was to be used in case of a 'simultaneous' attack by Russia and France. However, how 'simultaneous' was defined by Schlieffen is not clear. *Aufmarschplan I* incorporates troops fighting a delaying action in the east, which indicates that Schlieffen believed it could be used even in a two-front war.[43] Given Schlieffen's previous beliefs about the necessity of a rapid victory and that this appeared most likely in the west, it seems probable that he would have instituted *Aufmarschplan I*, with its western bias, if Russia did not attack Germany very soon after a war's outbreak. This unlikely event would have occurred only if political constraints prevented an outbreak of hostilities before the Russians had finished their lengthy mobilization. Regardless, the development of two plans allowed Schlieffen and the

German army a greater degree of flexibility in time of crisis.[44]

Reversing earlier assumptions, in his October 1898 memorandum Schlieffen now felt that the French would take the offensive, since the German deployment would take around four weeks to complete, while the French could complete theirs in two to three weeks. He believed that this French offensive would most likely come through Luxemburg and southern Belgium around the German fortresses of Diedenhofen and Metz. As with all of Schlieffen's plans, the goal of the campaign would be the rapid destruction of the French army. Thus, Schlieffen welcomed a possible French offensive through Luxemburg and Belgium, as it offered the opportunity to attack the French flank and 'detach the whole French army from its fortresses and to push it into the Upper Rhine'.

In case of a French attack, Schlieffen wrote that the armies of the German centre (3rd, 4th and 5th Armies, in total 12 army corps) were to allow the French to attack them. At the same time, the two armies of the German right wing (1st and 2nd Armies, altogether eight army corps) and the 6th Army (three army corps and two reserve divisions) on the left wing were to take in the French in a pincer attack (*Zangenangriff*). The armies of the right wing were to play a special part in the destruction of the French army. Schlieffen wrote, 'We must ... make our right wing strong and extend it as far west as possible. This will not be possible without violating the neutrality of Luxemburg and perhaps Belgium.'[45]

However, in the event that the French did not attack, Schlieffen wrote that the Germans would then have to take the offensive as soon as possible, and once again Schlieffen turned to his idea of a northern envelopment of the fortified Franco-German border, this time 'through Luxemburg, which possesses no army, and through Belgium, which will withdraw its relatively weak army into its fortresses'. However, Schlieffen felt that this envelopment should not extend too far as this wing had a dual role – 'Counterattack if the enemy advanced as soon as his deployment was finished or offensive if he remains standing behind his fortifications.'[46]

Schlieffen ordered that the two armies of the right wing (eight army corps) were to advance across the Maas between Donchery and Stenay and advance around the French fortress front from the north. The advance of the right wing was to be covered by a 7th Army formed from six reserve divisions on the right and the 3rd Army on the left. The 3rd Army (four army corps and two reserve divisions) was to follow across the Maas later. The 4th and 5th Armies (eight army corps), which had deployed between Saarbrücken and Saarburg were to advance against Nancy and, if possible, 'seize the position east of this city as well as the forts Frouard and Pt. St. Vincent'. These two armies were then to

INTRODUCTION

advance through the gap in the French front between Nancy/Toul and Épinal. The left wing army, the 6th, along with the forces mobilized in Upper Alsace (in total four army corps and six reserve divisions) had the task of covering the left flank of the German advance.[47]

This rather shallow and relatively weak envelopment corresponded to where the General Staff believed it would find the French army. In 1899, Plan XIV determined the deployment of the French army in case of war with Germany. It called for the French army to deploy in five armies along the Franco-German border. The 1st Army was to form the vanguard and was to deploy around Nancy, the 2nd was to be centred around Épinal, the 3rd from Mirecourt to Neufchâteau to Damblain, the 4th from Gondrecourt to Commercy to St Dizier, and the 5th behind the 3rd and 4th from Chaumont to Joinville. Additionally, three groups of reserve divisions were to deploy on both flanks and behind the main army. In all, the French would deploy 19 army corps and 12 reserve divisions against Germany.[48]

Despite getting some of the details wrong, the German General Staff had a fairly good picture of the deployments envisioned by Plan XIV thanks to agents in France. On 1 April 1898, the German Military Attaché in Paris was able to send to the 3rd Section of the General Staff, the section that had responsibility over intelligence against France, the mobilization plan for Plan XIV.[49] This intelligence arrived in time for the writing of Schlieffen's memorandum outlining how the German army would be employed in case of war in 1899 and had a clear influence over the formulation of Schlieffen's plan for his enveloping wing. A French army concentrated along the border and with no real cover along its left flank, meant the German envelopment from the north would not have to extend far westward or be as strong as later.

In the east, the weak German forces were to fight a delaying action until they could be reinforced from the *Westheer*. Schlieffen wrote:

> the more the days and weeks pass from the 1st mobilization day, the nearer come the Russians to our borders, and perhaps even reach the Vistula. With every day, the situation in the east becomes more doubtful and the necessity to intervene there with stronger forces, thus weakening the west, makes itself felt more and more.[50]

If necessary, wrote Schlieffen, the *Ostheer*

> must retreat behind the Vistula, and in such a retreat, one is better weak than strong. Everything depends upon fighting a decisive victory in the west – if this is successful, so one will see that which has been lost in the east won back again.[51]

ALFRED VON SCHLIEFFEN'S MILITARY WRITINGS
THE ENVELOPMENT PLAN

The two *Aufmarschpläne* developed in 1899/1900 would serve, with some minor modifications, as the German war plans until Schlieffen's retirement in January 1906. However, it seems that Schlieffen was not satisfied that they would result in the rapid, decisive victory he felt Germany required of any future war. Thus, shortly before his retirement, Schlieffen undertook a complete reappraisal of his plans. The year 1905, Schlieffen's last as Chief of the General Staff, saw an increase in both the number and complexity of wargames carried out under his direction, all of which were clearly designed to test various scenarios and different possible war plans.[52] In the early months of the year, Schlieffen carried out a *Kriegsspiel* covering a possible war in the east in which the numbers of German forces were very inferior to those of the Russians. This game tested three scenarios for a Russian invasion of eastern Germany – one covered a Russian invasion by two armies from the Narev and the Niemen Rivers, another with a Niemen Army advancing along both banks of the Vistula, and a third with the entire Russian army assembled at Warsaw for an advance on Berlin.[53]

In the summer of 1905, Schlieffen led a complex staff ride in the west based upon an altered *Aufmarschplan I*, in which he led the German side himself. Although recent commentators have seen no connection,[54] contemporaries of Schlieffen believed this staff ride to be an important test of his future war plan against France, the plan that would become known as the 'Schlieffen Plan'.[55] In this ride, almost the whole German army was deployed against France. Five German armies took up position along a line running from Wesel to Metz. A sixth army stood at Metz–Diedenhofen and a seventh covered Alsace. Schlieffen assumed that the French army, to be led in this ride by his subordinates, would deploy in four armies in the line Belfort–Nancy–Toul–Verdun–Sedan, i.e., further north and east than had been assumed when a German envelopment had been written into war plans in 1898.[56] The General Staff Chief intended to outflank the French army by advancing around their fortifications and thus bring about his desired decisive battle. As French forces were assumed to be deploying further north than in 1898, so the planned German envelopment would also have to be carried out further north. Schlieffen outlined his plan of operation to his subordinates:

> after one has outflanked the [French] position from the north, one faces a new position, a complete fortified system along the Lille–Maubeuge line and behind this La Fère, Laon and Reims. Before one arrives at this line, one must pass Antwerp and one's

advance is split by Liège and Namur. When one has overcome completely these considerable difficulties, one will find the entire French army before one. It is therefore advisable to bring the whole German army, or at least all of the active army corps, on to a line from Brussels to Diedenhofen.

From here, the German plan of operations is self-evident: one must stand firm at Metz–Diedenhofen and wheel left with the entire army, thereby always advancing right in order to win as much territory to the front and to the north as possible and in order to envelop the enemy, wherever he may be. Such a manoeuvre can only be made when the left wing is covered. Metz serves this function, a large Metz with a strong southern front.[57]

Schlieffen selected three different solutions to play out from those offered by his subordinates leading the French army. First, Hugo Freiherr von Freytag-Loringhoven proposed that the French shift their forces further north with their left flank resting on Lille. The main force would attack west of Metz in the direction of Luxemburg–Namur–Brussels. Next, Steuben put forward the plan that the French army would attack between Metz and Strassburg. Finally, Hermann von Kuhl wanted to launch a counterattack against the advancing German army at what he believed to be its most vulnerable point – the pivot at Metz–Diedenhofen. He proposed to send one French force to the west of the Moselle and another to the east. Each of these solutions resulted in the French army being forced away from its base of operations (Paris) and, in its complete defeat, seemingly vindicating Schlieffen's proposed northern envelopment of the French fortress line. However, Schlieffen himself came up with a French response that he believed might upset his plans – the creation of a new army to counter-envelop the right wing of the advancing German army. Indeed, it was just such a solution that the French employed in 1914.[58]

Finally, in November and December, Schlieffen directed a *Kriegsspiel* that tested the German deployment plan in a two-front war. This game differed significantly from his western staff ride of earlier in the year. German forces were split almost evenly between the two fronts, and the initial decision fell in the east. Moreover, German forces remained on the defensive on both fronts, allowing the Russians and French to invade German territory.[59] This game represents Schlieffen's best-case scenario and perhaps also a test of a revised *Aufmarschplan II* – a simultaneous attack by both opponents, a scenario he believed would result in an almost certain German victory. However, given the changed strategic situation in December 1905, it is unlikely that Schlieffen believed this to be the most probable scenario for a war in the coming years. Indeed, he himself stated in his critique of the game that the scenario upon which the game was based was 'unlikely, or better said, impossible'.[60]

Schlieffen conducted his reappraisal of his plans against the backdrop of a major change to Germany's strategic situation. In 1904, war broke out between the empires of Japan and Russia. As the war drew on, Russia began transferring greater and greater numbers of forces to the Far East, stripping its western provinces of the best and most modern troops. By 1905, the strategic situation had changed sufficiently to bring Schlieffen's *Aufmarschplan I*, the deployment of almost the entire German army in the west, undeniably to the fore. He clearly believed that the Russians were unlikely to pose a serious threat for the foreseeable future, writing in June that

> the East Asian war has shown that the Russian army is less competent than had previously been assumed by informed opinion and that the war has worsened the Russian army rather than made it more efficient ... It is very questionable whether or not an improvement will take place. They lack enough self-awareness to carry this out.[61]

The Russian revolution that broke out in 1905 seemed to make any army reform even less likely. Without a serious threat from Russia, Schlieffen could concentrate his forces in the west. In addition to the Russian situation, the construction of the new fortifications around Metz were almost completed that year, releasing additional forces for use elsewhere and adding protection to the German right wing's pivot,[62] and the additional railway capacity needed to carry a strong right wing was becoming available around Aachen and Trier.[63]

Yet, his almost continuous gaming throughout 1905 demonstrates a deep-seated uncertainty about the best way for Germany to conduct a future war, an uncertainty that had plagued him during his entire time as Chief of the General Staff. Clearly, Schlieffen believed his task would be made simpler if the French did him the favour of launching an attack into Germany. However, he had his doubts about whether the French would be so obliging. If they did not conduct such an offensive, then he believed that the Germans would need to conduct their own offensive in order to bring the war to a rapid end.

By 1905, a strong German right wing seemed to offer the best answer to Schlieffen's doubts. It would allow the Germans to retain the initiative in any future war and gave the best prospects for a rapid German victory. Additionally, the General Staff Ride of 1905 had proved that even a French advance into Lorraine could be defeated by

INTRODUCTION

a strong German right wing. However, even this scenario looked highly unlikely in 1905. In August, the 3rd Section of the General Staff produced a report that would reinforce a German envelopment plan. They believed that the Russo-Japanese War had made Russian intervention in a war against Germany unlikely and that this made a French offensive impossible. Further, they believed that the French anticipated a German offensive around the north of their fortifications. The 3rd Section concluded that the French would deploy their forces further north than previously in order to meet defensively the expected German offensive.[64] This supposed northern shift in the mass of the French forces clearly called for a shift in the mass of the German army, further reinforcing Schlieffen's decision to form a powerful right wing.

With all this in mind, in late 1905 and early 1906, Schlieffen wrote a memorandum that was to serve as the outline for a future *Aufmarschplan I* to be completed under his successor's direction. It called for almost the entire German army to be deployed in the west and for a powerful right wing that was to advance around the French fortifications to the north through not only Belgium and Luxemburg, but also the Netherlands, in an attempt to attack the French army in the rear. As in all his plans, Schlieffen aimed at forcing his enemy off balance and away from his sources of supply and thus to facilitate his destruction. He hoped that the French army could be forced away from Paris and against the Swiss border, much like Moltke the Elder had forced the Army of Châlons away from Paris against the Belgian border 35 years earlier. In case this did not happen, Schlieffen made provision for a possible siege of the fortress of Paris, but clearly hoped that such an operation would not have to take place.[65] At last, Schlieffen's long-desired envelopment plan had become a reality.

CONCLUSION

Throughout his 15 years as Chief of the General Staff, Schlieffen wrestled with the difficulty of fighting a two-front war against enemies overwhelmingly superior in numbers. Bounded by this strategic reality and his belief that Germany could only win a short war, he was forced to seek a decisive victory in the early days of any future war. For Schlieffen, Germany's position between its two enemies, one of whom would take much longer to mobilize than either Germany or its ally, offered a tantalizing prospect for success. If France, who would put its army into the field several weeks before its Russian ally, could be defeated rapidly, there was the possibility that Germany would be able to transfer her army to the east in time to meet the ponderous Russian bear. However, this rapid victory against the French would not be so easily accomplished. If France attacked Germany shortly after the beginning of hostilities, Schlieffen believed the prospects good. If France did not attack, as Schlieffen feared from 1891 to 1898 and then again in 1905, how was this rapid, decisive battle to be fought?

It is clear from his memoranda that, shortly after he began exploring an offensive in the west in 1892, Schlieffen wanted to bring the battle to the French by outflanking their fortress line from the north. Such an attack would make a lengthy, bloody breakthrough of the French fortress line unnecessary, would hit the French in their rear, their most vulnerable point, and perhaps best of all, would enable the Germans to maintain the initiative. In 1894, when Schlieffen first examined such an attack, the German army lacked the necessary manpower. However, the lure of a German envelopment of the French fortress line was too great for Schlieffen to resist and he continually came back to it in his memoranda and continually worked to raise the German army to the level where it could carry out such an offensive while maintaining enough troops to resist in the east.

Although the idea entered into his war plans in 1899, it was only on the eve of his retirement that the conditions were right for such an envelopment manoeuvre to become the prime element of the German war plan. The Russian enemy had been neutralized, the German forces available to conduct the envelopment had increased in size, and international politics ensured that the French army would remain on the defensive. Thus, in late 1905, Schlieffen began work on the memorandum that would become known as the 'Schlieffen Plan'. It called for a war against France to begin with a powerful German right wing sweeping around the fortified Franco-German border. This would take the French army in the rear and force it to fight a battle on unfavourable terms. The French army would be cut off from its base in the heart of France and defeated decisively. The basic features of this plan would serve as Moltke the Younger's operation plan in 1914 and would ultimately fail the Germans disastrously, as the French counter-enveloped the German right wing before it could bring about the decisive encounter Schlieffen hoped it would.[66]

11

Reports on the Russian Army, 1905

European observers paid close attention to the Russo-Japanese War taking place in the Far East during 1904 and 1905, and none paid closer attention than Russia's potential enemies, Germany and Austria-Hungary. The two reports below cast an interesting light on the conclusions of the German military, and in particular conclusions drawn by Schlieffen, regarding the state of the Russian army in the summer of 1905,[1] i.e., at the height of the First Moroccan Crisis.[2] Moreover, they are important to understanding the development of Schlieffen's war plan for 1906/7, the so-called 'Schlieffen Plan'. They set out clearly Schlieffen's belief that the Russian army would be a negligible force for the foreseeable future. With Russia unable to intervene effectively in Europe, Germany could safely concentrate the bulk of its military strength against France.

Berlin, NW 40
Moltkestrasse No. 8

10 June 1905

Chief of the General Staff of the Army
No. 471 Secret

To His Highness, the Chancellor,
 Fürst von Bülow

I have the honour of respectfully responding to Your Highness' letter of the 4th of this month.

Russia will, once peace has been concluded with Japan, return its army corps and divisions from the far east, and in the space of about six months, its army's strength in European Russia can be at the pre-war level once again. It will take rather more time to make good their expenditure of munitions and to refurbish their weapons and artillery. But in a short space of time, the Russian army, at least outwardly, will be refitted. However, inwardly there will still be differences.

For a long time, it was known that the Russian army possessed no significant leaders, that the majority of its officers were of limited value, and that the training of the troops could only be seen as insufficient. On the other hand, the individual Russian soldier was seen as one of the best in the world. His unquestioning obedience, his infinite patience, his quiet contempt for death were all recognized as inestimable characteristics.

Now, however, the experience of the war in the Far East has shaken greatly our belief in these characteristics. The Russian soldier's obedience proved not to be so blind. Many cases have come to light in which the officers did not command their troops, but rather begged, debated and entreated with them. In other cases, the troops resisted and turned against their superiors in the most insolent way. The authority of the Russian officers and the obedience of their troops are very questionable. Moreover, the Russian troops did not display their famous stoicism. In the Manchurian campaign, panic often broke out. The troops did not hold out until the very end. The war has shown that the famous Russian obedience was based less on attention to duty and a feeling of honour [*Pflichttreue und Ehregefühl*] than on dullness and a fatalistic resignation [*Stumpfsinn und fatalischische Resignation*]. Further, it has shown also that the inherited characteristics of the Slavic race last only so long, but then they degenerate into brutality.

Above all, the Russian soldier is not properly trained. He does not understand how to fire and manoeuvre in battle. In earlier times, one could still do something with brave but poorly schooled troops. Today, however, improvements in weapons require a soldier to possess careful and thorough training. Since the Russian soldiers did not receive this, they are not up to the standards of other armies and are altogether unfit for the offensive.

In short, the East Asian war has shown that the Russian army is less competent than had been assumed previously by informed opinion and that the war has worsened the Russian army rather than made it more efficient. It has lost all complaisance [*Freudigkeit*], all confidence [*Vertrauen*] and all obedience.

It is very questionable whether or not an improvement will take place. The Russians lack enough self-awareness [*Selbsterkenntnis*] to carry this out. They see the origins of their defeat not in their own imperfections [*Unvollkommenheiten*], but rather in the enemy's superiority in numbers and in the ineffectiveness of particular commanders.

The Russian army lacks the men capable of carrying out the required reforms and who possess the necessary moral fortitude.

Therefore, recent history would suggest that the Russian army will not improve, but instead will grow more ineffective. The current internal conditions of our great neighbouring empire will surely not help, but rather add to this development.[3]

This is not to say that Russia will refrain from becoming involved in all military entanglements in Europe. The desire to restore Russia to its former glory after the defeat suffered in East Asia through a cheap victory may well arise, and such a path could offer a way out of their internal difficulties.

Signed,
Graf Schlieffen.

Berlin, NW
Moltkestrasse No. 8

18 August 1905

Chief of the General Staff of the Army
No. 8353Z

To His Highness, the Chancellor,
Fürst von Bülow

Russia has made the greatest exertions to date to raise its forces in Manchuria to a respectable level. Already after the battle of Mukden, it had sent 212,000 men to East Asia, creating an army there of around 400,000. Now the IX and XIX Army Corps have been sent there and the XIII and XXI Army Corps are to follow immediately. This will bring the Russian strength in East Asia to about 512,000 men. They can be faced by approximately 420,000 Japanese.

To date, Russia has sent to, or made available for service in, East Asia ten of its 26 European army corps, six of its 38 reserve divisions, five of its eight rifle brigades.

There remains in European Russia only:
Guard Corps (St Petersburg)
Grenadier Corps (Moscow)
XXII Army Corps (Finland)
VII Army Corps (Crimea)

the two army corps in the Caucasus
the corps stationed on the Prussian and Austrian borders.

Moreover, the units remaining in European Russia have given up a great deal of personnel and equipment. They have lost the following percentages of their officers:

Infantry – 32.4 per cent
Cavalry – 16.1 per cent
Artillery – 20.4 per cent
Technical troops – 36.5 per cent.

The units had to surrender good commanders and long-serving personnel. These were replaced by recruits and reservists. Modern, rapid-fire artillery was taken from the corps which possessed it. Further, 28 per cent of the fortress and siege artillery and 60 per cent of the sapper battalions are being employed in East Asia.

In addition to great numbers of troops, considerable portions of the mobilization stores of the European artillery, engineer and munitions depots have been taken.

The above represents not only a great weakening of the Russian strength in Europe in terms of numbers and value, but also a great weakening of the army's organization.

Signed,
Graf Schlieffen

12

Memorandum of 1905: The Schlieffen Plan

What follows is the text of what has become known, somewhat misleadingly, as the 'Schlieffen Plan'. In fact, it was written by Schlieffen in late 1905 and early 1906 to serve as an outline for his successor's subordinates to follow when drawing up the detailed Aufmarsch- *and* Mobilmachungspläne, *and thus is not itself an operations order or final plan. Indeed, Schlieffen's successor, Helmuth von Moltke the Younger, accepted the memorandum's broad ideas – a German offensive against France by means of a powerful right wing that outflanked the French fortifications – and these ultimately served as the basic concepts behind the German plan of operations in 1914.*[1]

December 1905
Berlin

WAR AGAINST FRANCE

In a war against Germany, France will in all probability limit itself initially to the defensive, especially if it cannot depend on effective support from Russia. To this end, France has long prepared a defensive line, for the most part permanent, in which the fortresses of Belfort, Épinal, Toul and Verdun are the main strong points [Hauptstützpunkte]. This line can be sufficiently occupied by the powerful French army, and it offers great difficulties to the attacker.[2]

This attack will not be directed against the large fortresses, whose conquest requires a great siege apparatus [Belagerungsapparat], much time and much strength, especially as a complete encirclement is impossible and the siege can only be conducted from one side. The attacker will prefer to advance in the gaps between the fortresses. Two of these (Belfort–Épinal and Toul–Verdun) are filled with blocking forts [Sperrforts], which are, however, of limited value. More importantly,

Nature has already built strong positions within the gaps, in which sector lies behind sector. Additionally, the fortresses on the wings of the gaps hinder the attacker from carrying out an enveloping manoeuvre and at the same time threaten the attacker's flanks.[3]

The greatest chance of success is offered by an attack on the right wing of the Moselle front (Fort Ballon de Servance). However, we are not adequately prepared to overcome the difficult terrain found here. Moreover, even if we were able to do this, one would hardly wish to open the campaign with a siege of Ballon de Severance. In a later period of the war the capture of this fort might be of importance.

An attack against Nancy, which is mainly protected by field fortifications [*Feldbefestigungen*] and which is easily enveloped and bombarded, offers another prospect for success. However, once the city and the heights lying beyond the city are taken (Forêt de Naye), one finds oneself faced by the fortifications of Toul. Almost the only advantage offered by an attack against Nancy is that the French, in order to save the capital city of Lorraine, might be induced to come out of their fortifications and to fight a battle in the open field [*Feldschlacht*]. None the less, they would then have their defensive lines so close behind them that a defeat would harm them little and would bring the victor no great success. It would amount to a sortie from a fortress, which would result in about the same number of casualties for the besieger as for the defender and would leave the situation of both unaltered.[4]

Thus, a frontal attack against the Belfort–Verdun line offers little chance of success. An envelopment from the south requires a successful campaign against the Swiss and the reduction of the Jura forts – time-consuming undertakings during which the French would not remain idle.[5]

To prevent an envelopment from the north, the French intend to occupy the Meuse between Verdun and Mézières. However, contrary to what is said, they intend to offer the real resistance not here, but beyond the Aisne somewhere between St Menhould and Rethel. A intermediate position behind the Aire appears also to be under consideration. If the German envelopment reaches out even further, it will knock against a strong line of heights, the strong points of which are formed by the fortresses of Reims, Laon and La Fère.

Therefore, the Germans find before them:
(1) The line Belfort–Épinal–Toul–Verdun, with a continuation along the Meuse to Mézières – screening troops are pushed out to the Vosges, to the Meurthe River, to Nancy and to the Côtes Lorraines between Toul and Verdun
(2) The intermediate line an the Aire River
(3) The line on the Aisne
(4) The line Reims–La Fère.

THE SCHLIEFFEN PLAN

One would attack these positions with little confidence. An attack from the northwest directed against the flanks at Mézières, Rethel, La Fère and across the Oise against the rear of the line appears more promising than a frontal attack with an envelopment of the left wing. For this to succeed, the Franco-Belgian border on the left bank of the Meuse, with the fortified areas of Hirson, Maubeuge, three small blocking forts, Lille and Dunkirk, has to be taken. To accomplish this, the neutrality of Luxemburg, Belgium and the Netherlands has to be violated.

The violation of the neutrality of Luxemburg will have no important consequences other than protests. The Netherlands sees in an England allied with France no less of an enemy than does Germany. An agreement with them will be possible to achieve.[6]

Belgium will probably offer resistance. Its army[7] will, according to plan, withdraw to Antwerp in the event of a German advance north of the Meuse. It must be shut up there, and if possible the Schelde should also be blocked, cutting connections with the sea and with England.[8] Observation will be sufficient for Liège and Namur, which should only be weakly garrisoned. The citadel of Huy will be taken or be rendered harmless.[9]

If the Germans make a covered advance against Antwerp, Liège and Namur, they will find themselves up against a fortified border. However, this border is not as extensively and thoroughly fortified as that opposite Germany. If the French want to defend it, they will have to transfer corps and armies from the original front to the threatened front and replace them with reserves (for example, corps from the Alpine border). Hopefully, they will not be overly successful in this. Therefore, they might perhaps give up the attempt to occupy such an overextended line and instead take the offensive against the threatening invasion with all the troops they can muster. Whether they attack or defend, it is not improbable that it will come to encounter and to battle near the frontier close to the Mézières–Dunkirk line. It is the task of the Germans to be as strong as possible for this battle. Even if this battle should not take place and the French remain behind the Aisne, a strong German right wing would be of the greatest possible value for further operations.[10]

If one wants to attack the left flanks of the French positions at Mézières, Rethel and La Fère and from there take the French from the rear, it seems desirable to advance exclusively on the left bank of the Meuse through Belgium, to wheel left beyond Namur and then to deploy for the attack. However, there are too few roads and still fewer railways to bring the units into formation for such a narrow front. The limitations imposed by the railroads oblige a deployment of the German army mainly on the line Metz–Wesel. Here, 23 army corps, 12½ reserve corps and six cavalry divisions are to be assembled in order to advance immediately in a left wheel against the line Verdun–Dunkirk. The reserve corps of the northern wing will cover the right flank, chiefly against Antwerp, and the reserve corps of the southern wing will cover the left flank against an enemy advance on the left bank of the Moselle from the Toul–Verdun line. Therefore, the attack will not be directed exclusively against the flanks, but also against the left portion of the enemy's front.

Three and a half army corps and one and a half reserve corps will remain to the right of the Moselle. Initially, they are to draw as much French strength as possible on to them by means of an attack on Nancy and thus prevent the French from reinforcing their northern front. Later, however, they will cooperate in covering the army's left flank or in reinforcing the right flank.

Metz will form the strongpoint covering the left flank. Not the Metz of today and also not the Metz as it would be strengthened in the latest projects, but rather a Metz fortified largely through field fortifications, whose course will for the most part be determined by the course of the Moselle, the Saar and the Nied. It will receive a strong garrison force and *Landwehr* units reinforced by large numbers of heavy artillery, which will enable it to draw a considerable portion of the enemy's strength upon itself.

If possible, the German army's victory [*Schlachterfolg*] will be obtained through an envelopment with the right wing. Therefore, this will be made as strong as possible. For this purpose, eight army corps and five cavalry divisions will cross the Moselle along five routes below Liège and advance in the direction of Brussels–Namur. A ninth army corps (the XVIII) will join them after crossing the Meuse above Liège. To accomplish this, the XVIII Army Corps must make the Citadel of Huy untenable, as this covers the area where the XVIII Army Corps must cross the Meuse.

These nine corps will be followed by seven reserve corps, most of which are intended for the investment of Antwerp, while the remainder will initially give additional cover to the right flank. Moreover, there still remains the possibility of a reinforcement by the two army corps remaining on the right bank of the Moselle, which can be brought up by rail (German and Belgian) as soon as the lines are free and returned to service. They could bring the decision.

Six army corps and one cavalry division, followed by one reserve division will be set in march against the stretch of the Meuse between Mézières and Namur. Once they have crossed the river, between 15 and 17 army corps will have assembled left of the Meuse.

THE SCHLIEFFEN PLAN

Eight army corps and two cavalry divisions will advance against the Meuse front between Mézières and Verdun. Five reserve corps, leaning on Metz, will take over the protection of the left flank.

Ten *Landwehr* brigades will follow them north of the Meuse and another six south of the river; six will be in the war garrison of Metz, three and a half on the Upper Rhine and one in Lower Alsace.

It can be assumed that the deployment [*Aufmarsch*] of the German army will be completed undisturbed. At the most, it might be necessary to unload the reserve corps of the far left wing further back, instead of on or behind the Saar above Saarbrücken as planned. It will also be possible to start the advance of the whole army left of the Moselle according to plan. However, whether the French army will come out to meet us on the left or the right or on both sides of the Meuse, or whether and where it will merely await our attack is completely uncertain. Regardless, it is important that the defile between Brussels and Namur north of the Meuse is passed *before* a clash with the opponent, so that the deployment [*Entwicklung*] of the nine army corps can take place without interruption. Therefore, it is essential that the advance of the German right wing be accelerated as much as possible. Since a left wheel [*Linksschwenkung*] has to take place, the advance of the remaining parts of the army will slow down progressively toward the left.

The German armies advancing on the right bank of the Meuse have to be aware that a clash with the enemy on their side of the river could take place any day. At all times, it must be possible to form a front that is at least strong enough to fend off even a superior opponent. This will be made more difficult by a number of factors: by the fortresses of Longwy and Montmédy, which must be taken if possible or at least neutralized; by the wooded mountains that run across the land south of the Semois; and by the extensive forested area north of this river. It is necessary for the army commanders to be continually on the alert and distribute the march routes carefully. As the daily march distances need only be short, this task will be made easier. The troops can only fulfil their task if they are trained for movement [*Bewegung*] and for battle in woods and mountains.

When the Germans have broken through the French fortress belt left of the Meuse, be it after a successful battle on Belgian soil, after a successful assault against the fortified position, or without meeting serious resistance, they will, according to plan, turn against the left flanks of the French positions at Mézières, Rethal and La Fère. The forward position on the Meuse between Mézières and Verdun will likely be evacuated early. The French also will not wait passively in their positions on the Aisne and between Reims and La Fère for the German attack on their left flank. They will either seek a new position or make a counterattack.

The latter is the best for us. Provided that the two army corps from the right bank of the Meuse have been brought up, the Germans will have united their forces as much as allowed by prevailing circumstances. They will march in closed formation. Their left wing [will be] covered as much as possible. Their right wing [will be] strong. It is possible that the French, who first have to assemble their corps, will not be in good order. The position into which they will have been brought by the German envelopment through Belgium will have forced them to take hasty actions and more or less unjustified detachments. Once the Belgian and French fortresses of the northern border and the unfavourable terrain of the Ardennes have been overcome, the German situation has to be seen as more favourable. The German situation will be less favourable if the French await their opponent's attack in a prepared position or from behind a river line.

It would not be impossible for an army defeated in southern Belgium or in northern France to halt behind the Somme, which is connected with the Oise by a canal at La Fère, and offer renewed resistance. This would lead to a march by the German right wing on Amiens or even on Abbeville.

However, this is not very likely. The German advance against the stretch of the Meuse between Verdun and Mézières and further west in the direction beyond Hirson will bind the French in their positions behind the Aisne and between Reims and La Fère. However, these positions are untenable if the Germans advance directly against their left flank and rear from the direction of Lille–Maubeuge. The French have to cover this flank or they have to retreat behind the Marne or the Seine. They will do the latter only unwillingly. They will hardly decide to surrender northern France without a tough fight. Therefore, if they do not rescue their honour through a counteroffensive, they will probably prefer to form a defensive flank behind the Oise between La Fère and Paris rather than give up a great, rich country, their beautiful fortresses and the northern front of Paris. One can hardly say that it is impossible to take up a position behind the Oise. Since the main position Belfort–Verdun needs only to be weakly occupied, the available forces will suffice for the defence of the Aisne and the Oise. The position behind the Oise may not be very strong in front, but it rests its left flank on the colossal fortress of Paris. Even if it is overcome in front, even if the defender withdraws behind the Marne or the Seine, the victor must still submit to the necessity of investing Paris, first on the northern front and then on the other fronts, and is forced to continue the attack with considerably weakened strength against a numerically superior foe. To force the French out of their new position, he will turn the left flank, which rests on Paris, and thereby have again to use strong

THE SCHLIEFFEN PLAN

forces for the investment of the western and southern fronts of the gigantic fortress.

One thing is clear. If the French do not do us the good service of attacking, we will have to advance against the Aisne, Reims–La Fère and the Oise, and we will be forced, regardless of whether or not our enemies hold the Aisne–Oise position or whether they retreat behind the Marne or the Seine, etc., to pursue them with a part of our army and with another to go around Paris and invest this fortress. Therefore, we would be well advised to prepare for a timely crossing of the Seine below its juncture with the Oise and for the investment of Paris initially on its western and southern fronts.

However we may make these preparations, we will conclude that we are too weak to continue the operations along these lines. We will find the experience of all earlier conquerors confirmed – a war of attack [*Angriffskrieg*] demands and consumes a great deal of strength, and this strength diminishes constantly as the defender's increases. This is made worse by a land blocked by fortresses. The active army corps must be left intact for battle and should not be used for duties on the lines of communication [*Etappendienst*] or for investments and sieges [*Belagerung und Einschließung*] of fortresses.

When the Germans have reached the Oise, their supply area [*Etappengebiet*] will extend on the right to the sea coast and to the Seine below Paris. In front, it will be bounded by the Oise and the Aisne as far as the Meuse below Verdun. The course of the boundary from there to the Rhine depends upon what progress the French may have made on the right bank of the Moselle. The supply area comprises Luxemburg, Belgium, a portion of the Netherlands and northern France. In this wide area, numerous fortresses have to be besieged, invested or observed. For this task, the seven and a half reserve corps and the 16 *Landwehr* brigades will be used, with the exception, at most, of the two and a half reserve corps and two *Landwehr* brigades that are urgently needed for the reinforcement of the front and the covering of the flanks and rear of the main army.

(Under no circumstances is it possible to leave an army behind to cover against a landing at Dunkirk, Calais, Boulogne, etc. If the English land and advance, the Germans will halt, defend themselves if necessary, detach a sufficient number of corps to defeat the English, and then continue the operations against the French again.)[11]

It is calculated:

> For the investment of Antwerp – five reserve corps (perhaps not enough)
> For the observation of:
> Liège – two *Landwehr* brigades

Namur – two *Landwehr* brigades
Maubeuge – two *Landwehr* brigades
Lille – three *Landwehr* brigades
Dunkirk – three *Landwehr* brigades
Mézières, Givet and Hirson – one *Landwehr* brigade
Longwy and Montmédy – one *Landwehr* brigade.

However, the railways necessary for the supply of the army also have to be secured, and the large cities, the populous industrial provinces of Belgium, and the northwest of France have to be occupied. The whole area has to offer the army a secure base. For this, the *Landsturm* will be deployed. If the law is against this step, then the law must be altered as soon as possible after the beginning of mobilization.

Still more forces must be raised. We have as many *Ersatz* battalions as infantry regiments. From them and from the still available reserve personnel, and if necessary also from the *Landwehr*, fourth battalions must be formed, as in 1866, and from these and from the *Ersatz* batteries, divisions and army corps must be formed, again as in 1866.[12] In this way, eight army corps can be created. This reorganization should not be left until after the offensive has been taken when the need has become painfully apparent or when the operations are forced to a standstill, but rather immediately upon the completion of the mobilization of the other units.

Therefore, we have to make the *Landsturm* mobile enough to occupy the whole lines of communication area from Belfort to Maastricht, etc. We must pull out the *Landwehr* which have remained in the fortresses, and further we must form at least eight army corps. That is the very least that we are bound to do. We have invented universal conscription and the 'nation in arms' and have taught other nations the necessity of introducing these institutions. However, after having brought our sworn enemies to the point of increasing their armies out of all measure, we have slackened our own efforts. We boast of the great size of our population, of the millions who stand ready for our orders, but these millions are not trained or armed to the full number of able-bodied men they could yield. The fact that France with 39 million inhabitants fields 995 battalions in its active army [*Feldheer*], but Germany with 56 million fields only 971, speaks for itself.

The eight army corps are absolutely needed in or behind the army's right wing. How many can be brought up there depends upon the capacity of the railways. Those that cannot be brought up on the left of the Meuse and Sambre through Belgium and northern France, must be brought south of Liège–Namur on the Meuse between Verdun and Mézières. If this is not entirely possible, the remainder can be used according to need at Metz and on the right of the Moselle.

One must be able to count on there being available for the advance against the position Aisne–Oise–Paris, etc.

Army corps 25

Reserve corps 2½

Newly formed corps 6
_____

33½ corps

More than one third of these are necessary for the envelopment of Paris – seven corps for the actual envelopment and six of the new corps for the investment of Paris on the western and southern fronts. How the advance against and the attack on the position are planned is shown on Map 3 [not reproduced here].

If the enemy makes a stand, then the attack takes place on the whole line, especially though against La Fère, which is invested from two sides, and after a success against Reims, which is open towards the west. Across the whole line, the corps will seek to advance, as in a siege war [*Belagerungskrieg*], from position to position, by day and by night, advancing, digging in, advancing again, and digging in again, etc., and use every means of modern technology to dislodge the enemy from behind his cover. The attack must never come to a standstill as happened in the East Asian War.

France must be regarded as a large fortress. Of the outermost *enceinte*, the Belfort–Verdun section is almost impregnable. However, the Mézières–Maubeuge–Lille–Dunkirk section is only fortified in parts, and almost completely unoccupied. Here, we must attempt to break into the fortress. When we are successful in this, a second *enceinte*, or at least part of it, will become apparent – the position behind the Aisne from Reims to La Fère. However, this *enceinte* can be enveloped from the north. The builder of this fortress had anticipated a German attack from south of the Meuse–Sambre line, but not one from north of this river line. Any attempt to remedy this deficiency by extending the fortified Reims–La Fère line beyond Péronne along the Somme will be too late. The defender can meet the threatening envelopment with an offensive around the left wing of the position at La Fère. This counterattack, which can be accompanied by an advance from the whole front Verdun–La Fère, will hopefully fail. The defeated defender can then attempt to hold the Oise between La Fère and Paris. It is doubtful whether this stretch of the river can be defended. If this doubt is well founded or if the French do not defend the Oise and allow the Germans to cross the river with strong forces, then the second *enceinte* cannot be held. La Fère, Laon and Rheims, which is open to the west, the whole position along the heights designed against an attack from the northeast will be taken, and the Aisne position will have to be vacated. With this, the Meuse forts between Verdun and Toul, which can offer only limited resistance to an attack from the west, will be given up. Verdun and Toul will become isolated fortresses. The whole French fortress system directed against Germany will be threatened with collapse. Therefore, it is not unlikely that the French will seek to hold the Oise position despite all its deficiencies, and that they might be able to offer successful resistance. In this case, Paris has to be enveloped from the south. This will also be necessary if the French evacuate the Oise and the Aisne and retreat behind the Marne, the Seine, etc. If one allows them to proceed in this direction, it will lead to an endless war. Every attempt must be made through attack on their left flank to force the French in an eastern direction against their Moselle fortifications, against the Jura and against Switzerland.

The essential element of the entire operation is a strong right wing, the formation of which will help to win the battles and allow the relentless pursuit of the enemy and bring defeat to him again and again.

If the right wing is to be made very strong, this can only occur at the expense of the left, onto which will probably fall the task of fighting against a superior foe.

If success is to be achieved, the right wing must make great efforts. However, the roads to be used are in general very good. Also, billeting will be satisfactory in the numerous villages unless the corps of the right wing are forced to march so closely together that the densest population is not enough. On the other hand, provisions can hardly fail there. The rich land of Belgium and the rich land of northern France can yield much and they will produce anything they lack under suitable pressure from outside.

The increased claims on their resources will perhaps force the Belgians to refrain from all hostilities, to hand over their fortresses, and thereby reserve for the country all the advantages a third party gains as a bystander in a battle between two opponents.

At the start of the war, three army corps and one reserve corps with three cavalry divisions right of the Moselle will attack Nancy. Whether or not this attack succeeds depends on whether the French limit themselves to the defensive or whether they hold true to their principles and advance to counterattack. If they do the latter, the principal goal of the attack on Nancy – to bind as much French strength as possible on the eastern front – will have been reached. The more troops the French

THE SCHLIEFFEN PLAN

employ for the counterattack, the better it is for the Germans. However, the Germans must not allow themselves to enter into bitter engagements, rather they must recognise that their task is to draw as much French strength after them as possible and bind it with the help of the enlarged fortress of Metz. An army cut off on the right bank of the Moselle can hardly be in any danger. However, this army on the right of the Moselle could grow to be a danger to the main army if it possesses numerical superiority. The endeavour must be to tie down as much French strength as possible with as little German strength as possible.

If the French do not counterattack, two army corps from the outermost wing of the German army have to be transported to Belgium as soon as possible. Everything depends upon being strong on this wing. Only when 25 army corps are made available for the battle on the left of the Moselle – one cannot be strong enough – can one await the decision with calm certainty. The few troops remaining on the right bank of the Moselle, namely

an army corps
a reserve corps
the 30th Reserve Division (Strassburg)
eventually, two new corps
the *Landwehr* brigades on the Upper Rhine and out of Metz, if this is not attacked,
the 59th *Landwehr* Brigade (Lower Alsace)
six *Jäger* battalions in the Vosges,

have to be reinforced as much as possible. The fortress garrisons still offer material for new formations. Also, the south German *Landwehr* can by employed to cover the land left of the Rhine, to mask Belfort, etc. A new army must be formed, whose task will be to advance against the Moselle between Belfort and Nancy, while the five reserve corps of the left wing and two *Landwehr* brigades invest Verdun and attack the Côte Lorraine.

When the French hear during the course of deployment that the Germans are assembling on the Lower Rhine and on the Dutch and Belgian borders, they will have no doubt that the enemy intends to march on Paris and they will be wary of either advancing with all of their strength or with the main portion of their strength between Strassburg and Metz or, particularly, of invading Germany from the Upper Rhine. This would be akin to a garrison leaving the fortress at the moment when the siege is due to begin. If they take either of these courses regardless, it can only be welcome to the Germans. Their task will be thereby made easier. Best for them would be if the French choose to invade southern Germany through Switzerland. This would be one way of gaining a much-needed ally, who would draw a portion of the enemy forces upon himself.

In these cases, it will be advisable for the Germans to alter their operations plan as little as possible. None the less, the Lower Moselle between Trier and Coblenz has to be secured and the sector between the Moselle and the Meuse must be blocked level with the heights of Diedenhofen. The German army will seek to reach the general line Coblenz–La Fère with reserves on the right wing. The right bank of the Rhine from Coblenz upwards will be occupied. The right wing will attack.

If the French march over the Upper Rhine, resistance will be offered in the Black Forest. The troops, brought up from the rear, will assemble on the Main and the Iller.

The Germans can, if they persist in their operations, be sure that the French will quickly turn around, not north but south of Metz, in the direction from which the greatest danger threatens. Therefore, the Germans must be as strong as possible on the right wing, for here the decisive battle [*Entscheidungsschlacht*] is to be expected.

Signed,
Graf Schlieffen

13

Addendum to the Memorandum

Schlieffen's memorandum had concerned itself almost exclusively with a war against France and the French army. In February 1906, he wrote another memorandum to go with his first. This examined the impact of the involvement of British forces in a future war between Germany and France. Schlieffen makes it clear that even if the British were able to mobilize their small expeditionary force before the decisive battle had been fought against the French, he believed their intervention would have little meaningful impact on his plan of operations.[1]

Berlin
February 1906

If, in case of a war between Germany and France, the English should land more than 100,000 men in Antwerp, this can hardly occur in the first days of mobilization. The establishment of their three corps may not yet be well enough advanced, and their army organization and their defence system [Wehrsystem] have so many problems that one can barely conceive of their sudden appearance in the great Belgian fortress. However, even if they do land early on and advance against the Germans from the fortress, they will soon find the few routes that lead to the northern and eastern fronts from Antwerp through the peat bogs of northern Belgium and southern Netherlands occupied by the enemy. If they choose the southern front between the Nethe and the Dyle for the starting point of their attack, they will run into the eight German army corps that have crossed the Meuse below Liège.

As the Germans advance further, one fortress after the other will be sealed off. Every attempt by the combined English and Belgian forces to push back the investing corps will be frustrated by the support that these corps will receive from the advancing German army. Until the left wing army corps has finished the investment on the left bank of the Schelde, a number of German army corps will still remain ready to intervene in the fight [Gefecht].

The terrain before most of the front is not favourable for the development of English and Belgian sallies. They will have to work their way out of the defiles before they can deploy. If the Belgians carry out their intended inundations, the sectors of the fortress zone that favour a sally will be reduced.

If the English want to advance to the attack from Antwerp, they will have to undertake battles as hopeless as the numerous sallies made by the French before Metz and Paris.[2] It is certainly necessary that the corps earmarked for the investment strengthen their positions daily during the advance against the fortress, that they be always ready for an attack, and that they work as closely as possible up to the enemy works, improving their own positions until they are impregnable. The right and left wings will attempt to come as closely as possible together on the Schelde and to close off the fortress' last exit by water by means of artillery and sea mines. The possibility that the English might be shut up next to the Belgians if they enter Antwerp is not unfounded. They will be securely quartered in the fortress, much better than on their island where they represent a stark threat and standing danger to the Germans. The small fortress of Termonde does make the investment of Antwerp somewhat more difficult. None the less, it is neither strong nor in good repair and can at least be made untenable with the help of the heavy artillery of the next corps. Then it will be possible to complete the lines of investment of Antwerp between Termonde and Rugelmonde.

The battle for Antwerp will certainly be more difficult if the French are able to reach the Namur–Antwerp line early and, in cooperation with the English and the Belgians, prevent us from advancing farther on the left of the Meuse. An envelopment with the right wing would then be impossible, and the plan would have to be altered. A combined enemy can also be prevented from advancing north of Namur–Liège. If they want to throw us back, they also have to advance on the right bank of the Meuse, and, in so doing, they cannot help but present their right flank to a German attack. If the French come up at a later point, there is the possibility of a battle in two directions for the Germans, i.e., with one front directed against Antwerp and the other against the Hirson–Maubeuge–Lille line.

According to constantly repeated intentions, the French will advance in thick, deep masses. The saying of the late Field Marshal – a narrow front is in danger of being enveloped, while a broad front promises great results as long as precautions are taken against an enemy breakthrough – will be proved correct.

The English are also said to intend landing not in Antwerp but in Esbjerg. Others say the plan is to appear at an early stage on the coast

ADDENDUM TO THE MEMORANDUM, 1906

of Jutland; others that it is to delay the undertaking until German and French forces are completely engaged. Advantage is to be taken of the completely denuded state of Germany to advance on Berlin, perhaps with the support of some French corps.

In the first case, the Germans would not be able to complete their deployment if an English army arrived in the north while the deployment was in progress. The corps to the rear would have to stop, turn against the new foe, and annihilate him with their overwhelming superiority. The French would not remain passive when they could help their ally – they would give up their fortresses and positions and launch an offensive. Then, we would be faced with all the advantages of which we have convinced ourselves at different times in the event of a war on the left bank of the Rhine.

If the English await a favourable moment for their intended landing, they will hardly find this before the first battle. If this falls to the Germans, the English will probably give up their hopeless undertaking. Therefore, much depends on this battle and it would be a serious mistake if we left behind in expectation of the English an army, a corps or a division upon some distant future theatre of war which could bring a decision against the French.

However, if the English conduct their landing after our deployment is complete, be it before or be it after a battle, we must assemble all the forces remaining in the country, and they will be far from negligible, and crush the invading English. However, an organization of the forces left behind is necessary.[3]

Signed,
Graf Schlieffen

14

Comments by Moltke on the Memorandum, c.1911

Schlieffen's memorandum was left as a guide for his successor as Chief of the General Staff, Helmuth von Moltke the Younger. The following are Moltke's comments on Schlieffen's plan. On balance, Moltke accepts his predecessor's plan of operation, but also recommends some interesting changes, changes that would be reflected in the German advance in 1914. Moltke seems to have less faith in the plan than Schlieffen, and thus makes hints that a future war might not be ended as quickly as might have been hoped.[1]

One can safely assume that the next war will be fought on two fronts. France is our most dangerous enemy and can prepare the fastest. A reckoning with French forces has to come very shortly after deployment. If we are successful in defeating the French quickly and decisively, then troops will be available for use against Russia. I agree with the basic idea of opening the war with a powerful offensive into France while remaining initially on the defensive against Russia. If one desires a rapid decision with France, one cannot direct the attack solely against the strongly fortified eastern front of this country. If the French remain, as expected, on the defensive behind this front, there is no possibility of breaking through it quickly, and even if the breakthrough is successful, the German army, or a part of the army, will be exposed to attack from two sides. In order to find the enemy in the open [*im freien Felde*], the fortified border must be enveloped. This is only possible by way of an advance through Switzerland or through Belgium. The first would have great difficulties and, because of the defence of the mountain roads, would require a long time. However, a successful envelopment of the French fortresses could have the advantage of pushing the French army to the north. An advance through Belgium will push the French back into the heart of their hinterland. None the less, this is preferred, as we can count upon a more rapid advance there and upon the inefficient Belgian army being scattered, unless the Belgian army withdraws into Antwerp without a fight, which then must be sealed off.

COMMENTS BY MOLTKE, c. 1911

Naturally, it is important that the right wing be as strong as possible during an advance through Belgium. However, I cannot agree that, in order to carry out the envelopment, Dutch neutrality as well as Belgian needs to be violated. A hostile Netherlands at our rear could have disastrous consequences for the advance of the German army to the west, especially if England were to use the violation of Belgian neutrality to enter the war against us. If the Netherlands remains neutral, it secures our rear, as England could not violate Dutch neutrality after having declared war on us for a violation of Belgian neutrality – it cannot commit the same violation of the law for which it declares war against us. Moreover, it would be a great value for us to have in the Netherlands a country whose neutrality allows us to have imports and supplies. It must be the windpipe through which we can breathe.

However uncomfortable it is, the advance through Belgium must take place without the violation of Dutch territory. Essentially, this will only be possible when Liège is in our hands. Therefore, this fortress has to be taken immediately. I believe it possible to seize the fortress by a *coup de main*. The forward forts of the fortress are sited so unfavourably that they do not overlook the intervening terrain and cannot dominate it. I have had all the routes of advance that lead through them into the inner city, *which has no ramparts*, reconnoitred.[2] An advance with several columns is possible without them being observed by the forts. If our troops have entered the city, I believe that the forts will not bombard the city, but will likely capitulate. Everything depends upon the most exacting preparations and surprise. The undertaking will only be possible when the attack is made before the terrain between the forts is fortified. Therefore, it has to be launched with standing troops [*mit immobilen Truppen*] immediately after the declaration of war. Military history provides no examples of the taking of a modern fortress by a *coup de main*. However, it can succeed, and must be tried, since the occupation of Liège is the *sine qua non* of our advance. It is a hazardous enterprise [*Wagestück*] the success of which promises great results. In any case, the heaviest artillery has to be held ready to take the fortress should the storming fail. I believe the lack of an inner rampart will allow the fortress to fall into our hands.

The possibility of advancing without entering Dutch territory rests upon the success of the *coup de main*. The deployment of the army must be made accordingly.

(Troops for the *coup de main*, heavy artillery, mobilization preparations.)

Signed,
v.M[oltke].

B[erlin]. 1911

Part III:
THEORETICAL WRITINGS

Introduction

In a speech given on the 100th anniversary of Helmuth von Moltke's birth, Alfred von Schlieffen bemoaned the fact that Moltke had not left behind a substantial work of theory in which he elaborated his ideas about warfare.[1] A hundred years later, a student of Schlieffen could make a similar statement.[2] Like his mentor and unlike many of his contemporaries, Schlieffen never produced a single theoretical work that set out all his ideas about warfare. Instead, his ideas were scattered throughout his service writings and his post-retirement works. However, only the works he published after his retirement in 1905 were available for public consumption until his service papers were published in the interwar period. Thus, these works offer an important insight into the concepts that Schlieffen believed significant enough to continue to stress even after his retirement. Of these, three stand out – his 'War Today', 'Cannae Studies', and 'The *Feldherr*'. These three contain Schlieffen's ideas about Germany's contemporary strategic situation and how modern war would be fought, about how to bring about decisive victories, and about the role and responsibilities of an army's commander.

'WAR TODAY'

Not content to remain inactive after his retirement, Schlieffen turned to the pen to continue to influence the army that had been his life for well over 50 years. The most significant of the works he published after his retirement was undoubtedly his 'War Today'. This relatively short piece gives us the clearest indications of Schlieffen's views about Germany's strategic situation and about how he believed wars would be conducted. As such, it is the closest thing to a single theory of war that Schlieffen published. Moreover, perhaps because it reflected the beliefs of many of his contemporaries, this work was his most influential piece at the time.

Asked by the editors of the *Deutsche Revue* to write an article about the preservation of peace, Schlieffen responded by writing one on modern warfare.³ He began his essay by tracing the current political and military situation in Europe back to the rivalry between France and Germany created by the Franco-German War of 1870/71. To Schlieffen, the events of this war had created a permanent enemy in France. In turn, increasing German prosperity had led to the creation of an Anglo-German rivalry, and German success had led to fear among Germany's other neighbours. Germany's only true ally, in Schlieffen's opinion, was Austria, a fellow German nation. The result of all this was an 'encirclement' of Germany by enemies intent on bringing it and its allies down, a view shared by many, if not most, of Schlieffen's countrymen at the time.

This Franco-German rivalry had also, in Schlieffen's view, led to an arms race that had transformed the modern battlefield. Threatened by the German army, most European nations had introduced conscription. Moreover, each side attempted to outdo the other in technology, leading to the introduction of rapid-fire, long-range weapons with the capability of hitting almost any target on the battlefield. The combination of these two things had a great impact on how battles would be conducted. The lethality of modern weapons had led to the need to disperse on the battlefield, while the increase in the size of armies had led to more troops being available. According to Schlieffen, armies would therefore cover vast areas, and battles would often take place far from one another. Mass armies and modern weapons signalled the end of the days in which a commander could survey and fight his entire army from a convenient hilltop.

Up to this point, Schlieffen was largely reflecting the view of modern war prevailing within the German army at the time. The idea of the extension and the emptiness of the modern battlefield had been discussed since at least the end of the Franco-German War.⁴ However, Schlieffen's vision of how the challenges posed by this situation were to be tackled were unique, and it provides an important insight into how he envisioned his famous plan functioning.

Like most of his contemporaries, Schlieffen rejected the idea that the situation of the modern battlefield had made offensive action impossible.⁵ However, he did see that it changed fundamentally how armies would operate. The *Drill Regulations* of 1888 had introduced the idea that German formations from brigade downwards would fight from the march.⁶ In other words, they would no longer necessarily have the time to deploy into a specific order of battle, but at times would be forced to fight from the march upon encountering the enemy. Schlieffen now took this one step further and applied what had been intended for tactical application to the operational level. The vision of battle he outlined in 'War Today' had army corps, the smallest unit of the German

INTRODUCTION

army capable of supporting itself in independent action, going into battle directly from detrainment or from the march. Given the increased scale of the battlefield, Schlieffen acknowledged that individual corps or groups of corps might fight battles far removed from one another. However, it was the job of the *Feldherr* to give meaning to these disparate battles. It was the *Feldherr*'s role to set the overall goals of a campaign and to determine how these goals would be met:

> The essential task of the one who manages the battle [*Schlachtenlenker*] is fulfilled when, long before any clash with the enemy can come about, he can specify to each army and corps the roads and paths over which and the directions in which they must advance and give to them their general daily goals. The advance to battle begins as soon as the units have left the railway. From the railway stations, the corps and the divisions, some marching quickly, others somewhat more slowly, will seek to reach the place assigned to them by the order of battle [*Schlachtordnung*] ... Concentration for a battle will lose its significance. Those corps which strike at the enemy will have to fight without being able to reckon on further reinforcement.[7]

Thus, in response to the problem of mass armies, Schlieffen came up with a new concept of battle. Schlieffen viewed the clash of two mass armies as one huge battle spread over space and time, in which the smaller battles fought by the army corps, the *Teilschlachten*, would form the tactical encounters of traditional battles. These large numbers of battles that would take place far away from one another as the individual corps or groups of corps came into contact with the enemy would be welded together by the *Feldherr* into a *Gesamtschlacht*, or 'complete battle'. The *Teilschlachten* would be given significance by the *Feldherr*'s plan. Just as a commander of old gave units particular goals on the battlefields of days past, a modern *Feldherr* would give specific goals to his army corps. Each would play a part in the *Feldherr*'s overall plan. In Schlieffen's words: 'The success of battle today depends more on conceptual coherence than on territorial proximity. Thus, one battle might be fought in order to secure victory on another battlefield.'[8] The army corps would, in essence, play the role once assigned to battalions or regiments in traditional battles.

This radical new vision of war was significant to Schlieffen's war plan. Given this vision, his memorandum of 1905 must be seen as a plan for a gigantic battle. Although each individual army corps or army would be given independence to fight how it wanted, it was to be assigned its goals by the *Feldherr*, who might have used different means, but none the less directed the *Gesamtschlacht* as a commander might have directed a battle during the Napoleonic Wars. Schlieffen's plan of 1905 was designed to give structure to what would otherwise have been uncoordinated encounter battles. It was there to ensure that the sum of these battles was more than the sum of the parts.

Although it first appeared in print anonymously in the *Deutsche Revue* in January 1909, Schlieffen's essay had been passing around the higher echelons of the German army for some time before then and, hence, was well known among the Reich's highest military authorities. Schlieffen's successor as Chief of the General Staff, Helmuth von Moltke the Younger, first read a version in early December 1908. Schlieffen next sent a copy to the Minister of War, Karl von Einem, on 12 December. Although Einem thought he should pass the article on to the Chancellor's office for comment before publication, both he and Moltke essentially agreed with the manuscript's ideas and tone.[9] After their comments, Schlieffen next sent his essay to Kaiser Wilhelm II himself, who was so taken with it that he read the article to his corps commanders at a New Year's dinner on 2 January 1909.[10]

Indeed, there was much in Schlieffen's article with which his contemporaries would naturally agree. Moltke spoke for many when he replied to Schlieffen's piece: 'Your excellency's intention to trace and to represent for the German people the position of the Fatherland as it really is and how our security rests only on the strength possessed by our own army has been completely carried out by your words.'[11] Almost everyone in the German army could agree with Schlieffen's assertion that Germany was encircled by nations intent on doing Germany harm. Moltke even went so far as to write that he hoped that Schlieffen's article 'would be read and taken to heart by thousands'.[12] Moreover, Schlieffen's description of the extension and the emptiness of the modern battlefield was firmly in line with the thinking of his contemporaries, and thus found widespread acceptance.[13]

His vision of the conduct of battle, however, drew more criticism. Gottlieb Graf von Haeseler, the long-time commanding general of the XVI Army Corps and one of the *Kaiserheer*'s most respected officers, is reported to have declared of Schlieffen's *Gesamtschlacht* concept: 'You cannot carry away the armed strength of a Great Power like a cat in a bag.'[14] Schlieffen's vision also drew flak from one of Imperial Germany's best known military theorists, Friedrich von Bernhardi.[15] Although Bernhardi simplified Schlieffen's ideas, in his influential work, *Vom heutigen Krieg* (On War Today), he declared Schlieffen's view of combat to be 'mechanistic' and overly determinist. Fighting in the manner advocated, declared Bernhardi, 'can scarcely be any longer called an art. It becomes a trade, and the commander is, as it were, a mechanic.'[16]

INTRODUCTION

Another of the Imperial army's keenest minds, Sigismund von Schlichting, also spoke out against Schlieffen's view.[17] Although he was not as strident as some of Schlieffen's other critics, Schlichting felt Schlieffen's vision of battle was 'formalistic', 'schematic', and theoretical. In the end, Schlichting damned Schlieffen's article with faint praise, writing: 'I can certainly not see [Schlieffen's essay] as a fruitful and water-rich oasis in the desert sands of our evolution.'[18]

While the criticism of these authors must be taken seriously, it is also important to remember that they represented a distinct constituency within the *Kaiserheer*. They were all, at one time or another, corps commanders and could hope to be again upon the outbreak of a future war. Indeed, some could even aspire towards an army command. As the Reich's highest peacetime military commanders, these men had very considerable authority and autonomy. Schlieffen's vision of future battle relegated these men to the role once played by battalion or regimental commanders – although they would have licence to conduct their *Teilschlachten* as they saw fit, they would be playing a clear second fiddle to the overall commander. This subordination clearly rankled men used to independence. Thus, instead of Schlieffen's coordinated battle, Bernhardi wished to give 'free scope to the genius of command' to fight battles without restriction.[19] To carry out Schlieffen's plan with such men as subordinates, the future German *Feldherr* would clearly have to be a dominating personality.

'CANNAE STUDIES'

Shortly after the publication of his essay, 'War Today', Schlieffen began publishing his most significant work of history – 'Cannae Studies'. However, any examination of Schlieffen's historical writing must begin with that of one of Imperial Germany's most important historians, Hans Delbrück. In 1900, Delbrück published the first volume of his magnum opus, *Geschichte der Kriegskunst im Rahmen der politischen Geschichte* (History of the Art of War within the Framework of Political History) in which he dealt with warfare in antiquity. This volume contained an account of the battle of Cannae.[20] In this battle in 216 BC, the Carthaginian general Hannibal completely annihilated a Roman force superior in numbers by means of a double envelopment. The Romans lost around 50,000 of their original 80,000, and the Carthaginians lost only around 6,000 men. It was one of the most crushing and seemingly decisive battlefield victories of antiquity.[21]

This battle aroused Schlieffen's interest. While Schlieffen had brought out some historical works earlier,[22] he began publishing his first significant work of history, 'Cannae Studies', in the General Staff's quarterly journal, *Vierteljahrsheft für Truppenführung und Heereskunde*, in 1909. In this year, the 'Battle of Cannae' appeared, the first of Schlieffen's historical studies on how great commanders had gone about winning their battles. Influenced by Hans Delbrück's recently published account of the battle,[23] Schlieffen returned to a concept he had first elaborated in print in 1903, but which had underpinned his teachings throughout his time as Chief of the General Staff – annihilation of the enemy's army through envelopment.[24] Schlieffen put forward Hannibal's crushing defeat of the Romans at Cannae as a model for how such a victory should take place. In the *Vierteljahrsheft für Truppenführung und Heereskunde* over the next five years, Schlieffen published his historical studies, in which he claimed that all great *Feldherren* had as their goal the annihilation of the enemy and that these men had attempted to use flank attacks and envelopments to achieve this goal.[25]

In doing this, Schlieffen was engaging in a debate that had exercised the military establishment since the early 1880s. In 1879, Delbrück had published a work questioning the view accepted by the military that Friedrich the Great had attempted to annihilate his enemy's forces in all his battles.[26] In a debate that raged until the outbreak of the First World War, Delbrück argued that the annihilation of the enemy on the battlefield was only one goal in warfare. Instead of one, total goal (annihilation), he argued that in certain circumstances a more limited goal, one that did not involve the physical destruction of the enemy's armed forces, would be either desirable or necessary. He argued that great commanders sometimes did not aim to destroy completely their opponent's ability to wage war, and hence his ability to offer resistance, but might instead look merely to inflict enough damage to bring about a negotiated peace to a conflict. To support his viewpoint, Delbrück used the writings of Carl von Clausewitz, and this had the effect of transforming what had been largely a historical debate into one about the nature of strategy.[27]

While Schlieffen had engaged indirectly in the debate before,[28] his publication of 'Cannae Studies', with its strong emphasis on annihilation, was a clear public statement against Delbrück's interpretation of history and of strategy. However, Schlieffen went further in his work than merely countering Delbrück's interpretations; he attempted to use history not only to prove Delbrück wrong, but to demonstrate the exact methods by which *Feldherren* had gone about annihilating or seeking to annihilate their foes. He put forward his own historical interpretation that all great commanders had sought to annihilate their enemies by means of specific tactical or operational manoeuvres – flank attacks and envelopments. Schlieffen attempted to prove 'that which was achieved at Cannae floated more or less before [the eyes of all *Feldherren*] as a hazy but desirable goal'.[29] Moreover, according to Schlieffen, such methods were still relevant in the modern world. Although in the modern world surrender of the enemy army had taken the place of his slaughter, he wrote:

> a battle of annihilation can be carried out today according to the same plan devised by Hannibal in long forgotten times. The enemy front is not the goal of the principle attack. The mass of the troops and the reserves should not be concentrated against the enemy front; the essential is that the flanks be crushed. The wings should not be sought at the advanced points of the front, but rather along the entire depth and extension of the enemy formation. The annihilation is completed through an attack against the enemy's rear.[30]

To those German officers familiar with Schlieffen's critiques of wargames, the ideas he put forward in his 'Cannae Studies' were not new – Schlieffen had repeatedly stressed the importance of flank attacks and envelopments to his subordinates in the General Staff. However, their publication in an open journal, one read by many officers both inside and outside Germany, was new. Operational concepts that Schlieffen had been attempting to teach his subordinates were now available to anyone who wanted to read the General Staff's journal. This, however, was a double-edged sword. While the publication certainly brought Schlieffen's ideas to a wider audience, it also allowed a degree of criticism that had been impossible while Schlieffen was Chief of the General Staff, and this criticism was not long in coming.

First, astute officers criticized Schlieffen's historical methods. They argued that Schlieffen had used history selectively to illustrate concepts that he believed to be crucial and that he had failed to examine events in their proper context.[31] Even before the publication of 'Cannae Studies' Friedrich von Bernhardi had clashed with Schlieffen over his selective use of history.[32] However, one of Schlieffen's most strident critics was Sigismund von Schlichting, a recently retired corps commander who had published a considerable body of theoretical work on war.[33] Reflecting a growing disquiet about the use of history within the German army, Schlichting questioned what lessons for modern war could be learned from ancient warfare.[34] But more than this, Schlichting gave voice to what many believed. He felt that Schlieffen's historical method was fundamentally flawed: 'the defect of Schlieffen's doctrine is that he always generalizes lessons and experiences that suit a particular case'.[35]

This criticism was taken very seriously by Schlieffen's friends, in particular by Hugo Freiherr von Freytag-Loringhoven, the head of the Historical Section of the General Staff. From this position, Freytag was responsible for editing the *Vierteljahrsheft für Truppenführung und Heereskunde*. As Schlieffen published his work, Freytag attempted to soften some of Schlieffen's more outlandish assertions.[36] After their publication, Freytag and others attempted to claim that Schlieffen's work was not really a historical study. Instead, according to Freytag, Schlieffen's '"Cannae" consists of operational and tactical studies, which he constructed from historical facts. In it, he shows us how the concept of annihilation was realized or how it could have been realized in wars of the past.'[37] Thus, according to this viewpoint, Schlieffen's 'Cannae Studies' was really his attempt to impart to the next generation of officers the operational methods by which battles should be fought.

It was just this aspect that drew the fiercest criticism from Schlieffen's contemporaries. Schlieffen was accused of attempting to create a mechanistic doctrine within the German army, one that relied almost exclusively on one form of combat. Although flank attacks and envelopments were seen in the *Kaiserheer* as an important means of avoiding costly frontal attacks, they were none the less seen as two methods amongst many that a commander could choose.[38] This led officers within the army who had long had to put up quietly with Schlieffen's ideas to charge him with attempting to develop an 'envelopment mania'.[39] Friedrich von Bernhardi, one of Germany's best known writers on military affairs, believed that Schlieffen had attempted to form an overly schematic approach to combat. He wrote that modern combat demands 'now an envelopment be used, another time a flank attack, yet another a breakthrough, and at times a pure defensive or a decisive counterattack. A commander must be able to employ all means.'[40] Bernhardi was not alone in his criticism. Schlichting also made similar comments,[41] and Haeseler is reported to have proclaimed that Schlieffen had 'lost sight of the infinite variety of the military challenge in favour of a one-sided tendency'.[42] Once again, the corps commanders had rejected Schlieffen's view of combat.

'THE FELDHERR'

It was clear from Schlieffen's historical works that, in his opinion, the role of the commander in chief of any force was of decisive importance. According to him, this man stamped his mark on his army and determined the way in which it fought. The role of this commander had changed with time, and the creation of 'million-man armies' in the late

INTRODUCTION

nineteenth century had created new challenges for a modern-day commander in chief. With the commander playing such a central role in Schlieffen's concept of warfare, it is not surprising that he undertook a study of the institution. In the *Handbuch für Heer und Flotte*, a reference work edited by one of Schlieffen's former subordinates, Georg von Alten, Schlieffen published an essay entitled, 'The *Feldherr*', in which he examined what constituted a 'great captain'.

In Schlieffen's view, the *Feldherr* had to mould the army he commanded into a unique force: 'The *Feldherr* cannot stand at the head of just any force. He must have his own army.'[43] In the days of warrior-kings and small armies, this was easier to accomplish, as the king commanded the entire resources of the state. Thus it was that most of those Schlieffen categorized as 'great *Feldherren*' were kings – Alexander, Charlemagne, Gustavus Adolphus, Charles XII and Friedrich the Great. However, Schlieffen recognized that times had changed and that the days of warrior-kings was long past, necessitating the passing of military command to someone not of royal blood. Given the rise of the cult of personality around Paul von Hindenburg during the First World War, Schlieffen presciently recognized that there existed a danger of a successful army commander becoming too popular and that this popularity would threaten the power and legitimacy of a king. To avoid this happening and yet still to harness the abilities of non-royal men, Schlieffen put forward the General Staff system that had developed within Germany. In his view, this had solved the problem of rivalry between a king and his generals, as the king took nominal control of the army while his chief of staff acted only in his name and with his approval. The success of the Wilhelm I, Otto von Bismarck and Helmuth von Moltke team during the German Wars of Unification offered proof of this view: Wilhelm provided a figurehead under which his 'paladins' could do their work. Bismarck could manage the political sphere, while Moltke brought military victories.[44]

While Schlieffen put forward Moltke the Elder as a model for the military element of the modern '*Feldherr* triumvirate' in this essay and others,[45] there was at least one aspect of Moltke's style, that led Schlieffen to question whether or not he would have been able to dominate the army to the extent Schlieffen believed necessary to prosecute modern war. Moltke had developed within the German army the practice of 'directive command'. In this forerunner of today's concept of 'mission-command', a German commander would usually issue 'directives' to his subordinates in the place of 'orders'. Directives were not as prescriptive as orders, and a subordinate was to use his judgement as to how best to meet the objectives specified within his commander's directive. This procedure was designed to allow the commander closest to the action, and hence best informed about the actual circumstances, to take maximum advantage of opportunities as they presented themselves and not to have to wait for orders from above.[46] On the whole, this system had operated well during the Franco-German War of 1870/71, and Moltke's long tenure as Chief of the General Staff ensured its enshrinement in the German army.[47]

Although Schlieffen endorsed Moltke's system of 'directive command', he had, at times, criticized Moltke for not exercising enough control over his subordinates. During the German Wars of Unification, Moltke had had difficulty getting some of his subordinates to follow his directives. One particular instance stood out to Schlieffen.[48] Moltke had difficulty in getting the commander of the German 1st Army in 1870, Karl Friedrich von Steinmetz, to recognize his authority. As the German armies began their concentration in early August 1870, Steinmetz pushed repeatedly to attack before the 2nd and 3rd Armies were ready and before Moltke's plan of operations intended. Moltke had hoped that the French army could be encircled by the German 1st and 2nd Armies and pushed into the waiting arms of the 3rd Army. Instead of waiting and operating as Moltke intended, Steinmetz attacked before the other armies were in position and pushed the French back towards Paris rather than towards a waiting German army, thus ruining Moltke's planned encirclement near the German border. To make matters worse, Steinmetz' troops advanced across the 2nd Army's lines of communication in their attack, further throwing German plans into disarray.[49]

To Schlieffen, whose vision of battle put so much stress on the *Feldherr*'s plan of operations and the *Feldherr*'s role in shaping the *Gesamtschlacht*, such insubordination was unconscionable. Hence, he stressed over and over in his staff rides and staff problems the importance of lower-level commanders subordinating their own actions to the intentions of the commander in chief.[50] However, his essay 'The *Feldherr*' makes it clear that Schlieffen realized that blind obedience to authority is not enough for a successful general. As well as being respected, the successful *Feldherr* is also trusted and loved by an army that is pervaded by his spirit. With officers as independently minded as those who questioned the ideas Schlieffen put forward in his public writings, the challenge of finding someone who could carry off the role of *Feldherr* as Schlieffen saw it being played was clearly great.[51]

In August 1914, Germany put into effect a plan of operations largely based on the one Schlieffen drew up in 1905. Schlieffen's 1905 plan had at its core the ideas that he publicized in his writings after his retirement. As he had outlined how modern battles would take place in his 'War Today', Schlieffen's war plan of 1905 was in essence a plan for one

INTRODUCTION

gigantic battle. Although the individual armies would fight their own *Teilschlachten*, they would be guided by the plan's overall goals. Their individual successes would be nothing without the success of the *Gesamtschlacht*. Moreover, as outlined in his 'Cannae Studies', Schlieffen's plan called for an encirclement of the French forces as a means of annihilating them. It called for the bulk of the German army to march around the left flank of the French army, to attack its rear and to push it away from its base of operations.

However, one aspect that Schlieffen felt crucial to the success of such a plan was missing – a *Feldherr*. When war came in 1914, the one who was marked to play this important role, Moltke the Younger, neither filled the German army with inspiration nor controlled it in the way Schlieffen had desired. With even his closest subordinates, members of his own staff, doubting his abilities and health, it is not surprising that army and army corps commanders had little faith in Moltke. These men, senior officers with successful careers behind them, often acted as they saw fit, much as Steinmetz had done in 1870. Unlike his uncle in 1870, however, Moltke the Younger made little effort to impose his will upon these independent men in 1914. The result was that the operations of the German armies in Belgium and northern France slipped from his control. While it is questionable if even a strong-willed *Feldherr* could have rescued Schlieffen's plan in September 1914,[52] Moltke's hands-off leadership approach certainly did nothing to ensure its success.[53]

15

War Today, 1909

This essay represents the best source for Schlieffen's ideas about warfare and the strategic setting of his day and is the closest thing to a treatise on modern warfare that Schlieffen ever wrote. From this, it is evident that Schlieffen saw the 'encirclement' of Germany arising from an incomplete victory in the Franco-German War of 1870/71 and that this had created the strategic circumstances under which Germany would have to wage any war in the future. Moreover, Schlieffen recognized that modern inventions had changed fundamentally how wars would be conducted and his vision of the future battlefield contained here was in some ways reflected in the realities of the war that was to come five years after this essay's publication in the Deutsche Revue.[1]

The Peace of Frankfurt brought the battle between Germany and France to an end in appearance only.[2] If the arms of both sides remained laid down, there none the less existed still a cold war [*ein latenter Krieg*] between the two nations. If one of the two enemies found a faster firing rifle, a longer range gun, or a more effective shell, then he could be assured that the other would in rapid order produce a yet faster firing rifle, a yet longer range gun or a yet more effective shell. While each was endeavouring incessantly to outdo the other, in the end they succeeded in producing almost the same, barely to be out-classed weapons. Their zealous exertions were undertaken in order to win from the beginning in the imminent war of revenge [*Rachekrieg*] an advantage over the outsmarted enemy through superior rifles and cannon. Each was endeavouring to recreate a situation similar to that of 1866, when one enemy entered the arena armed with a needle-gun [*Zündnadelgewehr*] and the other armed only with a muzzle-loader.[3] Over the course of the years, there were moments when one or the other believed that he had reached his goal and when it only needed the right moment to send a declaration of war to the other camp. However, trust in the new weapons, made with the greatest of exertions, was never great enough to overcome all remaining considerations and doubts. Delaying gave the enemy the time to make good the lost advantage and even to win one for himself.

The other powers of Europe could not observe this rivalry with indifference. Any power that wanted to join in the dialogue in Europe, indeed across the whole globe, could not allow the armament of its troops to fall too far behind that of the two leading powers. However, it was not necessary to take part in every phase of the arms race. It was enough to exploit the essential lessons and achieve the same goals as the others with less effort and cost.

After the course of a few decades of Franco-German rivalry and of the arms specialists spurred on to their utmost, almost all armies, not only in Europe but also in the Far East and West, found themselves in the possession of pretty similar weapons. Rifles and cannon are [now] light and handy, can be loaded and fired quickly, are easily moved over long distances and range over a wide area. New powder does not give away either the rifle or the cannon through widely visible smoke. A shell of minimal calibre and weight allows a great deal of ammunition to be carried and permits a high rate of fire to be employed. It does not appear necessary to discover new inventions that will make weapons more effective. The conceivable has been achieved. A shot has barely reached its target before another follows. If the hand is sure and the eye is sharp, even the farthest target will be hit. The velocity is so great that almost the whole distance between the gun's barrel and the target is dominated. The bullet cannot be made smaller – without question it suffices to render *hors de combat* not only one of Nature's sons from a faraway land, but also a civilized European.

No unit in close order, no man standing free and upright can expose themselves to the rain of shot. Already at Mars-la-Tour, a Prussian regiment that advanced in close order lost 68 per cent of its strength in barely half an hour, and this against an imperfect and antiquated weapon. Three years ago, the Japanese Nambu Brigade advanced three times in a short space of time and had to count their losses at 90 per cent. In South Africa, a single covered rifle easily laid low 14 of the attackers storming it.

The science of arms is celebrating its most magnificent triumph. That for which both Germany and France endeavoured and that which all the remaining powers desired – an easing of battle [*Erleichterung im Kampfe*], a superiority over the enemy – was given to no one. While science gave its gifts simultaneously and impartially to all, it created for all the greatest of difficulties and brought for all the most considerable disadvantages. It was not difficult to say how one was to strike dead and to annihilate one's enemy with these effective weapons. How one was to avoid annihilation oneself; this was a problem not easily solved. A complete change in tactics proved to be necessary. It is no longer possible, as it was in the eighteenth century, to deploy against one another in two lines and to fire salvos into one another at not too great a distance. In the space of a few minutes, both armies would be eradicated from the Earth by rapid fire. It is no longer possible to storm the enemy position in Napoleonic columns, columns as wide as they are deep. They would be smashed by a hail of shrapnel. It is also not possible to overwhelm the enemy, as was recommended a short time ago, through the fire of thick swarms of skirmishers [*Schützenschwärme*]. These swarms would be quickly massacred. Only by the use of the cover of trees and houses, of walls and trenches, of elevations and depressions in the ground is it possible for the infantryman to advance on his enemy. First lying, then kneeling, then standing, he must try to hit the small and limited target offered to him, without himself being seen. He must suppress the fire of his enemy with his own fire then quickly move forward to new cover and from there take up the fight again. Yet, however much cover the battlefield may offer sooner or later an open, empty space covered by fire will extend out before the enemy. If the space is small, then the attacker will rapidly storm the defender, who will have been shaken by the continuous fire. If the space is wide, there will be nothing left for the attacker but to create cover for himself by the use of the spade and to advance, as in a fortress war, from trench to trench, when necessary by night.

It is the job of the artillery to assist this infantry advance. Their own fire will shield their hardworking, advancing infantry from the fire of the enemy artillery. They will seek out the hiding places of the enemy artillery with their shots and destroy the cover behind which they shelter. To work effectively, the artillery must seek cover from such devastating fire. Since it is not as easy to hide a gun as it is to hide a man, the artillery has to use the techniques of an earlier age and try to use an armoured shield to prevent at least rifle and shrapnel fire from doing any harm.[4]

In order to find enough cover, to fire a sure shot at a difficult-to-see target, and to advance quickly, the infantryman must have elbow room. In order to fight effectively, the infantry must not advance in close order, but in loose lines, with around a man to every metre, not in numerous thick files, but in one file. Further files follow in the not-so-close distance. These follow-on files come together in thick formations when the available cover permits. They are to make good the losses of the first file, fill in the holes in this line. They are to stand ready to serve as a reserve for unexpected events. If one does not want to field fewer combatants than in the past, the looser deployment will lead to an expansion of the front. This expansion will be even greater when one strives to bring into action as many effective rifles as possible. This will leave the ability of troops to attack or defend undiminished, since the smaller number of weapons of today are more capable than the many weapons of the past. It is only during the final assault with the bayonet that the constantly following reserve will advance into the loose front line.

Therefore, an immediate result of the improved firearms is a greater expansion of the battle front [*Gefechtsfront*]. Thus it is that while in the battles of the previous two centuries one could reckon on 10 to 15 men per metre in the battle line, including all arms and the reserve, and even 40 years ago ten men per stride was the norm, in the East Asian War of 1904/5, three men to the metre was usual, and even this declined according to need. Neither of the belligerents developed an established principle concerning the expansion of the battle front during the war or troubled themselves to bring into use their peacetime theories. The power of circumstances, a natural desire to protect themselves and to use their excellent weapons effectively brought forth the long battle fronts. Therefore, it is not to be doubted that that which occurred daily in the Far East will also be repeated in a European war. The battlefields of the future will and indeed must see a much greater expansion than those we have known in the past. Armies the size of which were employed during Königgrätz and Gravelotte–St Privat will today take up four times the room they did then. However, what impact would the 220,000 men of Königgrätz or the 186,000 men of Gravelotte have against the masses which are set to appear in a future war?

Forty years ago, universal conscription was the property solely of Prussia. A property that no one envied the petty military state [*der engherzige Militärstaat*]. However, since 1866 and 1870 almost every power has tried to make this secret of victory [*dieses Geheimnis des Sieges*] their own. Since then, every able-bodied man has been sent to the *kaserne*. In order to increase the size of the army, the time of service to the flag in peacetime was limited as much as possible, while the time in service for wartime was extended as much as possible.[5] No power could avoid striving to put forth the maximum number of battalions. He who remained behind had to fear being crushed.

Since Germany with 62 million inhabitants enlists 250,000 recruits annually for a 19-year term of service and France with 40 million inhabitants enlists 220,000 annually for a 25-year term of service, the former will have 4,750,000 men available for war and the latter 5,500,000! However, when one disregards those long since departed from service, these numbers are more or less imaginary. The man who has left the *kaserne* for the factory or the coal mine cannot remember the tactics taught to him on the parade ground of his garrison 15 years earlier. The rifle that the *Landwehr* soldier fired as a recruit on the rifle range has long since passed into the hands of a black warrior in the colonies. He regards the new rifle that is thrust into his hands with the same mistrust as one of the Old Dessauer's grenadiers would view a needle-gun.[6] The factory worker, who is used to spending his mornings at his work place and bicycling home in the evenings, will only do 30–40 kilometres per day loaded down with a rifle, ammunition and rucksack with great difficulty. *Landwehr, Landsturm*, Territorial forces and the reserves of the Territorial forces can only be counted as part of the nation in arms in a very limited and restricted way. Many of those who are useful from these groups must be left behind as fortress garrisons or as *Ersatz* troops.

When one examines the events of 1870, one finds that the *Landsturm* did not play a role in the war, that the *Landwehr* played a limited role, and that, of the total German strength of 1,200,000, only 500,000 made up the field army. From this, one can estimate that today we will have more troops, but not many more than a million. Still, such an army is large in comparison to those of earlier times and large for those who have to lead and manoeuvre it. It is small since it has neither secured superiority in weapons, as in 1866, nor superiority in numbers, as in 1870, over its enemies. It is only just large enough if it can be held together and made to work toward a common goal. Also, if this is achieved, it is not always necessary to have all the strength united on one battlefield, 20 times larger than that of Königgrätz. Indeed, the small battle of Dresden was composed of two separate parts. On 16 October at Leipzig three different battles were fought and at Le Mans a large number of encounters took place! The success of battle today depends more upon conceptual coherence than on territorial proximity. Thus, one battle might be fought in order to secure victory on another battlefield. Regardless, this much is certain: the total battle as well as its parts, the separated as well as the contiguous battles, will be played out on fields and across areas that dwarf the theatres of earlier martial acts.[7]

However, while these battlefields may be large, they will offer little to the eye. Nothing is to be seen across the wide desert. When the thunder of cannon does not deafen the ears, the direction of the artillery will only be betrayed by weak flashes of fire. One would not know whence came the rolling infantry fire, if now and then a thin line of infantry did not make a momentary appearance while springing forward, only to disappear again quickly. No riders are to be seen. The cavalry must seek its tasks away from the theatre of activity of the other two arms. No Napoleon stands upon a rise surrounded by his brilliant retinue. His white horse would be the easy target of countless batteries. The *Feldherr* finds himself further back in a house with a spacious office, where telegraphs, telephones and signals apparatus are to hand and from where fleets of cars and motorcycles, equipped for the longest journey, patiently await orders. There, in a comfortable chair before a wide table, the modern Alexander has before him the entire battlefield on a map. From there, he telephones stirring words [*zündende Worte*]. There, he receives reports from the army and the corps commanders, from the observation balloons and from the dirigibles that observe the movement of the enemy along the whole line and that look behind the enemy's positions.

These reports will be different from those of the past mainly in numbers, but also to a lesser extent in their content. Fairly predictably, they will read, as they have for centuries, that the enemy continually receives reinforcement, that the artillery has suffered heavy losses, that the infantry cannot advance, and that reinforcement is absolutely necessary. The *Feldherr* cannot give in to these desires. Even if he possesses a strong reserve, it will soon be used up if he met all legitimate calls for help that come in from all sides and from distances of many miles and many days' march. Since battles can only be conducted with comparatively small forces, the sending of strong reinforcement, who would be unable to find cover on the battlefield, would only increase losses. The essential task of the one who manages the battle [*Schlachtenlenker*] is fulfilled when, long before any clash with the enemy can come about, he can specify to each army and corps the roads and paths over which and the directions in which they must advance and give to them their general daily goals. The advance to battle begins as soon as the units have left the railway. From the railway station, the corps and the divisions, some marching quickly, others somewhat more slowly, will seek to reach the place assigned to them by the order of battle [*Schlachtordnung*]. Since their battle fronts [*Gefechtsfronten*] have expanded, the columns endeavouring to reach the battlefield will march in at least the width necessary to take part in any encounter [*Gefecht*]. Concentration for a battle will lose its significance. Those corps that strike at the enemy will have to fight without being able to reckon on further reinforcement. With 144 excellent cannon, compared with the 84 inferior cannon available in the past, and with 25,000 excellent rifles, every corps will be able to fulfil 10 times the number of tasks as its predecessor from the days of the muzzle-loader. If a corps covers three times the area as 40 years ago, this does not represent a dilution, but rather an increase in strength. It is completely within the power of such a force to attack, to maintain its gains, to cover losses of up to 50 per cent, and still to keep back a reserve for a final assault.

Certainly it will go on for a long time and it will be laborious, this fight in the front rank from cover to cover, this advance on the enemy, this persevering day and night, this always being ready to repulse a counterattack.

Not every corps will enter the encounter on the first day. At Leipzig, the evening of the third day had already fallen before the last of the Allied corps reached at least the neighbourhood of the battlefield. Battles lasting many days – Orleans, Le Mans, etc. – were the rule during the second half of the War of 1870/71. Also the battles of the future with their masses deployed over great areas will take up more, indeed many more, days, if not the 14 days taken up by the battle of Mukden. On every new day, the *Feldherr* will urge the armies and corps already engaged in action to new exertions, keep in their direction of march those not engaged, or direct them to new ones if the situation has changed.

These long-lasting battles will in no way be bloodier than those of the past. The daily battle losses of the East Asian War amounted to only 2–3 per cent as opposed to the 40–50 per cent during the days of Friedrich or Napoleon. The 14 days of the battle of Mukden cost the Russians and the Japanese less than the short hour at Mars-la-Tour cost the Germans and the French.

The Russo-Japanese War proved that an attack against an enemy's front can, despite all difficulties, succeed very well. However, the result of such an attack is, even in the best of cases, only limited. Indeed, the enemy will be pushed back, but he will renew his resistance in another place after a short space of time. The campaign will drag on. However, such a war is impossible today, when the existence of a nation is founded upon an unbroken flow of trade and industry and when the gears that have been brought to a halt must be brought back into motion by the means of a rapid decision [*eine rasche Entscheidung*]. A strategy of exhaustion [*Ermattungsstrategie*] is impossible when the maintenance of millions necessitates the expenditure of milliards.

However, to bring about a decisive and annihilating victory requires an attack against two or three sides of the enemy, i.e., against the front and against one or both flanks. While such an attack is comparatively easy to carry out for those finding themselves in possession of the greater numbers, it is difficult to reckon upon such a superiority under today's conditions. The forces necessary to carry out a powerful flank attack are only to be gained by making the forces employed against the enemy's front as weak as possible. However weak these are made, they must not be so weak that they only want to remain under cover and merely 'occupy' or 'hold fast' the enemy with fire delivered from a distance. Under all circumstances, the front must 'attack', and must also 'advance' forward. For this task, there is the rapid-fire, long-range rifle, a few of which can replace many earlier rifles and which is enough to meet all demands, so long as there is the necessary ammunition to hand. Instead of accumulating reserves behind the front, which must remain inactive and will be missed from the decisive point, it is better to attend to a plentiful supply of ammunition. Cartridges brought by trucks form the best and most reliable reserves. All the troops formerly retained to bring about the decision can now from the outset be led forward to attack the flank. The stronger the forces that can be brought up with that objective, the more decisive the attack will be.

In order to attack an enemy's flank, first one must know where it is to be found. In the past, it was the task of the cavalry to find this out. Hopefully, this mission will be carried out in the future by dirigibles, which can have a better view from the air than the cavalry, whose view is hindered by mountains, forests and villages. However, just as the cavalry used to have to clear the enemy from the field before it could carry out its reconnaissance missions, so these air ships must also meet their enemy in a battle in the high regions. Hopefully, the lighter built aircraft will succeed in climbing higher than its opponent, and then fire its annihilating incendiary shot down upon the enemy below, before distancing itself as quickly as possible so as not to be caught in the high-climbing flames.

The cavalry, essentially freed from its reconnaissance role, will attempt to carry the fire possessed by its artillery, machineguns and long-range carbines into the enemy's rear. As in the past, it will first have to strike and overcome the enemy cavalry in its way, before it can reach its main task. Much in the future will be more or less similar to the past: artillery will first fight artillery; cavalry will face cavalry; and air ships must be used against air ships, before all can unite with the infantry to help bring about the final victory.

However, battles of the future will not progress so simply. Since the end of the 1870/71 War, France and Germany have erected fortresses along their new common border, here to protect against a new invasion, there to guard against an act of revenge. The latter has restricted itself to the construction around the newly won fortresses of Strassburg and Metz. The former has constructed an almost unbroken barrier along the Upper Moselle and the Maas that is meant to cover the entire eastern border between Switzerland and Belgium. [Germany] was presented with a difficult situation. Even though it was free of any desire for conquest, it could not quietly watch while its vengeful hidden enemy waited for the most favourable moment to sally forth. The best defence is the offence. Germany had to remain free to use this means if forced to. Therefore, it could not set, as was advised, a fortified line against the French fortified line. Instead, it sought to procure a new instrument of attack. The heavy artillery was supplied with a high-explosive shot of previously unknown effect, against which no wall and no fortified magazine could stand. This did not remain a secret for long. Soon, similar annihilating projectiles were to be found on the enemy side. Since then, a long, bitter, and by no means finished battle has raged back and forth between the artillerists and the engineers. One discovers new, bigger, safer cannon and more effective shot, while the other constructs works capable of ever greater resistance.

Neighbouring states could no more ignore this race than they could the competition for rifles and field cannon. That peaceable Germany thinks constantly to make raids on the lovely plains of the Seine and the Loire generally went as given. If the direct path to this goal was blocked, then one could assume that a way around the offending obstacles would be sought through Switzerland or through Belgium. To prevent such an attempt on the right wing, the French have used fortified works to block the Jura passes since early on. On the left, the Belgians come to their assistance. They have cut the great routes [*Völkerstrassen*] along the Maas and the Sambre with concrete and armoured works and have erected an impregnable bulwark around Antwerp behind this line. The Netherlands sought through strength to support the efforts of its neighbours and to protect itself, like France, from a German attack.

All this was not enough. No so long ago, Italy lost a few provinces to France. That Italy would use a German invasion of France to win back its lost provinces was also taken for granted. Therefore, all the ways and paths that led through the high mountains separating France and Italy had to be blocked. Italy saw in France's fortress construction not a defence, but a threat, and hurried to match every fort, every battery and every rampart with a similar construction and to mirror the whole fortress system on the western side of the Alps with an exact replica on the eastern side. Barely two decades had passed since the Franco-German War before a Chinese Wall stretching from the Zuider See to the Mediterranean Sea had been built, meant to prevent the repeat of any terrible invasion.

Yet, it was still believed possible that the Italians would unite with the Germans on the other side of this Chinese Wall over the Alps and that this unified force would flow over the fortresses and the million-man armies in its path, like a river raging over its banks, into the coveted land. The Swiss could not hesitate to assist when this danger was imminent. The Gotthard Pass, the ways through the Rhône and Rhine Valleys, all paths between unapproachable glaciers and the sky-high mountains were barricaded with fortifications and the perpetually snow-covered forts were given garrisons.

The supposed lust for conquest, before which a bolt was effectively thrown on one side, was forced to look another way. If Germany was prevented from marching on Paris, it would be temporarily necessary to strike off on the path to Moscow. Russia felt itself forced to erect fortifications against Germany. Rivers, streams and swamps made this intention easier. At the same time, the German provinces on the Russian side of the Vistula were blocked off by a wide, swampy trench and the few paths through this were defended by walls and guns. It goes without saying that similar defensive measures were taken against Germany's ally – Austria.

Thus, the states of the Triple Alliance were cut off from the rest of Europe by lines in both the east and the west. In the north, Denmark has turned Copenhagen into a great place of arms and has taken control of the entry into the Baltic Sea. England possesses a powerful floating fortress that can be erected at any time in the North Sea and that can cover any sally port [*Ausfalltor*] along the coast of Jutland to Schleswig. Indeed, the production of so many border fortifications has had such an effect that Italy has fortified its borders with their ally Austria and vice versa. The iron ring thrown around Germany and Austria was only left open in the Balkans. However, even this exit has been filled by Turkey, Serbia and Montenegro, while Bulgaria and Rumania close in on the Austrian camp.

Thus is the military situation in Europe. In the centre stand Germany and Austria unprotected with the other powers surrounding them behind walls and trenches. The military situation corresponds to the political. Between the surrounded and surrounding powers there exist hard to remove differences. France has not given up the desire for revenge sworn in 1871. As this desire for revenge has called all of Europe to arms, it has also formed the cardinal point for all its politics. The powerful expansion of Germany's industry and trade has earned it another implacable enemy – Britain. This hatred of a formerly despised rival can neither be tempered by assurance of sincere friendship and cordiality nor aggravated by provocative language. It is not emotions, but questions of debit and credit that determine the level of resentment. Likewise, the inherited antipathy of the Slavs towards the Germans, the traditional sympathy with the Rumanians, and the need for loans will hold Russia to its old allies, and thus Russia throws itself into the arms of the powers that can do her the most harm. Italy, whose every expansion to the west is blocked off, does not believe that the foreign threat, which needs only cross the Alps to be on the fruitful fields of Lombardy, is over. It will endure the foreigners neither on the southern region of the Alps nor on the coast of the Adriatic Sea.

It has not been decided that these passions and these desires will be translated into powerful acts. However, a zealous endeavour is still underway to lead all these powers into a common attack against the centre. At a given moment, the gates will be opened, the drawbridges lowered, and the million-man armies will flow out over the Vosges, the Maas, the Königsau, the Niemen, the Bug, as well as over the Isonzo and the Tyrolean Alps, laying waste and destroying as they go. The danger appears immense. However, it diminishes somewhat when one examines it more closely.

England cannot destroy German trade without damaging its own trade. It understands well that profit requires that it allow its detested competitor, who is at the same time its best customer, to live. Before the advertised landing in a port in Jutland can take place, England will await telegrams from Africa, India, East Asia and America. If the world has been set alight, it will have better things to do than to allow its army to be arrested in Schleswig according to Bismarck's direction. Russia has all the strength and all the power necessary to oppose its allies' call for an attack; whether this attack now seems enticing after having become acquainted with the ways of modern war must be doubted. France was determined to take the pleasure of its now-cold revenge only in the company of good friends. All the doubts about the horrible cost, the possible high casualties, as well as the phantom of danger threatening from anarchism [*rotes Gespenst*] have emerged from the background. Universal conscription, which uses high and low, rich and poor alike as cannon fodder, has dampened the lust for battle. The supposedly impregnable fortresses, behind which one feels warm and safe, appear to have reduced the incentive to storm out and bare one's breast to combat. The arms factories, the cannon foundries, the steam hammers that harden the steel used in fortresses have produced more friendly faces and more amiable obligingness than all the peace congresses could. Everyone carries just as many doubts about attacking a numerous and well-armed enemy as fear of using their own destructive instrument, which has been laboriously created, but which they do not know if they understand how to handle. And even when all these doubts and all the difficulties have been overcome and when the decision is ripe to set out on the powerful advance against the centre from all sides, questions must still be anxiously asked: Will the 'others' also come? Will the faraway allies intervene at the right time? Will we be abandoned and left to face the hammer blow of a superior power alone? These doubts force a pause, a delay, the revenge to be postponed, the drawn sword to be put back into its scabbard.

'The coalition is dead', is called from the other side of the Channel. That they will proceed to war is thoroughly doubtful and is for the moment not necessary. The position which the allied powers have taken up is so favourable that its very existence forms a constant threat and automatically affects the German nervous system through the economic battle and the business crisis. In order to meet this pressure, Germany has had to be prepared to give in, to yield to demands, to allow others to win advantages.

While the battle was being fought in this way, the picture suddenly changed. As a result of the most recent experience in the Balkan peninsula, Austria sees itself bound to Germany's side for a long time. It requires support from its ally, who cannot grant such a request. The enemy tactic has been successful: one of the two allies has been directed towards an intended theatre of war and has been tied down there. Now with unified, annihilating superiority first one then the other can be destroyed. Russia reserves for itself the right to deliver decisions here and there with full strength.

Yet, despite a position that has become so favourable, the enemies surrounding Germany still do not want to take up their arms. Their many doubts have not yet been conquered. Moreover, even separated, Austria and Germany are too strong. First, they are to be weakened by inner conflict. In Austria, the nationalities dispute will be diligently stirred up by the friendly introduction of diplomacy, by delegations encouraged to fight and by calls to arms published by the press. How the same goal can be reached in Germany by the means of a short newspaper article with deceitfully constructed time-worn accusations has recently been shown.[8] And yet, for the distant struggle, which may be fought by arms or by some other means, 'a united nation of brothers' is at least outwardly necessary, as well as a large, strong and powerful army, which is guided by a sure hand and full of confidence.

16

Million-Man Armies, 1911

In this short essay, which originally appeared in the Deutsche Revue *in June 1911, Schlieffen again discusses the international situation and the effects that the increased size of armies had upon it. Moreover, Schlieffen again stresses the importance of solid training and sound leadership and makes the point that size of armies has little impact upon quality of leadership.*[1]

'Million-man armies' are no modern discovery; rather they have developed over a long period of time. It was still a barely 100,000-man army with which Friedrich the Great set to work transforming Germany, but in relation to the 2.5 million inhabitants of Prussia at that time, it substantially surpassed the uncounted masses that would follow the call to arms in today's Germany of 65 million. Even more onerous still were the sums of the levies of young and old that the completely exhausted and impotent Prussia in 1813 still had the strength to send into the field to throw off the yoke lying on them and all of Germany. From this depleted flock, Wilhelm I formed a solid army that was still much larger than the armies of Prussia's bigger, more powerful neighbours. With this army he won at Königgrätz, and from this army he formed the million-man army that defeated France. Only with the greatest resources and with the greatest of exertions are great things achieved and are great ideas realized, and also the German Empire was only brought together with the help of an army, the size of which appeared to consume the strength of a nation.

The defeated realized only too late what it was they lacked and what an unfair battle they had waged. Now all the powers of the European Continent have introduced universal conscription [*allgemeine Wehrpflicht*] in order to raise million-man armies with which to stand beside the German Empire and restore the earlier balance of power. They have now created million-man armies. However, the hopes set in these armies have not been realized. Supposedly, the general love of peace was too great to allow a war to break out. In truth, all the European powers have conducted wars over the past 40 years, even if only against weak, poorly armed and poorly trained peoples. Therefore, it was not the love of peace that prevented them from kindling the flame of war in Europe. They have shied away from using the powerful weapons that they have in their hands, but have never really trusted. Moreover, they found no joy in a war in which rifle fire does not distinguish between high or low, rich or poor. They feared that their allies would leave them, that the hated enemy would be stronger, that the war would last for an indeterminate time, and that it would have unforeseeable results. It is the same fear of the large, of the powerful, of the immense that leads time and again to peace.

Therefore, no country had less cause than Germany to limit its army. Except that the peace of Europe depended upon the fear that this army instilled. At that, the million-man army of the 65 million Germans is not substantially stronger than, for example, that of the 40 million French. The German army's image must, of necessity, have come from better training and better leadership. Certainly, leading a million-man army, it is maintained, is a barely solvable problem. Regardless, this much is true – commanding an army, be it large or be it small, has always been a clever feat [*Kunststück*]. However, it is difficult to accept that the problems in carrying-out this clever feat grow in proportion as the size of armies changes. There have been generals who have been completely lost with armies of 300,000 men. That is not to say, though, that they could have led 100,000 or 50,000 to victory. This much is certain, no *Feldherr* has yet created difficulties over too many troops being given to him, but all, without exception, have complained about having too few.

17

Cannae Studies

THE BATTLE OF CANNAE, 1909

This is the first, and most famous, part of Schlieffen's 'Cannae Studies', as well as the conclusion, originally published in the General Staff quarterly, Vierteljahrsheft für Truppenführung und Heereskunde, *between 1909 and 1913. This study also included accounts of the battles of Friedrich the Great and Napoleon, as well as more recent battles such as Königgrätz and Sedan. This 'historical study' represents Schlieffen's attempt to prove that victories derived primarily from flanking or encircling attacks – the apotheosis of which for Schlieffen was the battle of Cannae.*[1]

On 2 August 216 BC, Hannibal's army stood facing west against the army of Consul Terentius Varro on the Apulian Plain to the left of the Aufidus (Ofanto) in the vicinity of the village at the river's mouth, Cannae.[2] Varro, to whom had been transferred the daily changing command from the other Consul, Aemilius Paulus, had on hand:

<pre>
55,000 heavily armed soldiers
 8,000 lightly armed soldiers
 6,000 cavalry
──────
69,000
</pre>

and at his disposal in two fortified laagers:

<pre>
 2,600 heavily armed soldiers
 7,400 lightly armed soldiers
──────
10,000
</pre>

so that the total strength of the Roman army amounted to 79,000. Hannibal had available only

    32,000 heavily armed soldiers
     8,000 lightly armed soldiers
    10,000 cavalry
    50,000

With a considerably superior opponent to his front and the sea to his rear, Hannibal found himself in a by no means favourable position. Nevertheless, Aemilius Paulus, in agreement with Proconsul Servilius, wanted to avoid battle. Both feared the superior Carthaginian cavalry to which Hannibal principally owed his victories at Ticinus, at Trebia and at the Trasimene Lake. However, Terentius Varro wanted to seek a decision [*Entscheidung*] and avenge the defeats the Romans had suffered. He counted on the superiority of his 55,000 heavily armed soldiers against the enemy's 32,000 heavily armed men, of which only 12,000 were Carthaginian soldiers. The remaining 20,000 were poorly armed and trained Iberian and Gaullic auxiliaries.[3]

In order to conduct the attack with greater force, Terentius gave his army a new order of battle [*Schlachtordnung*]. According to Roman custom, the heavily armed soldiers would have been in three close-formed lines. The foremost two lines (the *hastati* and the *principes*) of this formation would be equal in strength with 4,000 men in the front and all together 12 columns,[4] while the third line (the *triarii*) would be only half the strength of the other two arrayed in 160 equally distributed columns of 60 men (ten in the front and six deep) immediately to the rear. This 18 file formation seemed to Terentius to be too broad. Therefore, he deepened it to 36 files, creating a front 1,600 men wide.[5] The cavalry he distributed on the wings. The lightly armed troops, who were appointed to begin the battle, to harass [*umschwärmen*] the enemy, and to support the cavalry, were barely considered by either side.

Against the enemy front, Hannibal set only his 20,000 Iberians and Gauls, which were probably only 12 files deep. The greater part of his cavalry were put on the left wing under the command of Hasdrubal. The Numidian cavalry was deployed on the right. Behind this cavalry, the 12,000 Carthaginian heavy infantry were deployed equally divided between the two wings.

Each army advanced against the other. Hasdrubal overwhelmed the weak enemy cavalry of the right wing. The Roman knights [*Ritter*] were cut down, driven into the Aufidius or scattered. The victor turned the enemy infantry and advanced against the Roman cavalry of the left wing, which until then had merely been skirmishing with the Numidian cavalry. Attacked from both sides, the Romans were also routed completely here. Upon the destruction of the enemy cavalry, Hasdrubal turned against the rear of the Roman phalanx.

In the meantime, the two masses of infantry advanced against each other. Pushed close together, the Gallic and the Iberian auxiliary forces were pushed back, not so much from the strength of the attack of the 36 Roman files as from their poor armament and lack of training in close combat. The Roman advance came to a halt as soon as the Carthaginian flanking echelons, which had so far been held back, came up and attacked the enemy on the left and right flanks and as soon as Hasdrubal's cavalry threatened the Roman rear. The *triarii* turned around, and the *maniples* of both wings turned outward. A long, complete square was forced to come to a halt, form fronts facing all sides, and face attacks on all sides from the Carthaginian infantry with their short swords, from the cavalry with javelins, arrows and slings, which never missed their mark in the compact Roman mass. The Romans were constantly pushed back and crowded together. Without aid and disarmed, they awaited death. Hannibal, his heart full of hate, circled the scene of the bloody work, here encouraging the zealous, there chiding the sluggish. Only after hours had passed did his soldiers let up. Tired of the slaughter, they took the last remaining 3,000 Romans prisoner. In a small area, 48,000 corpses lay in heaps. Aemilius Paulus and Servilius had both fallen, Varro had escaped with a few cavalrymen, some heavy infantry and the bulk of the light infantry. Thousands fell into the hands of the victors in the village of Cannae and in both camps. The Carthaginians had themselves lost around 6,000 men, mostly Iberians and Gauls.

A complete battle of annihilation [*Vernichtungsschlacht*] had been fought, made all the more marvellous by the fact that, in spite of all theory, it was inflicted by a numerically inferior force. 'Concentric action against the enemy does not suit the weaker', wrote Clausewitz. 'The inferior must not turn both flanks simultaneously', taught Napoleon. However, the weaker Hannibal had acted concentrically, if in an unseemly [*unziemlich*] manner, and had turned not only the wings, but even the rear of his enemy.

Armaments and the art of battle have changed completely since 2,000 years ago. One no longer attacks with a short sword, rather one shoots at thousands of metres; the bow has been replaced by the recoil gun, the sling by the machinegun. Capitulations [*Kapitulationen*] have taken the place of slaughters [*Metzeleien*]. However, the fundamental conditions of battle have remained unchanged. A battle of annihilation can be carried out today according to the same plan devised by Hannibal in long forgotten times. The enemy front is not the goal of the principal attack. The mass of the troops and the reserves should not be concentrated against the enemy front; the essential is that the flanks be crushed. The wings should not be sought at the advanced points of the front, but rather along the entire depth and extension of the enemy formation. The annihilation is completed through an attack against the enemy's rear. Here, the cavalry plays the principal role. They do not need to attack 'intact infantry'; they can first wreak havoc amongst the enemy masses through the use of long-range fire.

A condition of success is certainly that the enemy shorten his front by deploying in a deep formation with masses of reserves, thus deepening his flanks and increasing the number of combatants forced to remain inactive. It was Hannibal's luck to find himself opposed by Terentius Varro, who eliminated his superiority by deploying his infantry 36 men deep. Commanders of Hannibal's school have been found in all epochs, but not during the period when they would have been most desired by Prussia.

CONCLUSION, 1913

Finally with the battle of Sedan, a Cannae had been fought, a complete encirclement of the enemy had been achieved. None of the great *Feldherren* of the previous centuries had known the course of that battle on the Aufidus, but that which was achieved at Cannae floated before their eyes as a hazy but desirable goal. When he found he had enough strength for the task at the beginning of the Seven Years War, King Friedrich surrounded the Saxons at Pirna and the Austrians at Prague.[6] However, in doing this, he for the most part exhausted his own strength. With what was left to him, he did not feel strong enough to attack from all sides the Austrian army that was advancing to relieve the fortress. Instead, he limited himself to occupying the Austrian front at the battle of Kolin, while delivering the annihilating stroke against the Austrian right flank.[7] The advancing Prussian left wing, however, hit the extended Austrian front. The weak Prussian army was not up to a frontal attack against such a strong position and was itself encircled and suffered a total defeat. By way of repentance, at the battle of Leuthen, Friedrich left the enemy front completely alone. Instead, he took his 35,000 troops around Prince Karl of Lorraine's 65,000 men and turned against Karl's left flank. The Austrians wheeled precipitously to the threatened side and formed a compact, deep mass. They could now be attacked on the new front and also outflanked on the left and right. They were beaten and forced by this unwanted change of front into a costly withdrawal. At Zorndorf, the envelopment was so deep that the Prussian army stood, in the end, in the rear of the Russians, who were forced to make a rapid about face.[8] By means of an enveloping attack, first against the right wing and then against the left, the Russians were finally pushed against the Oder River. They were as good as encircled. One more assault and they would have been annihilated. However, such an assault would have barely left the Prussians as victors given the Russian army's great ability to resist. The Prussian army would have been worn out and made incapable of continuing the war. A door was opened for the Russians through which they could escape. They were not annihilated, but were defeated for this campaign. When they returned in the following year, Friedrich wanted to attack them from all sides at Kunersdorf and, despite their superiority in numbers, annihilate them finally.[9] The Prussian attack collapsed against an overwhelmingly strong Russian position and turned into a destructive defeat. However, much came from this failed Cannae: the Russians advanced to lay waste to the Prussian state, to burn and to fire. However, they would under no circumstances do battle with Friedrich and turned tail at the simple report 'The King is coming'.

At Torgau, Friedrich had to give up the attack against four sides and instead attempt an attack against the front and rear of his enemy.[10] Here and there, the assault was repulsed. However, the fire from the front and rear proved to be unendurable. The Austrians removed themselves during the night by way of their open flank. Only after peace with Russia had been concluded, which resulted in a Russo-Prussian alliance, did Friedrich return to his normal attack against his enemy's front, flanks and rear at the battle of Burkersdorf.[11] The Austrians, however, could see a means of escape from their encirclement, since the Russians, who were meant to attack the Austrian front or at least to pin it down, can be said to have limited themselves to a mere demonstration.

Napoleon also began his battles of annihilation with envelopments, which were not, however, carried out like Friedrich's with inferior numbers in the vicinity of the battlefield. Instead, Napoleon manoeuvred for days and weeks in a wide arc to bring his superior numbers to the enemy's rear. He then conducted a double envelopment or, better still, he allowed the weaker enemy to attack him in order to deliver the annihilating counterattack after the exhaustion of his foe. From the beginning, like Friedrich at Zorndorf and Torgau, he made Hasdrubal's decisive attack on the enemy's rear. He attacked his enemy on both flanks and in his rear and left open to the Austrians and the Prussians only the front facing France. They had to go in this direction, followed by his superior forces. At Marengo and at Ulm, this led to the immediate annihilation of the enemy.[12] At Jena, this occurred only after a lengthy pursuit. The battle, which was begun with the attack on Vierzehnheiligen, only reached its tragic end at Prenzlau and Ratkau.[13] Likewise, only Beresina left the stamp of a horrible Cannae upon Napoleon's march on Moscow and the breakthrough at Hanau formed the final act of the giant battle [*Riesenkampf*] of 1813.[14]

In the Preußisch-Eylau campaign, the envelopments were directed not against the rear of the enemy, but against the flanks of the enemy, who saw a limited wheeling movement as a way out of the pernicious attack. Napoleon then stood opposite his weaker enemy. A full-scale frontal attack, a weak attack against a flank and strong reserves held back were the solution to the simple situation. They were, ironically, brought about by the enemy, whose weak flank attacks led to himself being outflanked. Friedrich the Great was unsuccessful in some of his battles of annihilation because his forces [*Streitkräfte*] were too limited. None the less, he attempted it the most often. Napoleon failed at Preußisch Eylau because he lavished too much on an unfruitful frontal attack, held back too much strength in his reserves for contingencies, and ventured to employ too little on what should have been the decisive flank attack.

There is a risk connected with every envelopment and outflanking manoeuvre [*Umgehung*]. The enemies of Friedrich and Napoleon had to learn this, as they also wanted to conduct a battle of annihilation, outflank the enemy with superior forces, and fall upon his flank or rear. The plan failed at Roßbach, Liegnitz and Austerlitz, because the enemy being outflanked struck the head of the outflanking columns with superior strength.[15]

Napoleon fought an almost annihilating battle one more time. At Friedland, the enemy placed himself in a position exceedingly favourable for annihilation.[16] He stood with his back to the Alle, his front facing a doubly superior foe, and, on top of this, burnt the bridge that alone could allow him to escape. None the less, the annihilation did not succeed completely, as Napoleon limited himself to an attack against the front and one flank of the enemy and left one flank open, because he wanted to maintain a reserve that was as strong as possible. Indeed, this strong reserve did not win him the battle, but instead lessened his victory.

According to the principle of Cannae, a broad battle line advances against a narrower, but usually deeper, battle line. The overlapping wings envelop the enemy flanks and the advancing cavalry attacks the enemy rear. If the wings are for some reason separated from the centre, it is not necessary to bring them together again in order to advance together in the envelopment. They can be sent immediately against the flanks or the rear. This is what Moltke called 'concentration on the battlefield', and he declared it to be the best manoeuvre that a *Feldherr* could accomplish. It is also the most effective and, naturally, the riskiest. Most *Feldherren* and almost all able subordinates understand the danger that the parts will be beaten before they are able to unite and, hence, zealously endeavour to bring about the unification not on the battlefield, but as long as possible before the battle. In this way, they give up any chance of a decisive result from the act and must instead be satisfied with a more limited success or none at all. Napoleon experienced the former at Regensburg and, for the good of mankind, the latter at Groß Görschen.[17] Moltke would have experienced one or the other if he had followed the advice of his contemporaries and subsequent critics and had united all three of his armies on one base line [*Grundlinie*] at the battle of Königgrätz.

It is true that there exists the danger of a part being defeated on its own, or of it being pushed back. Cannae itself demonstrates this, as does Blücher at Löwenberg and Schwarzenberg at Dresden, and the Prussian 1st Army at Königgrätz might have proved it if Benedek had begun to attack Prince Friedrich Karl early in the morning on 3 July with his entire force [*Heeresmacht*].[18] However, the final result would have been that the victor, Benedek, would very quickly have had to leave the vanquished to turn against one of the enemies threatening his flanks. The 1st Army would then have reformed its front. Thus, though victory seemed assured, it would have led to the final encirclement of the Austrians and their annihilation would have been made the easier. This is shown by the campaign in the autumn of 1813 and by the wars of 1815 and 1866.

In order to annihilate a separated portion of an enemy army with a unified army [*mit versammelter Macht*], as at Prague in 1757, it is necessary for the remainder of the army to be so far away that support from it cannot be expected. If it comes too near, the unified army must be divided in order to defend itself. Detachments will then fight detachments. The weaker enemy standing in the centre no longer would have superiority [*Übergewicht*] anywhere and is lost as soon as it is possible to assemble the forces of the stronger opponent on the battlefield, as at Leipzig, Waterloo or Königgrätz. Also Friedrich, the weaker at Bunzelwitz, would have lost the battle had the Russians and Austrians, who had been intimidated by earlier experiences, not refrained from a difficult attack.[19]

In every Cannae, it is obviously desirable for one to have superiority in numbers. In 1870, Moltke had first to acquire superiority. A great, smothering coalition threatened to form against Germany. Moltke held fast to the principle tested in 1866 – no corps for observation, no armies where there was no enemy. Sixteen complete corps were sent against France. The French army assembled in Lorraine and in Alsace to cross the Rhine upstream from Karlsruhe and to fall on south Germany. It was easier for the Germans to oppose the invasion on the river.

However, as Napoleon had outflanked the front of the Prussian force assembled north of the Thüringer Wald by means of rapid marches, so Moltke used rail transports to outflank the front on the upper Rhine and appear on the middle Rhine between Karlsruhe and Coblenz. Napoleon's manoeuvre forced the Prussians onto the Saale. Moltke's forced the French against the Saar and the Lauter.[20] Both outflanked armies wanted to wheel about and hit back against one of the outflanking columns, as at Roßbach. This clever intention, undertaken by necessity, brought about a tragic end at Saalfeld in 1806 and would have led to the same end in 1870 – the French army advancing in the general direction of Mainz–Mannheim would have been fallen upon from all sides and would have barely made it back across the Saar.[21] Yet, a foreboding of what might come reached Napoleon III, and, thus, the German armies were able to advance to the Saar and the Lauter.

It would have corresponded to Napoleon's strategy in 1806, if the Germans in 1870 had crossed the Moselle with their advancing right wing and forced the French, whether they accepted battle or not, back in a southern direction against the Rhine and the Swiss border. However, the inadequate rail network of 40 years ago appears to have made such a manoeuvre impossible. The left wing had to be made strong at the expense of the right and it instead was to bring the decision. The 3rd Army had to advance to throw back the enemy forces that had assembled in Alsace and then to wheel left and attack the main French army in the flank and the rear, while, in the meantime, the German 1st and 2nd Armies were to advance against its front. The plan failed because the 1st and 2nd Armies attacked too early and the 3rd too late. The French army in Alsace was completely beaten, but the one in Lorraine could retire to Metz little harmed. The great superiority of the Germans would have made it simple for them to pursue the French and to envelop the French flanks with both far-outreaching wings after strong detached cavalry had brought the French retreat to a halt. The equipment and armament of the cavalry divisions at that time appeared not to permit such a course of action. Despite this, the German 5th Cavalry Division hindered the retreat of part of the French army at Vionville on 15 and 16 August. Indeed, it even forced the French to retreat. The cavalry would certainly have been able to fulfil the task set by General von Alvensleben for the III Army Corps early on the 16th – stop the enemy army, if necessary allow it to withdraw gradually to Verdun, but win enough time to allow German corps to take it in the flanks, or at least in one flank, and complete the Cannae. However, such unusual performance was not to be expected from the cavalry. Moltke, therefore, decided to outflank the enemy retiring on Metz to the south with all three of his armies, accompanying the French, if necessary, in a parallel pursuit until a suitable moment arrived to wheel to the left and force the French against the border with Luxemburg and Belgium. In this manner, the encirclement was to be completed. This plan was supported by the delay caused by the fortress of Metz and the battle of Colombey, which brought the French retreat to a halt, but was impaired by the slowness and the irresolute movements of both German armies, by the limited number of bridges across the Moselle, by the poor road net on the left side of the river and, not least, by Bazaine's careful delay in giving up connection with the cover of the fortress. The Marshal was convinced, not without reason, that the moment he relinquished the protection of Metz and moved into the open, he would be fallen upon from all sides and annihilated. Still, Moltke's intention would have been fulfilled had General Barnekow been allowed to advance through the Bois des Ognons and had the 25th Divisions been allowed through the Bois de Vaux to the Rezonville–Point du Jour road. Bazaine would hardly have ventured to use a route for his retreat that was, if not occupied by the enemy, then under his fire. He would have withdrawn in an northerly direction – just as Moltke wanted him to do. However, since Barnekow was used in an unfruitful frontal attack, as per the old custom, and since the 25th Division could only arrive too late at its appointed station, the main route of retreat remained open to the French. The Germans had to relinquish for the moment the annihilation of the French and, instead, be satisfied, albeit with hopes for the future, with their encirclement in Metz.

MacMahon was also to be pushed against the Belgian border and annihilated by means of an attack against his front and right flank. However, since neither the position at Châlons nor that at Reims offered enough advantages for the defence, MacMahon wanted to retire to Paris before he could be seriously threatened. The situation, which had been poor for the Germans, was changed completely by MacMahon's enforced march on Metz from Reims by way of Stenay. This gave the Germans the opportunity to attack from the south and outflank an army of comparatively limited strength marching from west to east and to push it against the nearby Belgian border. Since two corps remained in the reserve of the siege army, all the paths leading to the east and the south were very quickly blocked. Initially, only the path to the west was left open for retreat. MacMahon wanted to use this path when he came to find out about the German advance. However, he was immediately driven back by Paris to his public ruin. When the 10½ German corps advanced along all the available roads in line with their right flank above Longuyon along the Belgian border and with their left flank above Rethel, there was no doubt that the four French corps would be forced against the Belgian border, whether they marched forward or back, to the left or to the right. Whether they attacked or whether they offered resistance on this or that road, they came to blows with the German corps that were using the same roads to come in the opposite direction. The remainder marched in their original direction, at first, to determine whether or not they also had an enemy before them and, then, because only a march forward would enable them to win the enemy's flank and to support effectively their neighbouring fighting corps.

The Maas Army did not think to solve the task set for it for 30 August in such a simple way. They faced three enemies – one on the Sommauthe–la Beface road, one at Beaumont, one on the Mouzon–Stenay road, and possibly another at Carignan. If the two Bavarian corps had been allowed to continue along the Sommauthe–la Beface road and if the Maas Army had sent the IV Corps to Beaumont while the Guard and the XII Corps took the right bank of the Maas, they would have driven three or four enemies before them and, more importantly, would have blocked all exits to the east and to the south. However, the commander of the Maas Army did not want to divide his forces. Instead, he wanted to assemble his five corps, with three corps in the first rank and two in the second, before Beaumont. As a result of this, at least two enemy units were free, indeed were forced by the actions and failures of the Germans, to attack the German flank or at least to give an indication of what could have happened if in their place had stood a strong, united and determined enemy.

Since the attack against the French at Beaumont could not be carried out with the weight of 20 brigades, as it had been intended, but only with one or two brigades because of the limited space, the battle between the one Prussian brigade and the five French was called into question. It could perhaps have come to a very lamentable end, if a division commander had not, in his desire to get at the enemy, extended his front and thereby caused the outflanked enemy to give way. This also caused the planned French withdrawal to be somewhat hastened. However, this hastening was purchased at the cost of comparatively high casualties. In the end, the enemy, who should have been encircled without any difficulty, was freed from any pressure and could have removed himself off in two directions calmly and without any danger. Fortunately, he gave up the advantages he had and proved himself to be a generous enemy by halting again after a short march.

The superiority of the Germans was so great that they could complete the encirclement and could even accumulate masses in the closest area at their will and let nature take its course. Such extravagance would have been impossible if the enemy had extended himself somewhat, had he, say, occupied the Maas line between Sedan and Mézières. Then, the

Germans would have had to extend their left wing beyond Mézières. The strength at hand would still have been enough to set a corps advancing along every route, which would have allowed for the average size to be reached that Moltke believed necessary, according to the experience of 1870, for a proper deployment. Whether or not he would have stuck to this norm now that the length of a corps march column has grown from 15 to 29 kilometres must remain a matter of speculation.

A complete battle of Cannae is seldom found in the history of war. For its achievement, there must be a Hannibal on one side and a Terentius Varro on the other, both working together in their own way for the attainment of the great goal. A Hannibal must possess, if not superiority in numbers, then at least the knowledge of how to achieve this. It is desirable for such a purpose that the *Feldherr* combine in himself something of a Scharnhorst, a Friedrich Wilhelm or a Wilhelm I, who welded together a powerful army; something of a Moltke, who concentrated it solely against the main enemy; something of a Friedrich the Great, who brought all his guns and rifles into action; something of a Friedrich the Great or a Napoleon, who directed the main attack against the flanks or the rear; something of a Friedrich the Great or a Moltke, who replaced the absent Hasdrubal by a natural obstacle or the border of a neutral state. Finally, subordinates are needed, who are disciplined, well trained in their craft, and who possess an understanding of the intentions of the *Feldherr*.

A Terentius Verro has a great army, but he does not do his utmost to increase its numbers or to train it appropriately. He does not concentrate his strength against the main enemy. He does not wish to win through fire superiority from all sides, but rather by the weight of mass, arrayed in narrow and deep formations, seeing the enemy front, the side most capable of resistance, as most suitable for attack.

None of these desirable characteristics will be found together in a single person on either one side or the other. Some of Hannibal's characteristics and some of the means at his disposal have been possessed by other *Feldherren*. On the other hand, Terentius Verro has existed throughout history. Thus it happens that, with the exception of Sedan, no real Cannae has been fought, but only a whole series of nearly annihilating battles, and these are to be found right at the turning points of history.

18

The *Feldherr*, 1910

Throughout Schlieffen's time as Chief of the General Staff, he had stressed the importance of command to his subordinates. This essay, first published in the Handbuch für Heer und Flotte, *contains Schlieffen's ideas about what made up a great commander, a Feldherr. As Clausewitz wrote about a genius for war in his* On War, *so Schlieffen believed that a Feldherr was born to his position rather than appointed. However, he also felt that Prussia had found a possible alternative to a single great commander in the staff system created during the Napoleonic Wars.*[1]

At the head of an army stands a supreme commander, an all-highest commander, a *generalissimo*, a *général en chef*. The sovereign, the head of state, who makes such appointments, believes by this act he has acquired a *Feldherr*. Not infrequently he will be disappointed, for one is not appointed '*Feldherr*', but rather is born to, is predestined for, this office. For instance, the shepherd boy David, who would one day defeat the Philistines, was created king by Samuel, i.e., he was anointed as *Feldherr*. The nine-year-old Hannibal vowed to be an eternal enemy of Rome, and was ordained as *Feldherr* before the altar of Baal. No high priest came before Napoleon. Nor did he have to stand before the altar of Baal. Nevertheless, already as a young boy in Corsica, he was warmed by a *feu sacré*. The son of the Revolution had, like Prometheus, stolen the fire from heaven.

The task of the *Feldherr* is to annihilate or to defeat completely an enemy whose strength, location, direction and intentions are not known. He must not deviate from the path he chooses to carry out this task. He must overcome all obstacles in his way, and quickly find solutions for any diversions. He must strive his utmost to reach his goal and stand fast in the face of the vagaries of fate. To carry out his task, something superhuman or supernatural, call it genius or something else, must pervade the *Feldherr*. He must be conscious of the assistance and the support of a higher power. Caesar was certain of this assistance when he crossed from Brundisium to Dyrrhachium in a small boat in terrible weather, shouting out to his despondent navigator: '*Quid times?*

Caesarem vehis.'² Alexander believed himself to be a son of Jupiter. Constantine won '*in hoc signo*'.³ Cromwell believed himself to be God's 'chosen vessel'. Wallenstein observed the heavens to determine whether or not the stars were favourable to him. Napoleon clearly felt victory was his when the sun from Austerlitz broke through the clouds at Borodino. Friedrich the Great himself hoped that the saying 'Allow me to do with diligence that which I have been charged with doing' would bring about a success which could barely be achieved.⁴ Kaiser Wilhelm I saw in the most spectacular victory in the history of the world 'an expression of Divine Providence'.

However, if a *Feldherr* relies alone upon his holy calling, upon his genius, upon the assistance and support of a higher power, victories will not come easily. Only through hard work will he prepare himself for his high calling and only hard work will clarify his mental and intellectual faculties. Alexander tamed Bucephalus and trained himself through martial tournaments [*Waffenspielen*], but he also sat at the feet of Aristotle. Caesar was a philosopher, an orator and an author. Even today, no student can pass through Gymnasium without having worked through some of his *Gallic Wars*. Gustavus Adolphus spoke seven languages. Friedrich the Great had command of all areas of knowledge with the exception of orthography and the German language.⁵ Napoleon was said to have been a poor student of Latin when he was in Brienne, but he had '*du feu pour l'algèbre*'. The only thing Moltke lacked was time in a university and the titles 'doctor' and 'professor'.

What a degree of knowledge is demanded of a *Feldherr*! He not only has to understand how to lead an army to victory, but he must also understand how to move it, how to arm it, how to equip it, how to clothe it, how to train it and how to supply it in the field. Perhaps he might find others to undertake these tasks for him. However, in the end, he will not be thankful for this. The *Feldherr* cannot stand at the head of just any force. He must have his own army. Napoleon's remark 'mankind is nothing; a man is everything' means that the people, that is the soldiers, must be permeated to a man with the *Feldherr*'s spirit.

'Who is it that has forged us so tightly together,
That none can distinguish one from the other?
Why, no other man than Wallenstein!'⁶

proclaimed the sergeant-major in 'Wallenstein's Camp'.

It was not merely a Macedonian, but Alexander's phalanx that smashed the Persians at Granikus. It was not just any Roman legion, but Caesar's legion that crossed the Rubicon. Cromwell's 'pious dragoons' won at Naseby. Napoleon's grenadiers marched into Russia. Friedrich's 'Potsdamer Wachtparade' assaulted at Leuthen. Armies get sick, age and die with their *Feldherren*. As the spirit of the 'Philosopher of Sans Souci' flew off, the army went with it. Napoleon's army did not survive Waterloo. It was, after all, not Napoleon's army that perished at Sedan; just as it was not the army of Friedrich the Great that the Duke of Brunswick led at Jena.

An army alone, even if it is the best of armies, is not enough to conduct a war. War is only a means of politics. To make a war meaningful requires the preparation of a statesman. No one understood this better than Napoleon. In 1806, he had defeated the Prussians before a shot had been fired by the foremost outposts. 'Sire, you will be crushed', he wrote on 12 October – the recipient knew this as well as the sender. The battle of Jena was a mere formality, which honour would not allow to be bypassed. Therefore, the *Feldherr* must also be a statesman and a diplomat of the highest order. Further, he must be able to raise the enormous sums of money that are devoured by war.

Only a king can meet all of these demands, as he alone commands the entire resources of the state. The *Feldherr* must therefore be king. In the ranks of great *Feldherren* stand Alexander, Charlemagne, Gustavus Adolphus, Charles XII, Friedrich the Great, all of whom were kings by birth. Cromwell and Napoleon made themselves kings, after they had demonstrated their qualifications for high command. Caesar and Wallenstein would have done the same had not the strike of Cascas and the partisan Deveroux hindered the act. When ancient Rome found itself in danger, the Senate named a dictator with royal powers, thereby allowing him to be a *Feldherr* and crush his enemy. Hannibal was not a king and would not become king; thus, the Carthaginian Republic perished through want of a *Feldherr*.

As long as the primeval agreement of the concept of king and leader [*Anführer*] in war held up, there was no lack of material from which a *Feldherr* would arise. However, it failed when the tenants of the thrones of the first monarchies did not feel themselves able to or have received the call to stand at the head of their armies, yet they wanted to or had to conduct war. They believed it necessary to entrust a general with the most important of kingly prerogatives. This was not done without consideration. A general should win. However, if he won too many victories, if he showed himself to be a *Feldherr*, then royalty was endangered. One does not have to think back only to Macbeth or to Wallenstein. Already the cheer, 'Saul has slain thousands, but David has slain tens of thousands', did not fall well on the royal ear. To avoid the worst, the king would retain the conduct of the war in his hands. From the Viennese and the Versailles cabinets, armies were directed. Generals received only restrictive and limited tasks. They had to besiege a fortress or to destroy a city or to occupy a province, or now and then to fight a battle. A decisive battle [*Entscheidungsschlacht*] or a pursuit were carefully avoided.

In this manner, conventional strategy [*Kriegführung*] reached its state of perfection under Condé, Turenne and Prince Eugene of Savoy. They did not become *Feldherren*, for a *Feldherr* is the natural rival of a king. This threatening rivalry pressed Saul to take up the game of dice in order to nail his competitor to the wall. Belisarius was imprisoned, blinded and, in order to prolong his life, had to beg for an obolus from passers-by from his small jail window.[7] This after he had defeated the Goths and twice saved the empire! A French general who did not win would be recalled and sent back to his estates, and another, upon whom luck seemed to shine, would be sent in his place. Austrian generals who had received setbacks during the Turkish Wars wandered through fortress prisons; the victor of Aspern returned to private life.[8] A Russian general on his way back to the Motherland with half his army after having laid waste to East Prussia, Pomerania and the New Mark would be uncertain whether he would have to continue his journey on to Siberia or whether he would be awarded the Holy Order of Andreas, an audience with the Tsar and be given a large estate with thousands of serfs.

It was different in Prussia. The heirs to Friedrich's greatness believed it was inadvisable to lead their army into the field. Since neither Friedrich Wilhelm II nor Friedrich Wilhelm III felt themselves to be *Feldherren*, they named the Duke of Brunswick as 'supreme commander' [*Oberbefehlshaber*]. In this way, there formed two headquarters, a royal and a ducal, which frequently met for councils of war. The final decisions lay obviously with the King, and the Duke was often left to carry out decisions with which he did not agree or tasks which he did not want.

Into this stunted [*verkümmerte*] system broke Napoleon. The serious defeats he inflicted upon the powers of Europe could not produce any essential improvements. There emerged some competent generals, but no *Feldherren*. Yet in 1813, there still existed a titular 'supreme command' put together from two advisory boards, one composed of kings and emperors and the other of unemployed generals who had no responsibilities. Luckily, the allied army had at its head a man who possessed some of the essential properties of a *Feldherr*, even though he had not studied at the feet of Aristotle and did not possess a *feu pour l'algèbre*. Further, his failings were made good by his chief of staff. This '*Feldherr* duumvirate' made itself independent and carried the other army leaders along with it, thus enabling it to defeat the yet unbeaten but already old 'world conqueror'.[9]

The development of the idea of a chief of staff led to the revival of the belief that 'the king is the leader [*Anführer*] in wartime'. The sovereign no longer took the field merely as an onlooker who disturbed the company of the general named commander-in-chief. Rather, he took over the role of *Feldherr* and had a chief of staff at his side with whom he could hold council over the strategic situation and what decisions should be made. This system worked for Napoleon III in his war against Austria in 1859, but failed for his opponent. It failed the same Napoleon at the beginning of the campaign in 1870. The naming of a chief of staff itself is not enough. The bearer of the title must possess some of the properties of a *Feldherr*. Both France and Austria in 1859, Austria in 1866 and France during the course of the war of 1870 returned to an earlier method of command. They each had appointed a 'supreme commander' who had unlimited authority, but they had retained the traditional interference. Neither Benedek nor Bazaine had stressed their self-doubts before taking up the office of *Feldherr*. Only under pressure did they take over the office of command. Following this compulsion, they wanted very much to win, but did not have any clue as to how to bring this about. Since they, disobediently and stubbornly, did not win, one was condemned to a moral death and the other a physical punishment.

At last, the solution to the problem of the lack of a *Feldherr* was found in Prussia. The King himself rode at the head of the army he had created and made his own. At his side stood a statesman and a chief of staff. None of the three men possessed all the necessary traits of a *Feldherr*, but each possessed to a greater or lesser extent the required properties and each complemented the other.[10] The first task of this royal *Feldherr* with his two paladins was to set his armed forces [*Streitkräfte*] as soon as possible against his enemy under the most favourable strategic conditions. The accomplishment of this task will most often be sought through the winning of allies and through the formation of a coalition, an alliance or an entente. However, such alliances are often of limited value as each member attempts to make the other take on the lion's share of the task, while they themselves try to take the spoils of victory. Under such circumstances, Friedrich the Great destroyed the coalition formed against him by attacking one ally before the others could come to its support, by turning left and right against the individual advancing enemies. From 1805 to 1807, Napoleon defeated first the Austrians, then the Austrians and Russians, then the Prussians, and finally, once again, the Russians. Despite the fact that all his enemies added together were far superior to his forces in numbers, he knew, in the majority of cases, to battle against the [single] enemy who was vastly inferior. He himself valued his allies only if they were at the same time his vassals. He sought to keep other powers at a distance, to attend to their many-sided concerns, or to arrange that they take a portion of his enemy's strength away from his forces.

Bismarck operated similarly. To him, it seemed more advantageous for the Italians to occupy three Austrian corps in Italy than for them to fight by Prussia's side with twice the strength. France and Russia were content at first to be merely observers. To Bismarck, it was less important that these powers did not support Prussia than that they did not support Austria. The smaller German states were neutralized by three Prussian divisions that marched into Hessen and Hanover under General von Falckenstein. All other attempts to detach corps to cover distant provinces were resisted. The fate of the entire Prussian state was to be decided in the main theatre of war. There, seven Austrian corps and the Saxon corps were to be found. This force was roughly equal in number to the nine Prussian corps, but they were much more poorly armed. In this way, a Prussian superiority was built from the start. None the less, it was possible that one or more outside powers might intervene, as did Prussia in 1805, Russia in 1806, Austria and Sweden in 1813 and also in 1866, if the war lasted for a long period of time or the war took a decisive turn against one of the two combatants. Europe will quite happily stand by while two combatants weaken each other, but it will not hesitate to enter the conflict if one power threatens the other through the accumulation of too much strength and power. In this way, France, with wise forethought, intended to enter the fray at just the right moment as peacemaker and gain thereby a well-deserved reward. To prevent such an occurrence, Moltke sought to end the war quickly by means of a battle of annihilation [*Vernichtungschlacht*] that would present the world with a *fait accompli*.[11]

Whoever wants to annihilate his opponent must first know where this opponent is located. In practice, this knowledge is easy to obtain, especially now that the deployment of armies is essentially determined by rail networks. It is more difficult to ascertain where the enemy will go from his deployment area. As a rule, reports on enemy movements from cavalry and airships will arrive too late. The *Feldherr* must guess or calculate the intentions of his enemy. Napoleon often followed the practice of marching against his enemy's capital, certain in the knowledge that he would find what he was seeking along the way. In 1806, Scharnhorst wanted to attack Napoleon in his identified extended positions on the assumption that he would still be found there in 20 days. The French vanished before half of the deployment was complete. In comparison with this, Moltke marched his separated armies to the place where, according to his calculations, the Austrians had to arrive in ten days time.

To annihilate the enemy once located, Napoleon normally endeavoured to outflank his enemy and thus to force his enemy to fight with a turned flank. In this way in 1806 he was successful in making the

Prussian army conduct a withdrawal in an unfavourable, western direction and to force them into a position from which they could escape only by making a wide detour behind the Oder. In 1866, Moltke did not plan to force his enemy into making an unfavourable withdrawal, but rather he aimed at encircling and completely annihilating the Austrian force. This plan failed, not because Moltke had calculated wrongly and not because he lacked the necessary authority or the necessary energy, but because the army and corps commanders lacked training and discipline and because one of the armies advanced too slowly and entered into the decisive attack with only a part of its strength. The enemy found the time to evade this encirclement. The result was an Austrian withdrawal under unfavourable circumstances, as in 1806, rather than their annihilation. The Prussian commanders lacked the Napoleonic energy required to conduct the pursuit as it should have been conducted. None the less, the Austrians were forced, after making a great detour, to seek the safety of the Danube. While in 1806 the Prussian army was destroyed before it could reach safety on the far side of the Oder, the Austrian army in 1866 was able, with the help of railways, to evade their pursuers and make it, even if in terrible condition, across the Danube. There, an army was assembled which greatly outnumbered the Prussians. The situation seemed for Prussia even more unpleasant than for France in 1806, when Russia intervened. Then, Prussia still had a corps in reserve behind the Vistula River. A Russian army united with this corps in order to bring Napoleon's advance to an abrupt halt. In the end this attempt failed, but only after a long, bloody and strenuous campaign, which shook, for the first time, the foundations of Napoleon's edifice. Prussia alone had to bear the damage of defeat; the Russian army brought home a victory. In 1866, France thought in a similar way to Russia in 1806. It hoped to occupy the right bank of the Rhine and from there build a new Rhine League under its patronage. However, in 1866, France hoped to accomplish its goals not through battle, as the Russians had at Preußisch Eylau or Friedland, but through a diplomatic campaign. In this arena, though, Napoleon III was inferior to Bismarck, and after some vain efforts he was forced to retreat. Austria, thrown on to its own resources and threatened now by Hungary, had to reconcile itself to making peace after its generals had declared that the army would no longer attack.

A definite regularity in modern war, a definite consistency in the task of a *Feldherr* is difficult to discover. Also in 1870 there was a coalition planned against Germany. It would certainly have come about had there been long preliminaries, as in 1866, before the war began. The war broke out before the negotiations could be concluded; the thunder of cannon at Wörth removed all desire, did away with all opportunity.

This time, the battles of annihilation succeeded because Moltke's subordinates, at least some of them, had a certain understanding of Moltke's intentions.[12] Metz and Sedan were such spectacular feats of arms that the other European powers were convinced not to interfere in their neighbours' dispute. The fear of facing a similar catastrophe held their hand. A similar fear forced the portions of the French army that had survived and some of the newly raised French forces to flee to Paris. A battle for a fortress, which had been in ancient times the essence of war, but which had in the past 100 years seemed to play a minor part in war, became suddenly important again. The German forces were by no means prepared to besiege such a modern fortress. After all, the war was to have been brought to an end by means of a few powerful blows. Now, however, it would take time. The French had won the time necessary to raise new armies and for envious powers to consider and deliberate whether or not the new, rising power could be cast down. The normal second part of any war, which Napoleon had avoided through the defiantly obtained peace treaties of Schönbrunn and Pressburg, had to be conducted here as a siege. Only Moltke's quiet clarity could bring this second part of the campaign to an end and, even if it took far longer than it should have, he accomplished it just as brilliantly as the campaign's first phase.[13]

It does not appear as if battles for fortresses can be once again stricken from the programme of future warfare. The *Feldherr* will have to reckon with them in the future. In all of our great battles – Königgrätz, Gravelotte, Sedan, Paris – enemy fortresses have been of extraordinary assistance to Prussia and Germany. Fortresses draw in an enemy who cannot decide to attack, bring him to a halt and enable, or at least make easier, his encirclement. Therefore, it is difficult to wish for the flattening of fortress walls and battlements and the filling in of trenches. The attacker is not to be discouraged by them, but rather must use them in his own victory. Indeed, the difficulties, which the novelty of the appearance and the quantity of fortresses brings, are staggering. However, they will be overcome when the *Feldherr* sticks firmly to his task of not just pushing back his enemy, but of annihilating him. Success under today's conditions, as in earlier times, belongs to the true *Feldherr*. While the *Feldherr*–Triumvirate was successful in 1866 and 1870, this does not always have to be so. At least one of the committee that has today replaced the single *Feldherr* must have been touched by a drop of Samuel's anointing oil.

19

Helmuth von Moltke

In his essay, 'The Feldherr*', Schlieffen outlined the requirements of a great captain. In subsequent essays, he examined those who he thought met these requirements. While he did not publish a piece on the* Feldherr *with whom he was well acquainted, Schlieffen was called upon to talk about Moltke on two separate occasions, and the text of these two speeches was subsequently published in his collected works. Schlieffen makes clear in these that while Moltke was clearly a special individual, one who had been 'touched by a drop of Samuel's anointing oil', he was to serve as a role model for all General Staff officers.*[1]

SPEECH AT THE GENERAL STAFF BANQUET ON THE OCCASION OF FIELD MARSHAL GRAF VON MOLTKE'S ONE HUNDREDTH BIRTHDAY – 25 NOVEMBER 1900

Gentlemen! The Festschrift that the General Staff has to compose in the coming days will give expression to the regret that the late Field Marshal did not deal with the art of war scientifically; that he did not, like some others before him, write a theory of war. We all share this regret. A book is desired from which the searching intellect could read how the Field Marshal brought about victory in three campaigns, took whole armies captive and brought a war to an end in as many days as other *Feldherren* have required weeks, months and years. This desire, however, remains unfulfilled. The Field Marshal did not seek to solve the great strategic problems in numerous volumes, many chapters and countless paragraphs. Repeatedly, he limited his revelation of the art of war to the few words: 'Strategy is a system of expedients.'[2] This phrase seems to be a stone offered to the starving instead of bread or an answer of an oracle that confuses more than enlightens. The phrase seems to be nothing and is everything. However, it is a protest against those who seek salvation through a single theory or a single method alone – in interior or exterior lines, in envelopment or breakthrough. It is the assertion that for every situation the most appropriate solution must be sought. It is the expression of complete freedom for the leader [*Führer*] to do that which he believes must be done to win victory.

Through the course of the years, science [*Wissenschaft*] and the learned [*Gelehrten*] have erected a list of laws for war that are to be obeyed and that are not to be broken. Critics can never forgive the fact that the Field Marshal broke almost all these rules.

'*One must cover his flanks and his rear completely.*' However, the Field Marshal advanced into Bohemia and left, despite all remonstrances and, as one can say, all intrigues, only a single division and the garrisons of the western fortresses against enemies to the rear. Indeed, it was only in this way that 18 divisions (the strength of the Prussian field army at the time) could be brought to the battlefield.

'*One must hold his forces together.*' However, in the middle of June 1866 the Prussian army was spread out over 350 kilometres from Torgau to Neisse. Fourteen days later, 220,000 men were finally united at close quarters at Königgrätz. Only at Leipzig, not before and not after, had a similar event taken place.

'*Before the battle, one must amass his forces.*' However, only on the afternoon of 3 July 1866 did the army unite. Indeed, this delay caused the defeat of the enemy to be an annihilation.

'*The main enemy army is the goal against which one must march.*' The Field Marshal, however, marched on Vienna, not Olmütz. A more rapid conclusion of peace was the result.

'*The first thing a* Feldherr *must do is to secure his communications with his base of operations* [Basis].' This was not allowed, however; at Gravelotte the Field Marshal's forces faced Germany and again at Sedan their rear faced Paris.[3] It was only in this way that two armies could be taken prisoner.

Some say that he was assisted by luck – that he has luck alone to thank for victory despite making so many errors. However, luck only remains true to the clever. After all, was it really luck that the defeat of Trantenau fell at the time of highest tension or that the Guard Corps mechanically reached its march goals without worrying itself about the sound of cannon to its right and left or that the 1st Army did not advance despite all pressure? Even the most careful calculations cannot take into account such factors. Or was it luck that in the early days of August 1870 one of the army commanders knocked off too late and the other too early or that the 1st Army crossed over the march routes of the 2nd Army and threw everything into question?

And how did it go with the similar errors of other *Feldherren*? Did Napoleon have good communications with his base at Marengo? Did he not find himself at Jena in the most unfavourable position in the world? Can it be justified that on the morning of Leuthen Friedrich the Great marched along the Austrian front or that he marched almost a complete circle around the Russian position at Zorndorf? We will hardly arrive at the conclusion that he who makes many mistakes is a great military leader. However, we might reach the conclusion that whoever wants to achieve a decisive victory has to master the laws of strategy and must weigh up which of these he can ignore in a given situation and which to make use of for a daring undertaking.

It appears to me that it is not as dangerous to make such errors as it is to hold rigidly to this or that universal method. Napoleon, the praised master of concentration [*Massebilden*], had certainly massed his forces at Leipzig. However, this method, which had led to brilliant victories at Austerlitz and Wagram, failed against the concentric advance of the allies. Napoleon had begun his career as a *Feldherr* in 1796 with an operation on inner lines, in which he turned first left and then right, beating and destroying his separated enemies. Yet again in 1814, he marched here and there between the separated allied corps dealing out his hammer blows on all sides. However, such an operation on inner lines led to his defeat at Waterloo.

The Field Marshal bequeathed us one rule: 'Not *one* method, not *one* means, not *one* expedient [*Aushilfe*], but many.' The Field Marshal never lacked expedients, and he would never have lacked them. Everyone in the army was convinced of this. No one doubted or only hoped, everyone knew that even in the most difficult of positions, the man with the smooth, iron brow and the clear eyes would find the right method and that at the right moment the right decision [*Entschluß*] would be made.

The Field Marshal taught us that this decision must be simple [*einfach*], and his decisions were certainly simple, simple in content and in form. What could be simpler than the telegram of 22 June 1866: 'His Majesty has ordered that both armies advance into Bohemia and seek to unite in the area of Gitschin.' With these few words, he broke out of a doubtful position, forced upon him by a hesitant policy, and brought one of the boldest and most important decisions to fruition.

As lightly and smoothly as the words of the telegram roll off, the decision was not to be fought out in a lonely office, not to be gained by doubtful souls, for in war all is difficult. However, the Field Marshal looked upon setbacks and successes with equal confidence, with the full confidence of an anointed *Feldherr*. When on the afternoon of 3 July the Crown Prince absolutely did not want to advance, when the stragglers flowed out of the Swiep Forest, when the final batteries came to the heights where the King stood and where everyone rode around him in alarm and agitation, the Field Marshal reported that not only the battle, but the campaign had been won. His far-seeing spirit saw past the excited goings-on of his surroundings. He knew how the thing must certainly end and had already perceived a turning point in world history.

However, behind that philosophical calm, behind that steadiness of the learned man, burned the fire of a tenacious will to achieve victory, to rush wildly forward, a merciless desire to annihilate the enemy. This could only be recognized by the deed. His exterior kept the calmness and steadiness that it had throughout his life.

What a difference from other *Feldherren*, who lived their lives as dramas and who were ruined as heroes in a tragedy! He lacked the requirements – the passion, the ambition, the selfishness – for such an end. He lived not for himself. He lived not for existence, but for something higher. He was the servant of his king, one of the truest. As we celebrate his memory today, we cannot neglect to renew our vow of loyalty and devotion to our Warlord. Thus, we call: His Majesty, the King and Kaiser – Hurrah!

SPEECH AT THE UNVEILING OF THE MOLTKE MONUMENT ON THE KÖNIGSPLATZ IN BERLIN, 26 OCTOBER 1905

Your Imperial and Royal Majesties! The column here on this square is evidence of the great deeds of the great Emperor. Statues of two of his paladins have already been erected at the foot of this column.[4] A third, the construction of which was made possible by contributions from the whole German army, is to be unveiled today by order of His Majesty. This third paladin's destiny was to translate into deeds what the other two had introduced and prepared.

This man of action was already 65 years old when he was called upon to perform this deed for immortality. He came from the loneliness of the office desk. Few knew him. No one paid any attention to him. Even on the morning of 3 July 1866, now 39 years ago, a high-ranking officer asked, 'Who is this Moltke?'.[5] Forty-eight hours later, no one asked any longer. In the remotest villages, school children wrote his name in capital letters. What had happened? A battle had been fought, a victory had been won. Not a victory like so many others which required another victory after some time had passed and after which the situation remained basically the same as at the beginning of the act, but rather a victory that produced clarity, one that with one stroke cut the Gordian Knot which had confused *Feldherren* for centuries and to which for centuries *Feldherren* had sought a solution. This was a man of action.

He was not the *Feldherr*; he was only the Chief of the General Staff.

HELMUTH VON MOLTKE

He was not a commander; he was only an adviser. He never wielded a sword on the battlefield or held a staff, the symbol of high command, in his hand. He was a man of the map, of the compass, of the pen. Despite this, however, history has stood him next to his glorious Emperor in the ranks of the few great heroes who will stand the course of centuries. Yet posterity still questions whether he reached the level of Napoleon, whether he surpassed Napoleon or whether he remains behind. Certainly, he cannot boast of having made a 19-year promenade through Europe. However, the Field Marshal brought about the conditions necessary to encircle three brave armies within six weeks. His victories were not so numerous as those which began in 1796 and ended in 1815. However, in brilliance they outdo all others, for the Field Marshal did not merely win, he annihilated.

This 'Gray Eminence' lacked the fancy thrills and the legends that symbolized the military career of the young Corsican – the bridge of Lodi, the flag of Arcole, the crossing of the Alps, the Pyramids as a background to a battle.[6] However, he also lacked the sea of fire in Moscow, the horror of Beresina, the flight from Leipzig, the collapse at Waterloo.[7] Such stokes of fate need not worry the head of a man who made 'first weigh up, then work' the guiding principle of his deeds, thereby banishing misfortune and tramping defeat under his feet.

Was the Field Marshal too cautious in his actions? Did he place 'working' behind 'weighing up'? Certainly not. What could have been bolder than advancing into Bohemia with armies and army corps separated in the face of an enemy army?

It is said that he had luck. But was it really luck that, in the moment that demanded the utmost speed, one army advanced only slowly or that one army corps retired in the face of an inferior enemy, while another advanced to its march goals untroubled by the sound of cannon to its right and left? And was it really luck that, despite everything, the push forward was held on its course or that on the day of decision the army flowed together from three sides and stood united in one mass on the battlefield in a way that one could barely have foreseen and in a way in which no one got left behind or forgotten?

He who wanders over the heights west of Metz between Point du Jour and Amanweiler, who visits the Mance ravine and the slopes at St Privat today must say: 'Unattackable'. And this impregnable position was defended by an army whose military virtues had been recognized and praised by the whole world for centuries. And this position had to be attacked not from out of Germany, but from out of France, while at any moment a new enemy army might appear in the German rear. Despite this riskiest of all situations, the position was taken, the battle was won, the enemy was encircled.

One has only to remember [the scene at] any of the small fortresses along the Belgian border or to call out the dates 1 and 2 September in order to awaken in anyone the memory of an utter defeat and victory the likes of which had never before been known – a victory that appears to have been won with so little effort that one is tempted to call it easy, if only one did not know that in war even the simplest thing is the most difficult.

With a third of the troops with which he had crossed the border a few weeks earlier, the victor arrived at the largest and strongest fortress in the world, which was defended by no less than 400,000 men. The strength of his troops barely sufficed to embrace the powerful circumference of the fortress' outerworks with a thin line. Communication with home had to be established by means of a long, slender rail line that was still interrupted by enemy fortresses, which still had to be conquered, and by breaks, which still had to be repaired. Replacement of losses and reinforcement came only slowly and sporadically. Material for the siege was only gradually sent out and in insufficient quantities. Against this, new enemy armies, seemingly stamped from the earth, appeared on all sides. To anyone else, the situation would have seemed in doubt. Only the unshakable will to succeed, the terrible spirit of one who also knew how to find the simplest answer to the most complicated question and the simplest solution to the greatest difficulty, and the wonderful daring of this 70-year-old young man [*des 70 jährigen Jünglings*] could ensure that part of the enemy's army was annihilated and the other part scattered and that the gates to the fortress were opened and its defensive works taken.

Not for a long time had anyone doubted the happy ending. In the whole army, from first to last, no one believed that General von Moltke could fail. Everyone was convinced that, as bad as the situation might look, General von Moltke would find a solution that would seem completely obvious in hindsight, but that would suffice to bring the enemy to ruin. His subordinates might make mistakes and give rise to bad days, but General von Moltke would always put everything back on the right track again.

Such trust can only be given to a man who does not allow himself to be overwhelmed by the distresses of the moment, who holds steady to the look forward and who knows the future, not as a prophet or a seer, but rather as one who has learned to read carefully from the book of history what will, and indeed must, come to pass. Such trust can only be given to one who was able, when standing on the heights of Sadowa, while everything seemed to be going badly, when all around him were in dismay and asked fearfully 'How will this end? What will happen?', was able to report: 'Your Majesty has won the campaign.'

This elevated spirit had done his share to establish an edifice that is lasting, that will weather the storms of time and rise up ever prouder. It has not come to pass for him as it has for others – he was not to be entombed in the ruins of that which he triumphantly erected. This man, who did not know 'I' and 'Self', fought and worked not for himself or for his own ambition or for his own fame, but rather for something higher. His ambition was only directed at being not the first, but the truest servant of his King.

The army that has erected this monument in thankful remembrance of a man who has brought it so much fame and honour wishes to emulate him in every way, if not reach his level in everything. In one area, at least, we can all do as he did – selfless devotion to the All-Highest Warlord!

His Majesty, the King and Kaiser – Hurrah!

Appendix I

Schlieffen's Life and Career

28 February 1833	Alfred born in Berlin to Major Friedrich Magnus Graf von Schlieffen and Luise, neé Gräfin Stolberg-Wernigerode
1 April 1853	Joined 2nd Garde-Uhlan Regiment as 'one-year volunteer' in Berlin
13 December 1853	Promoted to *Portepee-Fähnrich*
16 December 1854	Promoted to *Sekondleutnant* in 2nd Garde-Uhlan Regiment
1858–61	Attended *Kriegsakademie* in Berlin
1861–62	Assigned as Adjutant to 1st Garde-Cavalry Brigade
14 October 1862	Promoted to *Premierleutnant*
1863–65	Assigned to the Topographical Section, Great General Staff
June–July 1866	Austro-Prussian War – General Staff officer of the cavalry corps (under Prince Albrecht of Prussia) of the 1st Army, saw action at battles of Münchengrätz, Gitschen and Königgrätz
12 July 1866	Promoted to *Rittmeister*, then *Hauptmann* in General Staff
November 1866	Appointed assistant military attaché, Prussian Embassy, Paris

1 April 1868	Named General Staff officer, X Army Corps, Hannover
8 October 1868	Married to cousin Anna Gräfin von Schlieffen
13 September 1869	Daughter Elizabeth born
December 1869	Assigned as squadron commander, 2nd Dragoon Regiment
August 1870	Franco-German War – General Staff officer to Grossherzog von Mecklenburg-Schwerin, saw action at battle of Noisseville, siege of Toul and Soissons, and in the winter campaign on the Loire, awarded Iron Cross, 1st Class
22 December 1870	Promoted to *Major*
March 1871	General Staff officer in the newly formed XV Army Corps, Strassburg
9 July 1872	Daughter Marie born
13 July 1872	Wife, Anna, died
1873	Staff of the Guard Corps in Berlin
20 September 1876	Promoted to *Oberstleutnant*
11 November 1876	Named commander of the 1st Garde-Uhlan Regiment, Potsdam
16 September 1881	Promoted to *Oberst*
25 March 1884	Chief of the 3rd Section, Great General Staff, Berlin
4 December 1886	Promoted to *Generalmajor*
4 December 1888	Promoted to *Generalleutnant*
22 March 1889	Appointed as *Oberquartiermeister*, Great General Staff, Berlin

APPENDICES

7 February 1891	Chief of the Great General Staff, Berlin
14 June 1892	Named Adjutant General to Kaiser Wilhelm II
27 January 1893	Promoted to *General der Kavallerie*
1896	Named *à la suite* to the 1st Garde-Uhlan Regiment
1897	Awarded Order of the Black Eagle
1 April 1903	Celebrated 50 years of service
11 September 1903	Promoted to *Generaloberst* (with the position of *Generalfeldmarschall*)
1904	Named life member of the Prussian Herrenhaus
1 January 1906	Retired
1 January 1911	Promoted to *Generalfeldmarschall*
4 January 1913	Died in Berlin

Appendix II

The General Staff, 1891–1905

PRUSSIAN GREAT GENERAL STAFF ORGANIZATION, 1891

Chief of the General Staff

Central Section (Personnel Matters)

Oberquartiermeister I
2nd Section (Mobilization and Deployment)
Railroad Section

Oberquartiermeister II
4th Section (Foreign Fortresses)
Geographical Section
German Section (*Kriegsakademie* and Staff Rides)

Oberquartiermeister III
1st Section (Russian, Balkans, Scandinavia)
3rd Section (France, Great Britain, the Low Countries, Switzerland, Italy, Austria)

Military History Section
Library Section
Archives Section
Land Survey Section

APPENDICES
PRUSSIAN GREAT GENERAL STAFF ORGANIZATION 1898

Chief of the General Staff

Central Section (Personnel Matters)

Oberquartiermeister I
2nd Section (Mobilization and Deployment)
Railroad Section

Oberquartiermeister II
5th Section (General Staff Rides)
8th Section (*Kriegsakademie*)

Oberquartiermeister III
1st Section (Russian, Balkans, East Asia)
3rd Section (France, Great Britain, the Low Countries)
9th Section (Austria and Italy)

Oberquartiermeister IV
4th Section (French Fortresses)
7th Section (Russian Fortresses)

6th Section (Kaiser Manoeuvres)
Military History Section K1 (Wars from 1870)
Military History Section K2 (War before 1870)
Map Library Section
General Library Section
Archives Section
Land Survey Section

Appendix III

German Army Corps at Wartime Strength

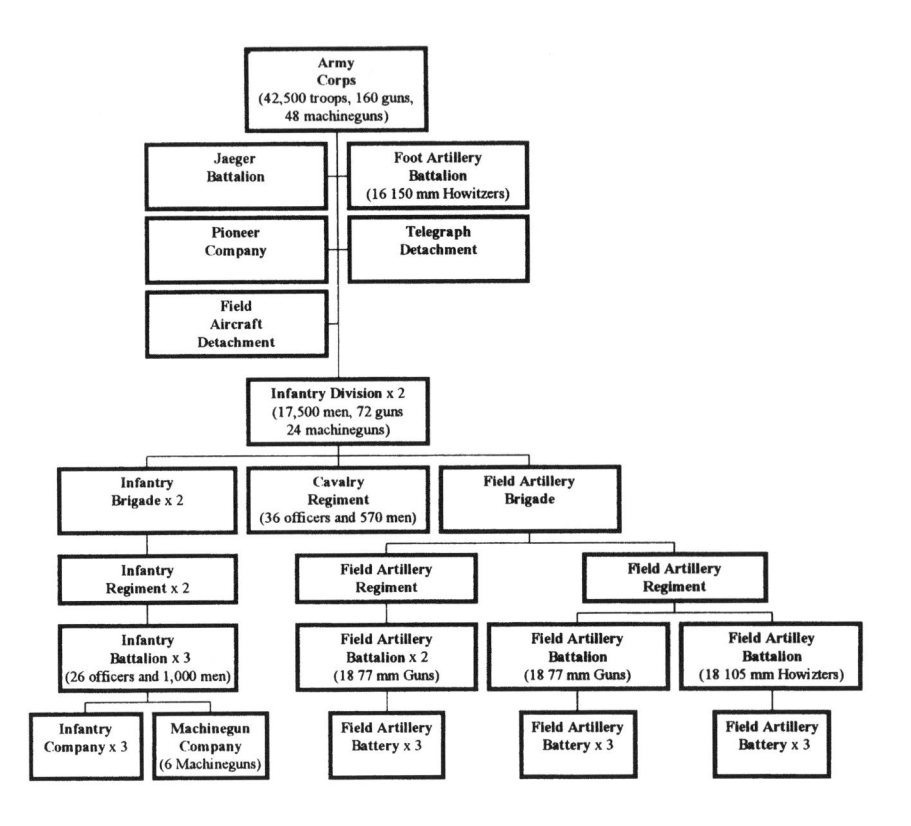

```
                    Army Corps
            (42,500 troops, 160 guns,
                48 machineguns)
                         |
    ┌────────────────┬───┴────┬──────────────────┐
    │                │        │                  │
Jaeger          Foot Artillery
Battalion         Battalion
              (16 150 mm Howitzers)

Pioneer           Telegraph
Company           Detachment

Field
Aircraft
Detachment
                         |
                Infantry Division x 2
                (17,500 men, 72 guns
                   24 machineguns)
                         |
    ┌────────────────┬───┴────────────┐
Infantry          Cavalry          Field Artillery
Brigade x 2       Regiment            Brigade
              (36 officers and 570 men)
    │                                    │
Infantry                    ┌────────────┴────────────┐
Regiment x 2          Field Artillery          Field Artillery
    │                    Regiment                Regiment
Infantry                    │                       │
Battalion x 3        ┌──────┴──────┐       ┌───────┴────────┐
(26 officers and 1,000 men)
    │            Field Artillery  Field Artillery  Field Artilley
┌───┴────┐       Battalion x 2     Battalion        Battalion
Infantry  Machinegun (18 77 mm Guns) (18 77 mm Guns) (18 105 mm Howizters)
Company   Company         │              │                │
 x 3    (6 Machineguns) Field Artillery Field Artillery Field Artillery
                         Battery x 3   Battery x 3      Battery x 3
```

Appendix IV

French Army Corps at Wartime Strength

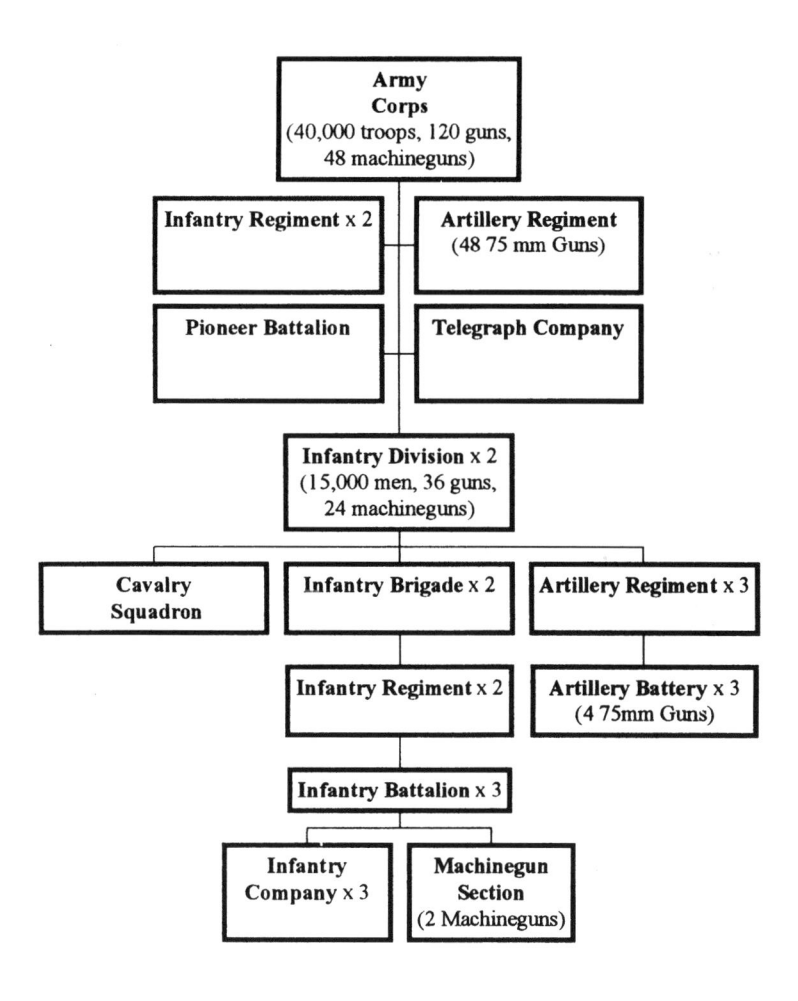

```
                    ┌─────────────────────────┐
                    │         Army            │
                    │         Corps           │
                    │ (40,000 troops, 120 guns,│
                    │    48 machineguns)      │
                    └─────────────────────────┘
         ┌──────────────────────┬──────────────────────┐
         │ Infantry Regiment x 2│ Artillery Regiment   │
         │                      │   (48 75 mm Guns)    │
         └──────────────────────┴──────────────────────┘
         ┌──────────────────────┬──────────────────────┐
         │  Pioneer Battalion   │  Telegraph Company   │
         └──────────────────────┴──────────────────────┘
                    ┌─────────────────────────┐
                    │   Infantry Division x 2 │
                    │   (15,000 men, 36 guns, │
                    │      24 machineguns)    │
                    └─────────────────────────┘
      ┌──────────────┬──────────────────┬──────────────────┐
      │   Cavalry    │ Infantry Brigade │ Artillery Regiment│
      │   Squadron   │       x 2        │       x 3        │
      └──────────────┴──────────────────┴──────────────────┘
                     ┌──────────────────┬──────────────────┐
                     │ Infantry Regiment│ Artillery Battery│
                     │       x 2        │  x 3 (4 75mm Guns)│
                     └──────────────────┴──────────────────┘
                     ┌──────────────────┐
                     │ Infantry Battalion x 3 │
                     └──────────────────┘
              ┌──────────────┬──────────────────┐
              │   Infantry   │    Machinegun    │
              │ Company x 3  │     Section      │
              │              │  (2 Machineguns) │
              └──────────────┴──────────────────┘
```

Appendix V

Russian Army Corps at Wartime Strength

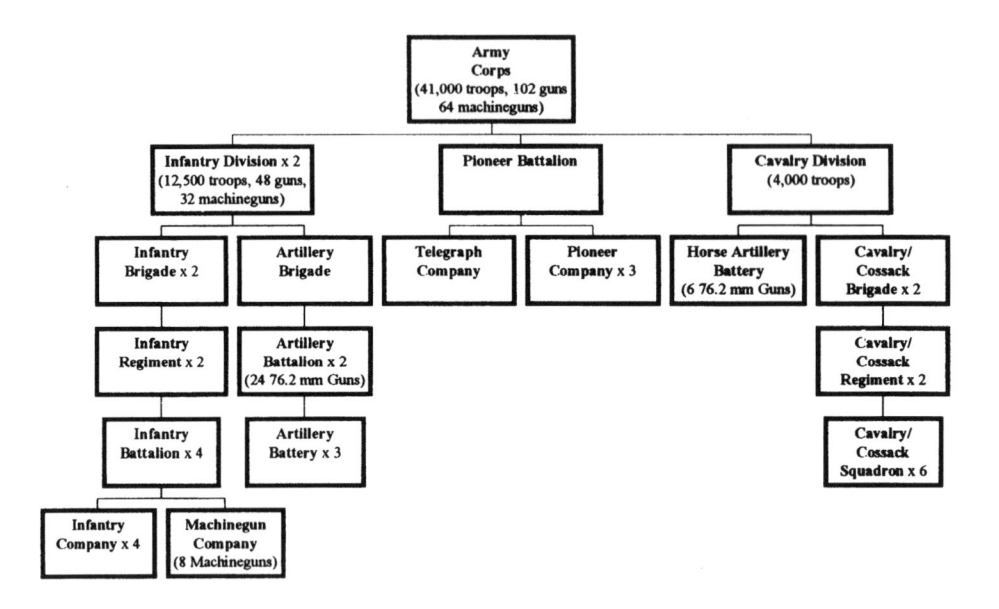

```
                          Army Corps
                   (41,000 troops, 102 guns
                       64 machineguns)
        ┌───────────────────┼───────────────────┐
   Infantry Division x 2   Pioneer Battalion   Cavalry Division
   (12,500 troops, 48 guns,                     (4,000 troops)
     32 machineguns)
    ┌──────┴──────┐              ┌──────┴──────┐      ┌──────┴──────┐
  Infantry      Artillery     Telegraph     Pioneer  Horse Artillery  Cavalry/
  Brigade x 2   Brigade       Company     Company x 3   Battery       Cossack
                                                      (6 76.2 mm Guns) Brigade x 2
     │             │                                                      │
  Infantry      Artillery                                              Cavalry/
  Regiment x 2  Battalion x 2                                          Cossack
                (24 76.2 mm Guns)                                      Regiment x 2
     │             │                                                      │
  Infantry      Artillery                                              Cavalry/
  Battalion x 4 Battery x 3                                            Cossack
                                                                       Squadron x 6
    ┌──┴──┐
Infantry  Machinegun
Company   Company
  x 4    (8 Machineguns)
```

242

Notes

Preface

1. Gerhard Ritter, *The Schlieffen Plan: Critique of a Myth* (trans. Andrew and Eva Wilson) (London: Oswald Wolff, 1958).
2. Alfred von Schlieffen, *Cannae* (Fort Leavenworth, KS: Command and General Staff School, 1931).
3. The debate began with a letter from one 'Alice von Schlieffen', supposedly the granddaughter of Alfred, but in fact the *nom de plume* of Mark Corby, in response to Correlli Barnett's article 'Oh What a Whinging War!', *Spectator*, 18 January 1997. It lasted until October 1997 with letters appearing in almost every intervening issue of the magazine. My thanks to Annika Mombauer for bringing this debate to my attention.
4. Robert T. Foley, 'Schlieffen's Last Kriegsspiel', in *War Studies Journal* 3, 2 (Summer 1998), pp. 117–33 and 4, 1 (Summer 1999), pp. 97–115.

Introduction

1. Hans von Seeckt, *Gedanken eines Soldaten* (Rev. Edn) (Leipzig: K.F. Koehler, 1935), pp. 22ff.
2. Ibid., p. 23. See also Friedrich von Rabenau, *Seeckt: Aus seinem Leben, 1918–1936* (Leipzig: v.Hase & Koehler, 1940), pp. 594ff.
3. On history writing in the General Staff, see Arden Bucholz, *Moltke, Schlieffen and Prussian War Planning* (Oxford: Berg, 1991), pp. 140ff. and passim. See also Constantin Hierl, 'Ziele und Wege für das Studium der Kriegsgeschichte', *Beiheft zum Militär-Wochenblatt*(1910), pp. 407–20.
4. Maximillian Yorck Graf von Wartenburg, *Napoleon as a General*, Vol.1 (London: K. Paul, Trench & Trubner, 1902), p. 1.
5. Hermann von Kuhl, *Der deutsche Generalstab in Vorbereitung und Durchführung des Weltkrieges* (Berlin: E.S. Mittler, 1920), pp. 150ff.; and Wolfgang Foerster, *Graf Schlieffen und der Weltkrieg* (Berlin: E.S. Mittler, 1921), pp. 21ff. For a recent reinterpretation, see Annika Mombauer, *Helmuth von Moltke and the Origins of the First World War* (Cambridge: Cambridge University Press, 2001).
6. Wilhelm Groener, *Das Testament des Grafen Schlieffen: Operative Studien über den Weltkrieg* (Berlin: E.S. Mittler, 1927); Groener, *Feldherr wider Willen: Operative Studien über den Weltkrieg* (Berlin: E.S. Mittler, 1931). This procedure was also followed by the authors of the German official history of the war. Reichsarchiv, *Der Weltkrieg 1914 bis 1918: Die militärischen Operationen zu Lande* (14 vols) (Berlin and Frankfurt: E.S. Mittler, 1925–56).
7. Wolfgang Foerster, *Aus der Gendankenwerkstatt des deutschen Generalstabes* (Berlin: E.S. Mittler, 1931); Friedrich von Boetticher, 'Der Lehrmeister des neuzeitlichen Krieges', in Friedrich von Cochenhausen, *Von Scharnhorst zu Schlieffen, 1806–1906: Hundert Jahre preußisch-deutscher Generalstab* (Berlin: E.S. Mittler, 1933) pp. 249–316; and Eugen Ritter von Zoellner, 'Schlieffens Vermächtnis', Sonderheft, *Militärwissenschaftliche Rundschau*, 3 (1938).

8. A.L. Conger, 'Introductory Note to German General Staff Problems', MSS in US National Archives, RG 165/320, discusses the use of Schlieffen's problems in the *Reichswehr* in the late 1920s; Alfred von Schlieffen, *Dienstschriften I: Die taktisch-strategischen Aufgaben aus den Jahren 1891–1905* (Berlin: E.S. Mittler, 1937); and A. von Schlieffen, *Dienstschriften II: Die großen Generalstabsreisen – Ost – aus den Jahren 1891–1905* (Berlin: E.S. Mittler, 1938).
9. Theo Schwarzmüller, *Zwischen Kaiser und 'Führer': Generalfeldmarschall August von Mackensen* (Paderborn: Ferdinand Schönigh, 1995), pp. 208ff. Mackensen, the onetime adjutant of Schlieffen and successful field commander in the First World War, was named as the society's first president.
10. Groener to Gerold von Gleich, 16 May 1935, quoted in Wilhelm Groener, *Lebenserinnerungen: Jugend, Generalstab, Weltkrieg* (ed. Friedrich Freiherr Hiller von Gaertringen) (Göttingen: Vandenhoeck & Ruprecht, 1957), p. 16.
11. See Roland G. Foerster, 'Military History in the Federal Republic of Germany and the *Bundeswehr*', David A. Charters, et al., *Military History and the Military Profession* (Westport, CT: Praeger, 1992), pp. 191–210.
12. For examples, see Gordon Craig, *The Politics of the Prussian Army* (New York: Oxford University Press, 1956); Walter Goerlitz, *History of the German General Staff, 1657–1945* (trans. Brian Battershaw) (New York: Praeger, 1957); and Karl Demeter, *The German Officer-Corps in Society and State, 1650–1945* (trans. Angus Malcolm) (London: Weidenfeld & Nicolson, 1965).
13. Gerhard Ritter, *The Schlieffen Plan: Critique of a Myth* (trans. Andrew and Eva Wilson) (London: Oswald Wolff, 1958).
14. Martin Kitchen, 'The Traditions of German Strategic Thought', *International History Review*, 1, 2 (April 1979), p. 163.
15. Jehuda Wallach, *Das Dogma der Vernichtungsschlacht: Die Lehren von Clausewitz und Schlieffen und ihre Wirkungen in zwei Weltkriegen* (Frankfurt: Bernard & Graefe, 1967); published in English as *The Dogma of the Battle of Annihilation: The Theories of Clausewitz and Schlieffen and their Impact on the German Conduct of Two World Wars* (Westport, CT: Greenwood Press, 1986).
16. Ritter, *Schlieffen Plan*.
17. Wallach, *Dogma*, pp. 35ff. See also Eberhard Kaulbach, 'Schlieffen: Zur Frage der Bedeutung und Wirkung seiner Arbeit', *Wehr-Wissenschaftliche Rundschau*, 13 (1963), pp. 137–49 and Günther Roth, 'The Thought of Annihilation in the Military Doctrine of Carl von Clausewitz and Count Alfred von Schlieffen', in Militärgeschichtliches Forschungsamt, ed., *Operational Thinking in Clausewitz, Moltke, Schlieffen and Manstein* (Bonn: E.S. Mittler, 1988), pp. 11–19.
18. Daniel J. Hughes, 'Schlichting, Schlieffen, and the Prussian Theory of War in 1914', *Journal of Military History*, 59 (April 1995), pp. 257–77; and Bucholz, *Prussian War Planning*.
19. Terence Zuber, 'The Schlieffen Plan Reconsidered', *War in History*, 6, 3, pp. 262–305; and Terence M. Holmes, 'Debate: The Reluctant March on Paris: A Reply to Terence Zuber's "The Schlieffen Plan Reconsidered"', *War in History*, 8, 2, pp. 208–32.
20. Antulio J. Echevarria II, *After Clausewitz: German Military Thinkers Before the Great War* (Lawrence, KS: University Press of Kansas, 2001), pp. 188–97.
21. Unfortunately, despite his significance, Schlieffen has not yet been the subject of a scholarly biography. The best to date is Friedrich von Boetticher, *Schlieffen* (Göttingen: Musterschmidt-Verlag, 1957).
22. A number of Schlieffen's relatives were high-ranking officials within the Reich's bureaucracy. See Eberhard Kessel, 'Einleitung', to Alfred von Schlieffen, *Briefe* (ed. Eberhard Kessel) (Göttingen: Vandenhoeck & Ruprecht, 1958), pp. 28ff.; and Bucholz, *Prussian War Planning*, pp. 109ff.
23. Hugo Rochs, *Schlieffen* (3rd edn) (Berlin: Vossische Buchhandlung Verlag, 1926), pp. 13ff.
24. Goerlitz, *General Staff*, pp.122–3; Gerhard Ritter, *The Sword and the Scepter: The Problem of Militarism in Germany*, Vol.II: *The European Powers and the Wilhelminian Empire, 1890–1914* (trans. Heinz Norden) (Coral Gables, FL: University of Miami Press, 1970), p. 130.

25. See Craig, *Politics*, pp. 255ff.; Goerlitz, *General Staff*, pp. 103ff.; and Ritter, *The Sword and the Scepter*, Vol.II, pp. 125ff.
26. In the years before the First World War, there was a saying that Europe was the home of five 'perfect' institutions: the Roman Curia, the British Parliament, the French Opera, the Russian Ballet and the Prussian General Staff. Mombauer, *Helmuth von Moltke*, p. 34.
27. On the development of the General Staff under Moltke, see Goerlitz, *General Staff*, pp. 69ff.; Bucholz, *Prussian War Planning*, pp. 39ff.; Kurt Jany, *Geschichte der Preußischen Armee vom 15. Jahrhundert bis 1914*, Vol.4: *Die Königliche Preußische Armee und das Deutsche Reichsheer 1807 bis 1914* (Berlin: Karl Siegismund, 1933), pp. 260ff.; Bronsart von Schellendorf, *The Duties of the General Staff* (4th edn) (London: HMSO, 1905), pp. 10ff.
28. Hans-Ulrich Wehler, *Das deutsche Kaiserreich* (Göttingen: Musterschmidt, 1973), pp. 69ff.
29. See below.
30. Ritter, *Sword and the Scepter*, Vol.II, pp. 123ff.
31. Schlieffen, *Briefe*, pp. 291–2, and Alfred Graf von Waldersee, *Denkwürdigkeiten des General-Feldmarschalls Alfred Graf von Waldersee* (ed. Heinrich Otto Meisner) (Stuttgart: Deutsche Verlags-Anstalt, 1923), p. 189.
32. See his speech at the celebration of his 50-year anniversary of service, Alfred von Schlieffen, *Gesammelte Schriften* Vol.II (Berlin: E.S. Mittler, 1913), p. 452. Although Schlieffen attributed this to Moltke, it appears as if he in fact borrowed it from Goethe, one of his favourite authors. See Bucholz, *Prussian War Planning*, p. 109. However, this expression is so emblematic of Schlieffen that his biographer took it as the subtitle to his book. Boetticher, *Schlieffen: Viel leisten, wenig hervortraten – mehr sein als scheinen*.
33. See Rainer Lahme, *Deutsche Aussenpolitik, 1880–1894. Von Gleichgewichtspolitik Bismarcks zur Allianzstrategie Caprivis* (Göttingen: Vandenhoeck & Ruprecht, 1990), pp. 100ff.
34. See William C. Fuller, *Strategy and Power in Russia, 1600–1914* (New York: Free Press, 1992), pp. 350ff.; and George F. Kennan, *The Fateful Alliance: France, Russia and the Coming of the First World War* (Manchester: Manchester University Press, 1984), pp. 136ff.
35. Ritter, *Sword and the Scepter*, Vol.II, pp. 122ff.; Holger Herwig, 'From Tirpitz to Schlieffen Plan: Some Observations on German Military Planning', *Journal of Strategic Studies*, 9, 1 (1986), pp. 53–63.
36. The important role played by Kaiser Wilhelm II in German policymaking has been the subject of much recent research. See John Röhl, *The Kaiser and his Court: Wilhelm II and the Government of Germany* (Cambridge: Cambridge University Press, 1994); Lamar Cecil, *Wilhelm II: Prince and Emperor, 1859–1900* (Chapel Hill, NC: University of North Carolina Press, 1989); and L. Cecil, *Wilhelm II: Emperor and Exile, 1900–1941* (Chapel Hill, NC: The University of North Carolina Press, 1996).
37. Bucholz, *Prussian War Planning*, p.135.
38. Although Schlieffen was on friendly terms with Friedrich von Holstein, the 'gray eminence' of the Foreign Office, Holstein appears to have used Schlieffen more as a technical adviser. See Peter Rassow, 'Schlieffen und Holstein', *Historische Zeitschrift*, 173 (1952), pp. 297–313. Cf. Ritter, *Schlieffen Plan*, pp. 126ff.
39. For a full discussion of Schlieffen's planning, see above, pp. 143ff.
40. Reichsarchiv, *Der Weltkrieg 1914 bis 1918: Kriegsrüstung und Kriegswirtschaft: Anlagen zum ersten Band* (Berlin: E.S. Mittler, 1930), 'Tabelle 4: Das Deutsche Heer in der Kriegsformation nach dem Stande vom Jahre 1888', pp. 461ff.
41. Douglas Porch, *March to the Marne: The French Army, 1871–1914* (Cambridge: Cambridge University Press, 1981), pp. 23ff. By way of contrast, Italy conscripted around 30 per cent of eligible men, Austria-Hungary 34 per cent, and Russia 44 per cent in 1900. Ritter, *Sword and the Scepter*, Vol.II, p. 23.
42. Schlieffen to his sister Marie, 13 November 1892, reprinted in Schlieffen, *Briefe*, pp. 295ff. Ultimately, a popular organization dedicated to the strengthening of the army by extension of conscription was founded by one of Waldersee's former 'pen hussars', August Keim. See Marilyn Shevin Coetzee, *The German Army League: Popular Nationalism in Wilhelmine Germany* (Oxford: Oxford University Press, 1990).

43. Max van den Bergh, *Das Deutsche Heer vor dem Weltkriege* (Berlin: Sanssouci Verlag, 1934), pp. 183ff. See also, Heinrich Otto Meisner, *Der Kriegsminister, 1814–1914* (Berlin: Hermann Reinshagen Verlag, 1940).
44. Reichsarchiv, *Kriegsrüstung und Kriegswirtschaft*, Vol.I: *Die militärische, wirtschaftliche und finanzielle Rüstung Deutschlands von der Reichsgründung bis zum Ausbruch des Weltkrieges* (Berlin: E.S. Mittler, 1930), pp. 26ff.; Jany, *Geschichte der Preußischen Armee*, pp. 289ff.
45. Schlieffen's colleagues at the Ministry of War were also wary of an influx of 'unreliable' Socialists that would inevitably follow an extension of conscription. See Stig Förster, *Der doppelte Militärismus: Die deutsche Heeresrüstungspolitik zwischen Status-Quo-Sicherung und Aggression, 1890–1913* (Stuttgart: Franz Steiner Verlag, 1985).
46. Bruce Gudmundsson, *On Artillery* (Westport, CT: Praeger, 1993), pp. 34ff.
47. Reichsarchiv, *Kriegsrüstung und Kriegswirtschaft*, I, pp. 42ff.
48. For details, see above, pp. 7ff. and pp. 149ff.
49. Paul Schneider, *Die Organisation des Heeres* (Berlin: E.S. Mittler, 1931), p. 66; Bergh, *Das deutsche Heer*, pp. 38ff.; Wiegand Schmidt-Richberg, 'Die Regierungszeit Wilhelms II', in Militärgeschichtliches Forschungsamt, ed., *Deutsche Militärgeschichte 1648–1939*, Vol.III: *Von der Entlastung Bismarcks bis zum Ende des Ersten Weltkrieges 1890–1918* (Munich: Bernard & Graefe Verlag, 1983), pp. 72ff.
50. For example, Sigismund von Schlichting, who commanded the XIV Army Corps from 1888 to 1896 and who had a great impact on the development of the operational art, developed a number of followers from within his corps who advocated his operational ideas even after his retirement. See Joachim Hoffmann, 'Die Kriegslehre des Generals von Schlichting', *Militärgeschichtliche Mitteilungen*, I (1969), pp. 5–35.
51. See above, pp. 186ff.
52. Schlieffen was reportedly so frustrated by the Ministry of War that he took to calling it the 'Ministry of Peace'. Rochs, *Schlieffen*, p. 55.
53. Bronsart von Schellendorff, *Duties of the General Staff*, 4th edn (London, HMSO, 1905), pp. 38ff.; Bucholz, *Prussian War Planning*, p. 159.
54. Steven E. Clemente, *For King and Kaiser! The Making of the Prussian Army Officer, 1860–1914* (Westport, CT: Greenwood Press, 1992), p. 193.
55. Herbert Rosinski, *The German Army* (ed. Gordon Craig) (New York: Praeger, 1966), pp. 107–9.
56. Kronprinz Wilhelm, *Meine Erinnerungen aus Deutschlands Heldenkampf* (Berlin: E.S. Mittler, 1923), p. 4. Emphasis added.
57. Schlieffen was called the 'master teacher of modern war' by a number of his subordinates. See Hermann von Kuhl, *Der deutsche Generalstabe in Vorbereitung und Durchführung des Weltkrieges* (Berlin: E.S. Mittler, 1920), p. 126; Friedrich von Boetticher, 'Der Lehrmeister des neuzeitlichen Krieges', in Friedrich von Cochenhausen, *Von Scharnhorst zu Schlieffen, 1806–1906: Hundert Jahre preußisch-deutscher Generalstab* (Berlin: E.S. Mittler, 1933), pp. 249–316.
58. See 'Tactical-Strategic Problems 1903', p. 107; and 'Kriegsspiel, 1905', pp. 138ff.
59. For details, see above, p. 7ff.
60. Friedrich von Bernhardi, *Denkwürdigkeiten aus meinem Leben* (Berlin: E.S. Mittler, 1927), pp. 220ff. Also Ritter, *Sword and the Scepter*, Vol.II, p. 113; and Dennis Showalter, 'Goltz and Bernhardi: The Institutionalization of Originality in the Imperial German Army', *Defense Analysis*, 3,4 (1987), pp. 306–7, 311–12.
61. Berthold von Deimling, *Aus der Alten in die neue Zeit: Lebenserinnerungen* (Berlin: Ullstein, 1930), pp. 49–50.
62. See James Corum, *The Roots of Blitzkrieg: Hans von Seeckt and German Military Reform* (Lawrence, KS: University Press of Kansas, 1992); and Robert M. Citino, *The Path to Blitzkrieg: Doctrine and Training the German Army, 1920-1939* (Boulder, CO: Lynne Rienner, 1999).
63. Herbert Rosinski, 'Scharnhorst to Schlieffen: The Rise and Decline of German Military Thought', *Naval War College Review*, 29 (1976), pp. 83–103; Wallach, *Dogma*, pp. 216ff.

Introduction to Part I: Wargames

1. See Reichsarchiv, *Der Weltkrieg*, Vol.II: *Die Befreiung Ostpreußens* (Berlin: E.S. Mittler, 1925), pp. 111–238; and for a recent account, Dennis Showalter, *Tannenberg: Clash of Empires* (Hamden, CT: Archon Books, 1991).
2. Showalter, *Tannenberg*, p. 329. For an example of the literature perpetuating the Hindenburg myth, see Joachim Franke, ed. *Hindenburg-Schläge und Hindenburg-Anekdoten* (13th ed.) (Stuttgart: R. Lutz, 1915).
3. See Paul von Hindenburg, *Out of My Life* (trans. F.A. Holt) (London: Cassell, 1920), pp. 81–99. For Ludendorff's position on the question, see his memoirs, *Ludendorff's Own Story: August 1914–November 1918* (New York: Harper & Bros., 1919), pp. 49–86. Likewise, see Max Hoffmann, *Tannenberg, wie es wirklich war* (Berlin: Verlag für Kulturpolitik, 1926).
4. The German army conducted one large-scale (corps-level) manoeuvre each September, the so-called *Kaisermanöver*.
5. 'The tactical education is, in the first instance, the task of the regimental commander.' Kriegsministerium, *Felddienst-Ordnung* (Berlin: E.S. Mittler, 1908), p. 10.
6. Kriegsministerium, *Felddienst-Ordnung* (Berlin: E.S. Mittler, 1888), p. 12.
7. *Felddienst-Ordnung*, 1908, p. 11.
8. On the history of war games, see (Jacob) Meckel, *Studien über das Kriegsspiel* (Berlin: E.S. Mittler, 1873); Werner Knoll, 'Die Entwicklung des Kriegsspiels in Deutschland bis 1945', *Militärgeschichte*, 20 (1981), pp. 179–89; and Arden Bucholz, *Moltke, Schlieffen and Prussian War Planning* (Providence, RI: Berg, 1991), pp. 85–93.
9. A good example of an 'education plan' has survived in the US National Archives. It was written by the commander of the Bavarian 6th Division. Pflauen, 'Ausbildung der Offiziere', 15 December 1905, USNA, RG242, T-78/Roll 21. (My thanks to Bruce Gudmundsson for bringing this document to my attention.) An example of a lecture appearing in print is August Keim, 'Kriegslehre und Kriegsführung', *Beiheft zum Militär-Wochenblatt* (1889).
10. See Hermann von Kuhl, *Der deutsche Generalstabe in Vorbereitung und Durchführung des Weltkrieges* (Berlin: E.S. Mittler, 1920), p. 126; Friedrich von Boetticher, 'Der Lehrmeister des neuzeitlichen Krieges', in Friedrich von Cochenhausen, *Von Scharnhorst zu Schlieffen, 1806–1906: Hundert Jahre preußisch-deutscher Generalstab* (Berlin: E.S. Mittler, 1933), pp. 249–316.
11. Paul Schneider, *Die Organisation des Heeres* (Berlin: E.S. Mittler, 1931), p. 66; Max van den Bergh, *Das Deutsche Heer vor dem Weltkriege* (Berlin: Sanssouci Verlag, 1934), pp. 38ff.
12. Alfred von Schlieffen, *Dienstschriften*, Vol.I: *Die taktisch-strategischen Aufgaben aus den Jahren 1891–1905* (Berlin: E.S. Mittler, 1937); and von Schlieffen, *Dienstschriften*, Vol.II: *Die Großen Generalstabsreisen – Ost – aus den Jahren 1891–1905* (Berlin: E.S. Mittler, 1938).
13. Friedrich von Rabenau (chief of the army archive) to all army archives, 22 May 1937, USNA, Alfred von Schlieffen Papers, RG242, M-961/Roll 1. The Reichsarchiv had also planned to publish Helmuth von Moltke the Younger's staff rides and tactical problems. However, like the final volume of Schlieffen's work, this too was destroyed in 1945.
14. Preface to Schlieffen, *Dienstschriften*, Vol.I, p. vii; Bergh, *Deutsche Heer*, pp.175–6; Wilhelm Groener, *Lebenserinnerungen* (ed. Friedrich Freiherr Hiller von Gaetringen) (Göttingen: Vandenhoeck & Ruprecht, 1957), pp. 67–9.
15. Hermann von Stein, *A War Minister and His Work: Reminiscences of 1914–1918* (London: Skeffington, n.d.), p. 44.
16. Kuhl, *Der deutsche Generalstab*, p. 126.
17. Preface to Schlieffen, *Dienstschriften*, II, p. vii; Bucholz, *Prussian War Planning*, p. 144.
18. Karl von Einem, *Erinnerungen eines Soldaten* (Leipzig: K.F. Koehler, 1933), pp. 46–7; Bucholz, *Prussian War Planning*, p.131.
19. Boetticher, 'Lehrmeister', pp.297–8.
20. In 1897, Schlieffen issued new orders for the conduct of staff rides that directed 'strategic' (what we would today refer to as 'operational') issues be dealt with more than 'tactical'. Einem, *Erinnerungen*, pp. 46–7.

NOTES TO PAGES 6-11

21. Schlieffen's critiques were legendary for not only their incisiveness, but also for their sarcasm. See Stein, *War Minister*, pp. 40–1; and General Hans von Beseler's opinion in Hugo Freiherr von Freytag-Loringhoven, 'Generalfeldmarschall Graf v. Schlieffen: Lebensgang und Lebenswerk', in Alfred von Schlieffen, *Gesammelte Schriften*, Vol.I (Berlin: E.S. Mittler, 1913), p. xxii. According to Freytag, Schlieffen often worked the entire night composing his critiques.
22. Quoted in Boetticher, 'Lehrmeister', p. 296.
23. No good study of the Military Society of Schlieffen's time exists. For an introduction see Charles White, *The Enlightened Soldier: Scharnhorst and the* Militärische Gesellschaft *in Berlin, 1801–1805* (New York: Praeger, 1989).
24. Eugen Ritter von Zoellner, 'Schlieffens Vermächtnis', *Sonderheft, Militärwissenschaftliche Rundschau*, 3 (1938), p. 46.
25. Schlieffen to his sister Marie, 13 November 1892, reprinted in Alfred von Schlieffen, *Briefe* (ed. Eberhard Kessel) (Göttingen: Vandenhoeck & Ruprecht, 1958), pp. 295ff.
26. See Reichsarchiv, *Der Weltkrieg 1914 bis 1918: Kriegsrüstung und Kriegswirtschaft*: Vol.1 (Berlin: E.S. Mittler, 1930), pp. 42ff.
27. Goßler to Schlieffen, 8 June 1899, printed in Reichsarchiv, *Kriegsrüstung und Kriegswirtschaft: Anlagen zum ersten Band* (Berlin: E.S. Mittler, 1930), pp. 57ff.
28. Goßler to Schlieffen, 19 October 1899, printed in Reichsarchiv, *Kriegsrüstung und Kriegswirtschaft: Anlagen* I, p. 68.
29. Grosser Generalstab, *Der Feldzug von 1866 in Deutschland* (Berlin: E.S. Mittler, 1867), pp. 45–8; Reichsarchiv, *Kriegsrüstung und Kriegswirtschaft: Anlagen* I, *Tabelle* 4: 'Das deutsche Heer in der Kriegsformation nach dem Stande vom Jahre 1888' and *Tabelle* 11: 'Das deutsche Heer in der Kriegsformation nach dem Stande vom Jahre 1902'.
30. See his 'War Today', pp. 218ff.
31. Schlieffen to Goßler, 19 August and 10 November 1899 printed in Reichsarchiv, *Kriegsrüstung und Kriegswirtschaft: Anlagen* I, pp. 60–7 and 77–9. See also Ludwig Rüdt von Collenberg, 'Graf Schlieffen und die Kriegsformation der deutschen Armee', *Wissen und Wehr* (1927), pp. 605–34.
32. 'Tactical-Strategic Problems 1903', p. 107. Cf. '*Kriegsspiel*, 1905', pp. 138ff.
33. See Moltke's 'Instructions for Large Unit Commanders of 24 June 1869', published in Daniel Hughes, ed., *Moltke On the Art of War* (Novato, CA: Presidio, 1995), pp. 183ff. See also Martin Samuels, 'Directive Command and the German General Staff', *War in History*, 2, 1, pp. 22–42.
34. This concept appears constantly in Schlieffen's critiques. For examples, see 'General Staff Ride, 1894', p. 23f., and 'General Staff Ride 1899', p. 48f.
35. From Schlieffen's critique of the General Staff Ride of 1904, quoted in Zoellner, *Schlieffens Vermächtnis*, p. 32.
36. Schlieffen was not alone in advocating flank attacks as a means of avoiding frontal assaults so costly in the face of modern weapons. See Sigismund von Schlichting, 'Über das Infanteriegefecht', *Beiheft zum Militär-Wochenblatt*, 2 (1879), pp. 38ff.; Wilhelm von Blume, *Strategie* (Berlin: E.S. Mittler, 1886), p. 169.
37. Contemporaries such as Sigismund von Schlichting and Friedrich von Bernhardi maintained that an 'envelopment mania' reigned in Schlieffen's General Staff. For discussions of contemporary opposition to Schlieffen's ideas see, Sigfrid Mette, *Vom Geist deutscher Feldherren* (Zürich: Scientia AG, 1938), pp. 163–220, which examines Schlichting's opposition to Schlieffen and includes many extracts from the now-destroyed Schlichting Nachlass; and Ernst Buchfinck, 'Feldmarschall Graf Haeseler', *Wissen und Wehr* (1936), pp. 3–9. The ideas of these critics were picked up by later observers. See Jehuda Wallach, *The Dogma of the Battle of Annihilation* (Westport, CT: Greenwood Press, 1986), pp. 35–68.
38. See above, his 'General Staff Ride, 1894', pp. 24ff.; 'General Staff Ride, 1901', pp. 51ff. '*Kriegsspiel*, 1905', pp. 119ff. and *passim*. Cf. Zoellner, *Schlieffens Vermächtnis*, pp. 30–1 for further examples.
39. See above, 'General Staff Ride, 1894', pp. 24f.; 'General Staff Ride, 1903', pp. 66f., '*Kriegsspiel*, 1905', pp. 126f.

40. Indeed, even 'Schlieffen's favourite disciple', Hugo Freiherr von Freytag-Loringhoven, maintained that encirclement was only one means of defeating an enemy. See Antulio J. Echevarria II, 'General Staff Historian Hugo Freiherr von Freytag-Loringhoven and the Dialectics of German Military Thought', *Journal of Military History*, 60 (1996), pp. 471–94. Cf. Oberstleutnant Brückner, 'Der Durchbruchsangriff vor dem Weltkriege in Anwendung und Theorie', *Militärwissenschaftliche Rundschau*, 5 (1938), pp. 586–601.
41. Although Ritter dismisses this objective, recent work by Bucholz has shown conclusively that Schlieffen's training exercises also had this planning role. Bucholz, *Prussian War Planning*, passim. Cf. Hugo Freiherr von Freytag-Loringhoven, *Menschen und Dinge, wie ich in meinem Leben sah* (Berlin: E.S. Mittler, 1923), pp. 102–3; and Erich Ludendorff, *Mein militärischer Werdegang* (Munich: Ludendorffs Verlag, 1933), pp. 96ff.
42. Quoted in Mette, *Feldherren*, p. 213.
43. Kuhl, *Der deutsche Generalstab*, p. 129.
44. While most of Schlieffen's *Schlußaufgaben* have been published, only five of his 31 General Staff rides made it into print, and each of these took place on the eastern frontier. Only one of his *Kriegsspiel* critiques seems to have survived two world wars and the division of Germany.
45. 'General Staff Ride, 1897', pp. 27ff.; 'General Staff Ride, 1901', pp. 51ff.; 'General Staff Ride, 1903', pp. 62f.; and '*Kriegsspiel*, 1905', pp. 120ff.
46. '*Kriegsspiel*, 1905', p. 126. See also 'War Today', p. 200.
47. Bruce Gudmundsson, 'The Battle of the Frontiers, 1914', unpublished paper presented at the Society for Military History Conference, Calgary, 26 May 2001; and Hew Strachan, *The First World War*, Vol.1: *To Arms* (Oxford: Oxford University Press, 2001), pp. 208–24.

1: General Staff Ride (East), 1894

1. This translation is from Alfred von Schlieffen, *Dienstschriften*, Vol.II: *Die Großen Generalstabesreisen – Ost – aus den Jahren 1891–1905* (Berlin: E.S. Mittler, 1938), pp. 38–50.
2. For the German deployment plans for 1893/94, see Wilhelm Dieckmann, 'Der Schlieffenplan', unfinished and unpublished manuscript in Bundesarchiv/Militärarchiv (BA/MA), W10/50220, pp. 28ff.
3. Schlieffen continually referred to the importance of railroads for an army's deployment. For example, see his 'Tactical-Strategic Problems, 1892', pp. 72ff.
4. The Germans made a distinction between mobilization (*Mobilmachung*) and deployment (*Aufmarsch*), although the two occurred simultaneously. Mobilization referred to the process of bringing units up to wartime strength, while deployment was the process of arraying units to carry out the war plan. Generally, the mobilization was the responsibility of the Ministry of War and the deployment was the responsibility of the General Staff. In practice, the two organizations worked together to ensure a smooth process. See Annika Mombauer, *Helmuth von Moltke and the Origins of the First World War* (Cambridge: Cambridge University Press, 2001), pp. 25ff.; and Arden Bucholz, *Moltke, Schlieffen and Prussian War Planning* (Oxford: Berg, 1991), passim.
5. In 1894, Russia was divided into a number of districts, each of which supplied upon mobilization the manpower for certain army formations. Some of these districts, however, had small pools of manpower from which to draw and hence they had to make up these shortages by 'borrowing' manpower from other, more densely populated districts. See Bruce W. Menning, *Bayonets Before Bullets: The Imperial Russian Army, 1861–1914* (Indianapolis, IN: University of Indiana Press, 1992), pp. 87–122.
6. In 1892, Russia and France signed a military convention obligating the one to come to the aid of the other if attacked by Germany. This convention was formalized by a treaty signed in January 1894, in which France agreed to face Germany with 1.3 million troops and Russia 800,000 by the 14th mobilization day. Schlieffen was here referring to this treaty. See William C. Fuller, *Strategy and Power in Russia 1600–1914* (New York: Free Press, 1992), pp. 350–62.

7. Like Russia, Germany was divided into districts that supplied manpower for the army. In 1894, Germany was divided into 20 districts (17 Prussian, two Bavarian, and one Württemberger), each of which provided for at least one active duty army corps, one reserve division, a *Landwehr* brigade, and various *Landsturm* units. Some districts provided additional units, depending upon available manpower. The I, XVII, II, V and VI Army Corps districts were on the eastern border. See Reichsarchiv, *Der Weltkrieg 1914 bis 1918: Kriegsrüstung und Kriegswirtschaft: Anlagen zum ersten Band* (Berlin: E.S. Mittler, 1930), p. 532.
8. The *Landsturm* made up the oldest classes of trained manpower. Following the reduction in terms of service from three years to two in 1893, in 1894 a German infantryman would serve two years on active duty beginning at age 20, at 22 enter the Reserve, at 28 enter the *Landwehr* I, at 32 the *Landwehr* II, and at 40 the *Landsturm*, where he would serve out his service to the age of 45. With each step up the ladder, time served with the colours per year reduced and requirements during wartime diminished. Wiegand Schmidt-Richberg, 'Die Regierungszeit Wilhelms II', in Militärgeschichtliches Forschungsamt, ed., *Deutsche Militärgeschichte, 1648–1939*, Vol.III (Munich: Bernard & Graefe Verlag, 1983), pp. 49–51.
9. This event was mirrored 20 years later at the battle of Tannenberg. For a recent description and analysis of the battle, see Dennis Showalter, *Tannenberg: Clash of Empires* (Hamden, CT: Archon Books, 1991).
10. The term *Armeeabteilung*, which is an *ad hoc* unit smaller than an army but larger than a corps, does not seem to have any direct corollary in English; therefore, I have left it in the original.
11. Throughout his staff rides and problems, Schlieffen brought up the problem of friction in war and how officers must learn to deal with never having complete information about the enemy. For other examples, see his 'General Staff Ride, 1899', pp. 48f.; and the 'Tactical-Strategic Problems, 1905', p. 112.
12. Helmuth von Moltke the Elder had written that 'a failure in the original assembly of an army can barely be made good during the course of a campaign'. (Quoted in Helmuth Otto, *Schlieffen und der Generalstab* (Berlin: Deutsche Militärverlag, 1966), p. 129.) Schlieffen combined Moltke's idea with concepts of battle developed in large part by Sigismund von Schlichting and elaborated in the drill regulations of 1888. These emphasized 'encounter battles', during which the formal deployment of forces prevalent in previous times would be impossible. Instead, German units would be forced to enter battle directly from march formation. See his 'War Today', p. 199; and Robert T. Foley, 'Attrition: Its Theory and Application in German Strategy, 1880–1916', PhD thesis, University of London, May 1999, pp. 61–6.
13. In the Imperial German army, the term '*Kommandierender General*' was reserved for the commanders of corps-level formations (army corps, reserve corps, cavalry corps, etc.).
14. Here, Schlieffen has outlined the basics of what has become known as *Auftragstaktik*, or 'mission-type orders'. However, unlike mission-type orders as they are understood today, Schlieffen has placed the responsibility of understanding the commander's overall intent upon the subordinates. For the development of this style of leadership, see Martin Samuels, 'Directive Command and the German General Staff', *War in History*, 2, 1, pp. 22–42; and Samuels, *Command or Control? Command, Training and Tactics in the British and German Armies, 1888–1918* (London: Frank Cass, 1995), *passim*.
15. Schlieffen refers here to the battle of Königgrätz (3 July 1866) during the Austro-Prussian War and the battle of Gravelotte–St Privat (18 August 1870) during the Franco-German War, both of which were considered 'decisive' (i.e., war-winning) battles for the Prussians/Germans.

2: *General Staff Ride (East), 1897*

1. This translation is from Schlieffen, *Dienstschriften*, Vol.II, pp. 93–104.
2. See Dieckmann, 'Schlieffenplan', pp. 107ff.
3. A rapid on rush of Russian cavalry and Cossacks aiming at cutting railways in the eastern

provinces and disrupting mobilization and deployment was a particular fear of the Germans at this time. See Dieckmann, 'Schlieffenplan', pp. 32ff.
4. Each German infantry division disposed of a regiment of cavalry, from which this new cavalry division was formed during this ride.
5. A distinction must be made between a *Befehl* (order) and a *Direktiv* (directive). The former was an order that had to be followed, while the latter allowed the subordinate latitude in execution. *Direktive* were integral to *Auftragstaktik* (which was also known as *Führung nach Direktiv*). See 'General Staff Ride, 1894', Note 13.
6. Throughout his tenure as Chief of the General Staff, Schlieffen struggled with the problem of not having enough forces to defeat both the French and Russians simultaneously. His solution in this game was to deal the French a serious, but not 'decisive', blow early and then shift forces to the east. There, they would take part in a decisive victory over the Russians before being transported west again for the final reckoning with the French. Cf. his 'General Staff Ride, 1901', pp. 51ff.; his '*Kriegsspiel*, 1905', pp. 119ff.; and his 'Memorandum of 1905', pp. 163ff., for variations on this theme.

3: General Staff Ride (East), 1899

1. This translation is from Schlieffen, *Dienstschriften*, Vol.II, pp. 163–74.
2. See Dieckmann, 'Schlieffenplan', pp. 125ff.
3. Although the rule was for each corps district to provide two active infantry divisions (a full corps), some districts had spare battalions, regiments and even divisions. See Reichsarchiv, *Der Weltkrieg: Kriegsrüstung und Kriegswirtschaft*, Vol.I: *Die militärische, wirtschaftliche und finanzielle Rüstung Deutschlands von der Reichsgründung bis zum Ausbruch des Weltkrieges* (Berlin: E.S. Mittler, 1930), pp. 46–55; and *Kriegsrüstung und Kriegswirtschaft: Anlagen zum ersten Band* (Berlin: E.S. Mittler, 1930), p. 478–9.
4. The German XX and XXI Army Corps had been constructed in the re-formation of the *Ostheer*.
5. In 1813, as the Allied armies pursued Napoleon back from Russia, the combined commanders decided that Napoleon was still too strong to be defeated in a great, decisive battle. Instead, his force was to be defeated in detail. Any Allied force that found itself attacked by Napoleon's main force was to withdraw, while the other armies converged on his lines of communication. This idea came to be called the 'Trachenberg Plan'. See David Chandler, *The Campaigns of Napoleon* (London: Weidenfeld & Nicolson, 1967), p. 901.
6. The question of manpower was always in Schlieffen's mind. The Franco-Russian Military Convention of 1892 pledged the French to send 1.3 million men and Russia '700,000 or 800,000' men against Germany. To face this, the Germans expected to deploy a field army of 1.6 million. Although Schlieffen could not know the exact strengths of his opponents, he clearly knew Germany would face enemies superior in strength. He used a formulation very similar to the one in this ride in a letter to the Minister of War, Heinrich von Goßler, dated 10 November 1899, in which he argued for army increases. Interestingly, Schlieffen was after an increase in the number of corps, rather than a simple increase in the army's manpower. It is clear from his exchange with Goßler and these staff rides that Schlieffen considered the number of corps important because by this time the General Staff believed the corps to be the basic warfighting unit. *Kriegsrüstung und Kriegswirtschaft: Anlagen* I, pp. 57–79.

4: General Staff Ride (East), 1901

1. This translation is taken from Schlieffen, *Dienstschriften*, Vol.II, pp. 222–30.
2. Dieckmann, 'Schlieffenplan', pp. 152–62.
3. The Triple Alliance, signed in 1882 and renewed every five years until the outbreak of the First World War, called for Germany, Austria-Hungary and Italy to support each other in case of war. This obliged France to maintain a small number of units along its border

NOTES TO PAGES 51-72

with Italy to guard against Italian attack. Moreover, the Italians agreed to send three army corps to Germany for an offensive against France in case of war. It is clear, however, that Schlieffen did not consider the Italians to be very reliable allies. Alfred von Schlieffen to Bernhard von Bülow, 12 March 1901, reprinted in Johannes Lepius, *et al.*, *Die grosse Politik der europäischen Kabinette, 1871–1914*, Vol.XVIII: *Zweibund und Dreibund 1900–1904* (Berlin: Deutsche Verlagsgesellschaft für Politik und Geschichte, 1924), pp. 691–5.
4. Schlieffen is referring to the battle of Solferino (24 June 1859) during the Franco-Austrian War. In this battle, a Austrian army under the personal command of the Emperor Franz Josef was defeated by a Franco-Piedmontese army in a bloody and indecisive battle in northern Italy. Although the Austrian army was not annihilated, the defeat did lead to negotiations to end the war. Two generals from either side who took part in the battle would later lose disastrously to the Prussians – Marie E.P.M. de MacMahon and Ludwig von Benedek. He also refers to the battle of Sedan (1 September 1870) in which the German forces annihilated MacMahon's Army of Châlons and the battle of Königgrätz (3 July 1866) in which Benedek's army was crushingly defeated by Moltke's army.
5. In reality, the French war plan (Plan XIV) did not envision a French offensive at the war's outbreak. See Ministère de la Guerre, *Les Armées Françaises dans le Grande Guerres*, I: *La Guerre de Mouvement*, Vol.1: *Les Préliminaires – La Bataille des Frontières*, 2nd edn (Paris: Imprimerie Nationale, 1936), pp. 26ff.; and A. Marchand, *Plans de Concentration de 1871 à 1914* (Paris: Berger-Levrault, 1926), pp. 140ff.
6. This is not the only time Schlieffen kept units near railroad loading sites in the west either for transport to the east or for use in the battle with France if needed. See the '*Kriegsspiel, 1905*', pp. 128ff.
7. This heavy artillery would have come from the Russian army's general reserve, rather than from any field unit.
8. This intervention by Schlieffen in the course of the game lends credence to the assertion that he was using these rides as much to test out specific operational ideas as he did as training tools. See above, pp. 11ff.
9. Emphasis in the original.

5: *General Staff Ride (East), 1903*

1. This translation is from Schlieffen, *Dienstschriften*, Vol.II, pp. 300–9.
2. Dieckmann, 'Schlieffenplan', pp. 162ff. This plan probably took into account the three army corps promised by Italy for use on the western front that were negotiated during the renewal of the Triple Alliance on 28 June 1902. Wolfgang Foerster, *Aus der Gedankenwerkstatt des Deutschen Generalstabes* (Berlin: E.S. Mittler, 1931), pp. 84–5.
3. Schlieffen is referring here to the battle of Leipzig (16–19 October 1813), in which the Prussians, Austrians and Russians all but encircled Napoleon and his Grand Army in the city and inflicted a serious defeat on them, and the battles of Gravelotte (18 August 1870) and Sedan (1 September 1870).

6: *Tactical-Strategic Problems, 1892*

1. This translation is from Alfred von Schlieffen, *Dienstschriften*, Vol.I: *Die taktisch-strategischen Aufgaben aus den Jahren 1891–1905* (Berlin: E.S. Mittler, 1937), pp. 7–16.
2. In 1892, the French deployment was determined by Plan XI, introduced in August 1891. Plan XI called for 17 army corps, nine reserve corps and six reserve divisions to be deployed against Germany. See Ministère de la Guerre, *Les Armées Françaises dans le Grand Guerre*, I, Vol. 1: *L'avant Guerre – La Bataille des Frontières* (Paris: Imprimerie Nationale, 1923), pp. 5–6. According to reports dated 4 October 1891 and 14 March 1892, the Third Section of the German General Staff believed that the French VI Army Corps was deployed in peacetime close to the border near Nancy, while units of the 2nd Cavalry Division were deployed in Lunéville. However, they had no information about

French units deployed in the Montmédy/Longwy area. See Archivrat Greiner, 'Welche Nachrichten besaß der deutsche Generalstab über Mobilmachung und Aufmarsch des franz. Heeres in den Jahren 1885–1914,' unpublished manuscript in BA/MA, W10/50267, pp. 52–8.

3. Schlieffen has here described the system employed by Moltke the Elder of marching divided but fighting united, used so effectively during the German Wars of Unification. For a good description of this technique (which became the model of combat for the German army before 1914), see Rudolph von Caemmerer, *The Development of Strategical Science During the 19th Century* (London: Hugh Rees, 1905), pp. 178ff.

7: Tactical-Strategic Problems, 1896

1. This translation is from Schlieffen, *Dienstschriften*, Vol. I, pp. 31–41.
2. In fact, Schlieffen refers to the 'northern' corps throughout this game. However, it is clear that he is referring to the Danes, so for clarity I have changed 'northern' to 'Danish'.
3. Schlieffen is referring here to events during the Franco-German War of 1870/71 – the battle of Spichern (6 August 1870), the battle of Vionville–Mars-la-Tour (16 August 1870), and the struggle against the improvised armies of the French Republic after September 1870.
4. Schlieffen is referring here to the battle of Rossbach (5 November 1757) during the Seven Years' War (1756–63). The Prussian victory in this battle over an Austro-French force allowed Friedrich the Great to turn against an Austrian army advancing on Breslau.
5. Here, Schlieffen is referring to Napoleon's attack against Field Marshal Gebhard von Blücher's Silesian Army during the Five Days' Battle. Napoleon forced the Prussian field marshal to retire and then turned on an Austrian force to the south. However, Blücher had not been defeated decisively and continued his advance on Paris once Napoleon had marched off to fight the Austrians.
6. Schlieffen is referring here to the battles of Ligny (16 June 1815) and Waterloo (18 June 1815) during Napoleon's One-Hundred Days' Campaign. At Ligny, Napoleon drove the Prussian forces from the field, before turning on the Duke of Wellington's Anglo-Dutch force at Waterloo. There, Napoleon was finally defeated after the late intervention of Blücher's Prussian forces.

8: Tactical-Strategic Problems, 1903

1. This translation is from Schlieffen, *Dienstschriften*, Vol. I, pp. 102–18.
2. See Michael Howard, *The Franco-Prussian War: The German Invasion of France, 1870–1871* (London: Rupert Hart-Davis, 1962), pp. 79–82, for the French attack on Saarbrücken. Cf. Helmuth von Moltke, *The Franco-German War of 1870–71* (trans. Clara Bell and Henry W. Fischer) (New York: Harper & Bros., 1892), p. 10.
3. Although Schlieffen proved himself to be a strong advocate of *Auftragstaktik* in his other staff rides and games, he clearly believed that a commander had to know when to issue definite orders, rather than the more flexible directives used in *Auftragstaktik*. Here, he is using Moltke's words to reinforce his belief. Cf. 'General Staff Ride, 1894', p. 23; and 'General Staff Ride, 1899', p. 49.
4. By 1903, Schlieffen was coming under criticism from some senior officers for setting such problems for the General Staff's junior officers. See Arden Bucholz, *Moltke, Schlieffen and Prussian War Planning* (Oxford: Berg, 1991), pp. 190–1; and Jehuda Wallach, *Dogma of the Battle of Annihilation* (Westport, CT: Greenwood Press, 1986), p. 37. Cf. 'Kriegsspiel, 1905', pp. 138f.

9: Tactical-Strategic Problems, 1905

1. This translation is from Schlieffen, *Dienstschriften*, Vol. I, pp. 133–43. These problems most likely come from one of the solutions to the *Kriegsspiel* Schlieffen directed early in 1905. See above, pp. 155f.

2. Once again Schlieffen is making reference to the friction of war and how officers must accept that they will not have perfect information upon which to base their decisions. Cf. 'General Staff Ride, 1894', pp. 21f.; 'General Staff Ride, 1899', pp. 48f.; and 'Tactical-Strategic Problems, 1905', pp. 112f.
3. The French maintained this tactic until the First World War. See Chef des Generalstabes der Armee, No. 15018, 'Die Taktik der französischen Armee', October 1912, in USNA, Captured German Records, Wilhelm Groener Papers, M-137, Roll 20. Cf. Jonathan M. House, 'The Decisive Attack: A New Look at French Infantry Tactics on the Eve of World War I', *Military Affairs* (December 1976), pp. 164–9; and Joseph C. Arnold, 'French Tactical Doctrine 1870–1914', *Military Affairs* (April 1978), pp. 61–7.
4. Schlieffen is referring to the battles of Leuthen (6 December 1757), in which a Prussian army under Friedrich the Great defeated a superior Austrian army under Daun; the twin battle of Jena/Auerstädt (14 October 1806), in which Napoleon's army crushed the Prussian army; and when Moltke defeated the Imperial French army in the space of the first six weeks of the Franco-German War.
5. Clearly, Schlieffen believed that any offensive into Russian Poland would be met with a fully prepared enemy and would make an Austro-German victory difficult to achieve. See Gerhard Ritter, *The Schlieffen Plan: Critique of a Myth* (London: Oswald Wolff, 1958), pp. 28ff.; Wolfgang Foerster, *Aus der Gedankenwerkstatt des deutschen Generalstabes* (Berlin: E.S. Mittler, 1931), pp. 54–9; and Schlieffen's exchange of letters with the Austro-Hungarian General Staff Chief, Friedrich Freiherr von Beck, printed in Helmuth Otto, *Schlieffen und der Generalstab* (Berlin: Deutscher Militäverlag, 1966), pp. 241–66.

10: *Kriegsspiel, 1905*

1. This translation is from a typescript entitled, 'Kriegspiel November/Dezember 1905– Schlußbesprechung', found in USNA, Captured German Records, Alfred von Schlieffen Papers, M-961, Roll 3. It appeared with commentary in two parts in the *War Studies Journal*, 3, 2 (Summer 1998), pp. 117–33 and 4, 1 (Summer 1999), pp. 97–115.
2. In 1905, Germany was divided into 23 different corps districts. From each district came an active duty corps (two divisions), a reserve division, and a number of *Landwehr* and *Landsturm* units. A typical German active duty army corps consisted of around 40,000 men and 144 artillery pieces (an additional battalion of heavy artillery was attached to some corps). See Reichsarchiv, *Der Weltkrieg 1914 bis 1918: Kriegsrüstung und Kriegswirtschaft: Anlagen zum ersten Band* (Berlin: E.S. Mittler, 1930), pp. 482–3.
3. Schlieffen was most likely referring here to the Russian General Aleksei Kuropatkin's conduct during the Battle of Liao-Yang in late August 1905 during the Russo-Japanese War. See German General Staff, *The Russo-Japanese War: The Battle of Liao-Yan* (trans. Karl von Donat) (London: Hugh Rees, 1909).
4. Cf. his 'War Today', p. 200 above.
5. Schlieffen was again referring to a battle during the Russo-Japanese War (the Battle of Sha-Ho, 5–17 October 1905). See German General Staff, *The Russo-Japanese War: The Battle of Scha-Ho* (trans. Karl von Donat) (London: Hugh Rees, 1910).
6. Field Marshal Helmuth von Moltke the Elder.
7. Schlieffen was referring here to a famous event during the Franco-German War. In late August 1870, Moltke learned of the movements of Marshal Patrice MacMahon's army from French and British newspapers. Based almost solely upon this information, Moltke set in motion plans which eventually resulted in the encirclement and destruction of the Army of Châlons at the battle of Sedan (1 September 1870).
8. The battle of Leuthen (6 December 1757) was one of Friedrich the Great's most brilliant victories. In the Wilhelmine army it served as a model for flanking attacks, and Schlieffen himself referred to it often in his critiques of wargames.
9. During the Franco-German War, Moltke's plans were often spoiled by the impetuosity of the commanders of the various German armies. In particular, General Carl Friedrich von Steinmetz, the commander of the 1st Army, refused to acknowledge the authority of the Chief of the General Staff. See Michael Howard, *The Franco-Prussian War* (London:

Rupert Hart-Davis, 1968), pp. 83–5, 128–91; and also the diaries of Moltke's chief of operations, Paul von Bonsart von Schellendorf, which gave a colourful picture of the relations between Moltke and Steinmetz, *Geheimes Kriegstagebuch, 1870–1871* (ed. Peter Rassow) (Bonn: Athenäum-Verlag, 1954).

10. Cf. 'Reports on the Russian Army, 1905', pp. 143ff.

Introduction to Part II: Memoranda

1. Bronsart von Schellendorff, *Duties of the General Staff*, 4th edn (London: HMSO, 1905), pp. 25–42; Walter Goerlitz, *History of the German General Staff 1657–1945* (trans. Brian Battershaw) (New York: Praeger, 1957).
2. Arden Bucholz, *Moltke, Schlieffen and Prussian War Planning* (Oxford: Berg, 1991), pp. 59–108.
3. Wilhelm Dieckmann, 'Der Schlieffenpla', unfinished and unpublished manuscript in BA/MA, W10/50220, p. 18 and p. 118; Erich Ludendorff, *Mein militärischer Werdegang* (Munich: Ludendorffs Verlag, 1933), pp. 94–5.
4. Hermann von Kuhl, *Der deutsche Generalstab in Vorbereitung und Durchführung des Weltkrieges* (Berlin: E.S. Mittler, 1920), p. 3.
5. Ludendorff, *Werdegang*, pp. 94–5.
6. Annika Mombauer, *Helmuth von Moltke and the Origins of the First World War* (Cambridge: Cambridge University Press, 2001), pp. 38ff. The General Staff also cooperated with the Ministry of War in developing a 'mobilization plan', which directed the call up of troops and the bringing of the army to wartime footing. Bucholz, *Prussian War Planning*, pp. 99ff. and passim; and Max van den Bergh, *Das Deutsche Heer vor dem Weltkriege* (Berlin: Sanssouci Verlag, 1934), pp. 45ff.
7. See Rainer Lahme, *Deutsche Aussenpolitik, 1880–1894: Von Gleichgewichtspolitik Bismarcks zur Allianzstrategie Caprivis* (Göttingen: Vandenhoeck & Ruprecht, 1990), pp. 100ff.
8. The convention pledged France to deploy an army of 1.3 million troops against Germany, while Russia was to deploy 700,000–800,000 against Germany by the 14th mobilization day. William C. Fuller, *Strategy and Power in Russia 1600–1914* (New York: Free Press, 1992), pp. 350–62.
9. Schlieffen to his sister Marie, 13 November 1892, reprinted in Alfred von Schlieffen, *Briefe* (ed. Eberhard Kessel) (Göttingen: Vandenhoeck & Ruprecht, 1958), pp. 295ff.
10. Ferdinand von Schmerfeld, ed., *Graf Moltke: Die Aufmarschpläne 1871–1890* (Berlin: E.S. Mittler, 1929) contains the texts of Moltke's guidelines for his deployment plans. The outlines of Waldersee's can be found in Hans Mohs, *Generalfeldmarschall Alfred Graf von Waldersee in seinem militärischen Wirken*, Vol. 2 (Berlin: E.S. Mittler, 1929). See also Reichsarchiv, *Der Weltkrieg 1914 bis 1918*, Vol. I: *Die Grenzschlachten im Westen* (Berlin: E.S. Mittler, 1925), pp. 49ff.; and Bucholz, *Prussian War Planning*, pp. 99–108.
11. See his 'War Today', pp. 197ff.
12. Gerhard Ritter, *The Schlieffen Plan: Critique of a Myth* (London: Oswald Wolff, 1948), pp. 23–4; Wolfgang Foerster, *Aus der Gedankenwerkstatt des Deutschen Generalstabes* (Berlin: E.S. Mittler, 1931), pp. 25–6; Eugen Ritter von Zoellner, 'Schlieffens Vermächtnis', Sonderheft, *Militärwissenschaftliche Rundschau*, 3 (1938), pp. 12ff.
13. Dieckmann, 'Schlieffenplan', pp. 10–11; Foerster, *Gedankenwerkstatt*, p. 49.
14. Dieckmann, 'Schlieffenplan', p. 12.
15. Ibid., pp. 18ff.; Friedrich von Boetticher, 'Der Lehrmeister des neuzeitlichen Krieges', in Friedrich von Cochenhausen, *Von Scharnhorst zu Schlieffen, 1806–1906: Hundert Jahre preußisch-deutscher Generalstab* (Berlin: E.S. Mittler, 1933), p. 263.
16. Dieckmann, 'Schlieffenplan', pp. 28–9.
17. The true extent of this major shift in policy was never completely communicated to Germany's Austrian ally. Schlieffen needed an Austrian offensive to keep Russia occupied, thus could not remain totally on the defensive in the east. See his letters and memoranda to Friedrich Freiherr von Beck, the Austrian Chief of Staff, reprinted in Helmuth Otto, *Schlieffen und der Generalstab* (Berlin: Deutscher Militärverlag, 1966), pp. 241ff. Also,

Otto, 'Zum strategisch-operativen Zusammenwirken des deutschen und österreich-ungarischen Generalstabes bei der Vorbereitung des ersten Weltkrieges', *Zeitschrift für Militärgeschichte*, 2 (1963), pp. 31–7; and Ritter, *Schlieffen Plan*, pp. 23ff.
18. Dieckmann, 'Schlieffenplan', pp. 48–51; Ritter, *Schlieffen Plan*, p. 38.
19. Foerster, *Gedankenwerkstatt*, pp. 26–7. On French war plans, see Ministère de la Guerre, *Les Armées Françaises dans le Grande Guerre*, I: *La Guerre de Mouvement*, Vol. 1: *Les Préliminaires – La Bataille des Frontières*, 2nd edn (Paris, Imprimerie Nationale, 1936), pp. 24ff.; and A. Marchand, *Plans de Concentration de 1871 à 1914* (Paris: Berger-Levrault, 1926), pp. 122–40.
20. Kaiser Wilhelm I to Bismarck, 2 October 1879, reprinted in Schmerfeld, *Aufmarschpläne*, p. 80.
21. See A. von Grabau, *Das Festungsproblem in Deutschland und seine Auswirkung auf die strategische Lage von 1870/1914* (Berlin: Junker & Dünnhaupt Verlag, 1935).
22. Cf. Terence Zuber, 'The Schlieffen Plan Reconsidered', *War in History*, 6, 3 (1999), pp. 262–305, who argues that Schlieffen never seriously considered such an operation. This author's conclusions seem to be at odds with the conclusions reached by the very document upon which he bases much of his argument, Dieckmann's 'Der Schlieffenplan'. The very structure of Dieckmann's work indicates that he believed Schlieffen was working throughout his time as Chief of the General Staff toward a northern envelopment of the French fortifications. It begins with a section entitled 'Der Umgehungsplan' (The Outflanking Plan), in which Schlieffen's *Aufmarschpläne* were discussed until 1903. In these years, Schlieffen toyed with the idea of a shallow outflanking movement around the French fortifications. Dieckmann was to conclude his manuscript with a section entitled, 'Der Umfassungsplan' (The Envelopment Plan), which, as its title suggests, would have taken Schlieffen's plans up to the famous memorandum of 1905 with its powerful right-wing envelopment.
23. Dieckmann, 'Schlieffenplan', pp. 18ff. Interestingly, despite its importance for future plans, this discussion by Schlieffen of an envelopment north of Verdun was not related in any other subsequent sources.
24. Ibid., p. 20.
25. Ibid., pp. 20–1.; Foerster, *Gedankenwerkstatt*, pp. 26ff.; Ritter, *Schlieffen Plan*, pp. 38ff.; Reicharschiv, *Weltkrieg*, I, pp. 51ff.
26. Quoted in Ritter, *Schlieffen Plan*, p. 40.
27. Dieckmann, 'Schlieffenplan', pp. 54–5.
28. Stig Förster, 'Der deutsche Generalstab und die Illusion des kurzen Krieges, 1871–1914: Metakritik eines Mythos', *Militärgeschichtliche Mitteilungen*, 54 (1995), pp. 61–95.
29. Curt Jany, *Geschichte der Königlich Preußischen Armee*, Vol. 4: *Die Königliche Preußische Armee und das Deutsche Reichsheer 1807 bis 1914* (Berlin: Karl Siegismund, 1933), pp. 314ff. See also Bruce Gudmundsson, *On Artillery* (Westport, CT: Praeger, 1993), pp. 34–5.
30. Jany, *Geschichte der Königlich Preußischen Armee*, pp. 300ff.; Reichsarchiv, *Der Weltkrieg 1914 bis 1918: Kriegsrüstung und Kriegswirtschaft*, Vol. 1 (Berlin: E.S. Mittler, 1930), pp. 31–42.
31. The new corps were to be the XVIII to the XXI and the III Bavarian. Reichsarchiv, *Kriegsrüstung und Kriegswirtschaft*, Vol. I, pp. 49ff.; Jany, *Geschichte der Königlich Preußischen Armee*, p. 296.
32. Dieckmann, 'Schlieffenplan', pp. 63–4.
33. For an example, see L.C.F Turner, 'The Significance of the Schlieffen Plan', in Paul Kennedy, ed., *The War Plans of the Great Powers, 1880–1914* (London: George Allen & Unwin, 1979) pp. 199–221.
34. See S.R. Williamson, 'Joffre Reshapes French Strategy, 1911–1913', in Kennedy, *War Plans*, pp. 133–54. For discussion in the contemporary press, see 'Tendencies in the German Army', *The Times*, 20 February 1911.
35. These intentions resulted in the so-called Luxemburg Crisis of 1867, in which France attempted to purchase the Grand Duchy of Luxemburg from the Duchy's ruler, the King of Holland. Indeed, it was only in the wake of this crisis that Luxemburg was declared neutral and her Prussian garrison withdrawn. See René Albrecht-Carrié, *A Diplomatic*

History of Europe Since the Congress of Vienna (rev. edn) (New York: Harper & Row, 1973), pp. 132—7; and A.J.P. Taylor, *The Struggle for Mastery in Europe, 1848–1918* (Oxford: Clarendon Press, 1954), pp. 171ff.
36. Bismarck made this enquiry to Waldersee in 1888. Alfred Graf von Waldersee, *Denkwürdigkeiten des Generalfeldmarschalls Graf von Waldersee*, Vol. I (ed. H.O. Meissner) (Berlin: Deutsche Verlags-Anstalt, 1923), p. 412.
37. This possibility appeared frequently in his wargames. For examples, see 'Tactical-Strategic Problems, 1892', pp. 72ff.; and *'Kriegsspiel, 1905'*, pp. 119ff.
38. Dieckmann, 'Schlieffenplan', pp. 59ff.
39. Ibid., pp. 63–73.
40. Ibid., pp. 88–106.
41. There were the XVIII and XIX Army Corps and the III Bavarian Corps.
42. There were the Gardereservekorps, and the XX to the XXIII Army Corps. Reichsarchiv, *Kriegsrüstung und Kriegswirtschaft*, Vol. I, pp. 52ff. Also, Ludwig Rüdt von Collenberg, 'Graf Schlieffen und die Kriegsformation der deutschen Armee', *Wissen und Wehr* (1927), pp. 605–34; and Michael Geyer, *Deutsche Rüstungspolitik, 1860–1980* (Frankfurt: Suhrkamp, 1984), pp. 50ff.
43. Dieckmann, 'Schlieffenplan', pp. 124ff. Cf. Zuber, 'Schlieffen Plan Reconsidered', pp. 276ff.
44. This procedure of producing two *Aufmarschpläne* would continue until 1913, when Moltke the Younger stopped working up *Aufmarschplan II*. See Mombauer, *Moltke*, pp. 100ff.; and Dennis Showalter, 'The Eastern Front and German Military Planning, 1871–1914 – Some Observations', *East European Quarterly*, 15, 2 (June 1981), pp. 163–80.
45. Dieckmann, 'Schlieffenplan', p. 122.
46. Ibid.
47. Ibid., pp. 122–3.
48. Plan XIV remained in effect from April 1898 to March 1903. See Ministère de la Guerre, *Les Armées Françaises*, I/1, pp. 7–8; and Marchand, *Plans de Concentration*, pp. 130–40.
49. Archivrat Greiner, 'Welche Nachrichten besaß der deutsche Generalstab über Mobilmachung und Aufmarsch des französischen Heeres in den Jahren 1885-1914? Wie wurden sie ausgewertet, und wie lagen die tatsächlichen Verhältnisse?', unpublished manuscript in BA/MA, W10/50267, pp. 85ff.
50. Dieckmann, 'Schlieffenplan', p. 124.
51. Ibid., p. 125.
52. The Railway Section alone carried out ten games during the course of the year. Bucholz, *Prussian War Planning*, p. 202.
53. Boetticher, 'Lehrmeister', p. 309. Unfortunately, no detailed description of his *Kriegsspiel* seems to have survived.
54. Zuber, 'The Schlieffen Plan Reconsidered', pp. 292–3.
55. Zoellner, 'Schlieffens Vermächtnis', p. 52; Ludendorff, *Werdegang*, p. 100; Boetticher, 'Lehrmeister', pp. 310–11.
56. This corresponded to where the 3rd Section believed the French to have moved their concentration areas. See Greiner, 'Nachrichten', pp. 95ff. In fact, the 3rd Section had overestimated the northern shift of the French forces.
57. Zoellner, 'Schlieffens Vemächtnis', pp. 49–50.
58. Ibid., pp. 48ff.; Boetticher, 'Lehrmeister', pp. 310ff.; Bucholz, *Prussian War Planning*, pp. 199ff.; and Wilhelm Groener, *Das Testament des Grafen Schlieffen: Operative Studien über den Weltkrieg* (2nd edn) (Berlin: E.S. Mittler, 1929), pp. 89ff. and Maps 9–11. Freytag-Loringhoven, at the time of this staff ride in the Historical Section of the General Staff, went on to be the *Generalquartiermeister* and adviser to Erich von Falkenhayn from January 1915 to August 1916 and then the Chief of the Deputy General Staff until the war's end. Hermann von Kuhl, in 1905 a member of the 3rd Section of the General Staff, went on to be the Chief of the General Staff of the 1st Army in 1914 and later the Chief of Staff to *Heeresgruppe Kronprinz Rupprecht*, from 1915 to 1918.
59. See *'Kriegsspiel, 1905'*, pp. 119ff.; and Robert Foley, 'Schlieffen's Last *Kriegsspiel*', *War Studies Journal*, 3, 2 (1998), pp. 117–33 and 4, 1 (1999), pp. 97–115. Cf. Ulrich Liss,

'Graf Schlieffen's letztes Kriegsspiel', *Wehrwissenschaftliche Rundschau*, 15, 3 (1965) pp. 162–6.
60. See '*Kriegsspiel*, 1905', p. 119.
61. See his 'Reports on the Russian Army, 1905', p. 160.
62. Schlieffen believed that Feste Lothringen, Kaiserin, Kronprinz and Graf Haeseler were needed for the fortress to play its intended role. Dieckmann, 'Schlieffenplan', pp. 103ff. Lothringen and Kaiserin were completed in 1903 and Kronprinz and Graf Haeseler were done in 1905. Oberst A.D. Heye, 'Die Festung Metz', in *Vierteljahreshefte für Pioniere*, 3 and 4 (1936).
63. Bucholz, *Prussian War Planning*, p. 167.
64. Greiner, 'Nachrichten', pp. 95ff.
65. For an excellent detailed analysis of the plan's operational ideas, including the role of the possible encirclement of Paris and Moltke the Younger's use of the plan, see Terence M. Holmes, 'Debate: The Reluctant March on Paris: A Reply to Terence Zuber's "The Schlieffen Plan Reconsidered"', *War in History*, 8, 2 (2001), pp. 208–32.
66. The lively post-war debate about Moltke the Younger's use of Schlieffen's plan is summarized in Mombauer, *Moltke*, pp. 42ff.

11: Reports on the Russian Army, 1905

1. The two reports are from the microfilms of the Auswärtiges Amt files in Public Record Office, Kew, GFM 10/89 (*Russland 72geh*/14: 'Militär und Marine Angelegenheiten Russland 3 Oktober 1896 – 31 Dezember 1906').
2. The French Foreign Minister, Théophile Delcassé, was forced to resign on 6 June, giving the Germans a great diplomatic victory.
3. In January 1905, revolution had broken out in St Petersburg, and it would not be until October that the Tsar would be able to bring order back to his Empire. It is clear that Schlieffen did not expect the Russians would be able to dedicate much time to improving the ability of their army while facing internal unrest.

12: Memorandum of 1905: The Schlieffen Plan

1. This translation comes from Generaloberst Graf Schlieffen, 'Denkschrift Dezember 1905', typescript in USNA, Captured German Records, Alfred von Schlieffen Papers, M-961, Roll 8.
2. Comments in the margin by Helmuth von Moltke the Younger: 'France's offensive or defensive stance will essentially be determined by the *casus belli*. If Germany brings about the war, France will probably remain on the defensive. If the war is desired and brought about by France, however, it will most likely conduct it offensively. If France wants to reconquer its lost provinces, it must advance into them, i.e., take the offensive. I do not take it for granted that France will remain on the defensive under all circumstances. The border fortresses laid out shortly after the war of '70/71 do indeed stress the defensive idea. However, this does not accord with either the offensive spirit inherent in the nation or with the teachings and views now prevalent in the French army.'
3. Notation in margin: 'France: 995 battalions, 444 squadrons, 705 batteries without Territorial troops and fortress garrisons. Germany: 971 battalions, 504 squadrons, 801 batteries without *Landwehr*, *Landsturm*, and fortress garrisons.'
4. *Moltke*: 'I believe it is certain that France will not surrender Nancy without a battle; in light of public opinion, the army command would never do this.'
5. *Moltke*: 'Of course, they are only conceivable if there is a simultaneous attack on the front.'
6. *Moltke*: 'If our diplomats bring this about, it will be a great advantage. We need the Dutch railways, and Holland would be of inestimable value.'
7. *Margin*: 'Three divisions.'
8. *Margin*: 'Three army corps.'

9. *Moltke*: 'An investment of Antwerp must be followed as soon as possible by a formal siege.'
10. *Moltke*: 'Liège and Namur by themselves have no meaning. Indeed, they may be weakly garrisoned, but they are capable of great resistance. They block the Meuse railways, whose use cannot therefore be counted upon during war. It is of the greatest importance, then, at least to capture Liège as quickly as possible in order to have use of the railway.'
11. This section in parenthesis is marked in the margin of the text 'Footnote'.
12. In Imperial Germany, not all eligible young men were conscripted. Those who did not complete their service were placed into the '*Ersatz* reserve', and were liable for call up in wartime. In 1914, the German army amounted to more than 4.4 million men. A further 6.7 million were available in the *Ersatz* reserve.

13: Addendum to the Memorandum, 1906

1. This translation comes from Generaloberst Graf Schlieffen, 'Denkschrift Dezember 1905', typescript in USNA, Captured German Records, Alfred von Schlieffen Papers, M-961, Roll 8.
2. Schlieffen is referring to the French attempts to break out of the sieges of Metz and Paris during the Franco-German War of 1870/71.
3. Cf. 'Tactical-Strategic Problems, 1896', pp. 82ff.

14: Comments by Moltke on the Memorandum, c. 1911

1. This translation comes from Generaloberst Graf Schlieffen, 'Denkschrift Dezember 1905', typescript in USNA, Captured German Records, Alfred von Schlieffen Papers, M-961, Roll 8. For more on Moltke the Younger's role in German war planning, see Annika Mombauer, *Helmuth von Moltke and the Origins of the First World War* (Cambridge: Cambridge University Press, 2001), pp. 106ff.
2. In 1908, Erich Ludendorff, at the time the head of the 2nd Section of the General Staff, personally conducted reconnaissance of the fortress of Liège. See Franz Uhle-Wettler, *Erich Ludendorff in seiner Zeit* (Berg: Hurt Vowinckel-Verlag, 1995), pp. 93ff.

Introduction to Part III: Theoretical Writings

1. See 'Helmuth von Moltke', pp. 227f.
2. Indeed, 40 years ago a student of Schlieffen made just such a complaint. Eberhard Kaulbach, 'Schlieffen: Zur Frage der Bedeutung und Wirkung seiner Arbeit,' *Wehrwissenschaftliche Rundschau*, 13 (1963), pp. 137–8.
3. Jehuda Wallach, *The Dogma of the Battle of Annihilation: The Theories of Clausewitz and Schlieffen and their Impact on the German Conduct of Two World Wars* (Westport, CT: Greenwood Press, 1986), pp. 65.
4. For an excellent discussion of the tactical debates within Germany before the First World War, see Antulio J. Echevarria II, *After Clausewitz: German Military Thinkers before the Great War* (Lawrence, KS: University Press of Kansas, 2001).
5. On the concept of the offensive in pre-war Europe, see Jack Snyder, *The Ideology of the Offensive: Military Decision Making and the Disasters of 1914* (Ithaca, NY: Cornell University Press, 1984).
6. Kriegsministerium, *Exerzir-Reglement für die Infanterie* (Berlin: E.S. Mittler, 1888), pp. 136ff.
7. 'War Today', p. 199.
8. Ibid., p. 198.
9. See Moltke to Schlieffen, 3 December 1908, and Einem to Schlieffen, 16 December 1908, reprinted in Alfred von Schlieffen, *Briefe* (ed. Eberhard Kessel) (Göttingen: Vandenhoeck & Ruprecht, 1958), pp. 308–9.

10. Friedrich von Bernhardi, *Denkwürdigkeiten aus meinem Leben* (Berlin: E.S. Mittler, 1927), pp. 292–3; Hugo Freiherr von Freytag-Loringhoven, *Generalfeldmarschall Graf von Schlieffen: Sein Leben und die Verwertung seines geistiges Erbes im Weltkriege* (Leipzig: Historia-Verlag Paul Schraepler, 1920), p. 117.
11. Moltke to Schlieffen, 3 December 1908, in Schlieffen, *Briefe*, p. 308.
12. Ibid.
13. Ironically, Schlieffen's ideas related closely to those of one of his fiercest critics, Schlichting. See Daniel J. Hughes, 'Schlichting, Schlieffen, and the Prussian Theory of War in 1914', *Journal of Military History*, 59 (April 1995), pp. 257–78.
14. Quoted in Wallach, *Dogma*, p. 118. See also Ernst Buchfinck, 'Feldmarschall Graf Haeseler', *Wissen und Wehr*, 1 (1936), pp. 3–9.
15. On Bernhardi, see Walter K. Nehring, 'General der Kavallerie Friedrich von Bernhardi – Soldat und Militärwissenschaftler', in Dermont Bradley and Ulrich Marwedel, eds, *Militärgeschichte, Militärwissenschaft und Konfliktsforschung* (Osnabrück: Biblio Verlag, 1977); and Dennis Showalter, 'Goltz and Bernhardi: The Institutionalization of Originality in the Imperial German Army', *Defense Analysis*, 3, 4 (1987).
16. Friedrich von Bernhardi, *Vom heutigen Krieg*, Vol.II (Berlin: E.S. Mittler, 1910), p. 163; Echevarria, *After Clausewitz*, p. 197; Wallach, *Dogma*, pp. 53–4.
17. See Werner Gembruch, 'General von Schlichting', *Wehrwissenschaftliche Rundschau*, 10, 4 (1960), pp. 188–96; and Joachim Hoffmann, 'Die Kriegslehre des Generals von Schlichting', *Militägeschichtliche Mitteilungen*, I (1969), pp. 5–35.
18. Quoted in Sigfrid Mette, *Vom Geist deutscher Feldherren: Genie und Technik 1800–1918* (Zürich: Scientia, 1938), p. 198. Mette was quoting from a document in Schlichting's now-destroyed papers. See also Egon Freiherr von Gayl, *General von Schlichting und sein Lebenswerk* (Berlin: Georg Stilke, 1913), pp. 350ff.
19. Echevarria, *After Clausewitz*, p. 198.
20. Delbrück's account of the battle of Cannae was in *Geschichte der Kriegskunst in Rahmen der politischen Geschichte*, Vol. I: *Das Altertum*, which had first appeared in 1900 with Georg Stilke Publishers, but was revised in 1907. This was published in English as *History of the Art of War within the Framework of Political History*, Vol. I: *Warfare in Antiquity* (trans. Walter J. Renfroe, Jr) (Westport, CT: Greenwood Press, 1985).
21. For a more recent interpretation, see Martin Samuels, 'The Reality of Cannae', *Militärgeschichtliche Mitteilungen*, 90, 1 (1990).
22. Schlieffen had also published '1806', in *Vierteljahrsheft für Truppenführung und Heereskunde* (hereafter V*fTH*) 3 (1906); 'Der Feldzug im Spätherbst 1806', 'Der Feldzug von Preußisch-Eylau', and 'Der Feldzug von Friedland', in V*fTH*, 4 (1907); and '1813', in V*fTH*, 5 (1908).
23. Freytag, *Graf von Schlieffen*, p. 75.
24. Grosser Generalstab, Kriegsgeschichtliche Abteilung I, *Der Schlachterfolg mit welchem Mitteln wurde er erstrebt?* (Berlin: E.S. Mittler, 1903). Schlieffen was disappointed that this did not have more of an influence over the army. See Freytag, *Graf von Schlieffen*, pp. 58–9, 88.
25. The 'Cannae Studien' appeared in Vols VI to X of the *Vierteljahrsheft für Truppenführung und Heereskunde* from 1909 to 1913.
26. Hans Delbrück, Review of 'Das militärische Testament Friedrichs des Grossen. Herausgegeben und erläutert von v. Taysen, Major im Grossen Generalstabe' in *Zeitschrift für preußische Geschichte und Landeskunde*, 16 (Jan.–Feb. 1879), pp. 27–32.
27. For accounts of this *Strategiestreit*, see Arden Bucholz, *Hans Delbrück and the German Military Establishment: War Images in Conflict* (Iowa City, IA: University of Iowa Press, 1985), pp. 52–85 and *passim*; and Sven Lange, *Hans Delbrück und der 'Strategiestreit': Kriegführung und Kriegsgeschichte in der Kontroverse 1879–1914* (Einzelschriften zur Militärgeschichte No. 40 Herausgegeben vom Militärgeschichtlichen Forschungsamt) (Freiburg: Rombach Verlag, 1995).
28. Schlieffen had directed Friedrich von Bernhardi while he was under Schlieffen in the Historical Section of the General Staff to counter Delbrück's theories publicly. See Bernhardi, *Denkwürdigkeiten*, pp. 142ff.
29. 'Cannae Studies', p. 211.

30. Ibid., p. 210. On the different conceptions of 'annihilation', see Echevarria, *After Clausewitz*, pp. 189–90.
31. Wilhelm Groener, *Das Testament des Grafen Schlieffen* (Berlin: E.S. Mittler, 1929), pp. 10–11.
32. Bernhardi, *Denkwürdigkeiten*, pp. 220ff.; Showalter, 'Goltz and Bernhardi', pp. 306–7, 311–12.
33. Schlichting's main theoretical work was *Taktische und strategische Grundsätze der Gegenwart* (3 vols) (Berlin: E.S. Mittler, 1898–99).
34. Gayl, *General von Schlichting*, pp. 339ff. Schlichting had long questioned the applicability of examples drawn from ancient history, and even from the Napoleonic period, to modern day warfare, as he believed that conditions had changed too much to make them useful. Schlichting and his followers were attempting to put forward their view of how history should be used in the army. The work by Schlichting's student, Rudolph von Caemmerer, *Die Entwicklung der strategischen Wissenschaft im 19 Jahrhundert* (Berlin: Wilhelm Baensch, 1904) is the most prominent example of this approach.
35. Quoted in Mette, *Feldherren*, p. 200.
36. See Schlieffen, *Briefe*, pp. 311ff.
37. Hugo Freiherr von Freytag-Loringhoven, 'Generalfeldmarschall Graf von Schlieffen: Lebensgang und Lebenswerk', in Alfred von Schlieffen, *Gesammelte Schriften*, Vol. I (Berlin: E.S. Mittler, 1913) pp. xxxvii–xxxviii. Cf. Freytag, *Graf Schlieffen*, p. 87. Similar statements can be found in the later writings of Schlieffen's other supporters.
38. For example, see Sigismund von Schlichting, 'Ueber das Infanteriegefecht', *Beiheft zum Militär-Wochenblatt*, 2 (1879) pp. 38–9; and Wilhelm von Blume, *Strategie* (Berlin: E.S. Mittler, 1886), p. 169.
39. Mette, *Feldherren*, p. 197.
40. Quoted in Emanuel von Kiliani, 'Die Operationslehre des Grafen Schlieffen und ihre deutschen Gegner (II.Teil)', *Wehrkunde*, 10 (1961), p. 135.
41. Gayl, *Schlichting*, pp. 370ff.; and Mette, *Feldherren*, pp. 196ff.
42. Quoted in Wallach, *Dogma*, pp. 72–3.
43. 'The *Feldherr*', p. 220.
44. For a modern interpretation of this team, see Stig Förster, 'The Prussian Triangle of Leadership in the Face of a People's War: A Reassessment of Conflict between Bismarck and Moltke, 1870–71', in Stig Förster and Jörg Nagler, eds, *On the Road to Total War: The American Civil War and the German Wars of Unification, 1861–1871* (Cambridge: Cambridge University Press, 1997), pp. 115–40.
45. 'Helmuth von Moltke', pp. 227ff.
46. This system of command was promulgated by Moltke in his 'Verordnungen für die höheren Truppenführer' (Instructions for Large Unit Commanders) issued on 24 June 1869. See Daniel J. Hughes, ed. and trans., *Moltke on the Art of War: Selected Writings* (Novato, CA: Presidio Press, 1993), pp. 171–224.
47. Martin Samuels, 'Directive Command and the German General Staff', *War in History*, 2, 1 (1995), pp. 22–42. Moltke's 'Instructions' remained in effect until their revision in 1910, but their spirit continued throughout German doctrine until 1945. Cf. Hughes, *Moltke*, pp. 171–2.
48. Schlieffen mentioned this numerous times. For examples, see 'Tactical-Strategic Problems, 1903', pp. 106f.; '*Feldherr*', pp. 225f.; and 'Helmuth von Moltke', pp. 230f.
49. See Michael Howard, *The Franco-Prussian War: The German Invasion of France, 1870–1871* (London: Rupert Hart-Davis, 1961), pp. 82ff. Cf. Helmuth Graf von Moltke, *The Franco-German War of 1870–71* (trans. Clara Bell and Henry W. Fischer) (New York: Harper & Bros., 1892), pp. 12ff.
50. See above, pp. 9ff.
51. Indeed, Schlieffen's son-in-law, Wilhelm von Hanke, wrote after the war that Schlieffen's writings about *Feldherren* before the war were a warning about the unsuitability of Helmuth von Moltke the Younger. See Hanke to Freytag-Loringhoven, 5 May 1924, BA/MA, Nachlaß Hanke (NL36)/10.
52. By the time of the battle of the Marne in early September 1914, the German troops were exhausted and at the end of their supply lines. Even if a French counterattack had not

taken place, they would have had to pause to re-group and re-supply. See Hew Strachan, *The First World War*, Vol. I: *To Arms* (Oxford: Oxford University Press, 2001), pp. 242ff.; Martin van Creveld, *Supplying War: Logistics from Wallenstein to Patton* (Cambridge: Cambridge University Press, 1977), pp. 109ff.

53. The view that Moltke the Younger was not up to the task of *Feldherr* was put forward by Schlieffen's supporters after the war as a prime reason for the failure of Schlieffen's plan in 1914. See Wilhelm Groener, *Der Feldherr wider Willen*. Also see Annika Mombauer, *Helmuth von Moltke and the Origins of the First World War* (Cambridge: Cambridge University Press, 2001).

15: War Today, 1909

1. This translation comes from Alfred von Schlieffen, *Gesammelte Schriften*, Vol. I (Berlin: E.S. Mittler, 1913), pp. 11–22.
2. The Treaty of Frankfurt, signed on 10 May 1871, brought an end to the Franco-German War of 1870/71. Its terms were harsh – France was forced to cede Alsace and part of Lorraine to the new German Empire and to agree to pay an indemnity of 5 billion gold francs.
3. During the Austro-Prussian War of 1866, the Prussian forces were armed with a breech-loading rifle, while the Austrians had only an antiquated muzzle-loader. The breech-loader allowed the Prussians to firer faster and from a prone position, thereby giving a tactical advantage. See Dennis Showalter, *Railroads and Rifles: Soldiers, Technolgy, and the Unification of Germany* (Hamden, CT: Archon Books, 1976), pp. 121ff.
4. The experience of the German War of Unification had convinced the European powers that cannon were vulnerable to small arms fire. From the early twentieth century on, they fitted shields to their guns to provide protection for the gun crews. See Bruce Gudmundsson, *On Artillery* (Westport, CT: Praeger, 1993), pp. 8–9.
5. Here, Schlieffen is discussing the practice of limiting the time served by conscripts during peacetime, but extending their obligation to return to the army in case of war. The German army in Schlieffen's day required conscripts to serve two years active duty, but then a further 17 in the various reserve formations.
6. Schlieffen is referring to Friedrich the Great's grenadiers, who were led by Prince Leopold of Anhalt-Dessau (the 'Old Dessauer') during the First and Second Silesian Wars (1740–42 and 1744–45).
7. In the original this sentence reads: 'Nicht auf die örtliche Berührung, sondern auf den inneren Zusammenhang, darauf kommt es an, dass auf dem einen Schlachtfeld für den Sieg auf dem anderen gefochten wird. Soviel ist indes gewiß, die Gesamtschlachten wie die Teilschlachten, die getrennten wie die zusammenhängenden Kämpfe werden sich auf Feldern und Räumen abspielen, welche die Schauplätze früherer kriegerischer Taten um ein Gewaltiges übersteigen.'
8. Schlieffen is referring to the '*Daily Telegraph* Affair' of 1908, when Kaiser Wilhelm II gave an inflammatory interview to the British newspaper and caused a worsening of Anglo-German relations and deep damage to Wilhelm's reign. See Lamar Cecil, *Wilhelm II*, Vol. II: *Emperor and Exile, 1900–1941* (Chapel Hill, NC: University of North Carolina Press, 1996), pp. 131ff.

16: Million-Man Armies, 1911

1. This translation comes from Schlieffen, *Gesammelte Schriften*, Vol. I, pp. 23–4.

17: Cannae Studies

1. This translation comes from Schlieffen, *Gesammelte Schriften*, Vol. I, pp. 27–30, 259–66. Notes 2, 3, 4 and 5 are those of Schlieffen's original.
2. Hans Delbrück, *Geschichte der Kriegskunst*, Vol. I.
3. The heavy infantry (*hopilites*) were equipped in general with helmet, breastplate, leg

plates, round shield, spear and short sword. The Iberians and the Gauls had as defensive equipment only helmets and large shields.
4. The formation into lines was not made in one connected line, but rather in six-file *manipel* columns with short intervals.
5. Both formations, the broad as well as the deep, required 57,600 men. Therefore, they were 2,600 men below required strength.
6. On 29 August 1756, Friedrich the Great began the Seven Years' War with an invasion of Saxony. His army occupied Dresden and forced the weak Saxon army to fall back to its camp at Pirna on the Elbe, where it was besieged. In April 1757, Friedrich invaded Bohemia and met an Austrian army at Prague on 6 May. Friedrich's initial attack on the Austrian battle line was defeated, but he enveloped their right flank with his cavalry. As the Austrians extended to meet this threat, a gap was created in their line into which the Prussian infantry advanced. This 'Prague Manoeuvre' split the Austrians and resulted in their defeat.
7. On 18 June 1757, Friedrich met an Austrian army under Field Marshal Leopold von Daun advancing to force the Prussians to left their siege of Prague. The weak Prussian force was defeated and Friedrich was compelled to raise his siege.
8. On 25 August 1758, Friedrich fought an inclusive battle at Zorndorf against a Russian force under the command of Wilhelm Count Fermor. Friedrich attempted to use his famed oblique order to outflank the Russians, but was met by a new Russian front. In the end, the Russians withdrew after suffering heavy casualties, but the Prussian army had also suffered badly and was unable to pursue.
9. Friedrich again fought the Russians at the battle of Kunersdorf on 12 August 1759. Friedrich attempted a double envelopment of the Russian defensive position, but his enveloping wings were unable to attack in concert. Despite continual attacks, the Prussians achieved nothing but their own attrition. Losing more than 19,000 men, 172 guns and 28 regimental colours, this was one of Friedrich's greatest defeats.
10. At the battle of Torgau on 3 November 1760, Friedrich again attempted an outflanking manoeuvre, this time against an Austrian position. The King led the enveloping army himself, while his general Hans von Ziethen was to lead a force against the Austrian centre. After a confused battle, Ziethen's attack finally drove the Austrians from the field, but only after high Prussian casualties.
11. On 9 July 1762, Friedrich again fought and defeated his Austrian nemesis, Daun, at Burkersdorf in Silesia.
12. On 14 June 1800, Napoleon encountered a superior Austrian force at Marengo. After being pushed from the field, Napoleon sent his army against the flank of the complacent Austrian force and all but annihilated it. During the Ulm campaign in late September/early October 1805, Napoleon led his army around the flank of an Austrian army centred on Ulm. Cut off, this army was forced to surrender on 17 October.
13. Schlieffen is referring here to the Jena campaign in October/November 1806 in which Napoleon crushed the Prussian army, first in the twin battles of Jena and Auerstadt (14 October) and then after a pursuit.
14. During the crossing of the Beresina River (26–28 November 1812) during Napoleon's retreat from Moscow, the French lost some 30,000 men to relentless Russian attacks. This action destroyed the remnants of Napoleon's invasion army. Schlieffen is also making reference to the battle of Leipzig (16–19 October 1813) during which Prussian, Austrian and Russian forces encircled Napoleon's army. At Hanau on 30/31 October, an Austro-Bavarian army attempted to cut off the French armies retreat from Leipzig, but was itself defeated.
15. At the battle of Roßbach on 5 November 1757, Friedrich met an Austro-French envelopment of his position with one of his own and completely routed their superior army. At the cost of 548 casualties, he inflicted over 10,000 on the Austro-French force. At the battle of Liegnitz on 15 August 1760, Friedrich was able of defeat a superior Austro-Russian force by falling on its components piecemeal. On 2 December 1805, Napoleon split the attacking Austrian front with a surprise manoeuvre and then proceeded to encircle the surprised Austrians, defeating them completely.
16. During the battle of Friedland on 14 June 1807, Napoleon attempted to annihilate a Russian army, but only succeeded in pushing over the Alle River in great disorder.

17. At the battle of Regensburg (also known as the battle of Ratisbon) on 23 April 1809, Napoleon was unable to catch and annihilate the retreating Austrians. On 2 May 1813, Napoleon was able to beat off an allied attack at the village of Groß Görschen (also known as Lützen), but was unable to defeat them decisively.
18. On 21 August 1813, Blücher encountered a superior French force at Löwenberg. There were no allied forces nearby to provide support, and he was forced to withdraw. On 26 August 1813, an Austrian army under Prince Karl Philipp von Schwarzenberg attacked a French force at Dresden. Napoleon arrived with reinforcement the next day and turned the Austrian left flank, defeating them.
19. In June 1761, Friedrich took up position at Bunzelwitz in Silesia in the face of superior Russian and Austrian forces. These forces, however, demurred from attacking Friedrich's heavily fortified camp, and Friedrich remained there until the fortress of Schweidnitz, which protected his rear, fell to Austrian assault in September.
20. See 'Tactical-Strategic Problems, 1903', pp. 108ff.
21. During the Jena campaign in 1806, Napoleon surprised the Prussian forces by carrying out a strategic outflanking manoeuvre that placed his forces between the Prussian army and Berlin. The Prussians first gained knowledge of this when a French corps overwhelmed a smaller Prussian force at Saalfeld on 10 October.

18: The Feldherr, 1910

1. This translation is from Schlieffen, *Gesammelte Schriften*, Vol. I, pp. 3–10.
2. 'What do you fear? You carry Caesar.'
3. '*In hoc signo vinces*' (With this sign thou wilt conquer) was the motto of the Roman Emperor Constantine.
4. '*Gib, dass ich tu' mit Fleiß, was mir zu tun gebühret.*'
5. Despite being one of Prussia's greatest kings, Friedrich II had a poor grasp of the German language. All his writing was done in French, and he is reported to have said: 'I speak French when discussing affairs of state, speak Italian with my mistress, and German to my horse.'
6. These lines come from the first part of Friedrich Schiller's *Wallenstein*, 'Wallenstein's Camp'. Friedrich Schiller, *The Robbers and Wallenstein* (trans. F.J. Lamport) (London: Penguin Books, 1979), p. 204.
7. Belisarius (505–565 AD) was the successful general of the Byzantine Emperor Justinian. He led Byzantine forces to victory in wars against Persia (524–532), against the Vandals (533–534), and against the Goths (534–554), and again against Persia (539–562). Justinian viewed his successes with envy and had Belisarius imprisoned for treason in 562. Justinian's conscience got the better of him, however, and after a year Belisarius was released and allowed to live out his life in obscurity.
8. Schlieffen is referring to the Austrian Archduke Karl, who commanded the Austrian force that defeated Napoleon at the battle of Aspern-Essling on 21/22 May 1809.
9. Schlieffen is referring here to Gebhard Fürst von Blücher and August Neidhart Graf von Gneisenau, the commander and chief of staff, respectively, of the Prussian army that fought against Napoleon during the Wars of Liberation.
10. Schlieffen is here referring to the Prussian command team of King Wilhelm I, Helmuth von Moltke and Otto von Bismarck that was so successful in the German Wars of Unification. For a modern interpretation, see Stig Förster, 'The Prussian Triangle of Leadership in the Face of a People's War: A Reassessment of Conflict between Bismarck and Moltke, 1870–71', in Stig Förster and Jörg Nagler, eds, *On the Road to Total War: The American Civil War and the German Wars of Unification, 1861-1871* (Cambridge: Cambridge University Press, 1997), pp. 115–40.
11. In fact, Moltke wanted to fight on to defeat the Austrians completely. Only Bismarck's intervention brought the war to a swift conclusion, albeit built upon Moltke's battlefield successes. See Eberhard Kessel, *Moltke* (Stuttgart: K.F. Koehler, 1957), pp. 482ff.
12. Schlieffen is making a backhanded reference to the problems of getting German commanders to follow Moltke's orders and directives during the Franco-German War.

Additionally, his comment, 'at least most of them', is directed at Karl Friedrich von Steinmetz, who as commander of the 1st Army during the Franco-German War had difficulty doing what Moltke wanted him to do. See Michael Howard, *The Franco-Prussian War: The German Invasion of France, 1870–1871* (London: Rupert Hart-Davis, 1961), pp. 83ff., 126ff., and p. 190.

13. Once again, Schlieffen is playing a bit fast and loose with history. As in 1866, Moltke was advocating a long campaign to destroy France once and for all, but was restrained by Bismarck. See Rudolph Stadelmann, *Moltke und der Staat* (Krefeld: Scherpe-Verlag, 1950), pp. 179ff.

19: Helmuth von Moltke

1. This translation comes from Alfred von Schlieffen, *Gesammelte Schriften*, Vol. II (Berlin: E.S. Mittler, 1913), pp. 439–42, 442–5.
2. This is one of Moltke's most famous expressions, one which he used repeatedly to his subordinates and in his writings on war. See his 'On Strategy' and his 'Strategy' in Daniel J. Hughes, ed. and trans., *Moltke on the Art of War: Selected Writings* (Novato, CA: Presidio Press, 1993), pp. 46 and 124.
3. At the battles of Gravelotte – St Privat (18 August 1870) and Sedan (1 September 1870), German forces circled behind the French cutting them off from Paris. Hence, the German forces 'faced Germany'.
4. Schlieffen is referring to the statues of Otto Fürst von Bismarck and Albrecht Graf von Roon. These three statues still stand around the Siegessäule in Berlin today.
5. On 3 July 1866, as the Prussian 1st Army reached the battlefield of Königgrätz, Moltke rescinded an order issued by its commander, Prince Friedrich Karl. When General Albrecht von Manstein, the commander of the 6th Division, received Moltke's counter-order, he famously replied, 'This is certainly in order, but who is this General Moltke?', Eberhard Kessel, *Moltke* (Stuttgart: K.F. Koehler, 1957), p. 480.
6. Schlieffen is referring here to a number of Napoleon's early victories in the Italian campaign: the battle of Lodi (10 May 1796), the battle of Arcola (15–17 November 1796) and the battle of the Pyramids (21 July 1798) during Napoleon's invasion of Egypt.
7. Here, Schlieffen refers to the defeats of Napoleon's later career – the burning of Moscow (14 September 1812); the crossing of the Berezina (26–28 November 1812) on the retreat from Moscow during which the French lost at least 30,000 men; Napoleon's defeat at the battle of Leipzig (16–19 October 1813), which opened the way for the allied invasion of France; and the battle of Waterloo (18 June 1815), Napoleon's final defeat.

Select Bibliography

Auwers, —. 'Einige Betrachtungen zu General Groeners "Testament des Grafen Schlieffen"', *Wissen und Wehr* (1927), pp. 146–72.
Beck, Ludwig. *Studien*. Stuttgart: K.F. Koehler, 1955.
Bergh, Max van den. *Das Deutsche Heer vor dem Weltkriege*. Berlin: Sanssouci Verlag, 1934.
Boetticher, Friedrich von. *Schlieffen: Viel leisten, wenig hervortraten–mehr sein als scheinen*. Göttingen: Musterschmidt Verlag, 1957.
Borgert, Heinz-Ludger. 'Grundzüge der Landkriegführung von Schlieffen bis Guderian', *Handbuch zur deutschen Militärgeschichte 1648–1939*, Vol. IX. Munich: Bernard & Graefe, 1979.
Bronsart von Schellendorf, Paul. *Duties of the General Staff*, 4th edn. London: HMSO, 1905.
Bucholz, Arden. *Moltke, Schlieffen and Prussian War Planning*. Oxford and Providence, RI: Berg, 1993.
Caemmerer, Rudolph von. *Die Entwicklung der strategischen Wissenschaft im 19. Jahrhundert*. Berlin: Wilhelm Baensch, 1904.
——. *The Development of Strategical Science During the 19th Century*. London: Hugh Rees, 1905.
Cochenhausen, Friedrich von, ed. *Von Scharnhorst zu Schlieffen, 1806–1906: Hundert Jahre preußisch-deutscher Generalstab*. Berlin: E.S. Mittler, 1933.
Craig, Gordon. *The Politics of the Prussian Army*. New York: Oxford University Press, 1956.
Demeter, Karl. *The German Officer Corps in Society and State 1650–1945*, Trans. Angus Malcolm. London: Weidenfeld & Nicolson, 1965.
Doerr, Hans. 'Der "Grosse Chef"', *Wehrkunde* 6 (1957), pp. 542–50.
Echevarria, Antulio J. *After Clausewitz: German Military Thinkers Before the Great War*. Lawrence, KS: University Press of Kansas, 2001.
——. 'Neo-Clausewitzianism: Freytag-Loringhoven and the Militarization of Clausewitz in German Military Literature Before the First World War'. PhD thesis, Princeton University, 1994.

———. 'On the Brink of the Abyss: The Warrior Identity and German Military Thought before the Great War', *War and Society* 13, 2 (Oct. 1995), pp. 23–40.

———. 'Borrowing from the Master: Uses of Clausewitz in German Military Literature before the Great War', *War in History* 3, 3 (1996), pp. 274–92.

———. 'A Crisis in Warfighting: German Tactical Discussions in the Late Nineteenth Century', *Militärgeschichtliche Mitteilungen* (1996), 1, 55, pp. 51–68.

———. 'General Staff Historian Hugo Freiherr von Freytag-Loringhoven and the Dialectics of German Military Thought', *Journal of Military History*, 60 (July 1996), pp. 471–94.

Förster, Stig. *Der doppelte Militarismus: Die deutsche Heeresrüstungspolitik zwischen Status-Quo-Sicherung und Aggression, 1890–1913*. Stuttgart: Franz Steiner Verlag, 1985.

———. 'Facing People's War: Moltke the Elder and German Military Options After 1871', *Journal of Strategic Studies* 10, 2 (1987), pp. 209–30.

———. 'Der deutsche Generalstab und die Illusion des kurzen Krieges, 1871-1914. Metakritik eines Mythos', *Militärgeschichtliche Mitteilungen*, 54 (1995), pp. 61–95.

Foerster, Wolfgang. *Graf Schlieffen und der Weltkrieg*. Berlin: E.S. Mittler, 1925.

———. *Aus der Gedankenwerkstatt des Deutschen Generalstabes*. Berlin: E.S. Mittler, 1931.

———. 'Einige Bemerkungen zu Gerhard Ritters Buch "Der Schlieffenplan"', *Wehr-Wissenschaftliche Rundschau*, 1 (1957), pp. 37–44.

Freytag-Loringhoven, Hugo Freiherr von. *Generalfeldmarschall Graf von Schlieffen. Sein Leben und die Verwertung seines geistigen Erbes im Weltkriege*. Berlin: Historia-Verlag Paul Schraepler, 1920.

———. *Menschen und Dinge, wie ich sie in meinem Leben sah*. Berlin: E.S. Mittler, 1923.

———. 'Lebensgang und Lebenswerk des Generalfeldmarschalls Grafen v. Schlieffen', in Alfred von Schlieffen, *Cannae*. Berlin: E.S. Mittler, 1925.

Gat, Azar. *The Development of Military Thought: The Nineteenth Century*. Oxford: Clarendon Press, 1992.

Geyer, Michael. *Deutsche Rüstungspolitik, 1860–1980*. Frankfurt: Suhrkamp, 1984.

Goerlitz, Walter. *History of the German General Staff, 1657–1945*. Trans. Brian Battershaw. New York: Praeger, 1957.

SELECT BIBLIOGRAPHY

Groener, Wilhelm. *Das Testament des Grafen Schlieffen: Operative Studien über den Weltkrieg.* Berlin: E.S. Mittler, 1927.

——. *Der Feldherr wider Willen: Operative Studien über den Weltkrieg.* Berlin: E.S. Mittler, 1931.

——. *Lebenserinnerungen: Jugend, Generalstab, Weltkrieg.* Ed. Friedrich Freiherr Hiller von Gaertringen. Göttingen: Vandenhoeck & Ruprecht, 1957.

——. 'Das Testament des Grafen Schlieffen", *Wissen und Wehr* (1925), pp. 193–217.

Grosser Generalstab, Kriegsgeschichtliche Abteilung I. *Der Schlachterfolg, mit welchen Mitteln wurde er erstrebt?* Vol. III: *Studien zur Kriegsgeschichte und Taktik.* Berlin: E.S. Mittler, 1903.

Herwig, Holger. *The First World War: Germany and Austria-Hungary, 1914–1918.* London: Arnold, 1997.

——. 'From Tirpitz Plan to Schlieffen Plan: Some Observations on German Military Planning', *Journal of Strategic Studies,* 9, 1 (1986), pp. 53–63.

Holmes, Terence M. 'Debate: The Reluctant March on Paris: A Reply to Terence Zuber's "The Schlieffen Plan Reconsidered"', *War in History,* 8, 2 (2001), pp. 208–32.

Hossbach, Friedrich. *Die Entwicklung des Oberbefehls über das Heer in Brandenburg, Preussen und im Deutschen Reich von 1655–1945.* Würzburg: Holzner Verlag, 1957.

Howard, Michael. *The Franco-Prussian War: The German Invasion of France, 1870–71.* London: Rupert Hart-Davis, 1961.

Hughes, Daniel J. 'Schlichting, Schlieffen, and the Prussian Theory of War in 1914', *Journal of Military History,* 59 (April 1995), pp. 257–78.

Jany, Curt. *Geschichte der Preußischen Armee vom 15. Jahrhundert bis 1914.* Band IV: *Die Königliche Preußische Armee und das Deutsche Reichsheer 1807 bis 1914.* Berlin: Karl Siegismund, 1933.

Kaulbach, Eberhard. 'Schlieffen: Zur Frage der Bedeutung und Wirkung seiner Arbeit', *Wehr-Wissenschaftliche Rundschau,* 13 (1963), pp. 137–49.

Keim, August. 'Graf Schlieffen: Eine Studie in Zusammenhange mit dem Weltkrieg', *Politische und militärische Zeitfragen,* 32. Berlin: Georg Bath, 1921.

Kiliani, Emanuel. 'Die Operationslehre des Grafen Schlieffen und ihre deutschen Gegner', *Wehrkunde* 10 (1961), pp. 71–6, 133–8.

Kitchen, Martin. 'The Traditions of German Strategic Thought', *International History Review* 1, 2 (April 1979), pp. 163–90.

Kuhl, Hermann von. *Der deutsche Generalstab in Vorbereitung und Durchführung des Weltkrieges.* Berlin: E.S. Mittler, 1920.

——. 'Graf Schlieffen und der Weltkrieg', *Wissen und Wehr* (1923), pp. 1–8.
Liss, Ulrich. 'Graf Schlieffen's letztes Kriegsspiel', *Wehr-Wissenschaftliche Rundschau* 15, 3 (1965), pp. 162–6.
Luvaas, Jay. 'European Military Thought and Doctrine, 1870–1914', in *The Theory and Practice of War*. Ed. Michael Howard. London: Cassel, 1965.
Mantey, Friedrich von. 'Graf Schlieffen und der jüngere Moltke', *Militär-Wochenblatt*, Nr 10 (1935), pp. 395–8.
——. 'Schlieffen-Plan von 1905, Moltke-Pläne 1908 bis 1914 und Schlieffen-Plan 1912', *Militär-Wochenblatt*, Nr 16 (1935) pp. 651–4.
Meisner, Heinrich Otto. *Der Kriegsminister 1814–1914*. Berlin: Hermann Reinshagen Verlag, 1940.
Mette, Siegfried. *Vom Geist deutscher Feldherren: Genie und Technik 1800–1918*. Zurich: Scientia, 1938.
Mombauer, Annika. *Helmuth von Moltke and the Origins of the First World War*. Cambridge: Cambridge University Press, 2001.
Ostertag, Heiger. *Bildung, Ausbildung und Erziehung des Offizierkorps im deutschen Kaiserreich: Eliteideal, Anspruch und Wirklichkeit*. Frankfurt: Peter Lang, 1990.
Otto, Helmuth. *Schlieffen und der Generalstab: Der preussich-deutsche Generalstab unter der Leitung des Generals von Schlieffen, 1891–1905*. Berlin: Deutscher Militärverlag, 1966.
Rangliste der Königlich-Preußischen Armee und des XII (Königlich–Württembergischen) Armeekorps 1891–1906. Berlin: E.S. Mittler, 1891–1906.
Reichsarchiv. *Der Weltkrieg 1914 bis 1918: Die militärischen Operationen zu Lande*, Vol. I: *Die Grenzschlachten im Westen*. Berlin and Frankfurt: E.S. Mittler, 1925.
——. *Der Weltkrieg 1914 bis 1918: Kriegsrüstung und Kriegswirtschaft: Anlagen zum ersten Band*, Berlin: E.S. Mittler, 1930.
Ritter, Gerhard. *Der Schlieffenplan: Kritik eines Mythos*. Munich: Verlag R. Oldenbourg, 1956.
——. *The Schlieffen Plan: Critique of a Myth*. Trans. Andrew and Eva Wilson. London: Oswald Wolff, 1958.
——. *The Sword and the Scepter: The Problem of Militarism in Germany*, Vol. II: *The European Powers and the Wilhelminian Empire, 1890–1914*. Trans. Heinz Norden. Coral Gables, FL: University of Miami Press, 1970.
Rochs, Hugo. *Schlieffen*. Berlin: Vossische Buchhandlung Verlag, 1926.
Rosinski, Herbert. *The German Army*. Ed. Gordon Craig. New York: Praeger, 1966.

SELECT BIBLIOGRAPHY

——. 'Scharnhorst to Schlieffen: The Rise and Decline of German Military Thought', *Naval War College Review*, 29 (1976), pp. 83–103.

Rüdt von Collenberg, Ludwig. 'Graf Schlieffen und die Kriegsformation der deutschen Armee', *Wissen und Wehr* (1927), pp. 605–34.

Samuels, Martin. *Command or Control? Command, Training and Tactics in the British and German Armies, 1888–1918*. London: Frank Cass, 1995.

——. 'The Reality of Cannae', *Militärgeschichtliche Mitteilungen*, 1 (1990).

——. 'Directive Command and the German General Staff', *War in History*, 2, 1 (1995), pp. 22–42.

Schlieffen, Alfred von. *Gesammelte Schriften*, 2 vols. Berlin: E.S. Mittler, 1913.

——. *Cannae*. Berlin: E.S. Mittler, 1925.

——. *Dienstschriften*: Vol. I: *Die taktisch-strategischen Aufgaben*. Berlin: E.S. Mittler, 1937.

——. *Dienstschriften*: Vol.II: *Die grossen Generalstabsreisen – Ost – aus den Jahren 1891–1905*. Berlin: E.S. Mittler, 1938.

——. *Briefe*. Ed. Eberhard Kessel. Göttingen: Vandenhoeck & Ruprecht, 1958.

——. *Cannae*. Fort Leavenworth, KS: Command and General Staff School, 1931.

Schmidt-Bückeburg, Rudolf. *Das Militärkabinett der preussischen Könige und deutschen Kaiser*. Berlin: E.S. Mittler, 1933.

Schulte, Bernd F. *Die deutsche Armee, 1900–1914*. Düsseldorf: Droste Verlag, 1977.

Schwertfeger, Bernhard. *Die grossen Erzieher des deutschen Heeres: Aus der Geschichte der Kriegsakademie*. Potsdam: Akademische Verlagsgesellschaft Athenaion, 1936.

Seeckt, Hans von. *Gedenken eines Soldaten*. Berlin: E.S. Mittler, 1929.

Senger und Etterlin, Ferdinand von. 'Cannae, Schlieffen und die Abwehr', *Wehr-Wissenschaftliche Rundschau*, 13 (1963), pp. 26–43.

Showalter, Dennis E. *Tannenberg: Clash of Empires*. Hamden, CT: Archon Books, 1991.

——. 'Army and Society in Imperial Germany: The Pains of Modernization', *Journal of Contemporary History*, 18 (1983), pp. 583–618.

——. 'German Grand Strategy: A Contradiction in Terms?', *Militärgeschichtliche Mitteilungen*, 2 (1990), pp. 65–102.

——. 'The Eastern Front and German Military Planning, 1871–1914 – Some Observations', *Eastern European Quarterly*, 15, 2 (June 1981).

——. 'Goltz and Bernhardi: The Institutionalization of Originality in the Imperial German Army', *Defense Analysis*, 3, 4 (1987).

——. 'Army, State, and Society in Germany, 1871–1914: An Interpretation', in Jack P. Dukes and Joachim Remak, eds, *Another Germany*. London: Westview Press, 1988.

Snyder, Jack. *The Ideology of the Offensive: Military Decision Making and the Disasters of 1914*. London: Cornell University Press, 1984.

Staabs, Hermann von. *Aufmarsch nach zwei Fronten*. Berlin: E.S. Mittler, 1925.

Strachan, Hew. *The First World War*, Vol. I: *To Arms*. Oxford: Oxford University Press, 2001.

Tunstall, Graydon A. *Planning for War Against Russia and Serbia: Austro-Hungarian and German Military Strategies, 1871–1914*. New York: Columbia University Press, 1993.

Turner, L.F.C. 'The Significance of the Schlieffen Plan', in Paul Kennedy, ed., *The War Plans of the Great Powers, 1880–1914*. London: Allen & Unwin, 1979.

'Ueber militärisches Schrifttum im preussisch-deutschen Heere von Scharnhorst bis zum Weltkriege', *Militär-Wissenschaftliche Rundschau*, 4, 3 (1936).

Wallach, Jeduda L. *Das Dogma der Vernichtungsschlacht: Die Lehren von Clausewitz und Schlieffen und ihre Wirkungen in zwei Weltkriegen*. Frankfurt: Bernard und Graefe, 1967.

——. *The Dogma of the Battle of Annihilation: The Theories of Clausewitz and Schlieffen and their Impact on the German Conduct of Two World Wars*. Westport, CT: Greenwood Press, 1986.

Weerd, H.A. *Great Soldiers of the Two World Wars*. New York: W.W. Norton, 1941.

Zoellner, Eugen Ritter von. 'Schlieffens Vermächtnis', *Militär-Wissenschaftliche Rundschau* Sonderheft, 1938.

Zuber, Terence. 'The Schlieffen Plan Reconsidered', *War in History*, 6, 3 (1999), pp. 262–305.

Index

Aachen, 127, 156
Adolphus, Gustavus, 191, 220, 221
Adriatic Sea, 203
Africa, 204
aircraft, 199, 201, 224
airpower, 201
Aisne River, 164, 169, 171, 172
Albrecht, Herzog von Württemberg, 26
Alexander the Great, 191, 199, 220, 221
Alle River, 32, 125
Allenstein, 19, 20, 22, 23, 31, 32, 33, 53, 57, 124
alliances, 223
Alps, the, 120, 202, 203, 204, 231
Alsace, 93, 96, 97, 99, 105, 106, 145, 153, 167, 173, 214, 215
Alten, Georg von, 25, 50, 191
Alvensleben, Constantin von, 215
America, 204
Amiens, 168
amphibious landing, 82, 84, 85, 90, 91, 120, 169, 175, 176, 177
amphibious raid, 85
anarchism, 204
annihilation, xv, xxvii, 10, 12, 15, 16, 30, 45, 58, 63, 64, 67, 70, 79, 84, 91, 94, 95, 105, 113, 116, 120, 121, 126, 127, 136, 177, 188, 189, 190, 193, 195, 200, 210, 211, 212, 213, 214, 216, 224, 225, 226, 228, 230, 232
annihilation, battle of, 210, 212, 213, 218, 224, 226
Antwerp, 129, 130, 131, 132, 133, 134, 136, 154, 165, 166, 169, 175, 176, 178, 202
'applicatory method', xvi
archives, 5
Ardennes, 168
Aristotle, 220, 222
arms race, 184, 194–5, 201–2
army corps, xxiv, xxv, 8, 9, 149, 151, 155, 169, 218
army expansion, xxii, xxiii, 7-8, 9, 149, 151, 170–1, 197

artillery, xxii, 17, 41, 46, 54, 66, 69, 75, 78, 83, 87, 147, 148, 149, 160, 162, 176, 194, 195, 196, 198, 199, 201–2
Aspern, battle of, 222
attrition, 63, 84, 121, 126, 200
Aufmarschplan (deployment plan), 11, 13, 27, 39, 51, 61, 143, 145, 146, 151, 154, 156, 163
Aufmarsch (deployment), 13, 29, 51, 63, 72, 73, 75, 76, 77, 78, 92, 93, 110, 120–1, 128, 152, 153, 154, 157, 167, 178, 224
Auftragstaktik (mission command), 10, 98, 191–2
Austerlitz, battle of, 213, 220, 229
Austria, xx, 89, 223, 224, 225
Austria-Hungary, xx, xxiii, 13, 39, 51, 61, 68–9, 120, 144, 159, 184, 203, 205
Austro-Prussian War (1866), xx, 8, 170, 194, 198, 214, 223, 224, 225, 226
'authoritarian polycracy', xx
automobiles, 199

Bagenski, *Major* von, 25
Balck, Wilhelm, 71
Balkan Peninsula, 203, 205
Baltic Sea, 13, 203
Barnekow, Albert Freiherr von, 216
Barth, Royal Saxon *Generalmajor*, 70
Basedow, *Hauptmann* von, 25
Basedow, *Major* von, 50
Bavaria, xxiii
Bazaine, François Achille, 88, 216, 223
Beaumont, battle of, 217
Belgium, 73, 119, 128, 130, 149–50, 152, 157, 165, 168, 169, 170, 173, 175, 178, 179, 193, 201, 202, 216
Belisarius, 222
Benedek, Ludwig Ritter von, 214, 223
Beresina, battle of, 212, 231
Berlin, xix, 5, 32, 40, 143, 154, 161, 163, 177, 179
Bernhardi, Friedrich von, xxv, xxvii, 186, 187, 189, 190

Berthier, Louis Alexandre, 63
Bismarck, Otto von, xxi, 191, 204, 224, 226
Bitzthum von Eckstädt, Royal Saxon *Generalmajor* Graf, 59
Black Forest, 174
Blankenburg, *Generalmajor* von, 49
Blitzkrieg, xxviii
Blücher, Gebhard von, 89, 214
Boehn, *Hauptmann* von, 26
Boer War, 131, 195
Bohemia, 228, 229, 231
Borodino, battle of, 220
breakthrough attacks, 10, 24, 32, 42, 54, 56, 66, 76, 100, 123, 125, 126–7, 146, 149, 158, 178, 190, 227
Bredow, *Major* Graf von, 49
Breslau, 43
Brest Litowsk, 62, 69
British Cabinet, 150
British Expeditionary Force, 175–7
Brunswick, Duke of, 221, 222
Brussels, 136, 155, 167
Bug River, 69, 108, 109, 116, 204
Bulgaria, 203
Bülow, Bernhard Fürst von, 159, 161
Bülow-Stolle, *Hauptmann* von, 38
Bunzelwitz, battle of, 214
Burkersdorf, battle of, 212

Caesar, 219–20, 221
cabinet wars, 80, 221
Calais, 120, 128
Cannae, battle of, 187–8, 208–11, 212, 213, 214, 215, 218
Caprivi, Leo von, xxi
Carthage, 221
casualties, 3, 58, 164, 187, 189, 195, 199, 200, 204, 207, 209, 210
cavalry, 14, 18, 22, 23, 27–8, 30, 31, 33, 34, 41, 42, 44, 46, 53, 56, 64, 79, 118, 137, 162, 198, 201, 209, 210, 213, 215, 224
Chales de Beaulieu, *Hauptmann*, 25
Chales de Beaulieu, *Major*, 70
chance, 81, 228
Chancellory, xix, 186
Charlemagne, 191, 221
Charles XII, King of Sweden, 191, 221
Claasen, *Major*, 38
Clausewitz, Carl von, 120, 188, 210, 219
Coblenz, 129, 174, 215
Cologne, 127, 129, 130, 132, 133
Colombey, battle of, 216
command, xxvi, xxvii, 9, 10, 22, 23, 24, 37, 48–9, 98, 107, 123, 138-139, 160, 183, 184-5, 186, 187, 190–2, 193, 198–9, 206–7, 218, 219
commanding generals, xx, xxiv, xxv, xxvii, 5, 24, 31, 72, 73, 74, 75, 77, 78, 81, 82, 83, 88, 104, 138, 186, 187, 199, 225
commander's intent, 10, 23, 24, 49, 98, 138–9, 191–2
concentration of forces, xv, 14, 15, 18, 20, 29, 33, 41, 42, 43, 48, 65, 69, 76, 79, 84, 85, 102, 123, 127, 132, 135, 156, 168, 185, 192, 199, 200, 201, 210, 213–14, 218, 228, 229, 231
Condé, Prince Louis I of Bourbon and, 222
conscription, xxiii, 3, 8, 170, 184, 197, 204
Constantine, Roman Emperor, 220
Copenhagen, 203
Corsica, 219
counterattack, 14, 102, 125, 152, 155, 167, 172, 190, 200, 212
Cromwell, Oliver, 220, 221

Danish War (1864), xx
Danube River, 225
Danzig, 28, 41
David, 221
decisionmaking, 6, 9, 16, 24, 31, 49, 65–6, 78–9, 80–1, 107, 132, 135, 138–9
decisive victory, 8, 12, 31, 32, 33, 34, 42, 44, 46, 47–8, 51, 52, 59, 64, 93–4, 103, 121, 126, 145, 146, 148, 154, 155, 158, 174, 175, 177, 178, 183, 200, 209, 219, 221, 225, 229
declaration of war, 73, 194
defence, 76, 93, 124, 146, 155, 163, 168, 171, 172, 178, 190, 202
Deimling, Berthold von, xvii, 60
Deines, *Major*, 25
Deines, *Oberst*, 59
Delbrück, Hans von, 187, 188
Denmark, 82, 203
deployment, see *Aufmarsch*
deployment portfolios, 143
deployment transport lists, 143
Deutsche Revue, 183, 186, 194, 206
Dickhuth, *Major*, 59
Diedenhofen, 72, 73, 74, 75, 76, 77, 78, 79, 80, 98, 138, 152, 154, 155, 174
Diederichs, *Vizeadmiral* von, 50
discipline, 160, 225
Dittlinger, *Major*, 25, 38
Dittlinger, *Oberstleutnant*, 49
doctrine, xxiv, xxv, xxvii, 5, 11, 189
Dorrer, *Major*, 49
Dresden, battle of, 214
Drill Regulations, xxv, 5, 184
Dual Alliance, 51, 144
'dual command', xvi
Dunkirk, 120, 128, 165, 170, 171

274

INDEX

East Prussia, 3, 13, 27, 39, 40, 41, 45, 52, 222
Eben, *Oberstleutnant*, 70
Eberhardt, *Oberstleutnant* von, 59
economics, 12, 126, 168, 179, 200, 203, 204–5, 221
Edler von der Plantz, Heinrich, 148
Einem, Karl von, 6, 186
Einkreisung (encirclement of Germany), 186, 194, 203, 205
Elbing River, 30, 57
emptiness of the battlefield, 186, 196, 198–9
encirclement, 10, 53, 54, 57, 59, 63, 68, 70, 88, 125, 126, 127, 128, 133–5, 137, 163, 192, 208, 210, 211, 212, 214, 216, 217, 225
English Channel, 120, 150
envelopment, xxvii, 18, 24, 28, 34–6, 41, 42, 43, 46, 55, 56, 58, 59, 63, 65, 66, 69, 86, 87, 100, 102, 104, 106, 107, 114, 115, 116, 123, 124, 126, 127, 129, 131, 149, 153, 155, 157, 158, 164, 165, 166, 168, 171, 178, 187, 188, 189, 190, 200, 212, 213, 215, 227
Ersatz forces, 83, 84, 87, 170, 198
Esch, *Hauptmann* von der, 38
Esch, *Major* von der, 60, 70
Eugene, Prince of Savoy, 222
Eupatoria, 90
expansion of the battlefield, 23, 186, 196–7, 198
exterior lines, 227

Falckenstein, Eduard Vogel von, 224
Falkenhausen, *Generalmajor* Freiherr von, 25
Field Service Regulations, 4, 5
First World War, xvi, xvii, xxvii, xxviii, 4, 5, 6, 12, 150, 158, 178, 188, 191, 192, 193, 194
flank attacks, xxvii, 10, 29, 30, 56, 58, 63, 65, 66, 70, 77, 79, 91, 94, 96, 122, 125, 129, 133–5, 138, 146, 150, 154, 158, 166, 188, 189, 190, 200, 201, 208, 210, 211, 212, 213, 214, 215, 216, 217, 218, 224
Foreign Ministry, xix, xxii
foreign policy, xx, xxi, xxii, 144
fortresses, xxiv, 10, 27, 40, 52, 53, 61, 62, 73, 83, 98, 104, 114, 120, 121, 122, 127, 144, 146, 147, 148, 149, 150, 151, 152, 155, 157, 158, 162, 163, 166, 167, 168, 169, 170, 171, 172, 173, 175, 176, 178, 179, 201, 202, 203, 204, 216, 221, 226
fortress garrisons, 45, 75, 114, 127, 167, 170, 173, 198, 228, 232
France, xx, xxi, xxii, xxiii, 7, 13, 39, 40, 51, 52, 61, 72, 73, 76, 119, 120, 144, 148, 149, 150, 151, 154, 157, 158, 159, 163, 165, 168, 170, 171, 172, 175, 178, 184, 193, 194, 197, 201, 202, 203, 204, 206, 212, 214, 223, 224
France Militaire, 119
Franco-Austrian War (1859), 223
Franco-German War (1870/71), xix, xxiii, 8, 46, 77, 88, 92, 100, 106, 113, 132, 139, 144, 146, 148, 184, 192, 193, 194, 195, 198, 200, 201, 202, 214, 215, 218, 223, 224, 225, 226
Franco-Russian Military Convention (1892), xxi, xxii, 144
François, Hermann von, 3, 71
French Revolution, 219
Freytag-Loringhoven, Hugo Freiherr von, 59, 155, 190
Friedland, battle of, 225
Friedrich, Prinz von Sachsen-Meiningen, 38
Friedrich II (the Great), King of Prussia, xxi, 63, 113, 188, 191, 200, 206, 208, 211, 212, 213, 214, 218, 220, 221, 222, 223, 228
Friedrich III, King of Prussia and German Kaiser, 229
Friedrich Karl, Prince of Prussia, 214
Friedrich Wilhelm I, King of Prussia, 218
Friedrich Wilhelm II, King of Prussia, 222
Friedrich Wilhelm III, King of Prussia, 222
Friedrich-Wilhelms-Universität, 7
Frisches Haff, 17, 19, 29, 52, 53, 70
frontal attack, 80, 86, 94, 98, 103, 116, 122, 123, 127, 164, 165, 200, 210, 211, 212, 213, 216
Frossard, Charles Auguste, 88
Fuchs, *Hauptmann*, 38
Fuchs, *Major*, 49
Fußartillerie (heavy artillery), xxiv, 54, 55, 147, 148, 149, 166, 201–2

Galicia, 69
Gallic Wars, 220
Gayl, Egon Freiherr von, 11, 26, 38, 71
General Staff: 3rd Section, 153, 157; duties, xxvi; entry into, xxvi; expansion, xx, xxv–xxvi, 143; Great General Staff, xix, xxv, xxvi, 5; Historical Section, xvii, 5, 190; history in, xv–xvii, 92, 189; Railway Section, 143; structure, xxv, xxvi; training, xx, 4–7, 9, 10, 11, 12, 92; *Truppengeneralstab*, xix, xxv, xxvi, 5
General Staff Society Graf Schlieffen, xvii
genius (for war), 219, 220
Gesamtschlacht, 8, 185–6, 193, 198

275

Geschichte der Kriegskunst im Rahmen der politischen Geschichte, 187
Goeben, *Major* von der, 25
Goltz, Colmar Freiherr von der, xxv, 38, 49
Goßler, Heinrich von, 8, 9, 60, 149, 150, 151
Gotthard Pass, 202
Gravelotte, battle of, 24, 63, 197, 226, 228
Great Britain, xxii, 12, 91, 119, 120, 150, 165, 203, 204
Groener, Wilhelm, xvii, xxviii
Gronau, *Oberst*, 38
Gronau, *Oberstleutnant*, 26
Groß Görschen, battle of, 214
Gründell, *Major* von, 26
guerrilla war, 79

Haeseler, Gottlieb Graf von, xxv, 186, 190
Hahndorff, *Major*, 59
Hahnke, Wilhelm von, 70
Hamburg, 83, 86, 90, 91
Handbuch für Heer und Flotte, 191, 219
Hanover, 224
Hannibal, 187, 189, 208, 209, 210, 211, 218, 219, 221
Hartmann II, *Major* von, 26
Hasdrubal, 209, 218
Hausen, *Generalmajor* Freiherr von, 25
Haxthausen, *Hauptmann* von, 49
Heavy artillery, see *Fußartillerie*
Heeringen, *Oberstleutnant* von, 26
Henk, *Hauptmann* von, 25
Hesse, 224
Heye, *Hauptmann*, 71
Hindenburg, Paul von, 3, 191
Hirschberg, *Major* Freiherr von, 60
Hoeppner, *Major*, 71
Hofacker, Royal Württemberg *Major*, 59
Hoffmann, Max, 3
Holstein, 82, 83, 90
Hungary, 225
Hutier, *Major* von, 38

India, 204
Industrial Revolution, 3
industry, 12, 170, 179, 200, 203, 204
infantry, 17, 41, 43, 44, 89, 162, 196, 199, 209, 210, 211
initiative, 156
intelligence, 48, 56, 75, 78, 79, 81, 85, 112, 117, 132, 153, 157, 199, 201, 223
interior lines, xxii, 12, 51, 52, 62–3, 89, 120, 122, 135, 157-8, 227, 229
Ismaïlia, 90
Isonzo River, 204
Italy, 51, 120, 144, 202, 203

Japan, 156, 159
Japanese Minister of War, 113
Jena, battle of, 212, 221, 228
Jochmus, *Major*, 59, 71
Jura Mountains, 172, 202
Jutland, 120, 177, 203, 204

Karl, Prince of Lorraine, 211
Karlsruhe, 214, 215
Kiel, 82, 83, 84, 86, 91
Kinzelbach, *Major*, 49
Klingender, *Hauptmann*, 25
Knoerzer, *Major* von, 60
Knoerzer, Royal Württemberg *Oberstleutnant*, 71
Kobbe, *Major* von, 71
Koenig, *Hauptmann*, 25
Königgrätz, battle of, 24, 52, 197, 198, 206, 208, 214, 225, 226, 228, 229–30, 232
Königsberg, 19, 28, 29, 45, 52, 53, 55, 57, 59, 62, 63, 64, 69, 70, 121, 122, 123, 124
Königsplatz, 143
Köpke, Ernst, 147, 148
Kolin, battle of, 211
Kolno, 62, 108, 110, 126
Kraewel, *Hauptmann* von, 25
Kriegsakademie, xx, xxvi
Krigesgeschichte, xvii
Kriegsspiele, xxvii, 4, 5, 7, 9, 11, 12, 34, 48, 108, 112, 119, 154, 155–6
Krosigk, *Major* von, 38
Kuhl, Hermann von, xxviii, 5, 11, 50, 155
Kunersdorf, battle of, 212
Kuropatkin, Alexi, 125

Lambsdorf, *Hauptmann* Graf von, 59
Landsturm, 14, 18, 28, 41, 43, 46, 61, 62, 64, 83, 121, 122, 170, 198
Landwehr, 18, 28, 41, 43, 46, 47, 61, 64, 83, 84, 87, 88, 121, 122, 124, 127, 133, 145, 150, 166, 167, 169, 170, 173, 197, 198
Lauter River, 93, 94, 95, 96, 97, 99, 215
laws of war, 228–9
Leipzig, battle of, 63, 198, 200, 214, 228, 229, 231
Le Mans, battle of, 198, 200
Lequis, *Major*, 71
Lessel, Emil von, 49
Leuthen, battle of, 138, 211, 220, 228
Leuthold, *Hauptmann*, 26
Leuthold, Royal Saxon *Major*, 70
Leutwein, *Oberst*, 113
Liegnitz, battle of, 213
Ligny, battle of, 90
Lille, 128, 155, 165, 168, 170, 171, 176

INDEX

Linde, *Oberst*, 25
Lithuania, 120
Lochow, *Major* von, 26
logistics, 88, 160, 169, 170, 179, 201, 232
Loire campaign (1870/71), 88
Loire River, 202
Lombardy, 203
Loos, *Oberst* von, 70
Lorraine, 77, 78, 156, 164, 214, 215
Löwenberg, battle of, 214
Lucius, Royal Saxon *Major*, 70
luck, 228, 231
Ludendorff, Erich, xxviii, 3, 5
Luxemburg, 72, 74, 77, 78, 79, 80, 150, 152, 155, 157, 165, 168, 216

Maas River, 146, 147, 149, 152, 201, 204, 217
Maastricht, 131
Macbeth, 221
machineguns, 201, 210
Mackensen, August von, xxviii, 5
MacMahon, Patrice, 132, 216
Main River, 174
Mainz, 128, 215
Manchuria, 121, 161
manoeuvres, 4, 84
manpower, xxii–xxiv, 7–8, 14, 80, 120, 144, 147, 149, 151, 157, 158, 170, 197, 198, 206–7, 213, 218, 232
Manteuffel, *Oberst* Freiherr von, 49
Marengo, battle of, 212, 228
Marienburg, 18, 28, 62, 63
Marne River, 168, 172
Mars-la-Tour, battle of, 200
Masurian Lakes, 121, 122, 126, 127
Matin, Le, 119
Mattiaß, *Major*, 37
Mauchenheim gen.Bechtolsheim, *Major* Freiherr von, 26
Meckel, *Generalmajor*, 25
Mecklenburg, 82, 83
Mediterranean Sea, 202
Meiß, *Hauptmann* von, 70
Messing, *Major*, 50
Metz, 72, 73, 74, 75, 77, 79, 80, 92, 97, 98, 99, 101, 127, 128, 129, 136, 145, 150–1, 152, 154, 155, 156, 166, 167, 170, 173, 174, 176, 201, 215, 216, 231
Metz, battle of, 113, 226
Meuse River, 62, 73, 127, 128, 129, 131, 132, 134, 135, 136, 137, 164, 165, 166, 167, 168, 169, 170, 171, 172, 174, 175, 176
Mikusch-Buchberg, *Generalleutnant* von, 25
Militargeschichte, xvii
Militärische Gesellschaft, 7

Military Cabinet, xx, xxi,
military history, xv, xvi, xvii, 92, 179, 187–90,
militia, 130
Millionenheere (million-man armies), 80, 202, 204, 206–7
Ministry of War, xix, xxiii, xxiv, xxv, xxvii, 5, 8, 149, 151, 186
mobilization, 4, 14, 27, 72, 75, 144, 148, 151, 153, 157, 163, 175, 220
modern battlefield, 131, 171, 184–5, 186, 195
modern weapons, 184, 195–7, 199, 201–2, 204, 210
Moltke, Helmuth Graf von (the Elder), xx, xix, xxii, xxv, xxvi, 5, 10, 63, 64, 92, 93, 96, 98, 106, 107, 113, 128, 132, 144, 145, 146, 157, 176, 183, 191, 192, 193, 213, 214, 216, 218, 220, 224, 225, 226
Moltke, Helmuth von (the Younger), xvi, 158, 163, 178, 179, 186, 193
Montenegro, 203
Moroccan Crisis, 159
Moscow, 120, 203, 231
Moselle River, 62, 74, 76, 77, 94, 96, 98, 100, 101, 102, 113, 127, 128, 129, 131, 132, 135, 136, 147, 151, 155, 164, 166, 167, 169, 170, 172, 173, 174, 201, 215, 216
motorcycles, 199
Mukden, battle of, 161, 200

Nancy, 72, 73, 77, 78, 97, 147, 148, 152, 153, 154, 164, 166, 172, 173
Napoleon I, xvi, 44, 63, 89, 113, 124, 139, 200, 208, 210, 212, 213, 214, 215, 218, 219, 220, 221, 222, 223, 224, 225, 226, 228, 229, 231
Napoleon III, 150, 215, 223, 225
Napoleonic Wars, 113, 186, 206, 214, 215, 219, 223, 224, 225, 229, 231
Narev River, 13, 14, 27, 32, 62, 114, 115, 116, 121, 126, 154
Naseby, battle of, 220
nation in arms, 170
naval bombardment, 85
Netherlands, 130, 132, 157, 165, 169, 175, 179, 202
Netze River, 40, 42
neutrality, 39, 72, 75, 77, 119, 130, 149–50, 152, 157, 165, 179
New Mark, 222
Niemen River, 13, 14, 27, 39, 121, 154, 204
North Sea, 203
Nowo Georgiewsk, 37, 40, 65, 67, 108, 109, 110, 117

277

Oberhoffer, *General der Infanterie*, 37, 49, 59
Oberhoffer, *Generalleutnant*, 25
Oder River, 40, 43, 44, 212, 225
On War, 219
operational art, xxvii, xxviii, 8, 9, 12, 184–5, 190
Orleans, battle of, 200
Osterode, 18, 21, 23, 54, 56, 62
Oven, *Oberstleutnant* von, 49

Paris, 98, 120, 129, 149, 150, 155, 157, 168, 169, 171, 176, 203, 216, 226, 228
Passarge River, 31, 56, 64, 65
Paulus, Aemilius, 208, 209, 210
Peh-Tang, 90
people's war, 80, 148
Pestel, *Oberstleutnant* von, 93
Pirna, battle of, 211
Plan XIV, 153
Poland, 13, 39, 51, 108
Pomerania, 222
Port Arthur, 113
Posen, 13, 40, 43, 45, 46
Potsdam, xx
Prague, battle of, 211, 214
press, 205
Pressburg, Peace of, 226
Preußisch Eylau, battle of, 225
prisoners of war, 126
Pritzelwitz, *Major* von, 26
Prometheus, 219
propaganda, 150, 205
Pursuit, 17, 18, 44, 48, 65, 67, 68, 80, 87, 89, 90, 118, 126, 129, 134, 169, 215, 225

railroads, xxii, 13, 14, 27, 29, 41, 45, 52, 54, 61, 62, 63, 72, 73, 75, 76, 85, 96, 97, 102, 104, 110, 114, 116–17, 121, 122, 126, 127, 130, 132, 143, 145, 156, 166, 170, 185, 199, 215, 223, 225, 232
Rasmus, *Oberstleutnant*, 26
Rath, *Hauptmann* von, 71
Rechenberg, *Generalleutnant* Freiherr von, 59
Rechenberg, *Generalmajor* Freiherr von, 37
Rechenberg, *Oberst* Freiherr von, 25
reconnaissance, 21, 22, 23, 33, 42, 43, 56, 65, 76, 79, 199, 201, 223
Regensburg, battle of, 214
Reichsarchiv, 5
Reichstag, xix, xxiii, 151
Reichswehr, xv, xxviii, 69
Reinsurance Treaty, xxi
Reitzenstein, *Rittmeister* Freiherr von, 26
reserves, 24, 137, 199, 201, 210, 213
retreat, 18, 19, 31, 32, 33, 37, 48, 66, 67, 68, 70, 88, 89, 90, 101, 102, 126, 129, 153, 169, 215, 216, 225
Rhine River, 106, 127, 128, 129, 132, 135, 152, 169, 173, 174, 177, 202, 214, 215, 225
Rhine League, 225
Rhône River, 202
Riga, 27
river crossings, 14, 17, 28, 29, 32–3, 65, 67, 100, 126, 169, 172
Roberts, Lord Frederick, 131
Rogge, *Major*, 38
Rome, 219, 221
Roos, *Major*, 38
Roßbach, battle of, 89, 213, 215
Rote Bude, 143
Rothe, *Generalmajor*, 38
Royal Navy, 82
Rubicon, 220
Rumania, 203
Russia, xxi, xxii, 12, 13, 14, 39, 51, 61, 119, 144, 151, 156, 159, 163, 178, 203, 204, 205, 212, 220, 223, 225
Russian General Staff, 139
Russian revolution (1905), 156
Russo-Japanese War, 113, 121, 125, 126, 121, 139, 156, 157, 159, 171, 194, 197, 200

Saalfeld, battle of, 215
Saar River, 77, 78, 93, 95, 96, 97, 99, 100, 101, 102, 105, 106, 107, 166, 167, 215
St Privat, battle of, 197
Samuel, 219, 226
Sauberzweig, *Major*, 71
Saul, 221, 222
Saxony, xxiii
Scharnhorst, Gerhard von, 218
Scheffer, *Generalmajor* von, 70
Schleswig, 82, 84, 91, 203
Schlichting, Sigismund von, xxv, 187, 189, 190, 223
Schlieffen, Alfred Graf von:
and army expansion, xxiii–xxiv, 7-9, 149–51, 170–1; and foreign policy, xxi–xxii; and the General Staff, xix, xxi, xxiv–xxviii, 4-7; and heavy artillery, 148-9; and the use of history, 92, 113–14, 187–90; attitude towards work, 5–6; influence of, xv–xvii, xxvii–xxviii, 4-7, 12; interpretations of, xv–xviii; on the British army, 130-1, 175-7; on cavalry, 23, 118, 201; on command, xv, 10, 23–4, 37, 48–9, 79, 80–1, 88, 98, 107, 134, 138-9, 185–6, 190-2, 198-9, 206, 218, 219-26; on decisionmaking, 16, 31–2, 44, 49, 65–6, 117, 132, 135,

INDEX

138; on the French army, 112, 176; on logistics, 170, 172; on importance of decisive victory, xv, 12, 33, 47–8, 52, 58–9, 63, 89–90, 91, 105, 120–1, 148, 153, 174, 177, 188–90, 200, 226, 230; on the importance of a strong right wing, 166–7, 172, 174; on methods of attack, xv, xxvii, 10–11, 34, 42, 45, 46, 58–9, 64, 76–7, 78, 98, 103, 112, 113–14, 126–7, 138, 171, 189–90, 200–1, 210–11, 211–18, 227–9; on the modern battle, 8–9, 184–6, 192, 195–201; on neutrality, 75, 77, 130, 149–50, 165, 173–4, 202; on reconnaissance, 22–3, 76; on the Russian army, 116–17, 139, 156, 159–62; on the use of *Landwehr* in combat, 84–5; opposition to, xxiii–xxv, xxvii, 186–7, 189–90; promotion of, xviii–xix; strategic assumptions of, xxii–xxiii, 7–8, 11–12, 13–14, 27, 32–3, 51–2, 62–3, 80–1, 116–17, 120–2, 126, 143–6, 148, 149–50, 152, 156–7, 183–7, 201–5; writings of, 5, 183–93
Schlieffen Day, xv, xvi
Schlieffen myth, xv–xvi
Schlieffen Plan, xvi, xvii, xviii, 147, 154, 158, 163, 193
Schlieffen School, xvi–xvii, xviii
Schmettow, *Major* Graf von, 59
Schmidt, *Major*, 49
Schmidt von Knobelsdorf, Constantin, xxvii
Schönbrunn, Peace of, 226
Schwarte, *Hauptmann*, 38
Schwarte, *Major*, 59
Schwarzenburg, Karl Philipp Prinz von, 214
Second World War, xvii, 5
Sedan, 217
Sedan, battle of, 46, 52, 63, 113, 132, 208, 211, 218, 226, 228, 232
Seeckt, Hans von, xv, xxviii, 5
Seine River, 168, 169, 172, 202
Serbia, 203
Servilius, Proconsul, 209, 210
Seven Years War, 211
Shaho, battle of, 126
Siberia, 222
Sick, *Generalmajor* von, 26
Silesia, 40, 42, 43, 89, 145
simplicity, xv, 87, 229, 232
Solferino, battle of, 52
Somme River, 171
Sommer, *Oberst*, 25
South Africa, 131
speed, xxvii, 12, 102, 117, 139, 144, 147, 148, 178, 231
Speidel, Royal Bavarian *Major* Freiherr von, 59

Staabs, Hermann von, 38, 70
staff problems (*Schlußaufgaben*), xvi, xxvii, 4, 5–7, 9, 11, 12, 119
staff rides, xvi, xxvii, 4, 5, 6, 7, 9, 11, 12, 34, 48, 119, 154–5, 156
Stein, *Oberstleutnant*, 70
Steinmetz, Karl Friedrich von, 192, 193
Stengel, *Major*, 60
Steuben, *Oberstleutnant* von, 60
Strassburg, 66, 102, 104, 127, 128, 129, 145, 155, 173
strategic consumption, 120, 169
strategic planning, 11, 51, 119, 143
strategy, 63, 98, 113, 120, 188, 222, 227, 229
Strölin, Royal Württemberg *Major*, 71
Studnitz, *Hauptmann* von, 38, 59
superiority, numerical, xxii, 7–8, 46, 48, 80, 88, 95, 107, 115, 121, 127, 131, 134, 136, 138, 144, 157, 160, 167, 168, 177, 200, 205, 212, 214, 217, 218, 224
surprise, 95, 132, 138
surrender, 68, 189, 210
Sweden, 223
Switzerland, 172, 173, 178, 201, 202
Sydow, *Oberleutnant*, 60

tactics, 8, 10, 42, 98, 112, 113, 126, 131, 184, 195–6, 197, 199–200, 209–10, 211
Tannenberg, battle of, 3, 6, 13
Teilschlacht, 185, 187, 193
telegraph, 14, 199
telephone, 199
Tettau, *Major* Freiherr von, 71
Thorn, 14, 16, 28, 29, 30, 34, 40, 43, 53, 54, 62, 63, 68, 70, 109, 122
Tilsit, 19, 27, 122
Tokyo, 113
Torgau, battle of, 212
training, xxv, 3–4, 5–6, 92, 160, 206, 218, 220, 225
trench warfare, 121, 126, 148, 196
Treusch von Buttlar-Brandenfels, *Major* Freiherr, 49
Triple Alliance, 51, 120, 144, 203
Trossel, *Major* von, 38
Troy, 114
Turkey, 203
Turenne, 222
Twardowski II, *Major* von, 26
two-front war, xxi, xxii, xxiii, xxv, 12, 52, 59, 62, 63, 119, 120, 144, 148, 155, 157, 178

Uckermann, *Major* von, 71
Ulm, battle of, 212
Umfassungssucht (encirclement mania), 10, 190

uncertainty, 6, 16, 21, 22, 24, 33, 37, 48, 56, 75, 76, 80, 81, 112, 117, 132, 135, 137, 156, 219, 223
Unger, *Major* von, 25, 37

Varro, Terentius, 208, 209, 210, 210, 218
Verdy du Vernois, Julius, xxiii, xxiv
Versailles, Treaty of, xvii, xxviii
Vienna, 228
Vierteljahrsheft für Truppenführung und Heereskunde, 188, 190, 208
Vistula River, 14, 15, 16, 27, 28, 29, 32, 33, 34, 36, 37, 39, 40, 41, 42, 44, 52, 53, 54, 62, 63, 64, 65, 67, 70, 108, 109, 116, 118, 121, 122, 153, 154, 203, 225
Volkmann, *Hauptmann* von, 37, 49
Vom heutigen Krieg, 186
Vosges Mountains, 72, 107, 128, 129, 164, 173, 204

Waenker von Dankenschweil, *Oberstleutnant*, 38
Wagram, battle of, 229
Waldersee, Alfred Graf von, xviii, xix, xx, xxi, xxii, xxv, 144, 145, 146, 147
Wallenstein, Albrecht Graf von, 220, 221
Wangemann, *Hauptmann*, 25, 38
Wars of Unification, xx, 9, 191, 192
Warsaw, 28, 29, 32, 39, 62, 67, 68, 108, 109, 110, 112, 114, 115, 116, 117, 126, 154

Waterloo, battle of, 90, 214, 221, 229, 231
Wegner, *Hauptmann*, 25
Wehler, Hans-Ulrich, xx
Wei-Hai-Wei, 90
West Prussia, 13, 27, 52
Wilhelm, Crown Prince, xxvi
Wilhelm I, King of Prussia and German Kaiser, xxii, 191, 206, 218, 220, 226, 229
Wilhelm II, King of Prussia and German Kaiser, xviii, xix, xxi, xxii, xxiv, xxvi, 7, 12, 150, 186
Wilhelmshaven, 82
Wilna, 28
Winterarbeit, 4, 7
Wittken, *Oberst* von, 38
Witzleben, *Major* von, 25
Wörth, battle of, 225
Wundt, *Hauptmann*, 38
Württemberg, xxiii
Wussow, *Major* von, 50

Yorck von Wartenburg, Maximillian Graf, 38

Zahn, *Major*, xxi
Zitzewitz, *Major* von, 49
Zorndorf, battle of, 211, 212, 229
Zuider See, 202

Printed in Great Britain
by Amazon